CONSTITUTIONAL POLITICS

For Michael
with warm regards,

Sot

CONSTITUTIONAL POLITICS

ESSAYS ON CONSTITUTION MAKING, MAINTENANCE, AND CHANGE

Edited by Sotirios A. Barber and Robert P. George

PRINCETON UNIVERSITY PRESS   PRINCETON AND OXFORD

Library of Congress Cataloging-in-Publication Data

Constitutional politics : essays on constitution making, maintenance, and change / edited
by Sotirios A. Barber and Robert P. George.
   p. cm.
   Includes bibliographical references and index.
   ISBN 0-691-08868-3 (alk. paper) — ISBN 0-691-08869-1 (pbk. : alk. paper)
   1. Constitutional history—United States. [1. United States—Politics and government.] I. Barber, Sotirios A. II. George, Robert P.

KF4541 .C589 2001
320.473—dc21

2001036378

This book has been composed in Galliard

Printed on acid-free paper. ∞

www.pup.princeton.edu

Printed in the United States of America

10 9 8 7 6 5 4 3 2 1

10 9 8 7 6 5 4 3 2 1
(Pbk.)

THE AUTHORS AND THE EDITORS DEDICATE THIS VOLUME TO

Mary Therese ("Terry") Murphy

Contents

Acknowledgments

Our thanks to the Bouton Fund of Princeton's Department of Politics for its generous funding of the conferences whose results are represented in this volume. Our thanks to Denise Stauber of Chicago for coordinating a long and complex correspondence between authors, editors, and PUP and for compiling the essays and preparing them for publication. Our thanks to Tim Vaughan of Princeton University Press for shepherding our work through to publication. Our thanks for the helpful criticisms and suggestions of two anonymous reviewers for the Press. And special thanks, from ourselves and our authors, to Walter Murphy for founding a conversation in constitutional theory that has fruitfully continued at Princeton for many years, for inspiring and contributing to this collection, and for carefully reading and commenting on earlier drafts of almost every essay.

CONSTITUTIONAL POLITICS

Introduction _____

IN THE LATE 1970s political scientists with a "Princeton connection" began producing works in constitutional theory and politics that departed in content and perspective from the preoccupation of other scholars in these fields. While mainstream students of public law and judicial politics pursued court-centered or litigation-minded research (doctrinal and behavioral), the Princeton group explored such questions as the nature of the American Constitution, the sources of constitutional obligation, the philosophic implications of the Constitution's amendability, and forms of constitutional maintenance beyond institutional arrangements like "checks and balances."

With a sense that there might be something distinctive about this developing body of work, members of the Princeton group began discussing the question in the mid-1980s. These conversations occurred under the urging and patronage of Walter F. Murphy, Princeton's McCormick Professor of Jurisprudence until his retirement in 1995. Murphy cultivated a sense of community among his former students and faculty colleagues by inviting them back year after year for colloquia and to address his graduate seminars. This effort in community building resulted in two conferences, in the spring of 1993 and 1995. The first of these conferences asked such questions as what, if anything, the substantive theoretical concern was uniting this group of some twenty scholars; what might be the broader academic and civic value of this unifying concern; and how might it be presented to the larger communities of political science and academic law. Although the first conference was somewhat inconclusive on the question of what defined the participants as a group, the conferees tentatively planned most of the essays collected here. After a year's delay draft essays started accumulating, talk of a "Princeton School" increased elsewhere in political science and academic law, and Murphy called the second conference to renew the question of unity and to discuss the early drafts of most of the essays published in this volume.

Each of these essays either explores or has immediate implications for what the authors have come to see as the concerns that define them as a group: (1) the normative, conceptual, and empirical study of *constitution making*, *constitution maintenance*, and deliberate *constitutional change* as aspects of a distinct form of political activity termed *constitutional politics*, and (2) judicial behavior and doctrine studied from the point of view of a concern for constitution making, maintenance, and change. This concern for constitution making, maintenance, and change is at once civic-minded yet somewhat liberated from the normative sway of any particular civic constitution. It takes the goodness or rectitude or efficiency of no constitution for granted. It flows from commitments not to any particular constitution but to constitutionalism itself. It aspires not only to understand constitution making, maintenance, and change, but ultimately to cultivate the skills and the virtues of these categories of action as varieties of political competence. Ours is a *constitutionalist's* concern for constitution making, maintenance, and change.

Yet we must acknowledge a reservation about a "constitutionalist's concern for constitutional politics" as an account of the public law scholarship by Princetonians over some three generations or more. Mention of Edward S. Corwin and Alpheus T. Mason is sufficient reminder of litigation-minded doctrinal commentary, court history, and judicial biography as facets of constitutional studies for which writers touched by Princeton's tradition have provided decades of leadership. Further, with his earlier research in judicial strategy and comparative legal systems, Murphy himself helped lead a behavioral movement in political science whose ambitions pointedly excluded practical political ends. Are major works of Corwin, Mason, and Murphy suddenly to be counted out of the "Princeton tradition"?

There is no quarrel here with this objection. Reducing a long and complex tradition to its more recent preoccupations would indeed misrepresent that tradition, and in a manner too obvious to mislead. For our part, therefore, we the editors refer to the "Princeton group"—i.e., the group here collected—not *the* "Princeton School" of which others may choose to speak. As editors we will have to accept what further label, if any, the future affixes to our authors' reflections on the elements of "constitutional politics."

Those reflections begin with such questions, why should anyone prefer constitutional democracy to other regimes? What is a constitution? How do different answers to the What question affect our views of the nature of constitution making, maintenance, and change? If we should conclude, for example (and unlike any of our authors), that for Americans "the Constitution" is essentially a contract between sovereign states, we would ask whether a competent strategy of constitutional maintenance would seek ways to discourage a sense of national community or, alternately, to encourage local attachments and sociopolitical identifications among the general population. Could such an arrangement make sense on paper? Has something like this worked for other nations? Under what socioeconomic and international conditions has it worked or might it work? What might the organic public policies of such a "nation" be? What might its basic institutions be?

The behavioral and comparative components of such questions are at least as obvious and pressing as the conceptual and normative. And if the former are worth asking, they're worth trying to answer in the only rational way—(social) scientifically. Scholars in the field of "public law" who accept the invitation of this collection of essays must therefore become more than mere scholars in public law. Just as they have recently acquainted themselves with fields like literary and ethical theory, they must now acquire the skills of comparative politics and public policy, or at least learn enough of these disciplines to communicate with their resident scholars. And although few if any of the authors in this volume claim to have satisfied the intellectual ambitions implicit in their view of constitutional studies, most believe that the times and the subject demand the setting of new goals, for themselves as well as others, and they submit these essays as first steps.

We reiterate that scientific though our aspirations may be when confronting scientific questions, we do not view constitution making, maintenance, and change as mere events to be studied by observers with both feet outside their subject. We see the elements of constitutional politics as categories of deliberate, deliberative, and cooperative action to be studied by individuals who link them with arts that the nation needs, now as much as ever, and as opportunities for personal intellectual and moral fulfillment. It is with this attitude that we offer these constitutionalist reflections on constitutionalism and constitutional politics.

To start things off, Walter Murphy's essay, "Alternative Political Systems," canvasses the question of "Why constitutional democracy?" and previews questions of constitution making and maintenance. By critically examining the experiences of other nations, Murphy challenges us to justify our preference for the political system we call constitutional democracy. His essay thus manifests a belief in the need to revive and perpetuate that aspect of the constitution maker's perspective that seeks alternative ways for a community to get what it wants and needs. Like Publius at his moment of "reflection and choice," Murphy sees the necessity of relevant information from outside the American experience.

John E. Finn follows with an essay that shows how different basic conceptions of what the American Constitution is influence a wide range of issues. Finn argues that a full understanding of the Constitution requires first a distinction between, and later a recombination of, two conceptions: the Juridic (or legal) Constitution and the Civic (or political) Constitution. He shows how the view from each of these two dimensions of the Constitution influences our beliefs on many traditional issues of constitutional theory, including "the relationship of the constitutional text to the constitutional order," who is responsible "for protecting and maintaining that order," whether constitutional interpretation is best conceived as a form of constitutional maintenance, "who bears final institutional authority in matters of constitutional interpretation," the nature of citizenship in a constitutional democracy, and the "vision of the community we claim citizenship in." At the conclusion of his analysis, Finn offers further argument for recombining the Juridic and Civic Constitutions in a way that favors the latter.

Christopher Eisgruber's essay on the revolutionary impact of the Fourteenth Amendment also implicates the question of what the American Constitution is. He suggests that writers who narrowly define a "constitution" as a particular text assume an answer to What, no less than writers who find constitutions in actual political practices and patterns of belief. Eisgruber shows that beliefs about the kind of text that analysts and political actors are dealing with influences their judgments about relationships among governmental institutions and their competing claims to legitimate power. Eisgruber's theory of the impact of the Fourteenth Amendment serves his broader point that amendments initially thought to be alterations of a larger whole can actually change the essentials of the entire system.

James Fleming's essay criticizes Bruce Ackerman's view of the American Constitution and illustrates the importance of perspective in constitutional analysis. Ackerman's treatment of the What question concludes that unlike Germany's Basic Law, the American Constitution values democratic processes above fundamental rights. This conclusion, Fleming argues, flows from dubious assumptions about "entrenchments"—founding decisions to place specific rights or practices beyond the reach of formal constitutional amendment. Ackerman assumes that entrenchment of a specific value marks it as constitutionally fundamental and that a value not so entrenched is not fundamental. Fleming disagrees. Taking a constitution maker's perspective, he finds other reasons for entrenchment and cites the histories of America and Germany to prove that entrenchment has in fact served purposes beyond those Ackerman identifies. By thus inviting Ackerman to rethink his contention that the American constitutional text is "democratic first, rights-protecting second," Fleming displays the advantages of looking at written constitutions from the perspective of actors who structure constitutional architecture to achieve political, social, and economic results.

Constitution making on the American model can be conceived as a form of collective self-limitation. As such, it suffers paradoxes of the kind that Jefferson addressed in his call for "revolution" every generation. If constitutional texts are planning documents that must eventually fail due to a humanly uncontrollable environment, and if generations are as equal as the individuals who comprise them, Jefferson may well have asked why one generation should bind another. The *Federalist* No. 49 tries to answer this question by claiming that the founding of the 1780s was a unique historical moment imbued with a special historical spirit, and that social stability is best served by living with tolerable errors rather than changing constitutional structure with each newly perceived defect. Other answers to the problem yield unexpected possibilities for constitutional change, even "revolution," in sources ranging from ordinary judicial interpretations to critical elections. With some writers (Bruce Ackerman comes to mind), these possibilities legitimate constitution making by depicting it as something less than the future-binding activity it appears to be. The adequacy of these different answers is a question that has generated much of the literature of American constitutional theory.

Jeffrey K. Tulis complicates matters further with an observation about the American Revolution and the Constitution that leaves in doubt the very coherence of constitution making as a type of action. He argues that constitution making in America presupposes revolution and that liberal legitimacy depends on the continuing possibility of revolution. Yet, Tulis contends, the organic policy commitments of the American constitutional system have extinguished the possibility of revolutionary liberals. The system thus undermines liberal legitimacy while inviting such revolutionaries as presently populate the "militia movement." The further difficulty for constitutional theory is whether liberal constitution making could have avoided this problem. Can a constitution be liberal without the continuing possibility of revolution by liberals? Can it be functional for a constitution of *government* to perpetuate revolutionary possibilities and attitudes? A negative answer to either question could vitiate a prescriptive theory of constitution making by indicating that constitution making, on the American model, is not a fully rational activity.

Suzette Hemberger's analysis of the founding debate between Federalists and Antifederalists exposes two opposed models, or "logics," of constitution making: constitution making as empowering government *versus* constitution making as limiting government. She observes that modern Americans have been able to assume that constitutions are instruments of limitation only because the post–New Deal consensus tended to make questions of power irrelevant and invisible. Now that a majority of justices of the Supreme Court appear willing to revitalize the Tenth Amendment and reopen questions of state vs. federal power, American constitutional thought may be more receptive to Hemberger's argument that constitutionalism in America has always at bottom been a matter of who governs and for what substantive purposes.

In other works, several of our authors (Macedo, Murphy, George) have proposed that constitution making is at least implicitly normative not only for institutional arrangements but also for human character and the ways of life that foster civic virtue. As the editors prefer to put it, an adequate constitutional plan must be linked to some theory of civic virtue and involve, however indirectly, a strategy for creating and perpetuating the "private attitudes" that support what the regime conceives as good citizenship. The point applies to liberal constitutions no less than to others. In his essay for this volume, "Notes on Constitutional Maintenance," Sotirios Barber elaborates a version of this point.

Stephen Macedo takes matters further. In an essay taken from his book, *Liberalism, Civic Education, and Diversity,* he shows how orthodox liberal assumptions "obscure the extent to which a liberal constitutional order is a pervasively educative order" and how a liberal regime, to succeed, "must constitute the private realm in its image . . . and . . . form citizens willing to observe its limits and able to pursue its aspirations." He goes on to defend as an unavoidable consequence of the concern for liberalism's survival what writers like Stephen L. Carter and Sanford Levinson have criticized as liberalism's political marginalization of conservative religious believers who would deny primacy to liberal values. Macedo would allow some accommodation of illiberal religious practices, but only to the extent justified by what advances liberal values and fosters liberal attitudes. Levinson responds to Macedo with a list of accommodations to religion that he believes secular liberals ought to make. He argues that anything less is politically unsustainable and inconsistent with liberal principles.

One can disagree with specific proposals for accommodating religion without disagreeing that constitutional maintenance involves an educative function and depends as much or more on a people's psychology and moral and spiritual commitments as on the arrangements of its governmental institutions. But most observers believe that modern constitutionalism forbids government's turning education into thought control. Education for citizenship in a constitutional democracy must allow not only for popular criticism of government but even for popular initiation of constitutional change. Maintaining such a system may thus mean maintaining openness to change, even radical change. Harry Hirsch's contribution to this volume develops this suggestion by considering recent efforts to deploy civil rights laws in civil litigation against pornography and racism. Hirsch argues that restrictions on speech must be enforced in a content-neutral way, and that attempts to restrict the rights of "bad guys," such as pornographers and neo-Nazis, are eventually likely to "ensnare good guys." Hirsch's essay illustrates how constitutional analysis that respects the perspective of constitution makers can influence the doctrines of those who administer constitutional provisions: constitution making favors a strong First Amendment because it actively assumes the revolutionary possibility of new constitutions.

Interpretation as maintenance and openness to fundamental change, and the role of minorities in constitutional maintenance are themes of Wayne D. Moore's article, adapted from his book, *Constitutional Rights and Powers of the People*. Exploring the attributes of constitutional citizenship, Moore draws on principles of popular sovereignty to maintain that "citizens"—as members of "the people"—may shape and vindicate constitutional norms against official practices through unofficial interpretive practices. He cites the case of Frederick Douglass. According to the Supreme Court's decision in *Dred Scott v. Sandford*, Douglass did not qualify as a "citizen." Yet Moore claims that the former slave made himself a citizen by at once shaping and vindicating foundational principles through his actions and his radical antislavery arguments. Douglass's life thus demonstrates that constitutional maintenance can involve far more than preservation of the status quo.

The volume continues with an essay by Keith E. Whittington that shows how a constitution maker's view can influence analysis of the political conditions for maintaining institutional arrangements. An interest in "how constitutions are maintained in politically fractious environments" brings Whittington to enlarge upon an observation of *The Federalist*: political actors must have political incentives for supporting institutional arrangements and prerogatives over time. Keeping formal legal arrangements in the background and focusing on the strategic political situations of American presidents vis-à-vis the Supreme Court, Whittington explores the political incentives that account for presidential domination of constitutional politics in some seasons, and presidential deference to the Supreme Court in others.

Deliberate constitutional change takes different forms and serves different purposes. Change can occur through formal amendment, formal interpretation by courts or other authoritative bodies, informal practices of public officials, the will of the voters in critical elections, or revolution. Theorists, of course, differ as to the legitimacy of all of these methods other than formal amendment as methods of constitutional change, and some may even hold that a specific emendation is constitutionally invalid. The effects of formal amendment may range from repair of verbal defects in the constitutional text to revolutionary changes in the larger political order. And it is the latter case that raises most questions of legitimacy.

The current literature of constitutional theory attends admirably to these problems, as is evident in the volume Sanford Levinson edited in 1995, *Responding to Imperfection: Theory and Practice of Constitutional Amendment*. Yet constitutional scholars have seldom addressed the abstract problem of constitutional failure, perceived instances of which precede the need for constitutional change. Neglect of this problem may reflect a reluctance to confront an additional question: the criteria for constitutional success. In his essay for this volume, Mark E. Brandon observes that Americans "do not like to be made to feel unhappy, especially about their Constitution." But, as he also observes, eventual constitutional failure is inevitable, and a theory of constitutional failure is a necessary part of any general theory of constitutional government. In a "preliminary exploration" of the issues, Brandon indicates the complexity of the notion of constitutional failure and some of the philosophic problems that await theorists who confront it.

Some of our authors (Levinson, Murphy, Fleming, Barber) have suggested in other works that one test of constitutional failure may be the inability of responsible bodies of citizens, like some economic, racial, and religious minorities, to reaffirm the constitutional order as a reasonably effective means to ends like justice and the general welfare. In the concluding essay of this volume, Robert George asks how citizens who believe legal abortion to be a grave injustice against the unborn can affirm a constitution which self-identified authoritative interpreters tell them includes abortion as nothing less than a fundamental right. George asks whether these citizens can treat such a state of affairs as anything less than a matter of constitutional failure. From the other side of the abortion issue, some people on the left fear that the rise of religious conservatism portends constitutional failure.

How to define constitutional failure and identify its instances are difficult questions, and Americans generally, including many in constitutional studies, may not want to think about them. We would count this as a sign, one of several, that the effort is past due.

1

Alternative Political Systems

WALTER F. MURPHY

> To inquire into the best form of government
> in the abstract (as it is called) is not a
> chimerical, but a highly practical employment
> of scientific intellect; and to introduce in any
> country the best institutions which, in the
> existing state of that country, are capable of, in
> any tolerable degree, fulfilling the conditions,
> is one of the most rational objects to which
> practical effort can address itself.
> —John Stuart Mill

THIS CHAPTER, a segment of a book on constitutional democracy, focuses on some of the choices open to political leaders guiding an imaginary nation, *Nusquam*, out of an oppressive political system.[1] Unlike John Rawls's "free and rational persons" operating behind a veil of ignorance, these founders know who they are and hope to become. They are also aware of the values they hold; and they want to establish a constitutional order that will promote those values. These leaders, styling themselves the Caucus for a New Political System, are practical men and women concerned more about the real-life consequences of their choices than the philosophical grounds for their values. Because *Nusquam* has deep religious divisions, these founders wish to avoid decisions based on theology. They realize, however, that because some of their politically relevant values rest on their own differing religious convictions, sooner or later they must face up to those divisions among themselves and the nation as a whole. Nevertheless, they now prefer to confront such difficulties later.

Members of the Caucus understand that they are operating not only under conditions of uncertainty but also under economic, military, geographic, and social constraints. Although they hope to create a new people, they know that different groups of citizens will retain different collective histories and memories. Because *Nusquam* has not one but several cultures, the Caucus must pay careful attention to varied "inclinations, riches, numbers, commerce, manners, and customs."[2] *Pace* William Graham Sumner, stateways can change folkways; but only with considerable violence can a government quickly create a new public "genius." The founders understand that what they want and what they can persuade their people to accept may differ. Although to most Americans constitutional democracy seems the obvious choice, it may entail heavier costs than *Nusquam* is willing—or able—to bear, forcing the Caucus to consider alternative systems.

Patriotism, the founders realize, does not automatically entail attachment to a particular constitutional order. During the lifespan of the United States, France has endured two periods of royal rule, several emperors and dictators, five republics, and more than a dozen constitutional texts. Germany, Italy, Japan, Poland, and Russia have similar histories, and none lacks patriotism. The Caucus assumes that most citizens see a constitutional order not as an end but as an instrument, which, if inefficient, should be discarded.[3] Nations have reservoirs of "diffuse support," and a constitutional order may build up similar, if less deep, reserves to survive crises. But, especially when new, political systems also need "specific support"—the backing citizens offer in return for recent or immediately expected benefits.[4] Thus the founders give heavy weight to a system's economic promise.[5] Tocqueville's high moral claim that "The man who asks of freedom anything other than itself is born to be a slave"[6] may seem like gospel to "a people of plenty"; but, where poverty is rife, citizens may deem that message—and leaders who follow it—perilously wrong.

Still, as Gigi complained about another fixation, "there must be more to life than this." What more—and how much—pose difficult questions; but the founders have already made some preliminary choices. They want a political system that promotes not only prosperity but also: freedom from governmental oppression and the rapaciousness of other citizens; peace with other nations; domestic stability; and citizens who value social justice and mutual obligation as well as personal autonomy. This cluster eliminates not only Communism and Fascism but also plebiscitary democracy, which can easily degenerate into elected dictatorship. Because of limits on space, this essay will consider only four options: constitutional democracy, representative democracy, consociational democracy, and coercive (or guided) capitalism.

Constitutional Democracy: Promises and Reality

Constitutional democracy differs significantly from representative democracy.[7] Although they accept many of the same principles, like the necessity of free elections, they disagree about how to protect substantive rights, like private property and freedom of religion, against government.

Following Jefferson's dictum that the "mass of citizens is the safest depository of their own rights," representative democrats would rely chiefly on voters. Constitutionalists prefer Jefferson's claim that "An elective despotism was not the government we fought for";[8] and would establish networks of institutional checks, typically including a bill of rights, judicial review, and several interdependent governmental departments. Blending constitutionalism and democracy poses huge difficulties, but the promises are also huge: a just society that offers a fair chance for citizens to work together peacefully for a good life for themselves and their families.

Freedom from Oppression

The amount of freedom from governmental oppression, equality before the law, and political participation citizens enjoy in constitutional democracies is, of course, vastly larger than under authoritarian regimes. But constitutional democracy's record is far from perfect. Americans' love for personal liberty was long accompanied by slavery, savage mistreatment of Indians, and rejection of women's social, legal, and political equality with men.[9] Most other constitutional democracies have committed similar sins. Moreover, some critics contend, by braking elected officials' authority to rule until the next election, constitutionalism's protections of individual freedom restrict the people's right to self-government. And constitutionalism's focus on governmental oppression exposes some individuals' rights to abuse by private citizens and corporations. What doth it profit a person to live under limited government when drug dealers imperil the lives of children and corporate downsizing threatens families' livelihoods in the name of economic efficiency?

There is truth in Lee Kuan Yew's comment that American society, which spends more public money for prisons than higher education, is menaced by "guns, drugs, [and] violent crime."[10] Nor is this situation unique to the United States. Crime "has become an obsession in the new South Africa,"[11] with a murder rate seven times that of America. Eastern Europe's incidence of crime has also multiplied since 1989; while in Russia, "The terror of a police state is gone, but it has been replaced by a fear of gangsters and corrupt police officers."[12] The Russian rate of violent felonies more than doubled between 1987 and 1992. By late 1999, various Russian *mafiosi* were conducting a cacophony of extortion, murder, bribery, robbery, and money laundering that reached beyond the private sphere into the highest levels of the Kremlin and to London, Zurich, and New York.

Although political liberalization in the 1990s was accompanied by a rise in crime, connections between crime and freedom are complex. Under dictators, as in Haiti, Kenya, Paraguay, and Zaire, violent crime has been a common way of life, and is apparently growing under some authoritarian Islamic regimes. Of course, the upsurge of crime in the old Soviet Union is partially a function of more accurate reporting and different concepts of what constitutes crime. The Old Regime tended to deny the existence of a serious problem with crime, though foreign journalists and tourists were very much aware of the violence. Furthermore, much of the bribery and extortion currently branded as criminal were standard practices under socialism; now they have been privatized. Another cause of real increase in crime in the former Soviet bloc lies in the Old Regime's failure to generate civic virtue; yet another cause may, indeed, be that wider liberty and lower probability of being punished lead people into temptation. Edward S. Corwin sketched the dilemma: "we enjoy *civil liberty* because of the restraints which government imposes upon our neighbors in our behalf." Freedom, he added, "may be infringed by other forces as well as by government; indeed, [liberty] may require the *positive intervention* of government against these other forces."[13]

On the promise of individual freedom as *Nusquam*'s founders conceive it, constitutional democracy's record is mixed. It offers great liberty against government, but citizens pay for that benefit by sacrificing some self-government. On the promise of freedom from fellow citizens and conscienceless corporations, constitutional democracy's grades would range only from "fair" to "good."

Peace

"Democratic Republicanism," Sam Adams said, would bring the world "perfect Peace and Safety till time shall be no more."[14] Adams was overly optimistic. A nation may want peace, but aggressors are not noted for respecting others' wishes. Moreover, founders must worry about the systemic proclivities of any regime they establish: Democracies were no less likely than other kinds of regimes to be involved in wars during the period 1813–1980.[15]

Social science is of limited help in comparing regimes on this score. Most relevant studies analyze "*democracies* and peace," not "*constitutional democracies* and peace." For democratization, scholars have relied on Ted Robert Gurr's ranking of nations across almost two centuries; for war, they have depended heavily on the "Correlates of War Project" directed by Melvin Small and J. David Singer.[16] In defining democracy, Gurr specified institutionalized restrictions on government and protections of individual rights, elements the Caucus deems constitutionalist.

On the other hand, Gurr's "operational indicator" of democratic rankings includes only a small subset of these elements.[17] Hence, although research relying on his rich database may have great utility for many purposes, it cannot be conclusive for the Caucus.

The claim that democracies are not apt to fight each other does not hold for earlier eras. Between 1817 and World War I, there was "*no* significant relationship" between types of regimes that went to war with each other.[18] And, far more common than full-fledged wars are "militarized interstate disputes"[19] in which violence is overtly threatened, as in the Cuban missile crisis, or occurs at a low level, as in the American bombing of Iraq in 1998. Democracies have not been strangers to these actions. Indeed, before World War I, they were more likely to engage in such disputes with each other than were other types of regimes.[20] Since World War I, however, the pattern has changed dramatically. "Mature" democracies are quick to retreat from strategic overcommitments, they seldom fight "preventive wars," and they do not battle each other. When they fight others, they usually win.[21]

But becoming a representative or constitutional democracy usually takes decades. From 150 years of data, Mansfield and Snyder concluded that, during the early stages of democratization, "countries become more aggressive and war-prone, not less, and they do fight wars with [more mature] democratic states."[22] Furthermore, during that century and a half, states that had recently become more democratic were "much more war-prone" than those that underwent no change, and were "somewhat more war-prone" than those that became more autocratic.[23] And rapid passage did not lower risks of war. Comparing changes from autocracy to a mixed democratic-autocratic regime with those from autocracy directly to democracy, Mansfield and Snyder discovered the latter "more likely to promote wars."[24]

Nusquam's founders can conclude that recent history, at least, shows that constitutional democracies' promise of peace is realistic.[25] On the other hand, the caveat about belligerence and development remains relevant. Like human beings, would-be constitutional democracies might be better off skipping adolescence.

Prosperity

The Caucus confronts similar methodological difficulties in assessing constitutional democracy's economic performance. Directly relevant studies of political economy also speak about democracies generally. In addition, constitutional democracy and capitalism grew up together, often making similar justificatory arguments.[26] And, despite persistent affairs with mild forms of socialism and continuing efforts to dull capitalism's crueler edges, all constitutional democracies have retained some version of that economic system, making it difficult to sort out reciprocal causes and effects between economic and political systems.

Some social scientists believe that, in developing nations, authoritarian governance provides stronger bases for prosperity than do those governments that put strong emphasis on individual liberty outside the economic sphere.[27] The data are mixed. Dictatorships in sub-Saharan Africa have cheerfully coexisted with gross poverty. So, too, except in Chile, the military in Latin America have not proved models of growth and prosperity, despite what the World Bank chose to believe in the mid-1980s.[28] In Europe, the Thousand-Year Reich survived a mere dozen years, Mussolini's poverty-stricken Roman Empire barely twenty, and Franco's reign only about twice that long. None, however, consistently gave priority to economic theory over political domination. Initially, Hitler stroked Germany's economy so that his subjects suffered less from the Great Depression than did the French, British, or Americans;[29] but his megalomania soon produced total war and near-total destruction. After 1936, Spain tried to create a Fascist economy; but, like other Fascist leaders, Franco subordinated economic theory to personal power.[30]

Comparisons with such Marxist regimes as those of the Soviet Empire and Mao's China, where poverty was rampant and occasionally famine stalked, also demonstrate constitutional democracy's (or capitalism's) superiority. But, once Mao's successors began loosening economic control, real income began to rise, though neither constitutionalism nor democracy made a parallel advance. According to the World Bank, the average Chinese is almost twice as likely as the average citizen of India's constitutional democracy to be literate. Furthermore, a Chinese can expect to have a larger income, live five years longer, and have healthier children than an Indian. And China's recent per capita growth rate has been much higher than India's, indicating long-range imbalances. Then, there is the matter of Asia's Tiny Tigers, all of whom began as (and some remain) authoritarian states that for decades produced amazing economic development.

Nusquam's founders would be justified, then, in concluding that, although the economic records of constitutional democracy are rather good when compared to those of most authoritarian systems, they must make finer judgments after focusing on coercive capitalism.

Political Stability

Although constitutional democracies frequently rotate individual officials and alter particular subordinate governmental arrangements, the basic political system tends to endure. Even Italians, who changed governments 59 times in the Republic's first half-century, remain staunch constitutional democrats.

One common explanation for constitutional democracy's apparent stability stresses the legitimating power of public opinion. As Hume noted, all governance rests on public acceptance, if only as a lesser evil; and, more than any regime except representative democracy, constitutional democracy involves citizens in peaceful politics. Within broad limits, the electorate can even revise the rules of the political game. Institutional arrangements provide additional checks on government. "Separate institutions competing for power"[31] make it difficult for majorities to oppress minorities, and judicial review (or its functional equivalent) allows losers in the political processes to appeal to judges rather than to heaven. By restricting the power of elected officials as well as of bureaucrats, constitutional democracy lowers the stakes of politics. If life, liberty, and property depended on the outcome of the next election, thoughtful citizens might be reluctant to accept that decision-making process unless it were grounded in a political culture that limits power and guarantees continued opportunities for political participation. A related explanation for constitutional democracy's alleged stability relates to the putative legitimizing effect of judicial review. Public policies often raise questions not only of wisdom but also of congruence with the polity's basic principles. In fact, however, in Germany, Ireland, Japan, and the United States, judicial review much more often than not sustains the validity of challenged policies.[32] Such decisions may quiet doubts among losers as well as neutrals.[33]

The record of "mature" polities during the past century and a third strongly supports constitutional democracy's claim to promote political stability. France might seem an exception, yet it has had only one change of regime since World War II, adding constitutionalist elements to its representative processes. Constitutional democracy is not, however, always successful. Latin America and sub-Saharan Africa have offered yawning graveyards for such regimes; and the records of Greece, Pakistan, the Philippines, South Korea, and Turkey are checkered. The most, therefore, the Caucus can reasonably expect of constitutional democracy is that it will facilitate political stability, *if* it takes root—a huge if.

A Civic Culture

Of the Caucus's goals, a civic culture in which duties and rights are "correlative, mutualist,"[34] rather than antagonistic, is the most difficult to define and achieve. These leaders have sketched rather than carefully mapped their version of the good life. That American constitutional democracy has not fully met these societal norms has been the claim not only of political candidates trumpeting "family values" but also of scholars like Daniel Bell, Robert N. Bellah, Mary Ann Glendon, and Michael J. Sandel. Underlying their critiques has been a pair of beliefs. The first is that capitalism functions as more than an economic order. It facilitates a culture that rejects the past and commits itself to "ceaseless change," accepts inequality, and works synergistically with its historic partner Liberalism to create an "acquisitive society" in which life is a competitive market of "possessive individualism."[35]

The second belief is that these characteristics make it very difficult to maintain a sense of community and civic obligation. In its American incarnation, constitutional democracy has come to be defined less in terms of public purposes like shared concerns for social justice and more in terms of protecting individual rights. Constitutionalism has joined with capitalism to produce a public philosophy that venerates "the unencumbered self,"[36] free from all obligations not personally chosen. The notion of common duties and values, shared not only with members of the current, but also past and future, generations—Bellah's "community of memory"[37]—has been succeeded by atomistic individualism and moral relativism. What has emerged is a double caricature: of Karl Marx's view of a bourgeois state built "upon the separation of man from man,"[38] and of a Protestant image of a society that has privatized and thereby marginalized not only institutional churches but also religious values.[39]

This culture, Sandel says, has spawned a "procedural Republic": Public philosophy appears concerned less with the substance of decisions than with processes of decision making. In fact, however, procedures shape substantive outcomes. And because the resulting substantive choices are often hidden behind a procedural screen, they seldom need to be justified. Liberalism's demand for governmental neutrality among most individual choices is either self-deceptive or hypocritical. Even government as "night watchman" supports current distributions of economic, social, and political power. Thus Glendon complains of individualistic "rights talk" as poisoning "the principal seedbeds of civic and personal virtue," impoverishing political discourse, enlarging social conflict, and inhibiting dialogue that might lead to discovery of common ground among individuals and groups.[40] Amy Gutmann and Dennis Thompson are less pessimistic, but they, too, label the discourse of interest-group politics as "impoverished."[41] *Nusquam*'s founders must ask if these critics are merely revealing transient manifestations of "American exceptionalism" or deficiencies inherent in constitutional democracy.

Some scholars claim that American culture was once much more civic-republican than it now is,[42] and data from other constitutional democracies are mixed. Italy, especially the south, suffers from greater civic defects than does the United States, though these are rooted in familial loyalty rather than liberalism.[43] On the other hand, Canadian, German, and Irish versions of constitutional democracy operate in cultural settings quite different from those of the United States and the *Mezzogiorno*. While the broader American constitution stresses individual liberty, Donald P. Kommers argues, the broader constitution of Canada underscores "fraternity" and community. The German constitutional order emphasizes human dignity, the incalculable worth of each person, demonstrated not only through rights but also duties.[44] Although Irish culture is less pious than when James Joyce wrote "O Ireland, my one and only love, where Christ and Caesar are hand in glove," that polity still reflects the social teachings of papal encyclicals: Only within a just society can men and women exist as fully human; an objective morality binds every person in public as well as private affairs; and all people have a duty to take care of one another.

Ireland's embedding political institutions into a religious culture raises issues the founders wish to avoid: To what extent does the kind of civic cohesion they want depend on religiously grounded beliefs?[45] Can a secular political theory perform that function?

Alternative Systems: Representative Democracy

The Nature of Representative Democracy

Representative democracy, the closest alternative to constitutional democracy, shares the latter's objectives: a political system responsive to its citizens' wishes and still respectful of individual rights. Moreover, representative democrats claim, their regime will achieve these goals without infringing on the fundamental right of the people to govern themselves. Officials, freely elected for limited terms, enact public policies without such constitutionalist restrictions as judicial review.

Theorists speak, often simultaneously, of several different versions of representative democracy.[46] One is the Westminster model under which elected officials exercise what Coke and Blackstone called "absolute despotic power."[47] In this version, Walzer states, "it is right that they [the people] make the laws—even if they make them wrongly," as judged by moral philosophers or adversely affected minorities. The people are "successors of gods and absolutist kings."[48] The majority's governance, Antonin Scalia adds, means it confers and removes putative rights at its pleasure.[49] And this arrangement allows a majority of the community to be judge in its own case, not only to enact the substantive policies it prefers but also to restrict rights to political participation. And the new, truncated, majority can again restrict participational rights until eventually a dictatorial clique rules. To prevent that outcome, some theorists create a second model of representative democracy, which limits the majority's power: It may not restrict participational rights.

A third model emerges when scholars turn an American-style descriptive theory of interest group politics into a normative formula: Majorities tend to be fragile and fluid; seldom monolithic, they are typically formed by negotiations *among* different groups, who act much like firms under oligopolistic competition. Political processes channel struggles, bargaining, and compromises among a multiplicity of ethnic, religious, geographic, social, and economic interests whose divisions crosscut rather than slice in the same direction. Alliances coalesce and disintegrate as various groups combine, drift apart, and (re)combine to form transient majorities to enact specific policies. Justice and the public interest lie in the processes themselves, allowing expression of the temporary and variegated majority's will—in sum, Sandel's procedural republic.

This third version, representative democrats assert, directly and indirectly protects substantive rights: directly because a coalition that threatens interests of other groups sparks counter-alliances; indirectly because group leaders know their coalitions are typically highly mutable. If today they restrict others' participational rights, tomorrow's coalition may legitimately restrict theirs. For their part, elected officials know they also have a vital personal interest in the regime's openness. If they ruthlessly push one set of interests, they may well be the next victims. The system thus imposes the prudent course of brokering compromises rather than pushing for full advantage. Furthermore, professional politicians have their own specialized version of democratic culture. They accept (and expect to be accepted by) opponents as equally (if misguidedly) patriotic and equally entitled to play by the rules of the democratic game. They should be listened to, reasoned with, bargained with, and, if these efforts fail, outvoted on substantive issues of public policy; but they should not be silenced or denied the right to appeal to the voters at the next election. This form of pluralist politics supposedly both draws on and reinforces respect for basic liberty and human dignity.

Proportional representation, which can exist under various constitutional orders, is an effort to increase democratic protections of minorities. The way votes are counted and elective offices allocated allows smaller parties to be represented in the legislature. The frequent necessity of forming coalition governments broadens the range of interests sharing power and furthers negotiation and compromise. Groups outside the coalition, however, lack bargaining strength except when the ruling alliance is brittle. And this exception reveals a serious weakness of proportional representation: It encourages proliferation of political parties, and multiparty governments may not be able to govern effectively, as happened in

Weimar Germany and the Third French Republic and still happens in Israel and Italy.[50]

A fourth model of representative democracy, another variant of Sandel's procedural republic, comes from theorists who believe that democratic government carries heavy moral authority. "The supposed failure of the democratic process to guarantee [morally] desirable substantive outcomes," Dahl claims, "is in important respects spurious."[51] Procedures are pregnant with moral significance; and, "given certain assumptions, the democratic process itself is a form of justice: It is a just procedure for arriving at collective decisions."[52] Nevertheless, some theorists find elections and bargaining among groups inadequate guarantors of moral decision making. Gutmann and Thompson, for instance, argue that the legitimacy of democratic decisions is constrained by respect for individual liberty and each person's fair opportunity to succeed in life.[53] They conceive representative democracy as "deliberative," requiring discussions among governmental officials and the public about what justice requires as well as about what interests are at stake. Like Dahl and Walzer, however, Gutmann and Thompson would entrust correction of substantive democratic errors to popular debate rather than to constitutionalist institutions like judicial review.

The critical difference between constitutional and representative democracy lies in means to protect substantive rights. Distrusting "the procedural republic" and fearing tyranny of the majority, most constitutional democrats would fracture governmental power and entrench a bill of rights interpreted in large part by officials not directly responsible to an electorate. When, however, rights pertaining to political participation are involved, differences between most constitutional and representative democrats narrow. The "democratic process obviously could not [long] exist," Dahl concedes, "unless it were self-limiting, that is, unless it limited itself to decisions that did not destroy the conditions necessary to its own existence."[54] Recognizing the difficulties of self-limitation, he, Walzer, and others would allow a nondemocratic institution to intervene to protect those processes, though they make this concession somewhat begrudgingly. Indeed, Dahl assents through *litotes* rather than direct affirmation: "for an independent body to strike down laws that seriously damage rights and interests that[,] while not external to the democratic process[,] are demonstrably necessary to it would not seem to constitute a violation of the democratic process."[55]

Comparative Costs and Benefits of Representative Democracy

Not only are many goals of constitutional and representative democracy the same; their institutional demands are not always sharply distinct. Regarding judicial review, constitutional democracy need not—even Germany does not—give judges unrestrained authority to interpret the constitution. On the other hand, allowing judges to police the fairness of political processes leads a constitutionalist camel into the democratic tent. Constitutional inquiry cannot be neatly divided between participational and substantive rights. As John Hart Ely demonstrates—perhaps unintentionally—oversight of political equality opens vast vistas for imaginative judges.[56]

Second, it is difficult to find representative democracies untinctured by constitutionalism. Belgium, Denmark, Finland, the Netherlands, New Zealand, Norway, Sweden, Switzerland, and the United Kingdom are the most obvious candidates. Some of these, however, have constitutionalist institutions like judicial review;[57] some have separate institutions sharing power; some, like Britain, are members of the European Union and subject to its Court of Justice; most have signed the European Convention on Human Rights and accept the jurisdiction of the tribunal at Strasbourg. Furthermore, in 2000, the United Kingdom made that Covenant part of its domestic law. New Zealand and possibly Britain's former colonies in the Caribbean provide the best, perhaps the sole, exemplars of representative democracy—a small sample for comparative analysis.[58]

A third set of methodological difficulties arises, as already noted, from the fact that the best studies of connections among political systems, peace, and prosperity have equated constitutional and representative democracy. Separating these regimes and comparing their records over time would require the Caucus to reconstruct huge databases. Comparing records on individual liberty, self-government, and civic culture also leaves answers unclear, not only because of the paucity of representative democracies but also because these concepts invite different conceptions. When comparing Britain and the United States before World War II, it is hard to demonstrate which was less protective of rights. Both discriminated against some minorities and protected others. So, too, it is difficult to show that today New Zealanders are more or less free than Canadians or Irish.

Representative democrats might contend that their system, insofar as it functions in accord with its principles, better protects the basic right to self-government than does constitutional democracy.[59] That argument would be much stronger if the qualification "functions in accord with its principles" always held. But only ideal models function ideally. Criticisms of constitutional democracy are not based on how it would operate in a perfect world, but on how it has been run by flawed men and women. And majorities have often kept minorities from effective political participation. Canada, Germany, Ireland, Japan, and the United States have each needed judicial intervention to bring majoritarian practices into line with democratic principles. Because this extra-democratic remedy for majoritarian mistakes moves the regime toward constitutional democracy, founders might believe that they can try representative democracy, with judicial protections for open political processes. If that system slides into constitutional democracy, they will have lost little. There is, however, no assurance a destabilizing representative democracy will evolve into constitutional democracy. Other alternatives are open: if Charles de Gaulle had been ten years younger when the Fourth Republic collapsed in 1958, his ego—"I am France,"[60] he claimed—might have pushed him to go down in history as Napoleon IV.

Nusquam's founders must also ask whether constitutional or representative democracy would more effectively promote their kind of civic culture. During the 1920s, when the United Kingdom's regime was closer to the Westminster model, critics like Beatrice and Sidney Webb and R. H. Tawney attacked Britain for fostering selfishness and greed, sins similar to those that current critics lay on American constitutional democracy. More positively, both systems encourage citizens to be politically aware and to participate energetically in public affairs, and so each should nourish a sense of belonging to and caring for a national, as well as a local, community. Representative democracy might do better at these tasks because the absence of safety nets like judicial review raises the stakes of politics and so might spur citizens to more active and more informed participation in public affairs.

On the other hand, judicial (or other non-elected) guardians can nourish the system's values. By explaining why certain governmental acts do or do not violate the constitutional order, judges can act as "school masters,"[61] if not directly to the electorate then to other public officials, scholars, journalists, and attorneys.

Although the Caucus cannot make an exact accounting of the relative costs and benefits of constitutional and representative democracy, a choice between the two could have enormous consequences. The critical factor would be the people's capacity to adopt and adapt to democratic virtues. Declaring "we are a democratic people" will not automatically create those virtues; they must be learned, often slowly and painfully. The Caucus must divine how rapidly its people will accept the restrictions on their power needed for a representative democracy to work. How soon can groups within the community agree that their power requires responsibility both to the political system and to fellow citizens? How quickly will they and their representatives accept that they will sometimes lose on issues that hurt their wallets and/or egos and, when they lose, work peacefully through democratic processes?

The more the founders doubt their people's potential here, the more attractive constitutional democracy, with its additional institutional restrictions, will become. But at least two critical conditions must obtain for constitutional democracy to survive: First, officials who check popular rule must accept restrictions on their own authority. They must allow the majority to govern even when it acts unwisely, intervening only when that governance seriously threatens the integrity of political processes or fundamental substantive rights. The second condition is like unto the first: minorities must realize that many of their claims to rights are contestable and, when they lose in both the electoral and judicial processes, accept those losses until they can form new majorities through peaceful persuasion. If representative democracy's chief danger is that elected officials will mistake themselves for "the people,"[62] constitutional democracy's chief danger is that officials not responsible to the electorate will conflate their own values with those of the political system.

Both constitutional and representative democracy demand a complex political culture. But culture is not a constant. Dahl's claim that life in a representative democracy is a form of political education also holds for constitutional democracy. And, as he admits, a democratic education does not ensure happy solutions: "The democratic process is a gamble on the possibilities that a people, in acting autonomously, will learn how to act rightly."[63] Constitutional democracy entails a similar gamble, but one on which society hedges its bet. As Madison wrote in *Federalist* No. 51: "A dependence on the people is . . . the primary control on government; but experience has taught mankind the necessity of auxiliary precautions."

Alternative Systems: A Consociational Regime

Consociational systems represent efforts to cope with volatile ethnic or religious divisions that stifle a sense of common citizenship. Even if neighbors, members of other groups may see each other as strangers or even enemies. Consociational regimes utilize a set of agreements among leaders of adverse groups to enable the state to function peacefully. Although some such regimes display constitutionalist and/or democratic elements, a consociational political system need be neither democratic nor constitutionalist. When Austria became consociationalist, it already had judicial review and a bill of rights along with free and open elections, while the Netherlands had only democratic processes. On the other hand, Yugoslavia under Tito had a strongly authoritarian consociational regime; and Malaysia, a consociational coercive capitalist state, has only trappings of free political processes and little constitutionalism.

When linked with democracy, consociationalism seeks to maintain at least a mask of popular government while lowering the stakes of politics to make coexistence possible; its essential mark is cooperation among leaders of hostile groups, who govern largely through a benign conspiracy.[64] Political parties may campaign on platforms that are mutually threatening, but leaders of the major factions agree, like principals in a cartel, to settle most divisive issues through consensus among themselves. These regimes usually have four characteristics:

> (1) grand coalition governments that include representatives of all major linguistic and religious groups, (2) cultural autonomy for these groups, (3) proportionality in political representation and civil service appointments, and (4) a minority veto with regard to [policies directly affecting] minority rights and autonomy.[65]

Many aspects of consociationalism are attractive, for most nations are now multicultural. Although intergroup hostility seldom reaches levels seen in Rwanda or the shards of Yugoslavia, ethnic enmity often imperils public peace, as in India and newly reconstituted South Africa. Moreover, by definition, constitutional democracies try to protect minority rights and usually list some consociational safeguards in their constitutional texts. Elected officials typically augment these with informal arrangements. Pluralist politics in the United States displays consociational features, as in federalism and policies like "affirmative action" and appointments of members of minorities to important public offices. Canada provides even clearer examples of such efforts: The formal political structure is federal; French is an official language along with English; the constitutional text allows public support of religious schools (in fact, mostly Catholic); by custom, three of the nine justices of the Supreme Court are from Quebec; that province retains its Civil Code; and the two largest parties take pains to promote Quebeçois to influential—and visible—positions. Prime ministers have frequently been Francophones, Pierre Trudeau and Jean Chrétien being only the most recent in this line.

Because fully consociational states are few in number, are relatively recent in operation, and have included representative and constitutional democracies as well as authoritarian regimes, it is difficult to compare their records on peace, prosperity, and stability with those of other political systems. Only India, a consociational constitutional democracy, has waged wars of conquest. The others have been too small or weak to threaten anyone or even to defend themselves if attacked by a major power. Economically, Malaysia did extremely well for several decades, then toppled into a deep recession in 1997, from which it had largely extricated itself by late 1999. India, despite recent economic growth, remains mired in poverty; other consociational states, like the Netherlands, have ranked among the wealthier nations. Stability is consociationalism's great promise, and it has delivered on much of that pledge.

Only Lebanon erupted in civil war, and it did so partly because of Arab-Israeli conflicts. On the other hand, the scale and frequency of India's inter-ethnic violence indicate that consociationalism does not provide a panacea.

As far as freedom from government is concerned, consociationalism presents three problems. First, when constitutionalist controls are lacking, the only minorities likely to be able to demand close protection are those represented in the grand coalition; and that alliance shields only the rights leaders have agreed to honor.[66] Political culture might supply a functional equivalent of constitutionalist checks; but it is precisely the absence of such a culture that argues for consociationalism. A second difficulty is that while autonomy for particular minorities may ease certain problems, consociationalism may also leave some members of minorities without rights available to other citizens. India, for example, allows Muslims to be governed in many respects by Islamic law and so permits Muslim men to deny alimony and custody of children to their divorced wives. Canada has also had problems with equal rights between men and women within organizations of indigenous peoples.

Consociationalism's third problem is familiar to critics of constitutionalism. Insofar as consociationalism operates through an informal cartel of elites, it "inevitably reduces the importance of elections and even of the direct accountability of leaders . . . presuppos[ing] that the electorate on the whole plays a rather passive role as both a condition for and a consequence of stable politics in divided societies."[67] This arrangement strikes at democracy's central norm: The people should govern either directly or through elected representatives.

Consociationalism's record on substantive and participatory freedoms has been better than these problems indicate. On the one hand, the liberties of Netherlanders have not been much different from those of Americans. On the other hand, some consociational states have had major problems. Although Mrs. Gandhi's attempt to institute a dictatorship was an aberration, India's subjugation of the rights of Muslim women to male-centered Islamic law seems permanent. Furthermore, India has been quick to use troops to quell ethnic violence and slow to return affected regions to civilian rule.[68] Malaysia's authoritarian regime has committed similar violations. Among the government's chief tasks has been equalizing wealth between the richer Chinese and poorer Malays so as to maintain a fragile *modus vivendi* between what Lucian W. Pye calls "two incompatible cultures."[69] To keep that peace—and themselves in power—Malaysia's rulers crack down hard on dissent: "Indefinite detention; rallies only by permission; no real opportunity to criticize."[70] Cultural norms discouraging open disagreement with authority reinforce governmental intolerance of opposition.

In sum, the great benefits of consociationalism are domestic peace and autonomy of diverse ethnic groups. Its great costs are electoral unaccountability and uneven protection of individual rights. Where secession, civil war, or ethnic violence are clear and present dangers, consociationalism may offer a welcome option. It may well be that some diverse groups sharing the same territory, as in the United States in 1861 or in modern Bosnia, Burundi, Rwanda, Malaysia, or Ulster, cannot govern themselves by the rules of democratic or constitutionalist principles.[71] There are, however, countervailing considerations. Although some consociational measures are useful, even necessary, for multicultural societies, India is the sole large nation that has fully deployed consociational arrangements. This singularity may indicate that consociationalism is an option safely available only to small states. More significantly, there is no assurance that consociational governments will remain benevolent over the long haul. History offers scant comfort for those who want to believe that rulers who can ignore constituents will use power benignly. The danger here is of oligarchic wolves camouflaged in clothing freely donated by the sheep.

A more ominous threat to consociational democracy, indeed to all political systems in multicultural states, may be lurking in "a clash of civilizations," which, Huntington argues, is replacing the old rivalry between superpowers: "peoples and countries with similar cultures are coming together. Peoples and countries with different cultures are coming apart."[72] To the extent he is correct, consociationalism may be dysfunctional. By encouraging divergent groups to continue their solidarity—to identify as Hindus or Sikhs rather than as Indians, or as Chinese or Malays rather than as Malaysians—consociationalism could hasten the doom Huntington predicts. Its homeopathic remedy for a society's divisions could stunt the growth of a more inclusive sense of identity. If such a movement would create a congeries of small, tolerant countries, the founders might be satisfied; but there is small evidence that monocultural constitutional orders moderate either the rapacity of the nation-state or the bigotry that fuels political disintegration.

Alternative Systems: Coercive Capitalism

Nusquam's need for economic development requires the Caucus to look closely at coercive capitalism, a regime that protects, while closely regulating, rights of property.[73] Although the World Bank, an institution with a history of cozy relationships with dictatorships, concedes that coercive capitalist states tend to be "authoritarian or paternalistic,"[74] it portrays their economies as cooperative ventures between official technocrats and entrepreneurs. Public officials not only encourage entrepreneurs, they lead the economy in directions they think most fruitful and do so with minimal regard for any constitutional rights, beyond some claims to private property, their own citizens might think they have.

There is a temptation to dismiss such regimes as Fascist, but their differences are significant. First, although Soeharto of Indonesia basked in public adulation and Lee Kuan Yew of Singapore and Mahathir Mohamad of Malaysia still do, coercive capitalism does not need a charismatic *Führer*, *Duce*, or *Caudillo* in command. No more nor less than any other political system, it may require a charismatic leader to initiate the regime, but running it requires quiet, efficient economic experts, not a demagogue. Second, coercive capitalism does not proclaim a world view or overarching ideology, unless it is that it is better to be rich than poor. Third, coercive capitalism does not argue for ethnic or racial superiority, focus on territory *irredenta*, or hark back to a *volk*'s lost empire. Its memory is pragmatic and not euphoric. It tries to build society on a rational, commercial model rather than a military one. As such, it respects a truncated version of the rule of law; terror is taboo.

Nevertheless, coercive capitalist states all began as authoritarian. Officials reinforced economic domination by punishing words or deeds they deemed threatening to public order or, for them, its functional equivalent, their personal tenure in office. As a senior advisor to Human Rights Watch described Soeharto's Indonesia, citizens were "expected to refrain from political activity, except for once every five years when, in what the government calls 'a festival of democracy,' they [re]elect the sitting parliament."[75] In Singapore, the ritual differs, not the result. During Korea's military rule, the government ostensibly tolerated some political dissent; but, in fact, the generals paid tame opponents to act out a charade. In Malaysia, Mahathir still runs a tight ship, even imprisoning his chief deputy in 1998 when he dared display independent judgment.

Of the seven Tiny Tigers—Hong Kong, Indonesia, Malaysia, the Republic of Korea, Singapore, Taiwan, and Thailand—Singapore is the paradigmatic case. In the 1950s, as colonial rule was ending, Lee helped organize the People's Action Party (PAP) and, by allying with the Communists, eventually won control of the new government. He then ousted all and imprisoned many of his erstwhile allies and used security forces to dominate labor unions.[76] His program for the city state was ambitious, his economics brilliant, and his control taut. Success brought enormous charisma: In mid-2001, Lee continued to personify Singapore, even though he had formally left office a decade earlier. Fareed Zakaria describes the regime as "'soft' authoritarian."[77] But Singapore soft can be Gibraltar hard: "The gallows and the cane are the merciless attendants of a rigorous judicial system."[78] Judges, attentive to Lee's wishes, sentence about a thousand defendants a year to caning. During the eighteen-month period ending in June 1995, 125 people were hanged, an annual average of 83 in a country with a population of less than 3.5 million. In the United States, 1995 saw the highest number of executions in thirty-eight years: 56. To have had the same per capita rate of executions, the United States would have had to kill 6,000 prisoners that year.

Dubbed "Asia's Moses,"[79] Lee acts out the twin roles of prophet and Confucian father. And, like the first Moses and many autocratic parents before and after, Lee has small use for discussion except with God and no use at all for dissent. His police strike swiftly at any hint of criticism. There are no *gulags*, but dissidents are apt to be hauled into court on trumped-up criminal charges or face libel suits over which his judges preside, unchecked by juries. Judgments tend to be huge; and, if a defendant flees the country, his assets in Singapore are forfeit. More generally, Lee unapologetically dictates his subjects' lifestyles. As he told them in 1986:

> I say without the slightest remorse, that . . . we would not have made economic progress if we had not intervened on very personal matters—who your neighbor is, how you live, the noise you make, how you spit, or what language you use. We decide what is right. Never mind what the people think.[80]

The government keeps the streets clean, quiet, and safe. The buses run on time. Most important, Singapore's policies have long yielded dramatic economic growth: low taxes, encouragement of foreign investment, compulsory savings for citizens, help in securing foreign markets, tolerance of monopolies, and a tame, disciplined, labor force that is increasingly well trained. (In 1996, the Third International Mathematics and Science Study ranked Singapore's students best in the world in science and mathematics, far ahead of Americans.)[81] Although the city did not escape East Asia's panic of 1997–98, it suffered less painfully and recovered more rapidly than its neighbors.

The mass of Singapore's citizens have shared in the boom. After a period of inviting transnational corporations to exploit cheap local labor, the PAP required that workers be well compensated[82] and protected by a form of social security.[83] Perhaps Lee's most visible accomplishment has been construction of public housing for more than 85 percent of the population—a symbol of paternal love for obedient children. Those accommodations, however, are also instruments of social and political control, as anyone familiar with the American company town would have predicted. "Sixteen Tons," Merle Travis's ballad about a coal miner, tells the story better than an equivalent weight of social science data:

> St. Peter, don't you call me,
> 'cause I can't go;
> I owe my soul to the company store.

"The owners" have equity in their houses but do not hold them in fee simple; they have only a 99-year lease subject to webs of regulations. Endorsing Chinese tradition, Lee has asserted that "the individual exists in the context of his family. He is not pristine and separate. The family is part of the extended family, and their friends and the wider society."[84] Yet his housing program forced massive resettlements that kept nuclear families together but dispersed extended families and weakened their potential check on his power. Moreover, after resettlement, housing developments became "working class barracks,"[85] facilitating state control of labor.

The government also operates large enterprises as well as joint ventures with foreigners, serves as the nation's largest employer, provides public utilities and port and airport facilities, censors the media, sets wages, and owns most of the land. Although Singapore has respected private property, it steers reinvestment of corporate profits into new technology and, building on the city's historic role as trader and banker, into developments in other countries. Public officials woo foreign corporations; they *direct* firms based in the city-state.

Soon after independence Singapore's per capita income exceeded— and continues to exceed —that of the United Kingdom; and for decades the average annual growth in real per capita gross domestic product has been far higher than that of the United States or Germany, as Table 1.1 demonstrates. In 1997, shortly before the epidemic of Asian Financial Flu, the World Economic Forum ranked Singapore ahead of all nations in economic competitiveness;[86] and in 1998 the Heritage Foundation placed the city-state second in economic freedom.[87]

Singapore and the other Tiny Tigers have done well on several other scores important to the Caucus. Like consociational regimes, coercive capitalist countries have usually been too weak to be aggressors except against their own citizens. Only Taiwan and Korea have been involved in serious international conflicts, and both were threatenees rather than threateners. In 1975, Indonesia provoked what could have become a war by seizing East Timor; but the Portuguese offered no military opposition, though locals did fight and 200,000 of them were killed. In 1999, Soeharto's successors allowed a referendum, which produced a 3–1 vote in favor of independence, and Jakarta soon, if slowly, began to keep its word.

Stability presents a less happy picture. Singapore has been the steadiest Tiny Tiger. Its political system, governing party, and even *de facto* leader have not changed since independence in 1965. Korea, now in its Sixth Republic since World War II, sits at the opposite extreme, though the current leadership's commitment to constitutional democracy seems more resolute than that of the past.[88] Between lie Taiwan, Thailand, Mal-

Table 1.1
Average Annual Real Per Capita Growth in GDP

Country	1980–1990	1985–1994
Singapore	5.2%	5.9%
Germany	2.1%	2.1%
United States	1.7%	1.6%

Source: James Gwartney, Robert Lawson, and Walter Block, *Economic Freedom of the World, 1975–1995* (Washington, DC: Cato Institute, 1995), pp. 145, 167, 197, and 221.

aysia, and Indonesia. The last was stable, though repressed, from the massacres following Soeharto's overthrow of Sukarno in 1965 until rioting forced Soeharto to resign in 1998.[89] Since then, the islands have been in turmoil, frequently beset by looting and raping mobs of soldiers and civilians. With large Muslim majorities, Malaysia and Indonesia remain vulnerable to Islamic fundamentalism's demands for a religiously orthodox state. Both nations have additional problems stemming from differences in wealth and work ethic between indigenous majorities and Chinese minorities. These antagonisms have occasionally erupted in violence, with the Chinese the victims.

Taiwan suffered bloodily after Chiang Kai-shek fled the mainland in 1949. A rabbit before Mao's soldiers, the Generalissimo was a lion before unarmed Taiwanese, murdering thousands of potential as well actual opponents. After several decades, however, Chiang's successors and the Taiwanese arrived at a trade-off: The Kuomintang's children control the military and civil service, while Taiwanese have a near-monopoly on commerce. By the mid-1980s, the government began easing authoritarian rule, allowing relatively free elections in 1995,[90] and peacefully left office in 2000 after being defeated at the polls.

Thailand has staggered toward political democratization, but the military has frequently intervened to restore its conception of order. Poorer peasants pose other kinds of dangers. So far, however, civilian and military officials as well as drug barons have remained strongly committed to a sort of free enterprise, even during the economic turmoil of 1997–98. Hong Kong's retreat from the beginnings of democracy the British belatedly instituted in the 1990s is a result of Beijing's refusal to tolerate restrictions on its power. Over the long run, the former Crown Colony may push China to pick up the cadence in its own march from Maoism toward coercive capitalism.

Prosperity is supposedly the prime benefit of coercive capitalism. Until mid-1997, it handsomely fulfilled its promise. Then, except in Singapore and Taiwan, effects of the panic were brutal: Indonesia's per capita gross domestic product fell by 80 percent; Malaysia's economy dropped by 25

Table 1.2
Life Expectancy at Birth

	1960	1990
Coercive Capitalist States		
Hong Kong	64	78
Indonesia	46	59
Korea	53	72
Malaysia	58	71
Singapore	65	74
Thailand	52	68
Other		
India	47	58
China	43	69

percent; South Korea and Thailand suffered similar losses; and even Hong Kong went into a recession.[91] Except in Indonesia, however, recovery was rapid. Moreover, the Tiny Tigers have been narrowing the gap in wealth between rich and poor, while it has been widening in the United States. The World Bank's accolade "the East Asian Miracle" has, by and large, been accurate. That marvel had also unfolded in more human terms, such as life expectancy, as Table 1.2 indicates. During this same period, life span also rose in other low-income nations from 36 to 49 years, while in Russia it decreased from 70 to 64 years between 1989 and 1994, with similar declines in other former socialist states.[92] On other criteria, coercive capitalism gets mixed grades. Especially in Singapore, it has increased freedom from oppression by fellow denizens. Although official figures are suspect, violent crimes reportedly occur there far less frequently than in the West and less often than under more relaxed rule in Taiwan and Thailand. But even under authoritarian governments, crime was a major industry in these two countries. And protection in all these states has been paid for by losses in due process.

Coercive capitalism has also imposed heavy costs in official corruption. Bribery of officials has been a normal operating expense in such states, with Singapore a notable exception. In Indonesia, Soeharto and his family had their hands in the till of almost every profitable enterprise. In Thailand, "politics is an expensive business. To win election, candidates buy votes, and then expect to see a return on their investment through kickbacks on government contracts and other perks of office."[93] Taiwanese officials also expect *kumshaw* and welcome locals' pirating American books, compact discs, and computer software. In 1998, two South Korean presidents were in jail for extorting bribes and the incumbent was implicated in another scandal. On the other hand, corruption is hardly a stranger to constitutional democracy; anyone doing business in Washington quickly learns that "campaign contributions" open many gates, including those to the White House.[94]

On this checkered record, the Caucus might conclude that:

1. Coercive capitalism provides discipline needed for economic growth, far beyond what any hyphenate democratic system can.

2. Business cycles are facts of life. During the boom years, coercive capitalism promoted more growth than did any other system; and, outside of Indonesia, these systems responded quickly to crisis. Singapore's unemployment rate of 4.5 percent in 1998 would have seemed Edenesque in South Africa, where almost a third of workers were out of jobs, and wonderful in Germany, France, and Italy, where about 11 percent were.[95]

3. Like all small countries, *Nusquam* would be impotent against the machinations of a global market, whatever political system it adopted; but it might learn from the Tigers' lesson and curb the greed of its own bankers and investors.

Still, coercive capitalism may, as does good Frascati, travel poorly. Lee claims Singapore's success is peculiarly Asian and Confucian.[96] Putting aside difficulties with concepts as vast as Asian or Confucian, there is exquisite irony in Lee's claim. First, he copied western, not Asian, political and economic institutions. Second, Lee himself is more British than Chinese. In the 1960s the British foreign secretary called him "the best bloody Englishman east of Suez."[97] Educated in the United Kingdom, where he was called "Harry," Lee was not fluent in Chinese when he formed the PAP; he played on "old boy" networks to ingratiate himself with colonial officials; and, once in office, he used the British Internal Security Act to crush opponents. Third, Lee's economic successes depended heavily on western money as well as technology. Fourth, when he decided that Singapore's schools should teach Confucianism, he had to import American scholars to teach the teachers.

Lee may, however, have described the sort of political culture coercive capitalism needs when he said: "[T]he majority of Chinese-Singaporeans do not want to be actively involved in political parties. It's not in their culture. What they want is to have somebody governing them well and producing things they want."[98] It is not clear how Asian or Confucian such an attitude is. It would not be farfetched to call Wilhelmine Germany a coercive capitalist state. And preferences for the primacy of prosperity echoed in the American presidential campaign of 1992—"It's the economy, Stupid"—and in bored public reaction to the salacious surroundings of President Clinton's public perjury in 1998. It is not impossible to believe that *Nusquam*'s citizens might willingly trade some freedom for more bread.

Without doubt, neither Singapore's tight control nor Indonesian and

Malaysian oppression reflects the Caucus's ideal civic culture. But, if the founders stay in power for many years, they might imprint their values on society and ride a wave of prosperity toward a more attractive system. Indeed, some economists believe that, while individual rights do not promote—may even retard—prosperity in underdeveloped countries, prosperity tends to promote individual rights. Thus Robert J. Barro views political freedom as a luxury: "Rich places consume more democracy because this good is desirable for its own sake and even though the increased political freedom may have a small adverse effect on [economic] growth."[99] On the other hand, he contends, if rights get far ahead of economic development, the system is likely to turn authoritarian.

Many political scientists disagree. "The emergence of democracy," Adam Przeworski and Fernando Limongi argue, "is not a by-product of economic development" but of political actors' choices and "can be initiated at any level of development." Chances of success, of course, increase when the country is rich, but the nation's "wealth is not decisive."[100] Linz and Stepan go further and conclude from their polls of public opinion in Eastern Europe that citizens can keep political and economic performance separate and that the former makes a heavier contribution to stability than the latter.[101]

The Tigers' records do not settle the issue. Although initially coercive capitalism everywhere opposed both constitutionalism and democracy, in some places that opposition has since eased. After economic success, Korea, Taiwan, Thailand, and Hong Kong before its reabsorption into China moved toward democracy, even constitutionalism. On the other hand, Soeharto was as opposed to constitutionalism and democracy when he was deposed as when he came to power; and neither Lee in Singapore nor Mahathir in Malaysia has become enamored of political freedom.

Furthermore, if the founders' tenure were short, their successors would have a similar opportunity to reshape political institutions and culture. Gods who give can also take away. To initiate a coercive capitalist regime expecting later to democratize and constitutionalize its politics takes heroic optimism—or enormous *chutzpa*.

Choices That Beget More Choices

The Caucus must carefully examine these and other alternative systems and decide whether to risk coercive capitalism's prospects of immediate economic growth against its authoritarianism. When weighing forms of representative democracy, they must judge whether their people and the officials they will choose have or can very quickly acquire a political culture that will, without constitutionalist checks, restrain political power. If

Nusquam's founders decide to establish constitutional democracy, they must explore the possibilities of creating a version that would: (a) contain consociational elements to reinforce protections for minorities; (b) guard citizens against one another more effectively than does the current American model; (c) encourage citizens to think not only in terms of individual rights but also of obligations; and (d) create political processes that would require political candidates, as well as stimulate citizens, to confront the questions of justice and wisdom that alternative public policies raise.

If the Caucus moves toward constitutional democracy, it must also address at least three other critical questions: (1) What are the political, social, and economic prerequisites for such a political system? (2) Can *Nusquam* now—or quite soon—meet these conditions? And, (3) if it can meet them, how should the founders lay foundations for institutions and processes best suited to generate and sustain their version the good society?

Notes

1. For a study of the same general problem from a very different set of perspectives, see Richard Rose, William Mishler, and Christian Haerpfer, *Democracy and Its Alternatives: Understanding Post-Communist Societies* (Baltimore: Johns Hopkins University Press, 1998).

2. Montesquieu, *The Spirit of the Laws* (New York: Harper, 1949), Bk. I, §3, p. 6.

3. See Juan Linz, *The Breakdown of Democratic Regimes* (Baltimore: Johns Hopkins University Press, 1978), p. 11, and *Federalist* No. 45.

4. David Easton's *A Systems Analysis of Political Life* (New York: Wiley, 1965) is the seminal work on diffuse and specific support; he revised his definition somewhat in "A Re-Assessment of the Concept of Political Support," *Br. J. Pol. Sci.* 5 (1975): 435. Joseph Tanenhaus and I co-authored a series of articles about public opinion and the U.S. Supreme Court that modify and operationalize those two concepts. We list the citations in "Publicity, Public Opinion, and the Supreme Court," *N'wn. U. L. Rev.* 84 (1990): 985.

5. See generally Gerald W. Scully, *Constitutional Environments and Economic Growth* (Princeton: Princeton University Press, 1992).

6. *The Old Regime and the French Revolution* (Stuart Gilbert, trans. from 4th ed., 1858; New York: Doubleday, 1955), p. 169.

7. See my "Constitutions, Constitutionalism, and Democracy," in Douglas Greenberg et al., eds., *Constitutionalism and Democracy* (New York: Oxford University Press, 1993). That essay and, even more so, *Constitutional Democracy* offer fuller discussions of the concept of constitutionalism, explaining that it is similar to but goes beyond Liberalism's theory of the minimal state. For a discussion of constitutionalism as authorizing as well as limiting power, see Suzette Hemberger's essay, ch. 6 in this volume.

8. The first quotation is from his letter to John Taylor, May 29, 1816; Paul L. Ford, ed., *The Works of Thomas Jefferson* (New York: Putnam's Sons, 1905), XI:527; the second from *Notes on Virginia*, Andrew A. Lipscomb, ed., *The Writings of Thomas Jefferson* (Washington, DC: The Jefferson Memorial Association, 1903), II:163.

9. For an excellent survey, see Rogers M. Smith, *Civic Ideals: Conflicting Visions of Citizenship in U.S. History* (New Haven: Yale University Press, 1997).

10. Quoted by Fareed Zakaria, "Culture is Destiny: A Conversation with Lee Kuan Yew,"' *For. Affrs.* 73 (March/April 1994):111.

11. *The Economist*, August 10, 1996, p. 30; May 31, 1997, p. 43.

12. Alessandra Stanley, "Gorbachëv's New Battle: Overcoming His Legacy," *New York Times*, March 10, 1995.

13. *Constitutional Revolution, Ltd.* (Claremont, CA: Claremont College Press, 1941), pp. 7, 67. (Italics in original.)

14. Quoted in Pauline Maier, "Review of Gordon S. Wood, *The Radicalism of the American Revolution*," *New York Review of Books*, March 1, 1992.

15. Henry S. Farber and Joanne Gowa, "Polities and Peace," *Intern'l Sec.* 20 (1995):123. For a fuller discussion, see Gowa, *Ballots and Bullets: The Elusive Democratic Peace* (Princeton: Princeton University Press, 1999).

16. *Resort to Arms: International and Civil Wars, 1816–1980* (Beverly Hills, CA: Sage, 1982).

17. Gurr's exact wording is important: "[O]ur operational indicator of democracy is derived from codings of the competitiveness of political participation, . . . the openness and competitiveness of executive recruitment, . . . and constraints on the chief executive." *Polity II: Political Structures and Regime Change, 1800–1986* [Computer file] (Boulder, CO: Center for Comparative Politics [producer], 1989; Ann Arbor, MI: Inter-University Consortium for Political Research [distributor], 1990), p. 38.

18. Farber and Gowa, "Polities and Peace," pp. 141–42. For a contrary conclusion, see Spencer B. Weart, *Never at War: Why Democracies Will Not Fight One Another* (New Haven: Yale University Press, 1998).

19. Charles S. Gochman and Zeev Maoz, "Militarized Interstate Disputes, 1816–1976," *J. of Conflict Resolution* 28 (1984):585.

20. Farber and Gowa, "Polities and Peace," p. 143.

21. Edward D. Mansfield and Jack Snyder, "Democratization and the Danger of War," *Intern'l Sec.* 20 (1995):5.

22. "Democratization and the Danger of War," p. 5. Mansfield and Snyder included colonial wars in their definition.

23. Ibid., 8.

24. Ibid., 17.

25. Colonial wars constitute another savage form of combat, but one in which two nation-states are not directly involved and so are not included in many studies. (For example, one of the most systematic studies of relationships between war and democracy limits its scope to "conflicts between two independent states." David L. Rousseau et al., "Assessing the Dyadic Nature of the Democratic Peace, 1918–1988," *Am. Pol. Sci. Rev.* 90 [1996]:512, n. 1.) Nevertheless, a plague of such conflicts afflicted constitutional democracies well into the second half of the twentieth century.

26. See Albert O. Hirschman, *The Passions and the Interests: Political Arguments for Capitalism before Its Triumph* (Princeton: Princeton University Press, 1977).

27. For instance: Robert J. Barro, *Getting It Right: Market Choices in a Free Society* (Cambridge: MIT Press, 1997); and Samuel P. Huntington and Joan M. Nelson, *No Easy Choices: Political Participation in Developing Countries* (Cambridge: Harvard University Press, 1976). See also Jon Elster, "The Necessity and Impossibility of Simultaneous Economic and Political Reform," in Greenberg, *Constitutionalism and Democracy*.

28. See Karen L. Remmer, "Democracy and Economic Crisis: The Latin American Experience," *World Pols.* 42 (1990):316.

29. See Avraham Barkai, *Nazi Economics: Ideology, Theory, and Policy*, trans. Ruth Hadass-Vashitz (New Haven: Yale University Press, 1990); Dan P. Silverman, *Hitler's Economy* (Cambridge: Harvard University Press, 1998); and, more generally, Ronald Wintrobe, *The Political Economy of Dictatorship* (New York: Cambridge University Press, 1998).

30. Whether Franco was merely an old-fashioned military dictator who exploited Fascist ideology or was a true Fascist is contested. See: Robert O. Paxton, "The Uses of Fascism," *New York Review of Books*, Nov. 28, 1996, pp. 48, 51; Paxton and Stanley G. Payne, *A History of Fascism, 1914–1945* (Madison: University of Wisconsin Press, 1996); and Walter Laqueur, *Fascism: Past, Present, and Future* (New York: Oxford University Press, 1996). For discussions of Franco's economic policies, see Victor M. Pérez-Diaz, *The Return of Civil Society: The Emergence of Democratic Spain* (Cambridge: Harvard University Press, 1993), chs. 1, 4; Howard J. Wiarda, *The Transition to Democracy in Spain and Portugal* (Lanham, MD: American Enterprise Institute for Public Policy Research, 1989), chs. 1, 8; and Phillipe Schmitter and G. Lehmbruch, eds., *Trends Toward Corporatist Intermediation* (Beverly Hills: Sage, 1979).

31. Charles Jones, "The Separated Presidency," in Anthony King, ed., *The New American Political System*, 2d ed. (Washington, DC: American Enterprise Institute, 1990), p. 3.

32. See: Robert A. Dahl, "Decision-Making in a Democracy: The Supreme Court As a National Policy Maker," *J. of Pub. L.* 6 (1957):279; and Charles L. Black, *The People and the Court: Judicial Review and Democracy* (New York: Macmillan, 1960), esp. ch. 3. The Japanese Supreme Court had, as of 1999, invalidated only a half-dozen of several hundred challenged statutes. Lawrence W. Beer and Hiroshi Itoh, *The Constitutional Case Law of Japan, 1970 through 1990* (Seattle: University of Washington Press, 1996), p. 24. Irish judges are less agreeable to the government than the Japanese, but still are more likely to sustain than invalidate a statute. In its first few decades, the *Bundesverfassungsgericht* invalidated more statutes that the U.S. Supreme Court had in its first century; nevertheless the German Court has upheld the validity of more than 2,000 challenged governmental acts. For more complete statistics on the work of European constitutional courts, see Alec Stone Sweet, *Governing with Judges: Constitutional Politics in Europe* (New York: Oxford University Press, 2000), esp. ch. 3.

33. For citations to some of the relevant literature, see Murphy and Tanenhaus, "Publicity, Public Opinion, and the Supreme Court," p. 989, n. 17. Our findings do not lend great support to the basic hypothesis.

34. Lawrence W. Beer, "Human Rights and 'Freedom Culture' in Eastern

Asia," in A. Anghie and G. Sturgess, eds., *Legal Visions of the 21st Century* (The Hague: Kluwer, 1998), p. 159.

35. Daniel Bell, *The Cultural Contradictions of Capitalism* (New York: Basic Books, 1976); R. H. Tawney, *The Acquisitive Society* (New York: Harcourt, Brace, 1920); C. B. McPherson, *The Political Theory of Possessive Individualism: Hobbes to Locke* (New York: Oxford University Press, 1962).

36. Michael J. Sandel, "The Procedural Republic and the Unencumbered Self," *Pol. Th.* 12 (1984):93, and *Democracy's Discontent* (Cambridge: Harvard University Press, 1996).

37. *Habits of the Heart: Individualism and Commitment in American Life* (New York: Harper & Row, 1985), pp. 152–55.

38. "On the Jewish Question," reprinted in Robert C. Tucker, ed., *The Marx-Engels Reader* (New York: Norton, 1972), 40.

39. See Stephen L. Carter, *The Culture of Disbelief: How American Law and Politics Trivialize Religious Devotion* (New York: Basic Books, 1993).

40. *Rights Talk: The Impoverishment of Political Discourse* (New York: The Free Press, 1991), p. 14.

41. *Democracy and Disagreement* (Cambridge: Harvard University Press, 1996).

42. E.g., Sandel, *Democracy's Discontent*, chs. 5–8; and Barry Alain Shain, *The Myth of American Individualism: The Protestant Origins of American Political Thought* (Princeton: Princeton University Press, 1994).

43. See Robert D. Putnam, *Making Democracy Work: Civic Traditions in Modern Italy* (Princeton: Princeton University Press, 1993). See also: Edward Banfield, *The Moral Basis of a Backward Society* (Glencoe, IL: The Free Press, 1958); Ann Cornelisen, *Torregreca* (New York: Holt, Rinehart & Winston, 1969) and *Strangers and Pilgrims: The Last Italian Migration* (New York: Holt, Rinehart & Winston, 1980); and, of course, Carlo Levi, *Christ Stopped at Eboli* (New York: Farrar, Straus, 1947). Despite Southern Italians' lack of attachment to the state, their commitments to family, neighborhood, and even city appear strong.

44. "Freedom of Speech, Democracy, and Constitutionalism: United States, Germany, and Canada," inaugural lecture for the Robie Chair, University of Notre Dame, Oct. 1994.

45. Carl J. Friedrich believed that constitutional democracy was "rooted in Christian beliefs." *Transcendent Justice: The Religious Dimension of Constitutionalism* (Durham, NC: Duke University Press, 1964), p. 17 and ch. 1 generally. If he is correct and if those roots can grow only in Christian soil, Africans and Asians should not seriously consider constitutional democracy. The experience of Japan and India offers hope, however.

46. There is insufficient space in this chapter to discuss Bernard Manin's brilliant critique of representative democracy: *The Principles of Representative Government* (New York: Cambridge University Press, 1997).

47. *Commentaries on the Laws of England* (facs. of the 1st ed. of 1765; Chicago: University of Chicago Press, 1979), I:156.

48. Michael Walzer, "Philosophy and Democracy," *Pol. Th.* 9 (1981):386.

49. Response to a question after a lecture at the Gregorian University, 1996. Although these remarks were supposedly off-the-record, they were widely quoted in the press. Justice Scalia kindly sent me a transcript.

50. See Ferdinand A. Hermans, *The Representative Republic* (Notre Dame, IN: University of Notre Dame Press, 1958), and *Democracy or Anarchy?* (Notre Dame, IN: University of Notre Dame Press, 1941).

51. Robert A. Dahl, *Democracy and Its Critics* (New Haven: Yale University Press, 1989), p. 175.

52. Ibid., p. 164.

53. *Democracy and Disagreement*, pp. 354–55. Carlos Santiago Nino offers a more constitutionalist interpretation of deliberative democracy: *The Constitution of Deliberative Democracy* (New Haven: Yale University Press, 1996); Ronald Dworkin's reading of democracy is also more constitutionalist and less morally agnostic than are most American democrative theorists: "The Moral Reading and the Majoritarian Premise," in Harold Hongju Koh and Ronald C. Slye, *Deliberate Democracy and Human Rights* (New Haven: Yale University Press, 1999).

54. *Democracy and Its Critics*, p. 154.

55. Ibid., p. 191. Walzer says: "The judges must hold themselves as closely as they can to the decisions of the democratic assembly, enforcing first of all the basic political rights that serve to sustain the character of the assembly and protecting its members from discriminatory legislation. They are not to enforce rights beyond these unless authorized to do so by a democratic decision." "Philosophy and Democracy," p. 397.

56. *Democracy and Distrust* (Cambridge: Harvard University Press, 1980), esp. ch. 6. Robert H. Bork was not the first to point to the open-endedness of Ely's supposedly limiting judges. *The Tempting of America* (New York: The Free Press, 1990), pp. 194–99.

57. For an argument that Britain has moved toward a subtle and unofficial form of judicial review, see Joshua Rozenberg, *Trial of Strength* (London: Richard Cohen, 1997).

58. One might include or exclude several other countries. Sweden, for instance, has judicial review, but courts exercise this authority so rarely as, perhaps, to make it a formal rather than a real power. See Barry Holström, "Sweden," in C. Neal Tate and Torbjörn Vallinder, eds., *The Global Expansion of Judicial Power* (New York: New York University Press, 1995). And some of the former Caribbean colonies have allowed appeal to the Privy Council in London, a form of judicial review.

59. Dworkin argues to the contrary: "The Moral Reading and the Majoritarian Premise."

60. Quoted in John A. Rohr, *Founding Republics in France and America* (Lawrence: University Press of Kansas, 1995), p. 26.

61. See Ralph Lerner, "The Supreme Court as Republican School Master," *Sup. Ct. Rev.* 1967:127; and John Semonche, *Keeping the Faith: A Cultural History of the Supreme Court* (Lanham, MD: Rowman & Littlefield, 1998), chs. 1–3.

62. See esp. Edmund S. Morgan, *Inventing the People* (New York: Norton, 1988).

63. *Democracy and Its Critics*, p. 192.

64. Hans Daalder, "The Consociational Democracy Theme," *26 World Pols.* 604, 607 (1974), says that, in a consociational system that has democratic ambitions, "elites must consciously eschew the competitive practices which underlie

the norms of British-style democracy. Instead, they must regulate political life by forming some kind of elite cartel."

65. Arendt Lijphart, "The Puzzle of Indian Democracy: A Consociational Interpretation," *Am. Pol. Sci. Rev.* 90 (1996):258. Lijphart is the leading scholar in this area. "The Puzzle" cites much of the literature; his earlier work includes: *The Politics of Accommodation: Pluralism and Democracy in the Netherlands* (2d ed; Berkeley: University of California Press, 1975); "Consociational Democracy," *World Pols.* 21 (1969):207; *Democracy in Plural Societies* (New Haven: Yale University Press, 1977); *Democracies: Patterns of Majoritarian and Consensus Government in Twenty-One Countries* (New Haven: Yale University Press, 1984). Hans Daalder has also been important in this field: "The Consociational Democracy Theme"; and "On Building Consociational Nations," *Intern'l Soc. Sci. J.* 23 (1971):355. See also G. Bingham Powell, Jr., *Conflict Resolution in Divided Societies* (Stanford: Stanford University Press, 1970).

66. Jacob Levy, "Consociationalism as a Substitute for Constitutionalism?" Seminar paper in Politics 561, Princeton University (1995).

67. Daalder, "The Consociational Democracy Theme," p. 608.

68. See the discussion in Stephen P. Cohen, "The Military and Indian Democracy," in Atul Kohli, ed., *India's Democracy* (Princeton: Princeton University Press, 1988).

69. The title of ch. 9 of his *Asian Power and Politics* (Cambridge: Harvard University Press, 1985).

70. Editorial, "The Shaming of Malaysia," *The Economist*, Nov. 7, 1998, p. 16.

71. See Timothy Sisk, *Power Sharing and International Mediation in Ethnic Conflicts* (Washington, DC: U.S. Institute of Peace, 1998).

72. Samuel P. Huntington, *The Clash of Civilizations and the Remaking of the World Order* (New York: Simon & Schuster, 1996).

73. See esp.: Alasdair Bowie and Danny Unger, *The Politics of Open Economies: Indonesia, Malaysia, The Philippines, and Indonesia* (New York: Cambridge University Press, 1997); W. G. Duff, *The Economic Growth of Singapore* (New York: Cambridge University Press, 1997); and Robert Wade, *Governing the Market: Economic Theory and the Role of Government in East Asian Industrialization* (Princeton: Princeton University Press, 1992).

74. A World Bank Policy Report, *The East Asian Miracle: Economic Growth and Public Policy* (New York: Oxford University Press, 1993), p. 13.

75. Jeri Laber, "Smoldering Indonesia," *N.Y. Rev. of Bks.* Jan. 9, 1997, p. 40.

76. For details, see Christopher Tremewan, *The Political Economy of Social Control in Singapore* (New York: St. Martin's, 1994), ch. 1; and Lee Kuan Yew, *The Singapore Story: The Memoirs of Lee Kuan Yew* (New York: Prentice Hall, 1998). See also the review of Lee's memoirs by Ian Buruma, "The Man Who Would Be King," *N.Y. Rev. of Bks.*, June 10, 1999, pp. 34ff.

77. "Culture Is Destiny: A Conversation with Lee Kuan Yew," *For. Affrs.* 73 (1994):109.

78. Henry Kamm, "In Prosperous Singapore, Even the Elite Are Nervous about Speaking Out," *New York Times*, August 15, 1995.

79. Jim Rohwer, quoted in "Singapore: Smelling of Moses," *The Economist*, Jan. 13, 1996, p. 37.

80. Speech at National Day Rally, 1986; quoted in Tremewan, *The Political Economy of Social Control in Singapore*, p. 4.

81. But only about 75 percent of Singapore's children attend secondary schools.

82. In 1995, the hourly cost for labor was $7.28 in Singapore, $31.88 in Germany, $17.20 in the U.S., 71 cents in the Philippines, 60 cents in Russia, and 25 cents in China and India. *The Economist*, Nov. 2, 1996, p. 77.

83. Worker and employer each contribute about 20 percent of salary to the "Central Provident Fund," in which each worker holds several kinds of accounts to pay for items like life and medical insurance, education, and pensions. Meanwhile, the government can use these billions of dollars. Tremewan, *The Political Economy of Social Control in Singapore*, pp. 53–55. For a succinct description of the Fund, see "Fiscal Providence, Singapore-style," *The Economist*, Jan. 13, 1996, p. 38.

84. Interview with Zakaria, "Culture Is Destiny," p. 113.

85. Tremewan, *The Political Economy of Social Control in Singapore*, ch. 3.

86. Http://www.ftvision.com/Today/Stories/wef4.htm. Hong Kong ranked second, the United States third, and Russia 53rd. Cited in Peter Passel, "Singapore Ranked to No. 1 Economy," *New York Times*, May 24, 1997.

87. Bryan T. Johnson, Kim R. Holmes, and Melanie Kirkpatrick, *1999 Index of Economic Freedom* (New York: Heritage Foundation and *The Wall Street Journal*, 1999). The *Index*, released in December 1998, ranked Hong Kong, before its re-annexation, as the most economically free.

88. James M. West and Dae-Kyu Yoon, "The Constitutional Court of the Republic of Korea: Transforming the Jurisprudence of the Vortex?" *Am J. of Comp. L.* 40 (1992):73.

89. See Adam Schwartz, *A Nation in Waiting: Indonesia in the 1990s* (Boulder, CO: Westview, 1994); Daniel Lev, "Social Movements, Constitutionalism, and Human Rights," in Greenberg et al., *Constitutionalism and Democracy*; and Charles P. Corn, *Distant Islands: Travels Across Indonesia* (New York: Viking Penguin, 1991).

90. See John F. Cooper, *The Taiwan Political Miracle* (Lanham, MD: University Press of America, 1997).

91. Paul Krugman has provided the most plausible explanation for the panic of 1997. As early as 1994, he had argued that East Asia's rate of growth would soon decline. The "Miracle," he said, was not driven by efficient use of resources but by two other factors: a surplus of local manpower and a flow of foreign investment. Between 1966 and 1990, for example, Singapore had enlarged the share of its employed population from 27 to 51 percent, a rate it could not continue, leaving sustained growth at the mercy of foreign investors. The immediate cause of the crash, Krugman reasoned in 1998, was bankers' greed in making chancy loans they thought would be protected by governments or the International Monetary Fund. When risks became realities and bailouts were not forthcoming, businesses and banks began to fail, starting a rapid downward spiral as foreign investors withdrew their money. "What Happened to Asia?" http://web.mit.edu/krugman/www/DISINTER.html (Jan. 1998). See also Krugman, *The Return of Depression Economics* (New York: Norton, 1999), in which he fine-

tuned his analysis. The region's dependence on foreign investment continues to be a serious concern. During the summer of 2000, the Association of South East Asian Nations refused to make public its annual report on investments allegedly because it showed a continued precipitous decline in 1999. Wayne Arnold, "Asian Group Declines to Release Study on Foreign Investment," *The New York Times*, Aug. 24, 2000.

92. See the data reported in *The Economist*, Aug. 3, 1996, pp. 45–46. For Russian males, the decline was even more dramatic: from 65 in 1989 to 58 in 1995. Ibid., Sept. 21, 1996, pp. 53–54.

93. "Thailand Gets the Bill," *The Economist*, Aug. 9, 1997, p. 31.

94. India and Japan have more than their share of corruption. Jacob Schlesinger, *Shadow Shoguns: The Rise and Fall of Japan's Post-War Political Machine* (New York: Simon & Schuster, 1997). Using surveys of business executives during 1996–97, Transparency International ranked 52 nations on a scale of official corruption. The United States came out as the 16th cleanest, well behind Singapore, 9th. Hong Kong was 18th, while the other Dragons lagged far behind: Taiwan 31st, South Korea 34th, Thailand 39th, and Indonesia 46th. India was 45th. The worst was Nigeria, followed by Bolivia, Columbia, Russia, and Pakistan. Http//www.transparency.de/documents/press-releases/1997.31.7.cpi.html.

95. *The Economist*, Oct. 24, 1998, p. 86, reports data from national statistics offices. Despite the turmoil, in late 1998 Singapore's reserves of foreign currency were one and a half times what they had been in 1993.

96. There is a double presence in all the Tigers, great and small, for even in Malaysia and Indonesia, the entrepreneurs behind economic growth have been mostly ethnic Chinese.

97. Quoted in Zakaria, "Culture Is Destiny," p. 125.

98. Quoted in Kamm, "In Prosperous Singapore."

99. *Getting It Right*, p. 11.

100. "Modernization: Theories and Facts," *World Pols.* 49 (1997):177. See also: Remmer, "Democracy and Economic Crisis"; and José Maria Maravall, "The Myth of the Authoritarian Advantage," and Barbara Geddes, "Challenging the Conventional Wisdom," both in Larry Diamond and Marc F. Plattner, eds., *Economic Reform and Democracy* (Baltimore: Johns Hopkins University Press, 1995).

101. Juan J. Linz and Alfred Stepan, *Problems of Democratic Transition and Consolidation: Southern Europe, South America, and Post-Communist Europe* (Baltimore: Johns Hopkins University Press, 1996). See also the results of the public opinion poll taken in Switzerland, indicating that, on the whole, people would prefer additional increments of political freedom to more money. Bruno S. Frey and Alois Stutzer, "Happiness, Economy, and Institutions," unpub. paper, 1999; available from Prof. Stutzer: astutzer@iew.unizh.ch.

2

The Civic Constitution: Some Preliminaries

JOHN E. FINN

Introduction

What is the Constitution?[1] There is an astonishing number of answers to this question. Among the more interesting (and not the least useful, insofar as they de-emphasize the jural nature of the text) are claims that the Constitution is a metaphor of political goodness or a "calculus of motives."[2] Alternatively, the Constitution has been likened to poetry, literature, scripture, theater, and art, all in an effort to determine what other "thing" the Constitution is *like*—a question not entirely on all fours with the question of what the Constitution *is*.

Implicit in these and other answers to the question of what the Constitution is or is like are particular and occasionally peculiar notions about what the "Constitution" includes, about who bears responsibility for its interpretation, and, sometimes, about how it should be interpreted. Perhaps less obvious, every answer to the question of what the Constitution is incorporates an understanding of the Constitution's authority. Likening the Constitution to literature, or to art, implies that its "authority" is largely a function of suasion and aesthetic coherence. The authority of *Billy Budd*, for example (or better, of any single interpretation of it), is tied to its capacity to persuade us of its probity. The authority of the "Constitution" thus conceived inheres in and is a function of its relationship with a model audience that it both constructs and is constructed by.[3]

Of course, we might say that an interpretation of *Billy Budd* is authoritative, in the sense that a community of readers embraces it. Similarly, the authority of the Constitution in this sense would depend finally on its capacity to persuade us that its vision of community is desirable. Clearly, however, this collegial authority differs in fundamental ways from the authority we usually ascribe to legal texts. Legal interpretation, unlike literary interpretation, comes attached with sanctions for mutiny backed by the coercive apparatus of the state.[4] It is precisely the troublesome nature of seeing literary texts as "binding" that has led some to liken the Constitution and other legal texts not to literary texts but to sacred texts, where, arguably, the relationship of text to community is somewhat different.[5] (Others, in turn, find the very lack of bindingness useful for understanding the relationship of the constitutional text to the larger political order, as we shall see in the section below on "The Civic Constitution.") Differences between literary, sacred, and legal texts thus raise issues about the nature of different kinds of authority, whether legal or collegiate. They also suggest that grounding the Constitution's authority in our "consent" to it tells us *why* we are bound but not—necessarily—*what* we are bound to. I am more interested here in the what than the why, less in the mechanisms for securing the Constitution's authority and more in the substantive nature of its authority.[6]

My concern, therefore, is not with what specific constitutional clauses, such as the First Amendment or the Fourteenth, should mean (although I will have something to say about Article VI), or with Supreme Court opinions on one or another of important constitutional issues. Instead, I focus less on the meaning of the words *in* the Constitution, and more on the essence and meaning of the Constitution as a whole and on the kind of political community the Constitution envisions. My focus, in other words, is on what we should call the "constitutional enterprise": The effort to create a particular type of political community, a constitutional democracy, that can survive the corrupting influences of time and fortune.

There are, I shall argue, two principal constructions of the Constitution and hence, two principal accounts of its authority. I shall distinguish between the Juridic (or legal) Constitution and the Civic (or political) Constitution.[7] The Juridic regards the Constitution primarily as a legal document, as the "supreme law of the land." It emphasizes legality and how law trumps (or transforms) politics. Insofar as the Constitution is law it is not—or it is more than—politics or policy. It "defines the rules of the game, not winners and losers; . . . it shapes the contours of politics, not the content."[8] The Civic Constitution emphasizes not the legal character, but rather the political character of the basic charter, its status not as supreme law but as political creed. It envisions a political order in which constitutional questions, although partly questions of law, are fundamentally and first questions about politics, about the broad principles and normative commitments that comprise our commitment to shared community. It also attaches a different meaning and significance to politics. The Civic Constitution thus finds its significance as a constitutive political act. Its essential character is identity, not legality.

The terms "Juridic" and "Civic" recall Corwin's distinction between the "juristic" and the "political" Constitutions and, more recently, Nagel's discussion of the "legal" and the "political" Constitutions.[9] I prefer Corwin's terminology to Nagel's because it does a better job of relating the Constitution's status as law to the institutional claims of judges to enforcement than does Nagel's use of the word "legal." I reject both Corwin's and Nagel's use of the word "political" in favor of "civic" for similar reasons. An unabridged discussion about what we mean when we say the Constitution is "political," in addition to its length, would add little to the argument I want to make. In contrast, the word "civic" emphasizes the preceptorial aspects of the Constitution that Jefferson identified when he called it a "text of civil instruction." So I use the terms "Juridic" and "Civic" to stress the Constitution's relationship to the people, or rather its relationship to the audience it constitutes, and to signify questions about who it imagines that audience to be.

In a complete sense, the Constitution is neither Juridic nor Civic, but both. A full understanding of the Constitution must incorporate both dimensions. There are important differences between the two dimensions, however, and no community that hopes to be self-governing should ignore or misunderstand those differences. My purpose in contrasting these different dimensions of constitutional authority is to show the different ways they address a variety of matters central to a comprehensive theory of the constitutional order. Such issues include the relationship of the constitutional text to the constitutional order writ large, as well as the determination of who bears responsibility for protecting and maintaining that order. Each understanding of the Constitution offers a distinctive way of thinking about what "protecting" and "maintaining" the Constitution means. Moreover, the Civic and Juridic Constitutions suggest different conclusions about the centrality of constitutional interpretation to the larger enterprise of constitutional maintenance. Similarly, they hint at different answers to the question of who bears final institutional authority in matters of constitutional interpretation. Finally, the Civic and Juridic Constitutions embody substantially different notions of citizenship in a constitutional democracy. Each has a particular vision of the community we claim citizenship in and of what citizenship entails.[10] Each constitutes "We the people" in a distinct way.

My objective is not to argue that we should reject one understanding of the Constitution and its claim to authority in favor of another. Instead, I want to argue for the re-invigoration of one strand of many that comprise American constitutionalism and the American Constitution. I want, in other words, to "shift the mix" between the Civic and Juridic Constitutions and to show why we should care about the mix, much as Thayer did when he sought "to reconcile the legal and political elements of modern constitutional law."[11] I cannot hope to provide a comprehensive account of the Civic Constitution and its implications for the constitutional enterprise here. Instead, I mean only to sketch the differences and implications in broad strokes.

In the next section I shall outline the main features of the Juridic Constitution. I will trace the development of the Constitution as supreme law from *Federalist* No. 78 to *Marbury v. Madison* (1803), and then explore how the Juridic Constitution's status as supreme law influences the projects of constitutional maintenance and constitutional interpretation. Next, I shall consider the Civic Constitution and the nature of its authority. The Civic Constitution offers a fundamentally different approach to the enterprises of maintenance and interpretation. I consider the implications of the Civic Constitution for the constitutional order and for what it means to be a citizen. My principal claim shall be that as *citizens*, we all bear a heavy responsibility for the constitutional enterprise. In the Conclusion, I shall consider a few of the objections that might be raised against reclamation of the Civic Constitution, such as charges that it inadequately protects individual liberties, and that it fails to "settle" constitutional controversies.

There is one objection, however, that I should acknowledge immediately. Some readers may regard a claim that citizens should shoulder responsibility for the Constitution as trite or self-evident. As we shall see, though, certain prominent accounts of constitutional maintenance, including one sketched in the *Federalist Papers*, envision the constitutional enterprise as a venture best kept from citizens. The prevailing scholarly view likewise envisions a constitutional enterprise that is first the province of governments and only secondarily that of citizens.[12] Independence Day speeches notwithstanding, it is hardly obvious that the constitutional enterprise should be entrusted to ordinary citizens. Indeed, the Juridic Constitution finds such claims acceptable only at the level of rhetoric and if not taken seriously as a prescription for constitutional design.

The Juridic Constitution

> This Society hath a peculiar Cant and Jargon
> of their own, that no other Mortal can
> understand, and wherein all their Laws are
> written.
>   —Jonathan Swift

The Juridic Constitution is a way of comprehending the fundamental law and its claim to authority. It is also a way of understanding the constitutional enterprise more generally, as well as who takes part in that activity. And as the quotation from Swift implies, there is an important sense in which the Juridic Constitution is a way of talking, a set of discursive practices with a distinct set of practitioners.[13]

The Juridic Constitution begins with, but is not coextensive with, the proposition that the Constitution is law. Few propositions seem as obvious or are shared as widely; certainly most contemporary scholarship on the Constitution takes for granted its status as law. Scholars as diverse as Robert Bork and Laurence Tribe, for example, both begin "from the premise that the Constitution is law." At a different level of abstraction we would want to be more precise about the meaning of "law"—and I will be later in this paper—but for present purposes no greater specificity is necessary.[14]

The chief textual support for the Juridic Constitution is Article VI's declaration that the Constitution is "the Supreme Law of the Land." The supremacy clause makes two claims explicitly, and it may imply a third. First, Article VI claims the Constitution is law. Second, Article VI also insists upon the supremacy of the Constitution. Like the claim that the Constitution is law, the Constitution's claim to supremacy does not ordinarily encounter dissent, although it has more than once nearly provoked a national crisis. Nevertheless, the implications of the claim to supremacy are largely unexplored, especially if we regard it as a claim about the Constitution as a political and not a legal instrument.[15] In addition, the declaration of supremacy has important implications for the Constitution's status as law, for it makes clear that the Constitution as law is superior to ordinary acts of legislation. Article VI thus envisions a hierarchy of law. The third claim, at best only implicit in Article VI, depends upon this hierarchy, or on the marriage of the two claims of supremacy and law. This proposition is that because the Constitution is supreme law, and because supreme law must control inferior law, federal judges possess a power of constitutional review.[16] The extent of that power has always been a matter of dispute.

Although it was not the first effort to tie the nature of the text to institutional responsibility to protect it, Marshall's opinion in *Marbury v. Madison* (1803) is the most familiar version of the argument. In *Marbury*, Marshall argued that "The Constitution is either a superior paramount law, unchangeable by ordinary means, or it is on a level with ordinary legal acts." And again: "Certainly all those who have framed written constitutions contemplate them as forming the fundamental and paramount law of the nation." Shortly following, Marshall chained the Constitution's status as superior law to the institutional prerogative of the Court. "It is," Marshall concluded, "emphatically the province and the duty of the judicial department to say what the law is."[17] Article VI offers some additional support for the claim insofar as it specifically directs "Judges in every State" to "be bound thereby."

Marshall also recognized that to the extent that the Constitution could not be conceptualized as law, or only law—in other words, to the extent that questions raised under it were in "their nature political"—then judges could claim no special authority or responsibility for preserving or protecting it. The claim of expertise, or institutional competence, was both the source and the limit of judicial responsibility for the text. This early use of the political question doctrine underscores the centrality of the Constitution's status as law to judicial claims to enforce it. (It also hints at a Constitution that is more than law. Nevertheless, at least for Marshall and certainly for most judges since *Baker v. Carr* [1962], the final decision about what is a matter of law or of politics rests with the Court. One might say that this underscores the subordination of politics to law.)

Marshall's argument borrowed heavily from *Federalist* No. 78, where Hamilton envisioned a federal judiciary with a broad and perhaps final authority of review. Unlike Hamilton, nowhere in the *Federalist Papers* did Madison clearly and forthrightly stake a position on judicial review. It is possible, however, to reconstruct Madison's views if we draw from a variety of sources, including *Federalist* No. 51 and his *Report on the Virginia Resolutions*. In the former, Madison envisioned an elaborate system of checks and balances, or institutional devices, to guard against constitutional abuses. The central characteristic of these devices was their very multiplicity. Nevertheless, Madison's list of checks on the abuse of national authority in *Federalist* No. 51 failed to list the judiciary. It is not likely that the omission was unintentional, especially given Madison's letters to Jefferson and others on the difficulties with judicial review.[18] Unlike Hamilton, who sought a centralized power of control, Madison sought security in institutional conflict and decentralization.[19]

Like Marshall later, Hamilton stressed the hierarchical structure of law contained in the supremacy clause. "No legislative act . . . contrary to the Constitution," he argued, "can ever be valid. To deny this would be to affirm that the deputy is greater than his principal."[20] And like Marshall, Hamilton stressed the Constitution's status as higher law. "A Constitution is, in fact, and must be regarded by the judges as, a fundamental law. It therefore belongs to them [judges] to ascertain its meaning as well as the meaning of any particular act proceeding from the legislative body."[21] And again in No. 78, "The interpretation of the laws is the proper and peculiar province of the courts. A constitution is, in fact, and must be regarded by the judges as, fundamental law. It therefore belongs to them to ascertain its meaning."[22] As the last quote makes clear, Hamilton, like Marshall, equated a particular answer to what the Constitution is (law) with an assertion about who bears responsibility for protecting and preserving it (judges). "Faithful guardians of the Constitution," independent judges are required to protect it against legislative incursions. Thus, "From the fact that the Constitution is a law comes the assertion that its interpretation must come from a court."[23] There are some differences between Hamilton and Marshall, but both accepted some form of judicial review as a logical inference from the twin claims of supremacy and law. All three claims are difficult, but it is the last that forms the centerpiece of the Juridic Constitution by soldering the Constitution as a legal text with the authority of judges to enforce it.

My point here is not to rehearse familiar arguments about the propriety of judicial review or to castigate the obviously shallow and oft-criticized reasoning Marshall offered in support of it. Instead, I want to emphasize how much of the argument in *Marbury* rests upon the assertion that the essential character of the Constitution is its status as written law. In Marshall's hands, judicial responsibility for the Constitution rested not on a Madisonian notion of checks and balances, but instead on the Constitution's status as law and on judicial claims of professional expertise.[24]

Perhaps because they are now so routine, we sometimes seem not to appreciate the significance of the twinned claims of law and supremacy and the edifice they provide for the claim of judicial review in *Marbury*. Recently, however, Snowiss has emphasized the extent to which Marshall's reliance on the Constitution's status as supreme law was "no part of the understanding of those who before *Marbury* supported a judicial check on legislation."[25] Indeed, throughout much of the founding, Snowiss argues, the concept of "fundamental law" was "understood to be a political instrument that could bind only politically and morally, not legally." Consequently, judicial enforcement of the fundamental law was subordinate to political or electoral enforcement—an understanding both of the Constitution and of the relationship between law and politics that wrestles with much of contemporary scholarship and teaching about the Constitution.

The Juridic Constitution As a Discursive Practice

As *Federalist* No. 78 and *Marbury* suggest, Article VI invites us to ground the Constitution in law. It then becomes reasonable (but not inevitable) to submit constitutional issues to judges and lawyers, who can fairly claim some expertise in resolving legal issues. Marshall's opinion in *Marbury* instated the development of the Juridic Constitution by claiming for the Court an authority to interpret the text. Marshall did not claim that judges had exclusive authority or even final authority, however. Nor did *Marbury* bring the Juridic Constitution into full bloom. "Judicialization" of the Constitution took place over a long period of time.[26] Its evolution was closely related to the development of law more generally as a profession.[27]

Legalization of the Constitution has had profound consequences for our understanding of it. Lawyers have made the text in their own image.

Consequently, "Our conception of the Constitution has been shaped by their [lawyers'] instincts and intellectual habits."[28] Those instincts and habits have also greatly influenced our sense of lawyers and judges as guardians of the temple. The exclusive nature of the legal profession is well established. Hamilton, for example, wrote how acquisition of the legal expertise necessary to interpret the law "demand[s] long and laborious study. . . . Hence it is that there can be but few men in the society who will have sufficient skill in the laws to qualify them for the station of judges."[29] Consequently, responsibility for constitutional interpretation rests not with "the whole society," but rather with those few who possess the professional skills needed to attend to the task. Hamilton's conception of the constitutional enterprise tells us what the Constitution is—a creature of law—and consequently to whom it belongs.[30] The Juridic Constitution is a Constitution about law and for lawyers. Its language is one of rules, commands, and penalties.[31]

Attended to and protected by the bar, the Juridic Constitution ordains for the constitutional order, more generally, an inherent inequality premised upon the unequal distribution of professional skills. Those of us who possess such skills are thus members of what the academy sometimes calls "interpretive communities."[32] An interpretive community is one whose members share certain skills or attributes. The interpretive community that surrounds the Juridic Constitution is comprised of members trained in law, of individuals who can think and talk like lawyers. Or, in the words of Strauber, "to be a member of the interpretive community is to question, clarify, formulate, categorize, and analyze the way lawyers do."[33] Consequently, "the community consists of the advocates . . . ; the judges . . . ; and the teachers and critics."[34]

To talk or to think about the Juridic Constitution one must be able to understand its essence as law—one must, in other words, know what law is. If we accept the claim that talk about, or interpretation of, the Juridic Constitution is legal in nature, then in a certain sense the Constitution is, as Levinson has suggested, "a linguistic system, what some among us might call a discourse."[35] It is, however, an extremely exclusionary discourse, a point acknowledged, indeed celebrated, in *Federalist* No. 78, but routinely overlooked by the many academic lawyers who have stressed the ways in which the Constitution structures public conversation.[36]

In truth, however, there is very little that is "public" about such conversations.[37] The point is clearest if we consider the work of Dworkin, who perhaps more than his colleagues has insisted upon the public or democratic character of constitutional discourse, most recently in *Freedom's Law*. In *Taking Rights Seriously*,[38] Dworkin's defense of civil disobedience was premised upon the possibility that *any* citizen can reach an informed and reasoned decision about what the law is and what it requires of us. As Dworkin noted, "a citizen's allegiance is to the law, not to any particular person's view of what the law is." Dworkin's defense of civil disobedience, then, rests upon a view of "the law" as a set of legal principles that require interpretation and application. Citizens no less than the law's practitioners are a part of the "interpretive community."

Apparently, Dworkin's interpretive community is an empire without borders, whether intellectual or physical, for Dworkin fails to acknowledge either kind. In the first instance, Dworkin simply does not account for the technical knowledge and professional skills that gain one entrance into the community, or that the community uses to regulate (limit) membership. As Fiss, Brigham, and others have concluded, "The community in law is very well defined, in comparison to other communities."[39] In part, that definition occurs at the abstract level of intellectual specialization and the evolution of law as a profession. Its physical manifestation is apparent in the existence of law schools, law libraries, and law courts.

In some ways, Dworkin's community without walls is wonderfully naive. There is little reason to think that citizens' views will carry much weight in such discussions, especially against the claims of superior knowledge made by experts. Even if we characterize such knowledge not as an understanding of technical law or constitutional history, but instead as knowledge of moral principle, as Dworkin suggests in *Freedom's Law*, it still unlikely that citizens will possess the kind of rhetorical skills and material resources necessary to play much of a role in the interpretive community. As Cotterrell and others have argued, "it is . . . profoundly unrealistic to consider non-lawyer citizens, on the one hand, and lawyers or judges, on the other, as part of the same community of legal interpreters."[40] Hence, the very existence of an interpretive community raises important issues concerning the distribution of political power.

Ackerman also wants to "enlarge" the community of discourse. He asks us "to behold . . . a pretty picture: an America in which a redis-covered Constitution is the subject of an ongoing dialogue amongst scholars, professionals, and the people at large."[41] His approach fails too, however, and for similar reasons. Ackerman's distinction between normal and constitutional politics gives a voice to citizens only in extraordinary constitutional "moments."[42] In the course of normal politics, the Court "speaks for" citizens in a "preservationist" function. Much of *We the People* is ceded to a discussion of the importance of "professional narrative" and how it might be changed or expanded to include a wider circle of scholars and disciplines. This professional narrative, notwithstanding Ackerman's effort to enlarge it, must still exclude citizens, who cannot be expected to play much of a role except in those extraordinary constitutional moments.

Imagine, however, another "pretty picture": that membership in the

Constitution's interpretive community is less exclusive than I suggest. Suppose we are all at least potential members of the interpretive community of the Juridic Constitution. We are not all equally literate in the law. And precisely because one's standing in the community is in large measure a function of one's ability to persuade others, some members of the community will be more equal than others. Further, some of the more important inequalities in our shared community are disparities in physical resources. "Settings like Yale," Brigham reminds us, "and of course others in the 'higher circles' have a special place."[43]

Even within the interpretive community, therefore, there are fairly identifiable disparities in status, disparities that raise important issues about the allocation of power. In a larger sense, the very existence of interpretive communities under the Juridic Constitution raises issues of power and politics. Legal language—the language of the interpretive community—is inescapably "a language of power" and social control.[44] It is, moreover, a specialized and private language, "the product of a society in which only a very limited class of 'legally competent' people can read the texts of that language."[45]

Consequently, the law, which is an important language, if not *the* language of political power in the United States, is the "peculiar province" of a few; the great majority of citizens is governed by what Learned Hand called an "alien tongue." This is an important part of political life, for "conscious choices between varieties of language have important political consequences, particularly when language skills are unevenly distributed."[46] Indeed, if language is constitutive, and not simply descriptive—if there is no such thing as an extralinguistic reality—then discursive practices must also be political practices.[47]

It is important to stress that this state results from a choice about how to understand the Constitution; it is not an inevitable or the only possible reading of the Constitution. We could reject the Juridic Constitution in favor of another understanding of the text, one that does not emphasize its status as law. Hence, we should recognize that the Juridic Constitution, notwithstanding its legal character, represents and embodies fundamental choices about the distribution of political power and self-rule.

Constitutional Maintenance, Interpretation, and Citizenship

Implicit in the Juridic Constitution is a conception of constitutional maintenance that largely reduces the enterprise to constitutional interpretation. Constitutional maintenance becomes the work of judges specially fit for the task.[48] For the most part, scholarship on and teaching about the Juridic Constitution—and perhaps the text itself—are equivalent to the study of judicial interpretations of the text. Even those who wish to draw analytical distinctions between the text and its judicial gloss find the distinction difficult to maintain.[49]

The Juridic Constitution makes constitutional interpretation the centerpiece of the constitutional enterprise. Indeed, in their recent works, Michael Sandel[50] and Cass Sunstein,[51] though they disagree in profound ways about the proper reach of judicial interpretation, both acknowledge the centrality of judicial responsibility for interpretation to the maintenance of the constitutional order as a whole. One of the consequences of this emphasis on constitutional interpretation is that it has made the Juridic Constitution even more mysterious and removed from anyone not trained in the law (just as Hamilton knew it would). The legal academy, following Hamilton, claims that skill in constitutional interpretation is an art or a matter of technique, attained only through long and rigorous study, manifest only when one can speak the language of law and whatever language (whether of literary criticism or moral philosophy) is fashionable in the interpretive community.[52] Skill in interpretation must be learned. And such skill "at assessing evidence about historical intent, at textual analysis, at harmonizing various provisions and cases, at clear and reasoned explanation—is thought to be a qualification for accurate and consistent interpretation."[53] I do not mean to suggest that there are no questions of degree here—the judicial minimalism of Sunstein's recent work, for example, represents an obvious effort to hitch a particular understanding of the judicial role to a reinvigorated conception of citizenship.[54] But the underlying premise of Sunstein's work is plainly hospitable to the argument I have made about the exclusivity and remoteness of professional constitutional interpretation.

Enforcement of the Constitution is thus conceived chiefly in terms of interpretation and entrusted to those who best understand it. This is a conception of constitutional maintenance that largely ignores citizens. Insofar as the Juridic Constitution is beyond the understanding of the people, it is less an instrument of self-government in the hands of citizens than a reverential and mysterious symbol for its subjects. Moreover, the focus on constitutional interpretation obscures the extent to which interpretation involves *political* choices. Every act of interpretation involves an act of choice, both about political values and norms and concerning who has the power to make such choices. The Juridic Constitution means that "'political' debate [must] be cast in a distinct judicial language and rhetoric."[55] Because it is so cast, debate over fundamental issues in American politics often takes place in arenas and in a language that excludes citizens. The Juridic Constitution teaches citizens that it is not their job to tend it so much as to revere it from afar.

The exclusion of citizens from the project of constitutional maintenance under the Juridic Constitution is at least compatible with, but not identical to, the conception of constitutional maintenance set forth in the *Federalist Papers*. As Robert Burt concluded, "the founders did not expect that the direct commandatory voice of the sovereign People would be heard very often in the daily affairs of governance. . . . This expectation has been realized in practice."[56] Both *Federalist* Nos. 78 and 49, for example, begin with the proposition that a citizenry whose passions are routinely engaged by constitutional matters is a matter for great apprehension. Madison captured the sense of this anxiety in *Federalist* No. 49, where he warned that "The danger of disturbing the public tranquillity by interesting too strongly the public passions is a still more serious objection against a frequent reference of constitutional questions to the decision of the whole society."[57]

In Madison's view, the constitutional enterprise is better served by a citizenry whose affection for the Constitution is not overly burdened by ongoing responsibility for it, because "every appeal to the people would carry an implication of some defect in the government, [and] frequent appeals would . . . deprive the government of that veneration which time bestows on everything, and without which perhaps the wisest and freest governments would not possess the requisite stability."[58] In *Federalist* No. 49, then (and elsewhere, notably in Nos. 10, 50, and 51), Madison described an approach to the constitutional enterprise that fancies constitutional quiescence and political stability.[59] It is an order "far more concerned with insuring domestic tranquillity and securing the blessings of liberty than it is with building cathedrals, spreading imperial domains, or grooming excellence in virtuous citizens."[60]

Madison's comments have important implications for how we should understand the role of citizens in the constitutional enterprise. First, Madison concedes that recourse to the people must be open "for certain great and extraordinary occasions," although he tells us little about how to know when such occasions are at hand. Second, Madison seems to acknowledge that constitutional questions, if not submitted to "the whole society," must nonetheless be submitted somewhere. Madison understood that it would be impossible for a constitution to anticipate every question of governance. He knew, therefore, that the periodic resolution of constitutional uncertainty is an integral part of the evolving constitutional enterprise. In *Federalist* No. 49 he made it clear that he did not favor frequent appeals to the people as the means for resolving constitutional controversies. Instead, "for Madison constitutional maintenance was to be achieved not by popular conventions but by properly designed institutional arrangements," free of "the risks attendant on perpetual public discussion of first principles."[61]

Thus, the Juridic Constitution anticipated and created a particular kind

of people, or in the words of Eco, a "model" citizenry. Wolin has written
that "Because the Constitution proposed to establish a centered system
of power, a national government, it had to create a new type of citizen."[62]
This new type of citizen must accept "the attenuated relationship with
power implied if voting and elections were to serve as the main link between citizens and those in power."[63] The new science of politics sought
a new citizen who would be less inclined to act in concert on public
affairs than to concentrate on the private pursuit of happiness. The
framers transformed a citizenry "into a pluralistic population pursuing its
multitude of private concerns. They remade 'the people' into a plural
noun"[64] and devised mechanisms to forestall "perpetual public discussion
of first principles."

The reason for this reconstruction was, at bottom, fear of unrest. Fear of
social and political conflict are recurrent themes throughout the *Federalist
Papers* (and not simply in Nos. 10, 41, and 49). Perhaps, as Hartz argued,
the fear was neurotic. Nevertheless, acknowledging that fear is a prerequisite to understanding the founders' juridical constitution and the manner
in which judges have appropriated and interpreted that constitution.[65]

Both Madison and Hamilton, in sum, conceived the constitutional enterprise as an activity largely unsuitable for the citizenry as a whole. Madison's account assumed that constitutional controversies if made democratic will unsettle the constitutional equilibrium. Hamilton made
constitutional maintenance the prerogative of experts. Madison distrusted
the temperament of citizens; Hamilton thought them unschooled. Both
feared the "turbulence" and "follies of democracy."[66] Consequently, they
sought a constitution "that put government at a distance from the people."[67] They knew that for such a strategy to work, the Constitution itself
must be beyond the daily press of politics; "frequent appeals [to the peo-
ple] would, in great measure, deprive the government of that veneration
which time bestows on everything." Lincoln went even further, arguing
that reverence for the Constitution ought to constitute a political religion.[68] In the end, therefore, and notwithstanding some important differences, both the Hamiltonian and the Madisonian conceptions of the constitutional enterprise lead to an understanding of the Constitution—the
Juridic Constitution—that is legalistic and beyond the ken of most
citizens.

It is wrong, however, to think that because the Constitution is the
Supreme Law, it is *only* law, or that lawyers and judges alone can discern
its meaning or have any special responsibility for maintaining the Constitution. It is, moreover, a mistake to think—as do most members of the
legal academy—that all or even the most significant problems in constitutional theory are questions about constitutional interpretation.[69] A
Constitution is more than a text in need of interpretation—it is a consti-

tutive act that both makes and is made by a larger political order. A complete understanding of the text must address, therefore, the interrelated activities of constitutional foundings, constitutional maintenance, and constitutional dissolution.[70] Constitutional interpretation is an element of each of these areas, but it is only one part of them, and not necessarily the most important one. One of my purposes in the next section will be to show how the Juridic Constitution impoverishes our understanding of the constitutional enterprise by neglecting those areas and others, such as civic education and political obligation, not easily understood as questions about interpretation.

The Civic Constitution

> A Constitution, founded on these principles,
> introduces knowledge among the People, and
> inspires them with conscious dignity, becoming
> Freemen.
> —John Adams

The Juridic Constitution constitutes the political order in the image of law. Its conception of constitutional maintenance, in turn, subordinates politics to law and privileges the application of law to politics. In the process, the project of constitutional maintenance becomes fundamentally exclusive, the province of professionals. Citizenship under the Juridic Constitution is largely a private affair; we are public actors only in carefully prescribed ways and at prescribed times.[71]

The Civic Constitution, in contrast, finds its identity in its status as political creed. The Civic Constitution is a statement of our collective identity—it defines who we are, first by calling into being the collective "We"[72] and second by articulating what "We" believe and that to which we aspire. The Civic Constitution is less about law and more about the polity, conceived in the republican sense of the body politic. Maintaining this Constitution is a matter of "tending" and active care,[73] more variegated, more affective, and less technical than judicial interpretation. Responsibility for the Civic Constitution is a broadly democratic matter; it cannot be delegated to or discharged by others more expert than ourselves. Citizenship acquires correspondingly more importance and requires more of us. The Civic Constitution (as Ackerman has observed but did little to advance in *We the People*), "presupposes a citizenry with a sound grasp of the distinctive ideals that inspire its political practice."[74]

The broad outlines of this creed are sketched in part in the Preamble, in part in the Declaration, and in the *Federalist Papers*, among other places. A comprehensive understanding of the Civic Constitution would require us to examine the substantive content and character of the creed. Unfortunately, limits of space preclude such an examination here.

Moreover, I am somewhat less interested here in exploring the substantive nature of the Constitution's political commitments than in emphasizing the educational and preceptorial role the text plays and the assumptions it makes about citizens' understanding of the Constitution. I use the term "civic," rather than "political," because I want to emphasize the Constitution's preceptorial aspects, or in Jefferson's words, its character as "a text of civil instruction." I use the phrase "Civic Constitution" to highlight this relationship between text and citizen.

Like the Juridic Constitution, the Civic Constitution embodies a distinct conception of who its audience is and how it interacts with that audience. But where the Juridic Constitution entrusts itself to legal and professional elites, the Civic Constitution is public, its meaning accessible and knowledge of it democratic. To discharge its function, to work as a creed or symbol of national identity, the Civic Constitution must not reduce to private knowledge, for "A knowledge cannot be at one and the same time accessible to the few and yet serve as the vital bond holding the entire community together."[75]

The Civic and the Juridic Constitutions augur particular kinds of citizens. The Juridic Constitution encourages and highlights our identity as private individuals and not our status as citizens. The Civic Constitution demands citizenship and thus demands more of its citizens. The conception of a citizen inherent in the Civic Constitution is far more complex. It requires greater knowledge and responsibility than does the Juridic Constitution. Citizenship under the Civic Constitution involves a type of public life more fertile than the barren conception of public life envisioned by the Juridic Constitution.[76] It assumes there is nothing about the Constitution that makes its meaning accessible only to those few schooled in the mysteries of law and legal logic. Because it assumes that no professional training is necessary to understand the Constitution, it regards responsibility for the constitutional enterprise as more diffuse or democratic. It anticipates a community in which constitutional issues of significance are matters of publicly debatable civic aspirations, not simply questions of law or legal interpretation. In contrast, the Juridic Constitution teaches that "constitutional problems . . . are technical, hence appropriate only for the experts."[77]

The Civic Constitution should thus be understood as an instrument whose primary purpose is to constitute and enshrine a particular kind of polity; it aspires to be a public affirmation of the shared principles of national self-identity.[78] (I do not, however, mean to suggest that civic identity is either single and static or entirely and simply a function of constitutional design.[79]) But because the principles that tell us who we are and what we believe are to some extent matters of contention, aspiring to know them is a collective and ongoing enterprise[80] that entails commitments to democracy and public reasonableness. The Civic Constitution, in other words, requires a particular kind of citizenry with a particular kind of competence that constitutes a particular kind of knowledge—a civic knowledge, or knowledge of what a *civis* is and of what *civitas* means.[81] Unlike the Juridic Constitution, then, the Civic Constitution seeks an active transformation of persons into citizens, of personhood into citizenship.[82] Implicit in the Civic Constitution, therefore, is a claim about the nature of the Constitution, as well as what it means to say we know or have knowledge of it. To know (and not just to revere or to celebrate) the Juridic Constitution we must know law.[83] The Civic Constitution is grounded in political identity. To know the Civic Constitution, we must know ourselves.

The Civic Constitution and Civic Knowledge

How does civic knowledge differ further from legal knowledge?

Different "kinds" of knowledge tend to take on reasonably distinct vocabularies. There is an important sense in which to know something is to know how to talk about it—a point that should be fairly obvious to anyone trained in any of the professions. Earlier I noted that law may be understood as a set of discursive practices. The Juridic Constitution is part of a set of discursive practices with a distinct community of practitioners. The common tongue of that community is law. Legal language is clannish. Its chief characteristic is not, as its proponents claim, precision.[84] Nor is its chief characteristic, as its detractors claim, its denseness. Instead, the dominant feature of legal language is its privacy. It is private because it is exclusive. "As an impenetrable discourse," Sumner writes, "it ranks second to none: at least sociology does not use latin."[85] As we saw in the section above on the Juridic Constitution, the interpretive community that talks the talk is an elite club. Only a fraction of the broader civic community can talk about or know the Juridic Constitution in any meaningful sense. Constitutional maintenance under the Juridic Constitution is a clubbish affair.

The language of civics, by contrast, is inclusive. To know what it means to be a citizen is to know something about a public identity that we share with others. A language about the *civis* must thus be a broadly shared language, a broadly common tongue.[86] Consequently, the Civic Constitution requires a theory of civic education. The Juridic Constitution educates its citizens to respect for authority or to what Lincoln saw as reverence for law. The Civic Constitution requires an approach to civic education that is far richer.[87]

By civic knowledge, therefore, I do not mean knowledge of a precise or particular set of institutional "facts," like how the electoral college works or how many states are required to call a constitutional convention. Nor does civic knowledge stress, as some advocates of political literacy have insisted,[88] citizens' knowledge of Supreme Court decisions, or of the precise language of specific constitutional provisions. Instead, civic knowledge consists of the deliberative competence and normative commitments of constitutionalism and constitutional government. Unfortunately, limits of space preclude any real examination here of what those commitments are, though other essays in this collection do take up that challenge. In general, I am less concerned with levels of public knowledge about the written constitution and its case law than with a working understanding of the constitutional enterprise.

Civic education thus helps us to make the transition from private to public, from person to citizen. What is included in civic education? We might, as Barber has suggested, imagine three sorts of civic education. The first consists of formal pedagogy, or formal schooling in civics, history, and government. The second kind of civic education, following de Tocqueville, consists of activity in the social sphere. Finally, there is a sort of civic education one gets by participating in politics.[89] Similarly, Janowitz distinguishes broad from narrow approaches to civic education. The narrow focuses "mainly on the relations of the student to the central agencies of government. Its methods are pedagogical and instructional." The broad conception, in comparison, has as its goals "an overview of fundamental values, practices, and interpersonal relations in a democratic society."[90]

It should be clear that the Civic Constitution envisions a form of civic education that resembles the broader definition proposed by Janowitz and the kind of participatory education envisioned by Barber.[91] It requires citizens whose knowledge resides less in recitation than in understanding the "central and political traditions of the nation."[92] How does the Civic Constitution make such citizens? It cannot do so from a conception of constitutional maintenance in which the public is remote and reverential. It cannot do so by calling into being a constitutional order in which the Constitution is not a citizen's concern. Instead, it must summon a system in which citizens can learn to embrace (or reject) constitutional values by taking responsibility for their realization.

Constitutional Maintenance and Constitutional Interpretation

As we saw in the preceding section, the Juridic Constitution confounds constitutional maintenance with legal interpretation. The Civic Constitution offers a different understanding: the constitutional enterprise is a broadly democratic affair, the province of every citizen. Once we approach constitutional maintenance as more than the application of rules to controversy—rather as the maintenance and transmission of constitutional norms and values from generation to generation—then it should be clear that constitutional interpretation in hard cases is just a part, albeit an important one, of the larger enterprise.

Although my argument subordinates constitutional interpretation to the larger enterprise of constitutional maintenance, it does have important implications for determining who bears responsibility for constitutional interpretation. Like Publius, Thayer, Hand, and more recently Dworkin, Sunstein, and Sandel, I begin with the (republican) assumption that the sort of citizenry anticipated by the constitutional enterprise is more likely to prosper under some types of institutional arrangements than others. A judicial monopoly over constitutional interpretation, as Jefferson first cautioned, is likely to teach other constitutional actors that their own powers of constitutional interpretation are insignificant or irrelevant.[93] A judicial monopoly (or any institutional monopoly, for that matter) decreases the number of arenas in which constitutional dialogue occurs; it is corrosive of constitutional literacy and consequently ill-suited to the Civic Constitution.[94] Again, the extent to which such corrosion will occur is plainly related to the circumstances and occasions of interpretation—judicial minimalization of the kind envisioned by Sunstein is less corrosive than judicial supremacy. Much will depend, too, on how we understand the nature of law—there are good reasons to think that Dworkin's understanding of law as moral principle, for example, may do more to promote a deliberative citizenry than some others.[95]

In *Constitutional Cultures*, Nagel argued that the predominance of the judiciary in giving the Constitution meaning, or what is the same, the triumph of the legal over the political constitution, undermines "both fidelity to constitutional principles and the general health of the political culture."[96] This is so because the realization of the Constitution and its basic principles depends upon "preserving the kind of tacit agreement that interpretation itself tends to break down."[97] Consequently, notwithstanding its purpose, a monopolistic judicial review unsettles the constitutional order, in part because it disturbs shared understandings, and in part because its technicality distances the text from public knowledge and appreciation.[98] One might respond that interpretation takes place only in those instances where there is no settled understanding, or that it is necessary because there is no shared understanding. I think this confounds "shared" with universal—the distinction is important, especially where, as in the United States, the ability to challenge a practice is not hinged in any meaningful way to support in another institution or substantial support in the community.

The extent to which judicial review unsettles or disturbs the constitutional order is in part a function of its scope, a point underscored by disputes between Hamilton and Madison, and later between Marshall and Jefferson, over the authority of judicial decisions to bind coordinate actors. I refer to the distinction between judicial supremacy and coequal review. Judicial supremacy means what it says—it ascribes to judicial decisions authority and finality.[99] Coequal review, or departmentalism, carves out for the Court a power of constitutional review, but not one necessarily superior to the interpretive powers of other branches. On this view, the Court's authority is *inter partes* only, and not conclusive of the issue raised by the case. Both versions of judicial review disturb and disable, but the former is ill-suited to constitutional maintenance under the Civic Constitution because it acts as a disincentive for other actors and citizens to engage the Constitution on their own. As Burgess has noted, "it is unclear how the public role in the process of interpretation will be maintained (or why the public should remain interested in interpretation) in the context of judicial supremacy."[100]

Judicial supremacy is suitable, if anywhere, only to the Juridic Constitution, where claims to finality match up well with claims about the hierarchical nature of law and the professional expertise of judges. Insofar as the Civic Constitution requires judicial review, it anticipates departmentalism, in which each branch is entrusted with the power of interpreting the Constitution. In recent years there has appeared a small but impressive literature on departmentalism as a way of assigning interpretive authority. Unfortunately, that literature has largely failed systematically to tie departmentalism to the larger issues of constitutional maintenance, especially concerning the issues that separate liberals and civic republicans.[101]

The Civic Constitution enables us to see the link clearly. Departmentalism is a preferable allocation of interpretive authority under the Civic Constitution because it increases the number of arenas in which constitutional issues receive expression. The presidency and the national legislature are more likely, under departmentalism, to constitute distinct and important arenas of constitutional discourse. I should add that departmentalism does not deprive the Court of the authority to interpret the Constitution—it is simply a way of understanding the breadth and limits of that authority. Departmentalism acknowledges and accepts, in other words, a power of judicial review. And to that extent, departmentalism accepts the claim that the Constitution is law. It denies, however, that the Constitution is only or exclusively law. Like Thayer, advocates of departmentalism start from the premise that the Constitution is fundamentally political in nature.[102]

This will have important consequences for civic education and the constitutional enterprise, because some measure of learning how to be a citizen comes from the experience of watching how political representatives address political issues. Congressional representatives who choose not to engage issues of constitutionality, for example, especially when they believe such issues are committed elsewhere, teach citizens that their own responsibility for the Constitution is slight. A judicial monopoly on the Constitution's meaning encourages us to retreat into our private lives and to delegate our public responsibilities to others.[103]

Conclusion

> The Court is not the Constitution. To accept
> the two as equivalent is to relinquish individual
> responsibility and the capacity for self-
> government.
>   —Louis Fisher

In this short work I can only profile the Juridic and Civic Constitutions. I do hope, though, to have penciled in enough to convince readers that there are substantial differences between the two. In doing so I have been quite critical of the Juridic Constitution. I reject the vision of the constitutional enterprise expressed in the *Federalist Papers*, for example, and I have criticized much contemporary scholarship on the Constitution. My treatment of the Civic Constitution by comparison has been favorable. Perhaps I should now consider a few objections to the Civic Constitution. Most inhere in the Civic Constitution's vision of constitutional maintenance and enforcement.

The most obvious objection to the Civic Constitution is its assumption that constitutional meaning is or can be accessible to ordinary citizens. The force of this objection depends on denying the very distinction I have proposed: the *juridic* constitution-cum-judicial gloss is inaccessible to most non-lawyers. But the *civic* constitution is not encrusted with legal technicalities. Its commitments to democracy and public reasonableness in the pursuit of broad constitutional principles can aspire to no more, and no less, than the shaping of the broader political culture that embraces judicial technicalities. This is the most comprehensive of constitutional aspirations to be sure; but it is not the only one.

A second and important objection concerns the need for finality and certainty in cases of constitutional controversy. This is a criticism directed against the practice of departmentalism in constitutional interpretation. Coequal authority, insofar as it denies judicial supremacy, seems to some to promise anarchy. In response, we might recall Jefferson's distinction, and Lincoln's, between respect for a decision in a particular case and with regard to the parties in the case, on the one hand, and acquiescence on the broader constitutional principle, on the other.

Some critics may find even this amount of institutional disagreement about the meaning and application of the institution unwelcome, insisting that the constitutional order requires finality both for the case and for the principle.[104] But one wonders whether this is so and why it must be so—it is a proposition that itself requires a justification. In the words of Madison, "This difference of opinion is an inconvenience not entirely to be avoided."[105] I would add that the justification must be careful to distinguish "finality" as a quality of judicial decisions from the "settlement" of controversies involving constitutional principles.[106] Insofar as an end to the dispute is the goal, it must be the former that we desire, for constitutional interpretation, even buttressed by judicial supremacy, hardly "settles" questions of constitutional principle.[107] Moreover, departmentalism would encourage judges and indeed other constitutional decision-makers to seek the strongest (and not simply the most convenient) arguments for their conclusions—arguments that could hope to persuade the widest possible audience. "Settlement" of disputes is more likely to be found in the civilizing influence of this broad public quest than in the mesmerizing power of any one set of decision-makers. The reason for this is that the finality of one decision-maker shuts down dialogue where controversy and dispute kindle it. True conversation of the sort Rostow, Dworkin, Tribe, and others want must take place among equals; agreement must be secured by persuasion and not by claims of superior authority.

A third difficulty with the Civic Constitution, some critics will argue, is that it fails to offer sufficient protection for individual liberties, especially of minorities or the unpopular. "It may simply permit the political processes to proceed, such as they are," write Fleming and McClain, "and to trample on or neglect basic principles of liberty and equality."[108] Any honest assessment of this criticism must agree to some extent with its rather dim appraisal of most citizens. And what little research we have on the matter seems to support the fear that most citizens would be unreliable guardians of individual liberty.[109] One might respond, however, that the Civic Constitution is not designed to displace the Juridic Constitution. Indeed, evidence dating from at least the fate of FDR's court-packing plan to Bork's nomination indicates that one principle of the Civic Constitution is a Court that is willing to oppose public opinion on matters of constitutional principle. To this one can add that if our citizenry is unfriendly to constitutional rights, we have the kind of citizenry the juridic monopoly helped to create.[110] Deprived of any significant opportunity or reason to apply constitutional norms, should we wonder that most citizens fail to embrace them as fully or as enthusiastically as we might like?

Constitutional maturity can be won only through the chance to exercise and learn responsibility.[111]

Finally, some readers may object that my position here is too conservative because it simply takes for granted the desirability of the constitutional enterprise. This I concede, at least in part. But unlike the Juridic Constitution, which asks mostly for our reverence, the Civic Constitution welcomes citizens who can think critically and even harshly about the constitutional enterprise. In that sense, it embodies an understanding of the Constitution's authority premised upon its ability to persuade us that its vision of who we are, and who we should be, is one that we should embrace.

Notes

1. I ask, "what is the Constitution?" not "what is a constitution?" In choosing the narrower formulation, I mean to limit my discussion to the Constitution of the United States.

2. Kenneth Burke, *A Grammar of Motives* (New York: Prentice-Hall, Inc., 1945), p. 377.

3. For a discussion of the ways in which every text constructs a "model reader," see Umberto Eco et al., *Interpretation and Overinterpretation* (New York: Cambridge University Press, 1992).

4. Laurence Tribe and Michael C. Dorf, *On Reading the Constitution* (Cambridge: Harvard University Press, 1991); see also Richard A. Posner, *Law and Literature: A Misunderstood Relation* (Cambridge: Harvard University Press, 1988). Especially useful, although dated, is the "Symposium: Law and Literature" issue of the *Texas Law Review* 60 (1982).

5. Michael J. Perry, *Morality, Politics, and Law: A Bicentennial Essay* (New York: Oxford University Press, 1988), pp. 136–145; Ronald R. Garet, "Comparative Normative Hermeneutics: Scripture, Literature, Constitution," *So. Cal. Law Rev.* 58 (1985):37.

6. In some ways, of course, the two must be interrelated; some conceptions of what the Constitution is necessitate or preclude some understandings of how and why it binds. In this case, however, the how and why—consent—can be subsumed under both conceptions of what the Constitution is.

8. H. Mark Roelofs, *The Poverty of American Politics: A Theoretical Interpretation* (Philadelphia: Temple University Press, 1992), p. 97.

9. Edward S. Corwin, *Court over Constitution: A Study of Judicial Review as an Instrument of Popular Government* (Princeton: Princeton University Press, 1938); Robert F. Nagel, *Constitutional Cultures: The Mentality and Consequences of Judicial Review* (Berkeley: University of California Press, 1989).

10. James A. Morone, *The Democratic Wish: Popular Participation and the Limits of American Government* (New York: Basic Books, 1990), p. 62.

11. Sylvia Snowiss, *Judicial Review and the Law of the Constitution* (New Ha-

ven: Yale University Press, 1990), p. 195. For a different use of the "mix" analogy, see H. Mark Roelofs, *The Tension of Citizenship: Private Man and Public Duty* (New York: Rinehart, 1957), p. 83.

12. I shall elaborate on and consider objections to this point later. See especially my discussions of Dworkin and Sunstein. See also Susan R. Burgess, *Contest for Constitutional Authority: The Abortion and War Powers Debates* (Lawrence, KS: University Press of Kansas, 1992), pp. 7–12; see also Alan Hunt, "Law's Empire or Legal Imperialism?" in Alan Hunt, ed., *Reading Dworkin Critically* (Providence, RI: Berg Publishers, Inc., 1992), pp. 9, 32.

13. By "distinct set of practitioners" I mean to highlight the exclusive or private nature of legal discourse, a point made admirably in Sumner's *Reading Ideologies*: "Legal discourse in modern societies is thus bureaucratized magic expressed in legalese. It is therefore not only a discrete phenomena but downright impenetrable." Colin Sumner, *Reading Ideologies: An Investigation into the Marxist Theory of Ideology and Law* (New York: Academic Press, 1979), 270.

14. Lawrence Tribe, "Contrasting Constitutional Visions: Of Real and Unreal Differences," *Harv. Civ. Rts.-Civ. Lib. L. Rev.* 22 (1987):95. Judge Easterbrook, conceding that the Constitution's status as law is a first premise, has similarly acknowledged that differences in understanding what law is will influence constitutional interpretation. Easterbrook distinguishes between a conception of law as rules and right answers and law "as reasoning of a certain form." *Politics and the Constitution: The Nature and Extent of Interpretation* (Washington: National Legal Center for the Public Interest, 1990), p. 23. See also Sanford Levinson, *Constitutional Faith* (Princeton: Princeton University Press, 1988), p. 68.

Agreement that the Constitution is "law" may mask a great deal of disagreement about what "law" is or means. As H. Jefferson Powell has noted in his study of Story's *Commentaries*, for example, accepting the Constitution as "law" might mean that the Constitution is a vessel for and a guarantee of justice, or, alternatively, an instrument designed to secure the will of the sovereign people. H. Jefferson Powell, "Joseph Story's Commentaries on the Constitution: A Belated View," *Yale L. J.* 94 (1986):1311. Alternatively, "law" in its constitutional sense might mean that constitutional interpretation should concern matters of history (originalism?) or questions of moral principle. This in turn will have important consequences for issues concerning institutional responsibility for interpretation and attendant conceptions of citizenship. I consider these points more fully later in this chapter. See, for example, Ronald Dworkin, *Freedom's Law* (1996); Samuel Freeman, "Original Meaning, Democratic Interpretation, and the Constitution," *Phil. & Pub. Aff.* 21 (1992):3; James E. Fleming, "Fidelity to Our Imperfect Constitution," *Ford. L. Rev.* 67: 1354, n. 88.

15. For a notable exception, *see* Sotirios A. Barber, *On What the Constitution Means* (Baltimore: Johns Hopkins University Press, 1984).

16. I say "constitutional review," and not the more widely used "judicial review," to distinguish clearly between the activity—review of constitutionality—from the institution, in this case courts, that undertakes that activity.

17. Compare Yates on this point: "the judges will be interested to expand the powers of the courts, and to construe the constitution as much as possible, in such a way as to favour it; and that they will do it, appears probable." Quoted in

Jackson Turner Main, *The Anti-Federalists: Critics of the Constitution* (New York: W.W. Norton & Company, 1961), pp. 125–26.

18. Robert A. Burt, *The Constitution in Conflict* (Cambridge: Harvard University Press, 1992), pp. 60–61.

19. Ibid., p. 68ff.

20. Clinton Rossiter, ed., *The Federalist Papers* (New York: Mentor, 1961), p. 467.

21. Ibid.

22. Ibid., p. 467 (No. 78).

23. John Brigham, *The Cult of the Court* (Philadelphia: Temple University Press, 1987), p. 43.

24. For an insightful discussion of this point, see Donald G. Morgan, *Congress and the Constitution: A Study of Responsibility* (Cambridge: Harvard University Press, 1966), pp. 84–85.

25. Snowiss, *Judicial Review*, p. 1.

26. The process took about a half-century to complete. Ibid., p. 5.

27. As Brigham has observed, "The Constitution as Higher Law and a maturing Bar carried the Supreme Court to its authoritative position." *Cult of the Court*, p. 35.

28. Nagel, *Constitutional Cultures*, p. 7. And as Sapir has noted, "forms of language predetermine for us certain modes of observation and interpretation." Edward Sapir, "Language," in Edwin R. A. Seligman, ed., *Encyclopedia of the Social Sciences*, vol. 9, 1933.

29. Rossiter, *Federalist Papers*, p. 471.

30. Hamilton's argument for judicial review was realized, of course, in *Marbury v. Madison* (1803), in which Chief Justice John Marshall claimed the power for the Supreme Court. *Marbury* is sufficiently vague, however, to support several quite different understandings of the role of judicial review in the constitutional enterprise.

31. Norman Jacobson made this point effectively in "Political Science and Political Education," arguing that the penal nature of the Constitution was even more stark in comparison to the "fraternal" character of the Articles of Confederation. *A.P.S.R.* LVII (1963):562.

32. See Ronald Dworkin, *Law's Empire* (Cambridge: Harvard University Press, 1986); Harry H. Wellington, *Interpreting the Constitution* (New Haven: Yale University Press, 1991).

33. Ira L. Strauber, "The Supreme Court, Constitutional Interpretation, and Civic Education," paper delivered at the Annual Meeting of the Midwest Political Science Association, April 9–11, 1992 (Chicago, IL), p. 5.

34. Harry H. Wellington, *Interpreting the Constitution*, p. 14.

35. Levinson, *Constitutional Faith*, p. 191.

36. If necessary, we could offer many examples of scholars who want to insist upon the "dialogic" or conversational character of constitutional interpretation— such a list would include Levinson, Dworkin, Powell, Fiss, Perry, Wellington, and others. Tribe and Dorf, for example, have asserted that part of what courts and scholars do is to "structure constitutional conversations." Tribe and Dorf, *On Reading the Constitution*, p. 31. See also James Boyd White, *Justice as Translation* (Chicago: University of Chicago Press, 1990), p. 267.

37. Strauber, "The Supreme Court," pp. 1–6; Roger Cotterrell, *The Politics of Jurisprudence: A Critical Introduction to Legal Philosophy* (Philadelphia: University of Pennsylvania Press, 1989), p. 177.

38. Ronald Dworkin, *Taking Rights Seriously* (Cambridge: Harvard University Press, 1977), pp. 206–22.

39. Brigham, *Cult of the Court*, p. 25.

40. Cotterrell, *Politics of Jurisprudence*, p. 178.

41. Bruce Ackerman, *We the People: Foundations* (Cambridge: Harvard University Press, 1991), 5. Notwithstanding Ackerman's aims, there is much that is confused about this effort. In addition to its inability to reconcile a court-centered professional narrative with a desire for a constitutionally mature citizenry, the book misunderstands the similarities between European and American constitutionalism, especially in its contest between the "democratic dualism" of the American Constitution and the "foundationalism" of some European texts. See, for example, John E. Finn, "Transformation or Transmogrification?": "Ackerman, Hobbes, and the Puzzle of *Changing Constitutional Identity*," Consti. Pol. Economy 10 (1999); James E. Fleming, "We the Exceptional American People," *Consti. Comm.* 11 (1994):355.

42. These moments are so extraordinary that Ackerman can find only three instances—the Founding, Reconstruction, and the New Deal.

43. Brigham, *Cult of the Court*, p. 27.

44. Peter Goodrich, *Legal Discourse* (New York: St. Martin's Press, 1987), p. ix.

45. Ibid., p. 81.

46. Brian Weinstein, *The Civic Tongue: Political Consequences of Language Choices* (New York: Longman, 1983), p. 3.

47. See Michael J. Shapiro, *Language and Political Understanding: The Politics of Discursive Practices* (New Haven: Yale University Press, 1981), p. 179.

48. Nagel makes a similar point, emphasizing the relationship between law and interpretation: "Because our conception of the Constitution is so shaped by [legal] argument about its meaning, interpretation seems indispensable." Nagel, *Constitutional Cultures*, p. 8.

49. The best discussion of this is in Barber, *On What the Constitution Means*, pp. 1–12. Candor compels acknowledgment that I am guilty of this failure, too. See Donald P. Kommers and John E. Finn, *American Constitutional Law: Cases, Essays, and Comparative Notes* (Boston: West/Wadsworth, 1999).

50. Michael Sandel, *Democracy's Discontent: America in Search of Public Philosophy* (Cambridge: Belknap Press of Harvard University Press, 1996).

51. Cass Sunstein, *Legal Reasoning and Political Conflict* (New York: Oxford University Press, 1996).

52. See Wellington, *Interpreting the Constitution*.

53. Nagel, *Constitutional Cultures*, p. 9.

54. Sunstein, *Legal Reasoning and Political Conflict*, pp. 4, 7, 37.

55. Sheldon D. Pollock, "Constitutional Interpretation as Political Choice," U. of Pitt. L. Rev. 989 48 (1987): 989.

56. Burt, *Constitution in Conflict*, pp. 50–51.

57. Rossiter, *Federalist Papers*, p. 315.

58. Ibid., p. 314. In *Federalist* No. 51, Madison also rejected "periodical ap-

peals" to a formal institutionalized body. His rejection was premised upon his reading of Pennsylvania's experience with the Council of Censors. Richard Burt has concluded, I think correctly, that Madison's comments on the Council of Censors suggest that he foresaw similar difficulties with entrusting constitutional enforcement to the Supreme Court. One should be careful, therefore, to distinguish between Madison's approach to the constitutional enterprise and Hamilton's. Burt, *Constitution in Conflict*, p. 59.

59. The Federalists' opposition to "populist" politics, of course, was manifest in far more than their opposition to the Articles of Confederation and their work in Philadelphia. As James Morone noted, this sort of opposition was also the animus behind the Alien and Sedition Acts. (Morone, *Democratic Wish*, p. 70.)

60. H. Mark Roelofs, *The Poverty of American Politics: A Theoretical Interpretation* (Philadelphia: Temple University Press, 1992), p. 48.

61. Snowiss, *Judicial Review*, p. 118.

62. Sheldon S. Wolin, *The Presence of the Past: Essays on the State and the Constitution* (Baltimore: Johns Hopkins University Press, 1989), p. 189.

63. Ibid., p. 189.

64. Morone, *Democratic Wish*, p. 65.

65. Burt, *Constitution in Conflict*, p. 44.

66. Morone, *Democratic Wish*, pp. 63–64.

67. Harvey C. Mansfield, Jr., *America's Constitutional Soul* (Baltimore: Johns Hopkins University Press, 1991), p. 177.

68. Ibid., pp. 180–81.

69. For a notable exception, see Nagel, *Constitutional Cultures*.

70. For a discussion of these three aspects of constitutional theory, see John E. Finn, *Constitutions in Crisis: Political Violence and the Rule of Law* (New York: Oxford University Press, 1991).

71. See Michael Walzer, *Obligations: Essays on Disobedience, War, and Citizenship* (Cambridge: Harvard University Press, 1970). See also Ackerman, pp. 3–33.

72. Contrast this with the state-centered opening of the Articles of Confederation.

73. As Wolin notes, "tending implies active care. Active care is not, however, a synonym for expert knowledge." *Presence of the Past*, p. 89.

74. Ackerman, *We the People*, pp. 3–4. *We the People* is paradigmatic of lawyerly scholarship on the Constitution. Ackerman "paints a pretty picture" of dialogue "amongst scholars, professionals, and the people at large," yet fails to understand how his own proposals make such a dialogue improbable. See Finn, "Transformation."

75. Sheldon S. Wolin, *Politics and Vision: Continuity and Innovation in Western Political Thought* (Boston: Little, Brown, 1960), p. 66.

76. Here I borrow heavily from Nancy L. Schwartz's description of citizenship as "the name for the public life." *The Blue Guitar: Political Representation and Community* (Chicago: University of Chicago Press, 1988), p. 10.

77. Morgan, *Congress and the Constitution*, p. viii.

78. A comparative analysis of constitutional texts would make this point clear. A common feature of twentieth-century constitutions is the inclusion of provisions that identify national languages, flags, anthems, and similar components that are best seen as autobiographical.

79. See the recent work on civic identity by Rogers M. Smith, *Civic Ideals: Conflicting Visions of Citizenship in U.S. History* (New Haven: Yale University Press, 1997), ch. 1.

80. Ibid.

81. E. Barker, ed., *The Politics of Aristotle* (New York: Oxford University Press, 1968), 1275a23, pp. 93–94.

82. On the role of loyalty oaths in making this transformation, see Levinson, *Constitutional Faith*, p. 112.

83. And to believe in the Juridic Constitution is to accept, at least implicitly, somewhat dubious claims about the integrity and autonomy of legal knowledge. Indeed, insofar as the Juridic Constitution seeks to insulate law from politics, it rests either upon a claim that law and politics are distinct, or that law is a distinctive kind of politics.

84. See, for example, David Mellinkoff, *The Language of the Law* (Boston: Little, Brown, 1963), pp. 24–33, 290–398; Murray Edelman, *The Symbolic Uses of Politics* (Urbana: University of Illinois Press, 1964), p. 138.

85. Sumner, *Reading Ideologies*, p. 271

86. See generally Brian Weinstein, *The Civic Tongue: Political Consequences of Language Choices* (New York: Longman, 1983).

87. I would not deny, though, that elements of reverence—or what Smith has called civic myths—are an important component of civic identity. I would insist that a fuller and richer understanding of citizenship requires ongoing critical reflection on the character of our shared identity in ways that simple subscription to myth does not. See Smith, *Civic Ideals*, pp. 31–32; 504–6.

88. See, for example, Jerry Combee, *Democracy at Risk: The Rising Tide of Political Illiteracy and Ignorance of the Constitution* (Cumberland, Va.: Center for Judicial Studies, 1984).

89. Benjamin R. Barber, *Strong Democracy: Participatory Politics for a New Age* (Berkeley: University of California Press, 1984), p. 233.

Ira Strauber has argued for a notion of civic education based on what Michael Walzer calls "casuistry," which presumably will help to create a political culture in which rulers will be forced "to justify their actions" against the standards of democratic and constitutional politics. Ira L. Strauber, "The Supreme Court, Constitutional Interpretation, and Civic Education," paper delivered at the Annual Meeting of the Midwest Political Science Association, April 9–11, 1992, Chicago, Illinois, pp. 13–15. Walzer's defense of casuistry is in "Political Decision-Making and Political Education," M. Richter, ed., *Political Theory and Political Education* (Princeton: Princeton University Press, 1980), pp. 159–76.

90. Morris Janowitz, *The Reconstruction of Patriotism: Education for Civic Consciousness* (Chicago: University of Chicago Press, 1983), p. 13.

91. I say "perhaps" because there is an Aristotelian sense of civic knowledge which consists in knowing how to rule and to be ruled in turn.

92. Barber, *Strong Democracy*, 194.

93. See, for example, Jefferson's letter to Judge Spencer Roane of September 6, 1819. Merrill D. Peterson, ed., *Thomas Jefferson: Writings* (New York: Library of America, 1984), pp. 1425–28.

94. The counterargument, I suppose, is that the Court itself is, or can be, an agent of civic education. Dean Rostow was the first to make the point nearly fifty

years ago, arguing that judicial review helped to initiate and structure "a vital national seminar." Eugene V. Rostow, "The Democratic Character of Judicial Review," *Harv. L. Rev.* LXVI (1952):193. For a more recent argument about the Court's obligation, see Paul R. Dimond, *The Supreme Court and Judicial Choice: The Role of Provisional Review in a Democracy* (Ann Arbor: University of Michigan Press, 1989).

I would not deny that the Court has a role to play in civic education. But as I wrote in the section "The Juridic Constitution," I do think it is profoundly mistaken to imagine the Court as engaged with "the nation" in any meaningful sense. In part, the very structure and complexity of judicial opinions precludes conversation. In this respect, it is worth consulting Joseph Goldstein's *The Intelligible Constitution: The Supreme Court's Obligation to Maintain the Constitution as Something We the People Can Understand* (New York: Oxford University Press, 1992).

95. See Fleming, "Fidelity to Our Imperfect Constitution," pp. 1352–54. Of course, a deliberative citizenry is not necessarily a citizenry that deliberates about public matters in exclusively constitutional terms. Such discussions might proceed upon some other basis, such as the public good, or what is ethical, or what is expedient. In such cases the conflict between constitutional ideals is at its clearest and raises profound questions about fidelity to and the limits of constitutional authority.

96. Nagel, *Constitutional Cultures*, p. 1.

97. Ibid., p. 23. For an argument that judicial review supports, rather than disturbs, see Christopher L. Eisgruber, "Disagreeable People," 43 Stan. L. Rev. 275 (1990).

98. Nagel, *Constitutional Cultures*, p. 25ff; 58.

99. Moreover, that authority is *erga omnes*—it binds all similarly situated—and not simply *inter partes*, or the parties to the case.

100. Burgess, *Contest for Constitutional Authority*, pp. 8–9.

101. Two useful studies, both of which understand the ways in which departmentalism is related to larger structural questions, are Burt, *The Constitution in Conflict*, and Burgess, *Contest for Constitutional Authority*. Burgess's book is a wonderful primer on the differences between judicial supremacy and departmentalism and why those differences matter. In general, Burgess cautiously concludes that departmentalism does offer some prospect for improved public understanding of constitutional issues.

102. See Wellington, *Interpreting the Constitution*, pp. 77–78.

103. It should be clear also that departmentalism will have important implications for how we approach issues concerning the separation of powers and federalism. The Civic Constitution counsels us to approach cases about separation of powers and federalism in ways that emphasize their capacity as agents of constitutional instruction. The Civic Constitution favors judicial approaches to cases involving separation of powers and federalism that promote the autonomy of other institutional actors because they are more likely to result in institutional actors keen to address constitutional issues on their own.

104. See, for example, Attorney General Edwin Meese's address at Tulane University, entitled "The Law of the Constitution," Reprinted in Louis Fisher,

Constitutional Rights: Civil Rights and Liberties (NY: McGraw-Hill, 1990), vol. II:1352–54.

105. "Helvidius No. II," in *Writings of Madison*, ed. Gaillard Hunt (New York: G.P. Putnam's Sons, 9 vols., 1900–10), 6:155.

106. For an interesting discussion of this concept, see Morgan, *Congress and the Constitution*, pp. 16–42.

107. See Morgan; Louis Fisher, *Constitutional Dialogues: Interpretation as Political Process* (Princeton: Princeton University Press, 1988), pp. 221–30 (describing noncompliance after the Court's decision in *INS v. Chadha* [1983]).

108. James E. Fleming and Linda C. McClain, "In Search of a Substantive Republic," Tex. L. Rev. 76 (1997):547.

109. The classic study is by Herbert McCloskey and Alida Brill, *Dimensions of Tolerance: What Americans Believe About Civil Liberties* (New York: Russel Sage, 1983); see also Michael G. Kammen, *A Machine That Would Go of Itself: The Constitution in American Culture* (New York: Alfred A. Knopf, 1986), pp. 24ff.

110. See generally Norman Jacobson, "Political Science and Political Education," A.P.S.R. LVII (1963):561.

111. See Nagel, *Constitutional Cultures*, p. 26

3

Judicial Supremacy and Constitutional Distortion

CHRISTOPHER L. EISGRUBER

HOW STRANGELY the Supreme Court reads the Constitution! Consider, for example, the curious debate between Justices Stevens and Thomas in *U.S. Term Limits v. Thornton*.[1] Voters across the country had been registering dissatisfaction with the nation's legislative process by limiting the terms of their federal representatives. The widespread popularity of such measures suggested a failure of public confidence in the American electoral system. By granting certiorari in *Thornton*, the Supreme Court put itself in a position to test term limits against constitutional principle and, one might have hoped, to quell or else legitimate growing doubts about the integrity of the Constitution's model of representation.

What the Court produced, however, was an historical debate about whether the Constitution derived its authority in 1787 from the authority of a single American people or from the multiple peoples of the several States. This was Hamlet without the Prince twice over. Absent from either Stevens's opinion for the majority or Thomas's opinion for four dissenters was any substantial discussion of normative issues about how term limits affect representation. And likewise absent was any discussion of how the Civil War altered the constitutional status of state sovereignty. Instead, the Supreme Court sought to resolve the constitutional controversy by combing the historical record for clues to what the framing generation might have thought about an issue it apparently never discussed.

Thornton is not unique. The Supreme Court regularly analyzes fundamental political issues by burying itself in historical and legalistic particularities. One cannot explain this practice as a result of the Court's obligation to be faithful to the constitutional text. Indeed, several constitutional clauses—e.g., the Preamble, the Guarantee Clause, the Ninth Amendment, the Citizenship Clause of the Fourteenth Amendment, and the Privileges or Immunities Clause of the same amendment—have been casualties of the Court's style, their grand abstractions ignored in the Court's quest to decide cases on the basis of historical and legalistic knowledge.

What explains this interpretive practice? I propose here that anxiety about how to justify judicial review has led the Court to distort the Constitution's meaning. Though the justices worry incessantly about the democratic legitimacy of their institution, they insist on absolute deference to their interpretations of the Constitution. This position might be defensible, but the justices have recoiled from candid examination of its premises. Instead, either by felt instinct or by conscious design, the justices have reconceived the Constitution to buttress their claim to interpretive supremacy. By treating the Constitution mainly as a set of legal restraints rather than an instrument enabling self-government, the Court has made more plausible the idea that constitutional interpretation is exclusively the province of lawyers—a professional elite who may have no special insight into justice or politics but who are expert at the manipulation of fine-grained rules.

Judicial Supremacy and the Fourteenth Amendment

The Fourteenth Amendment is oddly inconspicuous in much of the Supreme Court's jurisprudence. Indeed, were John Marshall alive today, he might exhort us "never to forget that it is *the Fourteenth Amendment* we are expounding."[2] The first paragraph of the amendment is the most obvious source of rights enforceable against the state governments, but we trace the Supreme Court's civil liberties jurisprudence largely to the Bill of Rights, mentioning the Fourteenth Amendment (if at all) only through an apologetic reference to the strained idea of incorporation.[3] Section 5 of the Fourteenth Amendment is a plausible source for many important congressional statutes, but we indulge the curious notion that the Commerce Clause authorizes everything from restrictions on local farming[4] to sweeping civil rights statutes.[5] Most striking is the Court's insistent refusal to consider how Reconstruction altered the principles of federalism. One would have thought it obvious that the "War between the States" reshaped American federalism in radical ways. But the Court typically reasons about federalism as though the Founding and the New Deal were the only constitutional events it need take into account.[6]

The Court has always been reluctant to take the Fourteenth Amendment at face value. Justice Miller, writing on behalf of the Court in the *Slaughter-House Cases*, looked into the amendment and foresaw a nation in which the federal government was ultimately responsible for "the security and protection of all . . . civil rights"; in which Congress would have power to legislate with respect to "the entire domain of civil rights heretofore belonging exclusively to the States"; in which Congress "may also pass laws in advance, limiting and restricting the exercise of legislative power by the States"; and in which the amendment would "constitute this court a perpetual censor upon all legislation of the States, on the civil rights of their own citizens, with authority to nullify such as it did not approve as consistent with those rights."[7] Justice Miller pronounced it unthinkable that the American constitutional order could take such a form: "We are convinced that no such results were intended by the Congress which proposed these amendments, nor by the legislatures of the States which ratified them."[8] But saying this did not make it so. The nation Justice Miller glimpsed in the Fourteenth Amendment is, in its main features, the nation that Americans inhabit today.

One might think that interpreters could revive the Fourteenth Amendment by citing the Fourteenth Amendment's Enforcement Clause rather than the Commerce Clause to justify federal civil rights legislation. But full acknowledgement of the amendment's potential would require a more thorough rethinking of contemporary constitutional practice. The Supreme Court's doctrinal tendencies are not purely a matter of historical accident or interpretive perversion. To discern the political logic behind the Supreme Court's constitutional style, we must first notice one respect in which the Fourteenth Amendment's description of American politics is incomplete.

Since the 1950s, the Court has insisted upon a judicial monopoly in constitutional interpretation. The Court's position is that other constitutional interpreters—citizens, the President, Congress, and the states—must all defer to its construction of the Constitution. In *Cooper v. Aaron*, the Court claimed that the obligation to defer applied even to nonparties. According to the Court, it was not simply the Constitution, but "the interpretation of the Fourteenth Amendment enunciated by this Court," that was "the supreme law of the land."[9] Later, in *Casey v. Planned Parenthood*, the Court announced that it, too, has an obligation to defer to rulings by past courts, *especially* when groups of citizens and members of the other branches have campaigned long and emotionally for reconsideration of the Court's decision.[10] Judicial supremacy (with or without *Casey*'s remarkable extension of the doctrine) thus entails considerably more than the power of judicial review elaborated by John Marshall in *Marbury v. Madison*.[11] If successful, Marshall's argument in *Marbury* establishes only that the Court may pass upon the constitutionality of laws; the argument does not say anything about whether (or when) other branches of the government must accept the Court's judgment as precedents governing their future conduct.[12] Nevertheless, the Court's claim to supremacy has been widely accepted.[13]

From the standpoint of judicial supremacy, the Fourteenth Amendment is an embarrassment. Section 5 of the amendment explicitly recognizes Congressional authority to enforce the Constitution or, at least, one very important part of the Constitution. By contrast, the Constitution remains silent about *judicial* authority to enforce the Constitution. The problem deepens if one recognizes Abraham Lincoln as a guiding spirit behind the Fourteenth Amendment. Lincoln sought election by contesting any suggestion of judicial monopoly in constitutional interpretation; inaugurated his presidency by exhorting the American people never to cede their Constitution to the Court; and directed one of his officers to resist a mandate issued by Chief Justice Roger Taney in a habeas corpus proceeding.[14] Whatever else the Fourteenth Amendment does, it underscores the need for some independent justification for judicial supremacy.

Indeed, when confronted with expansive interpretations of the Fourteenth Amendment's enforcement clause, the Court has sometimes reacted very defensively. For example, in *City of Boerne v. Flores*,[15] the justices reviewed portions of the Religious Freedom Restoration Act ("RFRA") that exempted some religiously motivated conduct from the reach of state and local law. Congress had characterized RFRA as an effort to use its enforcement clause power to implement an interpretation of the Free Exercise Clause (as incorporated into the Fourteenth Amendment) different from the Court's interpretation. The Court not only struck down RFRA, but contended that if Congress had "a substantive non-remedial power under the Fourteenth Amendment," then it would be free to "define its own powers by altering the Fourteenth Amendment's meaning." The Constitution would no longer be "superior paramount law, unchangeable by ordinary means."[16] Even if the justices were (as I believe[17]) correct to hold RFRA unconstitutional, they exaggerated the threat to judicial review. Several widely respected theories explain how Congress and the judiciary can share authority to interpret the Constitution without either endangering constitutional supremacy or losing the benefits of judicial review.[18]

Justifying a judicial monopoly over constitutional interpretation is therefore difficult. One way to do it is to argue that legal training and technique are crucial to understanding the Constitution. This has some immediate plausibility: lawyers are supposed to know what the law is, and the Constitution is a species of law. Lawyers specialize in developing and implementing technical language in instruments—wills, trusts, contracts, and statutes—designed to extend the present intent of parties into later circumstances. If the Constitution is itself such an instrument, perhaps lawyers are the best people to read it.[19] Lawyers will identify technical devices and conventions that render ambiguous language determinate, and they will engage in methodologically rigorous investigations that avoid disputed values and contests of political will.

But this argument holds only if the Constitution is indeed a technical document like a will, contract, or statute. If the Constitution is funda-

mentally different—if, for example, it is a statement of the American people's values and political character, or if it is a practical device that enables
Americans to govern themselves on the basis of their best current judgments about justice—then there is no reason to believe that lawyers will
read it especially well. The conventions of the profession might actually
deaden the political sensibilities of lawyers, making them ill-suited to
read the Constitution. Indeed, the American public is often suspicious of
lawyers' sense of justice.

Of course, we might be able to justify judicial review, and perhaps even
a monopolistic version of judicial supremacy, without claiming that the
Constitution is intelligible only to those schooled in legal methods. We
might, for example, believe that judges are likely to give the Constitution
a sounder reading because of their institutional position, rather than their
professional training. Alexander Bickel maintained that the justices "have
. . . the leisure, the training, and the insulation to follow the ways of the
scholar in pursuing the ends of government,"[20] and Lawrence Sager has
championed judicial competence in matters of political theory by identifying a resemblance between judicial reasoning and Rawlsian reflection.[21]
Or, putting aside questions about who has the greatest capacity to *understand* the Constitution, we might maintain that judges are most likely
to *vindicate* constitutional ideals, because life tenure frees them to insist upon justice even when the electorate favors other ends.[22] We need
not assess these arguments here. What matters for our purposes is that
however strong the case for judicial supremacy might otherwise be,
it becomes stronger if we understand the Constitution as a technical
instrument.

The Fourteenth Amendment fits uncomfortability with legalistic conceptions of the Constitution. One doesn't have to give a technical reading to its general and evaluative terms. Its allusions to equality and the
privileges of citizenship describe a polity constituted by and for a united,
self-governing people. At the core of the amendment's first section is a
vision of the American polity well articulated in ordinary moral terms by
Justice Harlan in his *Plessy v. Ferguson* dissent: Americans are a people
whose "destinies . . . are indissoluably linked together, and [their] interests . . . require that the common government of all shall not permit the
seeds of . . . hate to be planted under the sanction of law."[23] This idea of
an interdependent people with a common destiny could have justified
much of the civil rights jurisprudence of this century.[24]

Yet, recognizing the Fourteenth Amendment's transformative vision—
of a national community of values with authority to pursue positive projects that fall mainly within the competence of legislatures—would make
judicial supremacy harder to justify. Distorting the vision makes judicial
supremacy easier to justify. Consciously or not, the justices have chosen

to distort the Fourteenth Amendment, a choice that has enhanced their power.

Constitutional Distortion

State Sovereignty

Antebellum jurisprudence and political theory held that sovereignity entailed power to regulate community membership. Justice Benjamin Curtis articulated the most respected view in his famous *Dred Scott* dissent: under general principles of international law, sovereigns had the authority to determine the citizenship of persons born with their polity, and under the Constitution the states retained that power.[25] National citizenship, insofar as it existed at all, was derivative of state citizenship. The Fourteenth Amendment inverted that relationship. The national Constitution now defined citizenship for both the nation and the states. In its stunning first sentence, the Fourteenth Amendment identified personhood with United States citizenship and made state citizenship a mere incident of residency.

In the *Slaughter-House Cases*, however, the Supreme Court held that most important benefits of citizenship still attached to state, not national, citizenship. Even after the *Slaughter-House* decision, Justice Harlan was prepared in the *Civil Rights Cases* to uphold federal civil rights laws on the ground that the Fourteenth Amendment's Enforcement Clause authorized Congress to fulfill the promise of the Citizenship Clause.[26] But Harlan's arguments appeared in dissent. Justice Bradley, writing for the other eight justices, eviscerated the Enforcement Clause and implicitly disparaged the Citizenship Clause by omitting any discussion of it. Under the doctrine of the *Civil Rights Cases*, state sovereignty remains a potent constraint upon the scope of national citizenship and congressional authority. Constructions of the Fourteenth Amendment are wrong if they would "make Congress take the place of the State legislatures and supersede them."[27]

More than a century later, the Supreme Court continues to discuss constitutional federalism in terms of the states' pre-constitutional sovereignty.[28] In two ways, this rhetoric of state sovereignty has succored a technical, legalistic conception of the Constitution. First, the concept of state sovereignty diverts attention away from practical concerns about federalism and toward obscure (and perhaps incoherent) elements of eighteenth-century political and legal thought.[29] Second, by conceiving of the states as pre-constitutional entities, the Court has licensed analogies between the Constitution and one particular kind of legal instrument: a compact or treaty among multiple sovereign states. Justice Thomas employed that analogy explicitly in his *Thornton* dissent.[30] Thomas's position was extreme, but even the *Thornton* majority made no reference to the Fourteenth Amendment.[31] Likewise, in *United States v. Lopez*,[32] the majority and the dissenters alike analyzed American federalism as though the Civil War had never happened, parsing Federalist political theory and the lessons of the New Deal without reference to the Reconstruction amendments.

The Common Law

Another distortion might be called "common law fetishism." Despite Justice Miller's victory in the *Slaughter-House Cases*, it did not take the Court long to decide that the Fourteenth Amendment did indeed "constitute [the] court a perpetual censor upon . . . the States." In *Munn v. Illinois*, the justices began to embrace the idea that the Fourteenth Amendment protected a broad range of individual rights (in particular, economic rights). The Court reached this conclusion by invigorating not the Privileges and Immunities Clause but the Due Process Clause.

The conventional view maintains that in *Munn* and subsequent decisions the justices "simply wrote the dissenting opinions of Justices Swayne and Bradley in the *Slaughter-House Cases* into the Fourteenth Amendment."[33] In a subtle but important way, however, *Munn* departed from the *mode* of interpretation practiced by the *Slaughter-House* dissents (and, for that matter, the *Slaughter-House* majority). The *Slaughter-House* justices had disagreed about whether the Fourteenth Amendment assigned the national government primary responsibility for protecting all of the privileges and immunities of citizenship. The dissenters thought that it had done so; the majority insisted that most of those rights continued to depend upon state law. But the dissenters and the majority alike agreed upon the nature of the rights in question *and* the means for identifying them. Three opinions—Justice Miller's for the majority, and the dissents of Justices Field and Bradley—quoted Bushrod Washington's language from *Corfield v. Coryell*:

> We feel no hesitation in confining these expressions to those privileges and immunities which are, in their nature, fundamental; which belong, of right, to the citizens of all free governments; and which have, at all times, been enjoyed by citizens of the several States which compose this Union, from the time of their becoming free, independent, and sovereign. What these fundamental principles are, it would perhaps be more tedious than difficult to enumerate. They may, however, be all comprehended under the following general heads: Protection by the government; the enjoyment of life and liberty, with the right

to acquire and possess property of every kind, and to pursue and obtain happiness and safety; subject, nevertheless, to such restraints as the government may prescribe for the general good of the whole.[34]

The privileges and immunities of citizenship, within the meaning of the United States Constitution, are those which "belong as of right to the citizens of all free governments." Determining what these were and how to protect them required recourse to political theory as illuminated by American political experience. The *Slaughter-House* dissents pursued that course, largely by theorizing about the lessons of the Civil War.

Chief Justice Waite, for the majority in *Munn*, took a different tack. He treated the Fourteenth Amendment's phrases—such as "due process of law"—as defined by common law precedents that not only had nothing to do with the Civil War but, indeed, traced back to pre-revolutionary England. Thus, Waite injected into the opinion lengthy discussion of two old maritime treatises, Matthew Hale's *De Jure Maris* and *De Portibus Maris*.[35] Field, in dissent, seemed to take exception as much to the British sources of Waite's argument as to the test he derived from them. After answering the references to Hale on their merits, Field took up their relevance, and, as if to emphasize that old world treatises had little bearing on the meaning of a democratic constitution in the new world, he translated the titles:

> I do not doubt the justice of the encomiums passed upon Sir Matthew Hale as a learned jurist of his day; but I am unable to perceive the pertinency of his observations upon public ferries and public wharves, found in his treatises on "The Rights of the Sea" and on "The Ports of the Sea," to the questions presented by the warehousing law of Illinois, undertaking to regulate the compensation received by the owners of private property, when that property is used for private purposes.[36]

If one favors robust judicial authority, linking the Fourteenth Amendment to the common law has substantial advantages. Judges might know nothing more than legislators—indeed, perhaps less—about the rights appropriate to citizens of free governments everywhere. If, on the other hand, interpreting the Constitution required a familiarity with *De Portibus Maris*, then lawyers have fairly persuasive reasons for claiming that their technical skills give them special title to determine the Constitution's meaning. Robert McCloskey speculates that if Field's view had prevailed in *Munn*, confrontation with the "pressures of the welfare state would have forced the Court to scuttle [Field's doctrine] before long."[37] Waite, "whether instinctively or analytically does not matter," chose to emphasize traditional judicial functions rather than the transformative features of the Fourteenth Amendment. His recourse to common law "was a far more effective tool of judicial governance, not only because it was . . . more securely backed by use and wont, but because it was flexible enough to mean anything the judiciary wanted it to mean."[38] Here, then, is one way to save judicial supremacy while expanding constitutional protection of individual rights: interpret the Constitution as an expression of fundamental American commitments, while recognizing the Anglo-American common law as an essential clue to the content of those commitments.

There is, however, little reason to believe that the common law merits such a privileged role in constitutional interpretation. The common law's connection to American political authority has always been suspect. In England, the common law was respected because it was thought to be rooted in ancient custom. Eighteenth-century Americans realized that these roots were absent in their own polity. As Robert Ferguson observes,

> Arguably, there was no past to support the common law in America because the legal definition of custom beyond memory required origins preceding the reign of Richard the First. As St. George Tucker pointed out in his Virginia edition of Blackstone's *Commentaries*, North America had been settled four hundred years too late to qualify. The legitimacy of American law obviously required more immediate sources.[39]

Indeed, Blackstone himself denied the authority of the common law in America.[40] These difficulties reinforce a conclusion that might be thought obvious from common sense: if one is searching for the constitutive features of American liberty, one would do better to study the Declaration of Independence and the Gettysburg Address, not the technical treatises of Anglo-American common law. Americans had to invent the Constitution partly because their new nation lacked the foundation in custom presupposed by the English common law.

The common law's apparent irrelevance has not deterred the Supreme Court from invoking it regularly. Generations of justices have casually elided the distinction between American tradition and British legal tradition. An especially stark example is Justice Frankfurter's opinion for the Court in *Rochin v. California*, the case that gave us the "shocks the conscience" test. Frankfurter began by quoting Cardozo's view that due process protects liberties "so rooted in *the traditions and conscience of our people* as to be ranked as fundamental,"[41] but only two pages later he declared that the limits upon this formula derive from "considerations deeply rooted in reason and in *the compelling traditions of the legal profession*."[42] To deter critics, Frankfurter appended a textual footnote quoting Edmund Burke's assertion that "'*English jurisprudence* has not any other sure foundation . . . but in the maxims, rules, and principles, and juridical traditionary line of decisions.'"[43] Not surprisingly, Frankfurter thought that constitutional interpretation was essentially a matter for judges: interpreters must seek their guidance from "established standards of judicial behavior" and exhibit the judicial "habit of self-discipline and self-criticism."[44] For Frankfurter, the conscience that matters was not the ordinary citizen's "fastidious squeamishness or private sentimentalism" but rather the "hardened sensibilities" of good, tough legal minds.[45]

Much Supreme Court interpretation of the Fourteenth Amendment has transpired through the vehicle of "substantive due process," and many of the categories used to implement that doctrine find their wellspring in the common law.[46] The byzantine categories of economic due process germinated from seeds planted in cases like *Munn, Butchers' Union Co. v. Crescent City Co.*,[47] and *Mugler v. Kansas*,[48] where the Court struggled to devise public law categories "that were congruent with the common law of nuisance."[49] Even as the Court recognized the need to adjust common law doctrines in light of the novel demands of American industrialized society, it insisted that its constitutional jurisprudence was part of a continuous arc of meaning shaped by legal processes and traceable to English precedent.[50] In the Court's more recent privacy cases, the common law has figured prominently in the justices' analysis of tradition. The common law entered into the Court's justification for its position in *Bowers v. Hardwick*.[51] Justice Scalia's opinion in *Michael H. v. Gerald D.*, to take another recent example, has been much discussed for its controversial suggestion that only the narrowest core of tradition has constitutional significance.[52] Less noticed but perhaps more important is how Scalia investigated American tradition. He looked not to social histories but to treatises on the common law of bastardy, featuring quotations from such authorities as Bracton's *De Legibus et Consuetudinibus Angliae* and Boullenois's *Traité des Status*.[53] We can only wonder whether Hale's *De Portibus Maris* might have afforded any assistance.

Specific Clauses

A third interpretive distortion has already been mentioned: the Court favors provisions of the unreconstructed Constitution even when the Fourteenth Amendment is most obviously on point. This interpretive strategy, like Justice Waite's move in *Munn*, veils the grand political judgments called for by the Fourteenth Amendment and introduces instead arguments from textual and historical sources that appear more determinate. This display of concern with legally determinate sources often comes wrapped in the language of judicial restraint: constitutional language and history determine legal results and thereby "constrain" judges.

The judiciary's obsession with textual specificity has produced a series of interpretive gyrations that serve only to obscure constitutional meaning. While the justices insist that textual specificity is valuable because of its power to constrain judges, their interpretive practice demonstrates that specific clauses permit expansive constructions of individual rights. Indeed, one might say that specific clauses are to lawyers what the briar patch was to Brer Rabbit: protected by a thicket impenetrable to pursuers, they move about more freely than in an open field. The passion for specificity diminishes visibility without enhancing predictability.

Two examples should suffice. The first is, once again, *Rochin v. California*, where Black and Douglas met Frankfurter's nebulous borrowing from common law with a surprising invocation of constitutional text. After protesting Frankfurter's failure to moor his conclusion to a specific textual command,[54] both justices concurred in Frankfurter's conclusion on the basis of the Fifth Amendment's self-incrimination clause, which reads, "No person . . . shall be compelled in any criminal case to be a witness against himself." Said the arch-textualist Black, "I think a person is compelled to be a witness against himself not only when he is compelled to testify, but also when as here, incriminating evidence is forcibly taken from him by a contrivance of modern science."[55] One can debate whether Black and Douglas read the clause rightly. If one believes that the testimonial privilege depends upon a concern about the problem of coerced confessions, or upon solicitude for the special humiliation that might result from naming oneself as a criminal, then Black and Douglas might not fare well. But, however one comes out on this issue, the creative conclusion of Black and Douglas undercuts the idea of linguistic constraints that they use to criticize Frankfurter. They demonstrate that rights of bodily integrity may emerge from the concept of "witness." The question is whether "witness" best illuminates Rochin's complaint, not whether it is the most specific concept.

Our next example is more complex; it involves a line of several decisions about personal autonomy in which the Supreme Court drifted away from the Fourteenth Amendment and toward the First. In his *Poe v. Ullman* dissent, Justice Harlan observed that while an earlier Supreme Court relied upon the Fourteenth Amendment's general reference to liberty to vindicate parental autonomy, more recent Courts sought refuge in the specific language of the First Amendment. Harlan cited *West Virginia v. Barnette*[56] to buttress his suggestion, and that case provides a nice example of the trend he criticized. Read as a prohibition upon compelled speech, *Barnette* would fit comfortably under the heading of "the freedom of speech." Most people, however, read *Barnette* to stand for the more powerful idea that the government cannot prescribe what shall be orthodox, and that principle is not obviously derivative of free speech.

Indeed, in *Barnette*, Jackson and Frankfurter disagreed not about whether the government could compel speech, but about whether West Virginia had in fact compelled anyone to do anything. As Frankfurter pointed out, the flag salute requirement applied only in the public schools, and parents had a constitutional right to send their children elsewhere. Of course, parents may find it difficult to exercise that right without the government's cooperation, but the problem now appears as one of parental autonomy rather than children's speech. *Barnette*, commonly treated as a speech case or even a religion case, has at its core a question about the family, much like the question at issue in *Pierce v. Society of Sisters*[57] and *Meyer v. Nebraska*.[58] One can reconceptualize this question in terms of free speech, but doing so will not aid the cause of legal determinacy.[59]

This problem, relatively well hidden in *Barnette*, became more evident in later cases. The Court's textual reflexes simultaneously achieved precedential authority and a measure of self-parody with *Griswold v. Connecticut* and Justice Douglas's curious artifact, "penumbral rights." Douglas began his opinion by promising to avoid the error of *Lochner* and disavowing any intention to rely upon determinations appropriate to legislative, rather than legal, judgment. He then recharacterized *Pierce* and *Meyer* as First Amendment cases, exactly as Harlan had anticipated in *Poe*. Douglas nevertheless found a general right to privacy at the intersection of more specific zones of privacy created by several provisions of the Bill of Rights. Douglas's offhand use of the ill-conceived and somewhat comical "penumbra" metaphor makes it hard to take his opinion seriously.[60] It is tempting to regard Douglas's opinion as a clever legal argument aimed at duping those not savvy enough to realize that doctrine derived from specific clauses, no less than doctrine derived from common law technicalities, is "flexible enough to mean anything the judiciary want[s] it to mean."

A less grand but still odder effort to derive privacy from "the freedom of speech" is the Court's opinion in *Stanley v. Georgia*.[61] In *Stanley*, the Court held that the state could not criminalize the possession of obscene films within one's own home, even though the state might constitutionally prohibit their sale and distribution. To justify this result, Justice Marshall waxed poetic about every person's "right to . . . satisfy his intellectual and emotional needs in the privacy of his own home," and "to be free from state inquiry into the contents of his library."[62] "If the First Amendment means anything, it means that a State has no business telling a man, sitting alone in his own house, what books he may read or what films he may watch," concluded Marshall.[63] Only an obsessive fascination with the constitutional text could make such a claim appear plausible. Perhaps the First Amendment does protect the sanctity of the home. But, contrary to Marshall's suggestion, it is easy to imagine other meanings for "the freedom of speech," and equally easy to imagine other sources for a powerful privacy right.

Roe v. Wade

In *Roe v. Wade*,[64] common law fetishism and clausal fetishism blend to produce an ironic landmark. *Roe* deserves to be regarded as the paradigmatic test of modern constitutional practice, though not because it speaks to the so-called "countermajoritarian difficulty."[65] *Roe* exemplifies the interpretive distortions that result when the political concepts of the Fourteenth Amendment become submerged beneath technical stratagems arguably askew from constitutional ideals. The flaws in Justice Blackmun's opinion are legion and familiar: the largely irrelevant survey of abortion's history in the western world, the waffling indecision about the right's textual foundation; the dismissive refusal to discuss whether the state might have an interest in fetal life from the moment of conception; the focus upon the doctor's interests; the failure adequately to describe the woman's interests; and, finally, the flat prescription of a complex, quasi-statutory regulatory framework, including a blatantly circular justification for making viability the point at which the state acquires an interest in fetal life.[66]

For our purposes, one common thread linking these defects has special importance. Many if not all of the problems with Blackmun's opinion reflect an urge to transform the abortion problem from a political question about citizenship and liberty into a question peculiarly suited to legal expertise. Blackmun's survey of historical sources exposes this urge. The survey covered eight categories: "Ancient attitudes," "The Hippocratic Oath," "The common law," "The English statutory law," "The American law," "The position of the American Medical Association," "The position of the American Public Health Association," and, finally, "The position of the American Bar Association."[67] Three categories concern subjects— English and American law—within the professional expertise of lawyers, and the remaining four refer directly or indirectly to the judgments of professional historians. The emphasis on professional judgment in Blackmun's history sets the tone for the rest of the opinion, which shifts its focus away from the underlying ethical problems and towards problems for the competent legal analyst and historian.

Blackmun's treatment of the constitutional text might seem a departure from the patterns noted above. When describing the textual foundations of the privacy right, Blackmun referred in rapid succession to the First Amendment, the Fourth and Fifth Amendments, the "penumbras of the Bill of Rights," the Ninth Amendment, and the Fourteenth Amendment. He concluded this constitutional circuit by opining that the "right of privacy, whether it be founded in the Fourteenth Amendment's conception of personal liberty and restrictions upon state action, as we feel it is, or, as the District Court determined, in the Ninth Amendment's reservation of rights to the people, is broad enough to encompass a woman's decision whether or not to terminate her pregnancy."[68] This doctrinal indecision contrasts sharply with the opinions in *Stanley* or *Griswold*, where the Court was eager to pin its conclusion to some particular provision. Viewed from another perspective, however, Blackmun's textual fudging merely produces a new manifestation of the Court's clause-bound practice. Instead of elaborating specific provisions of the Bill of Rights or the Fourteenth Amendment's general guarantees, he implied, without demonstrating, that a competent lawyer would have no difficulty justifying the privacy right in any number of ways. Only the legally unsophisticated would be naive enough to believe otherwise. Such cynicism, if that's what it was, is not inconsistent with an understanding of the constitutional text as the property of lawyers.

We might view *Roe*'s weaknesses as nothing more than case-specific mistakes that will often occur when fallible judges confront hard issues honestly. But the particular mistakes made by the *Roe* majority are also intelligible as the natural consequences of a constitutional jurisprudence that has obscured the transformative features of the Fourteenth Amendment. By clinging to legalistic assumptions about the Constitution's role, the Court has obscured the legitimacy of constitutional principles protecting individual liberty while shoring up the case for judicial supremacy.

Casey's Constitution

Planned Parenthood v. Casey repaired some of *Roe*'s failures. The plurality opinion unequivocally declared its reliance upon the Due Process Clause of the Fourteenth Amendment.[69] It repudiated the idea that either "the Bill of Rights [or] the specific practices of States at the time of the adoption of the Fourteenth Amendment mark[] the outer limits of the substantive sphere of liberty which the Fourteenth Amendment protects."[70] The opinion faced up to the moral issues at stake. It included a sensitive examination of the liberty interests of pregnant women.[71] It also recognized a competing State interest in "the protection of potential life."[72] The opinion did away with *Roe*'s rigid regulatory framework.[73] Perhaps most strikingly, the plurality emphasized its obligation to decide the case so as to enable "the country . . . to see itself through its constitutional ideals,"[74] and described the Constitution as "a covenant running from the first generation of Americans to us and then to future generations," embodying "ideas and aspirations that must survive more ages than one."

Here at last, one might suppose, is a jurisprudence consistent with the Fourteenth Amendment. Having identified the Constitution not as a contract among states or long-dead framers, but as a vehicle through which Americans see what binds them together as a people,[75] the Court addressed questions of political value without cowering behind specific clauses or common law technicalities. *Casey* might warrant such a conclusion if it contained nothing more than the elements summarized thus far. But there is more. Much of *Casey* consists of a strong theory of *stare decisis*, one which requires the Court to give special deference to its own past decisions on landmark constitutional cases.[76] Indeed, the Court's reference to the "countr[y's] ability to see itself through its constitutional ideals" occurred in the course of its discussion of precedential authority, not in connection with its reading of the Fourteenth Amendment.

The Court's theory is remarkable. The Court traced its legitimacy to "a product of substance *and* perception."[77] The Court insisted upon the "need for principled action to be perceived as such."[78] When "the Court decides a case in such a way as to resolve the sort of intensively divisive controversy reflected in *Roe* . . . , only the most convincing justification under accepted standards of precedent could suffice to demonstrate that a later decision overruling the first was anything but a surrender to political pressure, and an unjustified repudiation of the principle on which the Court staked its authority in the first instance."[79]

Principled but contestable disagreement with an earlier landmark precedent is thus an insufficient ground for overruling. The Court reached this conclusion because it believed that ideas of judicial supremacy and of special legal competence to interpret the Constitution are essential to the political identity of the American people. Americans' "belief in themselves as . . . a people [who aspire to live according to the rule of law] is not readily separable from their understanding of the Court [as] invested with the authority to decide their constitutional cases *and speak before all others for their constitutional ideals.*"[80]

Here, then, is not the repudiation of the Court's legalistic, judge-centered interpretation of the Constitution, but rather the most self-conscious articulation of that practice. *Casey*'s substantive interpretation of Fourteenth Amendment liberty treats the Constitution as a guide to political ideals accessible to those without legal training. Its institutional theory, by contrast, champions the authority of the judiciary.[81] There is not so much tension between these principles as might at first appear. They fit together if the ideals of the American people revolve around respect for judicial processes. The Court's opinion presupposes a people who, as the Court says, are dedicated to the rule of law, and who, as the Court also says, understand the rule of law in terms of deference to the judiciary.

Casey's vision of the Constitution has the Constitution expressing the national identity but defining that identity in a way that subordinates citizenship and liberty to the virtues and processes of the judiciary. *Casey* thus supplies an alternative to the Fourteenth Amendment. For the lost portions of that amendment—the Citizenship Clause, the Privileges or Immunities Clause, and the Enforcement Clause—it substitutes legal tradition, Supreme Court authority, and consistency (understood as, among other things, respect for the *appearance* of principled behavior). *Casey's* Constitution is a Constitution fit for a people who care deeply about predictability, regularity, and the appearance of being good.

Conclusion

The power of judicial review has created a constitutional forum administered entirely by persons drawn from and shaped by the legal profession. The *Federalist Papers* recognize this link. In the same number where Publius defends judicial review, he also indicates that life tenure is essential to attract to the bench people who have engaged in "long and laborious study to acquire a competent knowledge" of the "very considerable bulk" of legal precedents relevant to the resolution of cases.[82] Of course, the legal profession has changed in ways that Publius likely never foresaw: by comparison to the citizen-lawyers at the Founding, the legal profession is more technical, more specialized, and less schooled in general principles of citizenship and statecraft.[83] The unintended character of these changes does not make them any less significant to the current shape of constitutional government. On the contrary, the evolution of the legal profession, through its effects on the Supreme Court, may well have helped to change the character of the American people and the nature of their polity.

Not surprisingly, the Supreme Court's self-serving assumptions about *who* should interpret the Constitution have influenced its views about *what* the Constitution is and *how* it should be interpreted.[84] The Court's connections among who, what, and how might be the result either of self-conscious reflection or unreflective impulse. Either way, if Americans are to be something more than the passive subjects described in *Casey*, they must themselves become self-conscious about the Constitution's character. They must decide to become the citizens promised by the Fourteenth Amendment; more specifically, they must find within themselves a commitment to the tumult of justice-seeking constitutionalism rather than to the stability, predictability, security, and uniformity promised by legalistic governance.

Notes

This essay is excerpted and adapted from Christopher L. Eisgruber, "The Fourteenth Amendment's Constitution," *So. Cal. L. Rev.* 69 (1995):47. I am grateful to the editors of the *Southern California Law Review* for their permission to reprint portions of that article here. The Filomen D'Agostino and Max E. Greenberg Faculty Research Fund at the New York University School of Law provided generous support for this research.

1. 514 U.S. 779 (1995) (term limits case).

2. Cf. *McCulloch v. Maryland*, 17 U.S. (4 Wheat.) 316, 406 (1819) ("we must never forget that it is a *constitution* we are expounding"; emphasis in original).

3. See, e.g., Akhil Amar, "The Case of the Missing Amendments," *Harv. L. Rev.* 106 (1992):152 ("the Fourteenth Amendment's general invisibility in 'First Amendment' discourse has blinded us to the myriad ways in which the Reconstruction Amendment has colored the way we think about and apply the First Amendment of the Founding").

4. *Wickard v. Filburn*, 317 U.S. 111 (1942) (upholding the Agricultural Adjustment Act).

5. *Heart of Atlanta Motel, Inc. v. United States*, 379 U.S. 241 (1964) (upholding federal civil rights legislation).

6. In *United States v. Lopez*, 514 U.S. 549 (1995), the first Supreme Court decision in more than fifty years to strike down a law on the ground that Congress had exceeded its power under the Commerce Clause, all six opinions focused on the Founding and the New Deal; none discussed the importance of the Civil War and the amendments that followed it.

7. 83 U.S. (16 Wall.) 36, 77–78 (1872).

8. Id. at 78.

9. 358 U.S. 1, 18 (1958).

10. 505 U.S. 833, 867 (1992) (the Court must abide by its watershed precedents when they are challenged, since "to overrule under fire in the absence of the most compelling reason to reexamine a watershed decision would subvert the Court's legitimacy beyond any serious question").

11. 5 U.S. 137 (1803).

12. See Christopher L. Eisgruber, "The Most Competent Branches: A Response to Professor Paulsen," *Geo. L. J.* 83 (1995):347, 349–53 (discussing the limits of Marshall's argument). A useful discussion of the relation between *Marbury* and *Cooper*, with extensive references to other views, appears in Laurence H. Tribe, *American Constitutional Law*, 2nd ed. (Mineola, NY: Foundation Press, 1988) secs. 3–4, pp. 32–42.

13. When Attorney General Ed Meese suggested that other branches might legitimately resist Supreme Court interpretations, conservatives and liberals joined

forces to condemn his position. See generally *Tul. L. Rev.* 61 (1987):979 ff. (reprinting Meese's speech with responses from several scholars).

14. See Eisgruber, "The Most Competent Branches," 362–63 (analyzing Lincoln's example).

15. 521 U.S. 507 (1997).

16. Id. at 527–29.

17. Christopher L. Eisgruber and Lawrence G. Sager, "Congressional Power and Religious Liberty after" City of Boerne v. Flores, 1997 Sup. Ct. Rev. 79.

18. See Tribe, *American Constitutional Law*, 342–50.

19. See Michael McConnell, "Book Review," *Yale L. J.* 98 (1989):1515 (analogizing the Constitution to wills, contracts, and statutes).

20. A. Bickel, *The Least Dangerous Branch* (Indianapolis: Bobbs-Merrill, 1962), pp. 25–26.

21. Lawrence G. Sager, "The Incorrigible Constitution," *N.Y.U. L. Rev.* 65 (1990):893, 958–59.

22. In my own view, this argument provides a strong ground for requiring other political actors to defer to most of the Court's interpretive judgments. For a preliminary consideration of the problem, see Eisgruber, "The Most Competent Branches," 353–64.

23. 163 U.S. 537, 560 (1896) (dissenting opinion).

24. For the connections between the Fourteenth Amendment and the idea of an inclusive political community, see Kenneth Karst, *Belonging to America* (New Haven: Yale University Press, 1989). With regard to the particular topic of race discrimination, see Christopher L. Eisgruber, "Political Unity and the Powers of Government," *U.C.L.A. L. Rev.* 41 (1994):1297, 1304–12, 1312–1326.

25. Dred Scott v. Sandford, 60 U.S. (19 How.) 393, 581–82, 585–86 (1857) (Curtis, J., dissenting).

26. 109 U.S. 3, 16 (1883).

27. Id. at 13.

28. See, e.g., *Alden v. Maine*, 527 U.S. 706, 713 (1999).

29. See Jack N. Rakove, "Making a Hash of Sovereignty," *Green Bag* 2 (1998): 35.

30. 115 S. Ct. 1842, 1875 (1995).

31. Justice Stevens's opinion in *Thornton* did include an apt reference to the Gettysburg Address. 514 U.S. at 821. The sole opinion in the case to give serious attention to the Civil War's impact upon federalism was Justice Kennedy's concurrence. Id. at 842–44.

32. 514 U.S. 549 (1995).

33. Robert G. McCloskey, *The American Supreme Court*, 2nd ed. (Chicago: Chicago University Press, 1994), p. 88 (quoting B. F. Wright). See also William E. Nelson, *The Fourteenth Amendment: From Political Principle to Judicial Doctrine* (Cambridge: Harvard University Press, 1988), p. 171 ("the Court adopted the essence of Justice Field's *Slaughter-House* dissent in *Munn v. Illinois*").

34. *Corfield v. Coryell*, 6 F. Ces. 546, 551–552 (C.C.E.D. Pa. 1823).

35. 94 U.S. 113, 126–29 (1876).

36. Id. at 150–51.

37. McCloskey, *The American Supreme Court*, p. 89.

38. Ibid.

39. Robert Ferguson, *Law and Letters in American Culture* (Cambridge: Harvard University Press, 1984), p. 21 (footnotes omitted).

40. William Blackstone, *Commentaries*, vol. 1, *105–6.

41. 342 U.S. 165, 169 (1952) (quoting Snyder v. Massachusetts, 291 U.S. 97, 105 [1934]).

42. Id. at 171. Frankfurter here cites Cardozo again, but this time he cites Cardozo's monographs on legal reasoning rather than Cardozo's constitutional opinions.

43. Id. at 171, n. 4 (quoting Report of the Committee of Managers on the Causes of the Duration of Mr. Hasting's Trial, *Speeches of Edmund Burke*, vol. 4, 201 [1816]).

44. Id.

45. Id. at 172.

46. Substantive due process is by no means unique in this regard; see, e.g., Ira C. Lupu, "Where Rights Begin: The Problem of Burdens on the Free Exercise of Religion," *Harv. L. Rev.* 102 (1989):966–77 (recommending the common law as a source of principles to guide Free Exercise jurisprudence).

47. 111 U.S. 746 (1884) (sustaining the constitutional power of New Orleans to abrogate the monopoly status which it had granted in the contracts challenged in the *Slaughter-House Cases*). The opinions in this case are especially interesting. Justice Miller, in the opinion of the Court, relies heavily on Kent's *Commentaries*, Id. at 747, 750, while Justices Field, Bradley, Harlan, and Woods concur in opinions that instead invoke the Declaration of Independence, Id. at 756–57 (Field, J., concurring); 762 (Bradley, J., concurring).

48. 123 U.S. 623, 664–65 (1887) (state liquor control ordinances upheld on the ground that the Fourteenth Amendment did not displace the state police powers recognized by the common law).

49. Morton J. Horwitz, *The Transformation of American Law 1870–1960* (New York, Oxford University Press, 1992), p. 27.

50. Holden v. Hardy, 169 U.S. 366, 385–93 (1898).

51. 478 U.S. 186, 192–94 and nn. 5–6 (1986) (constitutional right of privacy does not prohibit the state from prosecuting consensual homosexual sodomy). See also Id. at 196–97 (Burger, CJ., concurring) (quoting Blackstone and common law rules).

52. 491 U.S. 110, 127–28, n. 6 (1989) (Scalia, J.).

53. Id. at 124–25.

54. 342 U.S. at 175 (Black, J., concurring in the judgment) ("faithful adherence to the specific guarantees in the Bill of Rights insures a more permanent protection of individual liberty than that which can be afforded by the nebulous standards stated by the majority"); and at 179 (Douglas, J., concurring in the judgment) (complaining that the majority's test makes "the rule turn not on the Constitution but on the idiosyncracies of the judges who sit here").

55. 342 U.S. 175 (Black, J., concurring in the judgment). See also Id. at 179 (Douglas, J., concurring in the judgment) (same).

56. 319 U.S. 624 (1943) (holding unconstitutional compulsory flag salutes in public schools).

57. 268 U.S. 510 (1925).

58. 262 U.S. 390 (1923).

59. "'Specific' provisions of the Constitution, no less than 'due process,' lend themselves as readily to 'personal' interpretations by judges whose constitutional outlook is simply to keep the Constitution in 'tune with the times.'" *Griswold v. Connecticut*, 381 U.S. 479, 503 (1965) (Harlan, J., concurring in the judgment).

60. For sensitive criticism of the metaphor, see Henry Greely, "A Footnote to 'Penumbra' in *Griswold v. Connecticut*," Const. Comm. 6 (1989):251.

61. 394 U.S. 557 (1969).

62. Id. at 565.

63. Id.

64. 410 U.S. 113 (1973).

65. In a memorable article, John Hart Ely propounded the idea that *Roe* was an extreme example of the "countermajoritarian difficulty." Ely, "The Wages of Crying Wolf: A Comment on *Roe v. Wade*," Yale L. J. 82 (1973):920, 937–49.

66. 410 U.S. at 129–47, 153, 159, 163, 165. The Court's treatment of viability prompted a trenchant response from John Hart Ely: "The Court's defense [of the viability criterion] seems to mistake a definition for a syllogism." Ely, "The Wages of Crying Wolf," p. 924.

67. 410 U.S. at 130–47.

68. Id. at 153.

69. 505 U.S. at 846.

70. Id. at 848.

71. Id. at 852.

72. Id. at 871.

73. Id. at 872.

74. Id. at 868.

75. Id. at 901.

76. Id. at 860–69.

77. Id. at 865 (emphasis added).

78. Id. at 866.

79. Id.

80. Id. at 868 (emphasis added).

81. See, e.g., p. 853 ("the reservations any of us may have in reaffirming the central holding of *Roe* are outweighed by the explication of individual liberty we have given combined with the force of *stare decisis*").

82. The Federalist No. 78, at 471 (Alexander Hamilton) (Clinton Rossiter ed., 1961).

83. See, e.g., Ferguson, *Law and Letters in American Culture*, pp. 202–5 (lawyers have ceased to serve as "the ideological guardian of the culture" and have become instead "the increasingly technical representative of vested interests"); Robert W. Gordon, "The Independence of Lawyers," *B. U. L. Rev.* 68 (1988):1, 14–19 (describing how ideals of legal community changed from republican virtue to independent, professional excellence); R. Kent Newmyer, Harvard

Law School, "New England Legal Culture, and the Antebellum Origins of American Jurisprudence," in *The Constitution and American Life* (David P. Thelen ed., Ithaca: Cornell University Press, 1988), p. 154 (describing the rise of a professional legal culture). See also Anthony Kronman, *The Lost Lawyer: Failing Ideals of the Legal Profession* (Cambridge, MA: Belknap Press, 1993) (commenting on the decline of statesmanship in the legal profession during recent decades).

84. I draw these categories from the elegant organization of constitutional materials pioneered in Walter F. Murphy, James E. Fleming, and William F. Harris II, eds., *American Constitutional Interpretation* 1st ed. (Mincola, NY: Foundation, 1986).

4

We the Exceptional American People

JAMES E. FLEMING

> [The People of America] reared the fabrics of
> governments which have no model on the face
> of the globe.
> —*The Federalist* No. 14[1]

Introduction: "American Exceptionalism"

There is an academic movement afoot—one with a long historical pedigree—to attribute the vitality of the American constitutional order to
"American exceptionalism." The most prominent representative of this
school of thought is Bruce Ackerman, whose *We the People* opens with a
jeremiad against the "Europeanization" of American constitutional theory and urges us as Americans to "look inward" to rediscover our distinctive patterns, practices, and ideals.[2] He maps the terrain of theory as
being divided into monists ("Anglophiles"), rights foundationalists
("Germanophiles"), and dualists (red-blooded Americans).[3] Only dualists
have the "strength" to declare our American independence from British
and German models and philosophers.[4] Thus, as Sanford Levinson observes, Ackerman is reopening the question about "American exceptionalism" from Europe.[5]

Ackerman published *We the People* in 1991, during the bicentennial
celebration of the ratification of the Bill of Rights. Accordingly, it is
tempting to dismiss his rhetoric of American exceptionalism as little more
than patriotic flag-waving. But his argument that the American Constitution is dualist rather than rights foundationalist depends importantly
upon a contrast that he draws between the American Constitution and
the German Basic Law with respect to entrenchment of constitutional
provisions against subsequent amendment.[6] I shall assess this argument,
asking to what extent his contrast illuminates differences between the
American and German constitutional orders and adjudicates the conflicting claims of dualism and rights foundationalism to be the better account
of the American scheme of government. My conclusion is that, although
the American "fabrics of governments" may well be exceptional, Ackerman has not established his case for dualism over rights foundationalism.

Our Alienable Dualist Constitution?

Ackerman argues that the American Constitution is dualist rather than rights foundationalist. Dualists conceive the Constitution as "democratic first, rights-protecting second" in the sense that judicial protection of constitutional rights against encroachments by the ordinary law of legislation "depend[s] on a prior democratic affirmation on the higher lawmaking track" of the Constitution.[7] Rights foundationalists "reverse this priority," for they hold that "the Constitution is first concerned with protecting rights; only then does it authorize the People to work their will on other matters."[8]

Ackerman's argument for dualism over rights foundationalism emphasizes a contrast between the American Constitution and the German Basic Law concerning entrenchment. Our Constitution, he observes, "has never (with two exceptions . . .) explicitly entrenched existing higher law against subsequent amendment by the People."[9] The two exceptions are Article V's prohibition of amendments (1) affecting the African slave trade until 1808 and (2) depriving a state of equal representation in the Senate without its consent. The Basic Law, by contrast, "explicitly declared that a long list of fundamental human rights *cannot* constitutionally be revised, regardless of the extent to which a majority of Germans support repeal."[10] Article 79(3) entrenched unalienable human rights to dignity, the fundamental principles of free democratic basic order, and the basic structure of federalism.[11]

Ackerman submits that practices regarding entrenchment provide an important crucible for testing whether a constitutional order is dualist or rights foundationalist.[12] He contends that the absence of "German-style entrenchment" of fundamental rights in the American Constitution—and thus their repealability or alienability—is an "embarrassment" for rights foundationalists but not for dualists.[13] He also states that our constitutional experience with entrenchment, through the two exceptions involving slavery and federalism, has been "very negative" and has not served the cause of human freedom.[14] From these aspects of our constitutional document and history, he concludes that rights foundationalism "is inconsistent with the existing premises of the American higher lawmaking system."[15] For in America, "it is the People who are the source of rights,"[16] and We the People are not bound by a higher law than the higher law of the Constitution.[17] In the crucible of entrenchment, Ackerman argues, ours proves to be an alienable dualist Constitution, unlike the unalienable rights foundationalist Basic Law.

Should we be persuaded by Ackerman's argument for dualism from his contrast between the American Constitution and the German Basic Law?

Are practices of entrenchment a good crucible in which to test the basic commitments of a constitutional order? Or is Ackerman's test rigged in favor of a positivist dualism?

Early British legal positivists like John Austin believed that, to get to the bottom of a legal system, one had to find a sovereign, "a legally untrammelled will" behind the legislature that was free, "not only from legal limitations imposed *ab extra*, but also from its own prior legislation."[18] Sophisticated contemporary positivists like H.L.A. Hart have argued instead that the foundation of a legal system is an accepted rule of recognition specifying the ultimate criteria of legal validity.[19] Ackerman has stated that his aim in constitutional theory is to develop a "principled positivism" in the form of a theory of dualist democracy that would provide "principles of recognition" of higher lawmaking (by analogy to Hart's idea of rules of recognition).[20] Under Ackerman's positivist theory of popular sovereignty, We the People are free, not only from limitations imposed *ab extra* by unalienable rights, but also from our own prior higher lawmaking.[21]

With this background in mind, we should ask whether the fact that our Constitution lacks entrenchment clauses of the sort expressed in the German Basic Law proves, as Ackerman maintains, that it is dualist rather than rights foundationalist. In answering this question, we should consider the strong likelihood that an unrelenting positivist dualist applying Ackerman's crucible of entrenchment would contend that the German Basic Law, like the American Constitution, is ultimately dualist. According to such a positivist, Article 79(3) of the Basic Law would not, in Hart's terms, put a stop to the chain of inquiries concerning legal validity;[22] she or he would insist on pressing further to find the legally untrammelled will or sovereign standing behind the entrenchment clauses. (The proof of this speculation lies in Ackerman's suggestion that the Basic Law may have an "escape hatch" [Article 146] through which German dualists might prevail over German rights foundationalists by repealing the limitations of Article 79(3) and thereby modifying the Basic Law's foundationalist commitments.)[23] From the standpoint of such a positivist dualism, entrenchment clauses in a written constitution are—to quote Chief Justice John Marshall from an analogous context—"absurd attempts, on the part of the people, to limit a power, in its own nature illimitable."[24]

Furthermore, even a rights foundationalist could admit, as John Rawls writes, that "in the long run a strong majority of the electorate can eventually make the constitution conform to its political will."[25] But, Rawls continues: "This is simply a fact about political power as such. There is no way around this fact, not even by entrenchment clauses that try to fix permanently the basic democratic guarantees."[26] This fact about political power, however, is not the foundation of legitimacy in either the American or the German constitutional order.[27] Nor does it prove that, at bottom, our Constitution is dualist rather than rights foundationalist. Ackerman's crucible of entrenchment is a rigged positivist test.

If practices of entrenchment do not tell us whether we have a dualist or a rights foundationalist constitutional order, can they tell us anything? One way to explore this matter is to ask what the purposes of entrenchment are. Let us posit a positivist—less relentless than the one we just imagined—who believes that if you want to know the constitutive principles on which a constitutional order is founded (and nothing else), you must look at it as an entrenchment formalist, and examine what provisions are explicitly entrenched in the constitutional document against subsequent amendment.[28] Applying this test, the positivist would conclude from Article 79(3) of the German Basic Law that the constitutive principles of the German scheme of government were unalienable human rights to dignity, the fundamental principles of free democratic basic order, and the basic structure of federalism. But such a positivist would find Article V of the American Constitution cryptic (or deeply unjust) on first sight: for entrenchment of protection of the African slave trade until 1808 and equal representation of the states in the Senate hardly look like constitutive principles of a constitutional order.[29] This discovery might lead to either of two conclusions: that the American Constitution simply recognizes no fundamental rights as constitutive principles, or that in our constitutional document entrenchment performs a role other than that of securing constitutive principles. Ackerman basically draws the former conclusion; I shall pursue the latter.

What alternative role might Article V entrenchment play in the American Constitution? Perhaps Article V entrenches provisions that reflect deep compromises with our Consitution's constitutive principles: the protection of the African slave trade with the principle that all persons are created equal, and the equal representation of the states in the Senate with the principle of the equal representation of citizens.[30] The founders of the Constitution concluded that both compromises were necessary to "the forging of the Union": the slave states insisted upon the former, the small states upon the latter.[31] Thus, both imperfections were considered necessary "to form a more perfect Union" than the Articles of Confederation. From this standpoint, *contra* Ackerman, we can see that Article V entrenched features of the Constitution that were vulnerable to being repealed through democratic procedures, precisely because they manifested such deep compromises with our constitutive principles and ordained such an imperfect Constitution.

With this idea of the purpose of entrenchment on hand, we should reassess Ackerman's contrast between American and German practices.

Ackerman may make such haste to disparage the American experience with "German-style entrenchment," and to taint it by association with slavery, that he overlooks this alternative purpose of bolstering vulnerable features of a scheme of government. Moreover, his discussion obscures a deeper similarity: both the American and German founders expressly entrenched provisions of their new constitutional orders that they considered necessary to secure the transition to a more perfect union. Again, in making the transition from the Articles of Confederation to the Constitution, the small states insisted upon equal representation in the Senate, and the slave states upon protection of the African slave trade. In the aftermath of the failures of the Weimar Constitution and the atrocities of Nazism, the founders of the Federal Republic of Germany insisted upon entrenching certain unalienable human rights and structural principles that had been outrageously disregarded during the Nazi regime.[32]

The further point is that both countries expressly entrenched the features of their new constitutional orders that were feared to be in greatest need of bolstering, and at greatest risk of repeal through democratic procedures, given their historical circumstances. As it happens, the American Constitution explicitly entrenched provisions that deeply *compromised* its founding principles, while the German Basic Law explicitly entrenched provisions that profoundly *expressed* its reconstruction principles.[33] We should not, however, let this contrast concerning entrenchment clauses obscure similarities between the constitutive principles of the two constitutional orders.

In drawing this misleadingly strong contrast between the American and German constitutional schemes, and urging Americans to "look inward" to rediscover their distinctive dualist Constitution, does Ackerman seriously mean to imply that the idea of unalienable rights is alien to American constitutional theory, or that Americans have gotten this idea from looking outward to German models and philosophers? To the contrary, the idea of unalienable rights is far more congenial to the American constitutional tradition than to the German. For one thing, British legal positivists from Bentham to Hart have characterized American jurisprudence as marked by an anti-positivist emphasis on unalienable rights.[34] For another, the German Basic Law's explicit entrenchment of unalienable rights was a "forceful rejection of the legal positivism that grounded individual liberties in Weimar, where such rights found their source in the authority of the state."[35]

The reconstruction of constitutional democracy in Germany, upon "reflection and choice,"[36] was rooted not only in a rejection of Weimar constitutional theory and Nazism, but also in an acceptance of American constitutional theory and practice. After World War II, the American "fabrics of governments" served as a "model on the face of the globe."[37]

The German Basic Law (not to mention the Japanese Constitution) was in no small measure *made in America*.[38] To some extent, therefore, when Americans look outward to the German Basic Law, they look into a mirror of their own unalienable rights and constitutive principles. In other words, to a degree the unwritten American Constitution is written into the German Basic Law, and the unalienable rights and constitutive principles underlying the American constitutional order are expressly entrenched in the German constitutional document.[39]

In conclusion, the fact that the American Constitution, unlike the German Basic Law, does not explicitly entrench unalienable rights or constitutive principles does not prove that it is dualist, or "democratic first, rights-protecting second." Contrary to Ackerman's claim, the absence of provisions entrenching fundamental rights in the American Constitution is not an "embarrassment" for rights foundationalists.[40] To paraphrase the Ninth Amendment: The entrenchment in the Constitution, of certain compromises, shall not be construed to deny or disparage unalienable rights retained by the people.[41] Ackerman has failed to establish his claim that our "American exceptionalism" consists in the fact that we have an alienable dualist Constitution.

Our Imperfect Dualist Constitution?

Ackerman further argues that the general availability of repeal of fundamental rights protected in the American Constitution is an "embarrassment" for rights foundationalists but not for dualists.[42] He contends that our Constitution, again unlike the German Basic Law, is open to "morally disastrous" amendments repealing fundamental rights.[43] To test this contention, Ackerman conjures up two hypothetical Christianity amendments. The first establishes Christianity as the state religion of the American people, thereby repealing the fundamental right to liberty of conscience. The second forbids repeal of the first, thereby entrenching it and in effect repealing freedom of speech and dualist democracy itself.[44] Ackerman states that dualists would accept these amendments as valid, while rights foundationalists would reject them as unconstitutional. Asserting that in America, unlike Germany, "almost all lawyers" would consider "absurd" or "preposterous" the idea that an amendment to the Constitution might be unconstitutional, Ackerman claims that dualism better fits our constitutional order than does rights foundationalism.[45]

Having drawn this contrast through these two hypothetical amendments, Ackerman goes on to confess that, as a citizen and a political philosopher, he is a rights foundationalist who would be proud to be a member of the generation that "finally redeem[ed] the promise of the

Declaration of Independence by entrenching *inalienable* rights into our Constitution," including liberty of conscience and freedom of speech.[46] We should recall that his earlier writings include *Social Justice in the Liberal State*,[47] a work of rights foundationalist political philosophy that bears affinities to the liberal political philosophies of John Rawls and Ronald Dworkin, from whom he now wishes to distance himself as a dualist constitutional theorist.[48] Michael Klarman has suggested that Ackerman's confession that he yearns to move "beyond dualism" to a rights foundationalist constitutional order evinces a "glaring contradiction" that undermines his commitment to popular sovereignty and raises the question "why one should take seriously Ackerman's detailed exegesis of dualist democracy."[49]

Whether or not he falls into contradiction, Ackerman is straining mightily to prove his democratic and positivist mettle by proclaiming that he would uphold the validity of these hypothetical amendments as a dualist constitutional theorist, though he would hold them "morally disastrous" as a rights foundationalist political philosopher. With all the zeal of a born-again positivist who has seen the errors of his rights foundationalist past, Ackerman kneels before the altar of Henry Monaghan's "Imperfect Constitution,"[50] striving to show that his constitutional theory passes what Christopher Eisgruber has dubbed Monaghan's "no pain, no claim" test.[51] (Basically, the idea is that a constitutional theory has no serious claim on our attention unless the theorist putting it forward suffers some pain by acknowledging that the Constitution does not secure everything that she or he would protect in a perfect Constitution.)[52] Indeed, Ackerman does more than confess his past as a rights foundationalist, for he also admits his present temptation to move beyond dualism to rights foundationalism and to entrench a new Bill of Rights against subsequent amendment.[53] Yet he maintains that he does not succumb, proving his democratic and positivist virtue by unveiling his imperfect dualist Constitution.[54]

Through this argument for dualism from the two hypothetical Christianity amendments, Ackerman is attempting to deliver a *coup de grace* against rights foundationalists of the sort that would be made by Article V positivists like Robert Bork.[55] Their last move, in trying to place the American Constitution in the camp of popular sovereignty rather than unalienable fundamental rights, would be to assert that under the amending procedures of Article V, We the People have ultimate constitutional authority to "alter any feature of the [constitutional] document including its commitment to basic liberties and constitutional forms."[56]

Now, this type of move is to be expected from an Article V positivist like Bork. But such a move is, to say the least, surprising coming from Ackerman. After all, he has spent the last decade developing a complex theory of amending the Constitution outside Article V through structural amendments.[57] Yet here we find Ackerman talking like an Article V positivist with respect to repealability and entrenchment. In this essay, I can only briefly state three points in response.

The first point concerns Ackerman's evident strategy for winning acceptance of his complex constitutional theory among lawyers. He assumes that lawyers are low-level positivists who would reject out of hand rights foundationalist theories that presuppose that unalienable rights or constitutive principles are implicitly entrenched in the constitutional order (outside Article V), though not explicitly entrenched in the constitutional document (in Article V). Ackerman's tack is apparently to join such positivist lawyers and then to try to enlist them—through an appeal to lawyerly criteria of fit with our constitutional document and underlying constitutional order—on the side of dualism and against rights foundationalism.[58] The strategy is, basically, if you can't beat the positivist lawyers, join them, and then hope that they will join you. I mean to intimate shades of Suzanna Sherry's interpretation of Ackerman's dualism, in the guise of a liberal originalism, as "the ghost of liberalism past."[59]

Strategically, Ackerman would be prudent to ponder the great likelihood that positivist lawyers who would join him in rejecting rights foundationalist ideas of implicit entrenchment of constitutive principles or unalienable rights outside Article V as absurd or preposterous would also stand ready to join positivists like Bork in rejecting as preposterous and absurd Ackerman's own idea of amendment of the Constitution outside Article V. That is, lawyers who are Article V positivists regarding entrenchment are also quite likely to be Article V positivists concerning amendment. They are usually the sort of people who contend that the words of Article V "mean what they say"[60] or that the whole point of Article V is to have a "clear rule of recognition for constitutional change."[61] In short, such positivist lawyers—Ackerman's new-found allies—probably would use Article V as a *coup de grace* against his own theory of structural amendments. Ironically, notwithstanding Ackerman's attempt to portray himself as a positivist,[62] the positivists are the persons who are least likely to be persuaded by his theory.

My second point is that Ackerman himself, despite his best efforts, does not sound like an Article V positivist when discussing the two hypothetical Christianity amendments. For example, he does not say simply that the hypothetical amendment repealing liberty of conscience is valid, because it has been ratified through Article V procedures. Instead, he concedes that it would inaugurate a "deep transformation" of our Constitution: "on more or less the same order, though of a very different kind," as the transformations to new "regimes" within dualist democracy achieved by the Reconstruction Republicans and New Deal Democrats.[63]

Nor does Ackerman say simply that the hypothetical amendment en-trenching such a repeal is valid, because the voice of the People has duly spoken. Rather, he states that it would amount to a "repeal of dualist democracy itself."[64] That is, the latter amendment would go beyond the former's deep transformation within dualist democracy to a repeal of that order. It might amount to a constitutional breakdown or revolution, ush-ering in a new constitutional order altogether.[65]

The implication is that Ackerman himself acknowledges that principles such as liberty of conscience and freedom of speech, even if they are not explicitly entrenched in our constitutional document, are nonetheless fundamental rights that partly constitute the identity of regimes within our constitutional order or of that order itself. Indeed, on Ackerman's account, freedom of speech, at least as expressed in participation in the amending process, might be unalienable.[66] My claim is not that Acker-man here commits himself to a theory that the Constitution implicitly entrenches constitutive principles or fundamental rights outside Article V—only that his theory is not as far from such a conception as might appear on first sight.

This suggestion brings me to the third point: Just as Ackerman has elaborated a theory of "structural amendments" to the Constitution out-side the formal Article V amending procedures,[67] so one might develop a theory of "structural entrenchments" of fundamental rights or constitu-tive principles outside Article V. Ackerman rejects rights foundationalist theories that hold that certain fundamental rights are pre-constitutional principles that bind even constitutional framers and ratifiers at the found-ing, when they are establishing a constitutional order.[68] Whatever one thinks of such theories, one might advance a theory that certain constitu-tive principles or fundamental rights become entrenched against repeal through long and successful constitutional tradition and practice.[69] Re-sponding to Ackerman's hypothetical Christianity amendments along these lines, Rawls suggests that our constitutional tradition and practice over two centuries place restrictions upon the formal amending pro-cedures of Article V.[70] On this view, Ackerman's hypotheticals, instead of being valid amendments of the Constitution, would amount to a consti-tutional breakdown, or revolution in the proper sense.[71] Moreover, this view entails that entrenchment is not purely positivist and confined to Article V (any more than amendment is for Ackerman's theory).[72]

The possibility of a theory of this sort underscores an evident incon-gruity in Ackerman's theory: Ackerman supplements Article V where structural amendments are concerned but would invoke Article V as a positivist bar to structural entrenchments of fundamental rights at the founding or through constitutional tradition and practice.[73] I do not claim that a theory of structural entrenchments would permanently fix basic constitutional guarantees, or perpetually impose pre-constitutional principles upon We the People. In fact, structurally entrenched fundamental rights or constitutive principles, like explicitly entrenched ones, will give way to a strong majority that is determined to make the Constitution conform to its political will. But again, this is simply a fact about political power as such,[74] not a fact that unveils an ultimate rule of recognition or source of legitimacy in popular sovereignty in an imperfect American Constitution as distinguished from the (perhaps) more perfect German Basic Law.

The question *what is the Constitution*—and when does it become a different Constitution through breakdown or revolution?—is analytically distinct from the question *whether courts are empowered to declare amendments (or original provisions) unconstitutional.*[75] And so, even if we decide to reject Ackerman's Article V positivism concerning entrenchment of constitutive principles or fundamental rights in the Constitution, there remains his contrast between American and German judicial practices. He asserts that in America, judicial review invalidating "morally disastrous" amendments would seem "absurd" or "preposterous" to "almost all lawyers," whereas in Germany it would not.[76] From this contrast, Ackerman argues that our scheme of government is dualist, while the German scheme is rights foundationalist.

Ackerman overstates the significance of this contrast. Initially, one might express doubts whether hypotheticals concerning judicial review of unconstitutional amendments to our Constitution provide a good crucible in which to test whether almost all lawyers are dualists or rights foundationalists. After all, most American lawyers probably have never thought about the possibility of limitations on the amending power and, if asked about it, probably would simply make the immediate observation that the idea of an "unconstitutional constitutional amendment" seems like a contradiction in terms or a paradox. But this idea seems so only to those who beg the question by unreflectively assuming a false equivalence among the amending power, the Constitution, and the constituent power.[77] If pressed beyond this immediate reaction, almost all lawyers might also believe that to adopt an amendment purporting to repeal certain unalienable fundamental rights (such as freedom of speech and liberty of conscience) would be to repudiate our constitutional order, not merely to ratify a valid constitutional amendment.[78]

In any event, in assessing Ackerman's account of American judicial practice, we should distinguish between two types of situations in which an assertion regarding judicial review might be dismissed as absurd or preposterous. In the first, judicial review would seem absurd because it is unprecedented (or novel). In the second, it would seem absurd because it is contrary to well-established precedents (or settled). To illustrate the first situation: in 1946, Justice Frankfurter might have said that representation-reinforcing judicial review of malapportioned legislatures would be absurd;[79] or in 1922, a country lawyer named Hugo Black might have lamented that "absolutist" judicial review enforcing the First Amendment against both the state and federal governments would be absurd;[80] or again, in 1937, Ackerman's forebears might have despaired that President Franklin Roosevelt was launching a court-packing plan instead of seizing a crucial moment to amend the Constitution through the formal procedures of Article V, because the idea of structural amendments to the Constitution outside Article V would be preposterous.[81] To illustrate the second situation: today, one might argue, despite Richard Epstein, that judicial review invalidating the New Deal and the welfare state that has grown up on its foundations would be absurd.[82]

Which of these two types of situations does Ackerman mean to invoke in claiming that in America judicial review declaring amendments unconstitutional would seem absurd or preposterous to almost all lawyers? Evidently, the first rather than the second. Ackerman does not appear to argue that in America there is a well-established practice *against* judicial review of amendments to assure conformity with constitutive principles, only that there is no well-established practice *in favor of* such review.[83] To be sure, there are cases rejecting the idea that a duly ratified amendment might be unconstitutional (which Ackerman does not cite).[84] But those cases were easy. For example, one basically upheld the Eighteenth Amendment against an argument that it was beyond the Article V amending power to prohibit the manufacture, sale, transportation, importation, and exportation of intoxicating liquors for beverage purposes.[85] Another essentially upheld the Nineteenth Amendment against a contention that it deprived unconsenting states of their sovereign power to deny women the right to vote and thereby destroyed their autonomy as political bodies.[86] Furthermore, such cases date from an era—1920 and 1922, respectively—in which "representation-reinforcing" review of ordinary lawmaking might have seemed hardly less absurd than "sovereignty-reinforcing" review of higher lawmaking.[87] I mention these complex matters not to resolve them but rather to suggest that our practices regarding judicial review may not be as settled as Ackerman's argument presumes.

Put another way, the question whether the Supreme Court has authority to declare amendments (or original provisions) unconstitutional presents a case of what Hart would call uncertainty in the penumbra of the ultimate rules of recognition.[88] In resolving such questions, as Hart aptly put it: "Here all that succeeds is success. . . . Here power acquires authority *ex post facto* from success."[89]

In this light, the glaring difficulty with the idea of judicial review preserving the constitutive principles or fundamental rights of our Constitution against repeal is not so much absurdity or preposterousness as it is probable futility. We all know the standard moves concerning the impotence of the "least dangerous branch": for example, quotations from *The Federalist* No. 78,[90] President Andrew Jackson,[91] James Bradley Thayer,[92] Judge Learned Hand,[93] and John Hart Ely.[94] Yet we all also know the common countermoves: for example, hypotheticals about the possibility of judicial civil disobedience[95] and the observation that, our fears of futility notwithstanding, after ordered to do so in *United States v. Nixon*,[96] President Richard Nixon did turn over those tapes.[97]

To Ackerman's dualist claims about the absurdity or preposterousness of judicial review of morally disastrous amendments, and to fears about its futility, I offer three responses. The first is to repeat what Hart said concerning such situations: "Here all that succeeds is success."[98] The second is to imagine what Yogi Berra, paraphrasing Hart, might have said: "Here nothing succeeds like failure." By that paradoxical utterance, I mean to suggest the possibility that judicial review (or judicial civil disobedience) invalidating repeals of liberty of conscience and freedom of speech—whether successful or futile in a narrow legal sense—would succeed in dramatically signaling that a constitutional breakdown or revolution was occurring.[99]

My final response is to admit that—from a larger perspective outside our constitutional enterprise—constitutions, constitutional interpretation, and judicial review are themselves preposterous and absurd. As William F. Harris expresses it: "American constitutional interpretation takes for granted the elemental preposterousness of its subject—the presumption that a political world can be constructed and controlled with words."[100] And, in the face of a determined political will, constitutions—written or unwritten, with or without entrenchment clauses—may be "absurd attempts, on the part of the people, to limit a power in its own nature illimitable."[101] We should not, however, adopt such an external point of view in assessing the foundations of legitimacy in our constitutional order.[102] Our Constitution is underwritten by more than the fact of political power lying under an imperfect dualist Constitution.[103]

We the Exceptional American People?

The bicentennial celebration of the ratification of the Bill of Rights is over. James Madison rightly proclaimed in *The Federalist* No. 14: "[The People of America] reared the fabrics of governments which have no model on the face of the globe."[104] Two centuries later, though, these fabrics of governments have served as models for other countries (and will continue to do so if efforts like Ackerman's project of American imperialism, or exporting liberal revolution to the countries of Eastern Europe, make any headway).[105] Ironically, the upshot of Ackerman's project of "American exceptionalism" is that on his view We the People, the American popular sovereign, are ultimately quite similar to the "legally untrammelled will" of the sovereign that is envisioned in British legal positivism and that positivist dualists would find standing behind the entrenchment clauses of the purportedly rights foundationalist German Basic Law.[106] The American constitutional order may well be exceptional, but Ackerman has not established his case for dualism over rights foundationalism as the better account of the American scheme of government through his contrast between the American Constitution and the German Basic Law.

Notes

I am grateful to Bruce Ackerman, Akhil Amar, Sot Barber, Debby Denno, Chris Eisgruber, John Finn, Martin Flaherty, Ned Foley, Samuel Freeman, Will Harris, Bob Kaczorowski, Greg Keating, Sandy Levinson, Steve Macedo, Linda McClain, Walter Murphy, John Rawls, Paul Schwartz, Tony Sebok, and Bill Treanor for helpful comments concerning this chapter. I also would like to thank my research assistants Larry McCabe, Steven Shaw, and Sabrena Silver. Fordham University School of Law provided generous research support. I prepared an earlier version of this chapter for the Georgetown University Law Center Discussion Group on Constitutional Law, which was organized by Mark Tushnet. The chapter has been published in *Constitutional Commentary* 11 (1994): 355. Subsequently, I published another article on Bruce Ackerman's constitutional theory, "We the Unconventional American People," *U. Chi. L. Rev.* 65 (1998): 1513 (reviewing Bruce Ackerman, *We the People, vol. 2: Transformations* [Cambridge, MA: Belknap Press, 1998]).

1. *The Federalist* No. 14, 104 (James Madison) (all page references are to edition by Clinton Rossiter, New York: New American Library, 1961).

2. Bruce Ackerman, *We the People, vol. 1: Foundations* (Cambridge, MA: Belknap Press, 1991), pp. 3–6, 32–33.

3. Ibid., pp. 6–16, 32–33, 35–36. Monism emphasizes popular sovereignty over and against fundamental rights, and thus tends to equate popular sovereignty with parliamentary supremacy on a British model (pp. 7–10, 35). Rights foundationalism challenges the primacy of popular sovereignty, stressing constraints imposed by deeper commitments to fundamental rights on a German model (pp. 10–12, 35–36). Ackerman presents dualism as an "accommodation" between monism and rights foundationalism (pp. 12–13). Dualism distinguishes between the constituent power of We the People, expressed in the higher law of the Constitution, and the ordinary power of officers of government, expressed in the ordinary law of legislation. Dualism preserves, against encroachment by ordinary law, the fundamental rights ordained and established by We the People

in the higher law of the Constitution; to that extent, it is like rights foundational-ism. But it preserves only those fundamental rights; beyond them, it is like mo-nism in deferring to ordinary law (pp. 12–13, 32–33).

There are problems with Ackerman's map of the terrain of American constitu-tional theory. For purposes of this chapter, I shall put to one side the difficulties with his distinction between monism and dualism, and I shall accept his distinc-tion between dualism and rights foundationalism. Elsewhere, I have suggested that one can be a dualist in a general sense without being committed to dualism in Ackerman's specific sense—that is, without endorsing his complex apparatus of higher lawmaking through structural amendments to the Constitution outside the formal Article V amending procedures, and without accepting his purported distinction between dualism and rights foundationalism on the ground that the former theory but not the latter rejects the idea that a duly ratified amendment might be unconstitutional. See James E. Fleming, "Constructing the Substantive Constitution," *Tex. L. Rev.* 72 (1993): 287, n. 380; 290, n. 405. Furthermore, I have outlined a constitutional constructivism (pp. 217–20, 280–304), a theory that is neither as positivist as Ackerman's own theory of dualism nor as naturalist as his portrayal of rights foundationalism.

4. Ackerman, *We the People* 1:3.

5. Sanford Levinson, blurb on dust jacket of *We the People*, vol 1. See also Sanford Levinson, "Accounting for Constitutional Change," *Const. Comm.* 8 (1991): 429 (characterizing Ackerman's enterprise as "the most important and imaginative work now being done in the area of constitutional theory"). If Acker-man's *We the People* reopens the tradition of "American exceptionalism," perhaps his *The Future of Liberal Revolution* continues the tradition of American imperial-ism, attempting to colonize Eastern European countries (not to mention South Africa and Latin American countries) with American models and theories. See Bruce Ackerman, *The Future of Liberal Revolution* (New Haven: Yale University Press, 1992). Both works are thus in different ways characteristically American. Ackerman places himself in the tradition of American exceptionalism epitomized by Louis Hartz, stating: "I share with Louis Hartz an abiding skepticism about the power of European models to enlighten American politics without fundamen-tal conceptual reorganization." Ackerman, *We the People* 1:25 (referring to Louis Hartz, *The Liberal Tradition in America* [New York: Harcourt, Brace, 1955]).

6. Ackerman, *We the People* 1:13–16. Ackerman also discusses the German Ba-sic Law in his treatment of liberal revolution. See Ackerman, *The Future of Lib-eral Revolution*, pp. 101–12. In the aftermath of the unification of West Germany and East Germany, I shall speak simply of the "German Basic Law." For an anal-ysis applying Ackerman's constitutional theory to constitutional issues raised by German unification, see Paul M. Schwartz, "Constitutional Change and Consti-tutional Legitimation: The Example of German Unification," *Houston L. Rev.* 31 (1994): 1027.

7. Ackerman, *We the People* 1:13. Thus, Ackerman's theory of dualism seeks to reconstruct the classical, interpretive justification of judicial review, put forward in *Federalist* No. 78, pp. 467, 469 (Alexander Hamilton) and *Marbury v. Madison*, 5 U.S. (1 Cranch) 137, 177–78 (1803): Courts are obligated to interpret the higher law of the Constitution and to preserve it against encroachments by the ordinary law of legislation. See Ackerman, *We the People* 1:60–61, 72. In this

chapter, I shall not assess his distinctions between ordinary lawmaking and higher lawmaking, or between "normal politics" on the former track and "constitutional politics" on the latter track. pp. at 230–94. For discussions of these matters, see, e.g., Suzanna Sherry, "The Ghost of Liberalism Past," *Harv. L. Rev.* 105 (1992): 918 (reviewing Ackerman, *We the People, vol. 1: Foundations*); Terrance Sandalow, "Abstract Democracy: A Review of Ackerman's *We the People*," *Const. Comm.* 9 (1992): 309; Michael W. McConnell, "The Forgotten Constitutional Moment," *Const. Comm.* 11 (1994): 115. See also "Symposium on Bruce Ackerman's *We the People*," *Ethics* 104 (1994): 446.

8. Ackerman, *We the People* 1:13. For an argument that Ackerman's formulation presents a "false dichotomy" because both democracy and rights, or popular sovereignty and unalienable rights, are constitutive principles of our constitutional democracy, see Samuel Freeman, "Original Meaning, Democratic Interpretation, and the Constitution," *Phil. & Pub. Aff.* 21 (1992): 3, 41–42. For a similar argument, though not directed specifically against Ackerman, that our constitutional order is a hybrid scheme of democracy (majority rule) and constitutionalism (limited government), or constitutional democracy, see, e.g., Walter F. Murphy, James E. Fleming, and Sotirios A. Barber, *American Constitutional Interpretation* (Westbury, NY: Foundation Press, 2d ed., 1995), pp. 41–67; Walter F. Murphy, "Constitutions, Constitutionalism, and Democracy," in Douglas Greenberg et al., eds., *Constitutionalism and Democracy: Transitions in the Contemporary World* (New York: Oxford University Press, 1993), pp. 3–7.

9. Ackerman, *We the People* 1:13.

10. Ibid., p. 15 (emphasis in original).

11. Article 79(3) of the German Basic Law provides in relevant part: "Amendments of this Basic Law affecting the division of the Federation into Laender, the participation on principle of the Laender in legislation, or the basic principles laid down in Articles 1 and 20, shall be inadmissible." Articles 1 and 20 relate to the protection of unalienable human rights to dignity and the free democratic basic order—specifically, the right to resist any person or persons seeking to abolish the constitutional order, a democratic and social federal state. For a translation of portions of The Basic Law of the Federal Republic of Germany, see Walter F. Murphy and Joseph Tanenhaus, eds., *Comparative Constitutional Law: Cases and Commentaries* (New York: St. Martin's Press, 1977). For analyses of the constitutional theory of the Basic Law, and of its entrenchment of certain basic principles against subsequent amendment, see, e.g., John E. Finn, *Constitutions in Crisis: Political Violence and the Rule of Law* (New York: Oxford University Press, 1991), pp. 185–91; Donald P. Kommers, *The Constitutional Jurisprudence of the Federal Republic of Germany* (Durham, NC: Duke University Press, 1989), pp. 36–39, 52–55; Walter F. Murphy, "Excluding Political Parties: Problems for Democratic and Constitutional Theory," in Paul Kirchhof and Donald P. Kommers, eds., *Germany and Its Basic Law* (Baden-Baden: Nomos Verlagsgesellschaft, 1993), pp. 173–78.

12. Ackerman, *We the People* 1:13.

13. Ibid., p. 14. See also Bruce Ackerman, "Constitutional Politics/Constitutional Law," *Yale L. J.* 99 (1989): 453, 469 (using the stronger formulation "a very great embarrassment").

14. Ackerman, *We the People* 1:15 (referring to entrenchment of African slave

trade until 1808). See also p. 326, n. 21 (referring to entrenchment of equal representation of each state in the Senate and claiming that "[t]his effort to entrench federalism caused all sorts of trouble in the aftermath of the Civil War").

15. Ibid., p. 15.

16. Ibid.

17. In using formulations like that in the text ("We the People are not bound by a higher law") or in the title ("We the Exceptional American People"), I do not intend to personify the constituent power, that is, to conflate the citizenry (the people) with the constituent power (We the People). For a sophisticated treatment of the difference between the "Constitutional People" and the "sovereign constitution-making people," see William F. Harris II, *The Interpretable Constitution* (Baltimore: Johns Hopkins University Press, 1993), pp. 201–4.

18. H.L.A. Hart, *The Concept of Law* (Oxford: Clarendon Press, 1961), p. 145 (analyzing John Austin, *The Province of Jurisprudence Determined*, (ed. H.L.A. Hart [London: Weidenfeld and Nicholson, 1954 (1832)]). See also pp. 70–76 (analyzing the positivist idea of "The Sovereign behind the Legislature").

19. Ibid., pp. 97–107.

20. Bruce Ackerman, "Remarks at New York University School of Law Colloquium on Constitutional Theory," Nov. 16, 1993 (colloquy between Ackerman and Ronald Dworkin). Subsequently, Ackerman has characterized such a "principled positivism" as a "humanistic positivism." Ackerman, *We the People* 2:92.

21. Ackerman, *We the People* 1:13–16.

22. See Hart, *The Concept of Law*, p. 104.

23. Ackerman, *We the People* 1:326, n. 20. Ackerman observes that the Basic Law (Grundgesetz), in Article 146, allows for its replacement by a completely new Constitution (Verfassung). He writes: "Since the drafters of the Basic Law took this step to emphasize the provisional character of West Germany [pending reunification with East Germany], and not the provisional character of fundamental rights, it would be a great abuse of art. 146 to use the occasion of a new Verfassung to modify the entrenched provisions on human rights." He concludes: "Nonetheless, this technical possibility does provide an escape hatch through which German dualists might conceivably modify their Basic Law's foundationalist commitments."

Originally, Article 146 provided: "This Basic Law shall cease to be in force on the day on which a constitution adopted by a free decision of the German people comes into force." Murphy and Tanenhaus, *Comparative Constitutional Law*, pp. 22–23. As it turned out, the Basic Law was not replaced by a completely new Constitution during the process of reunification of West Germany and East Germany. For constitutional analyses of German reunification, see Peter E. Quint, "The Constitutional Law of German Unification," *Md. L. Rev.* 50 (1991): 475; Schwartz, "Constitutional Change and Constitutional Legitimation."

24. *Marbury v. Madison*, 5 U.S. (1 Cranch) 137, 177 (1803). In the quoted passage, Chief Justice Marshall is not discussing entrenchment clauses, but instead is advancing the classical, interpretive justification of judicial review under a written constitution. See *supra* n. 7.

25. John Rawls, *Political Liberalism* (New York: Columbia University Press, 1993), p. 233.

26. Ibid. See also Walter F. Murphy, "An Ordering of Constitutional Values," *S. Cal. L. Rev.* 53 (1980): 703, 757 (conceding that "[a]s a matter of sheer power, the people can give themselves a new constitutional order" by repudiating a constitutional document's protection of unalienable human rights to dignity, but contending that the terms of the current constitutional document "cannot supply legitimate procedures" for destroying the old constitutional order and creating a new one); Walter F. Murphy, "Merlin's Memory: The Past and Future Imperfect of the Once and Future Polity," in Sanford Levinson, ed., *Responding to Imperfection* (Princeton: Princeton University Press, 1995) (discussing the issue of the extent to which "the people can bind themselves").

27. I do not mean to deny that one could attempt to provide a justification for a constitutional theory of popular sovereignty or positivist dualism like Ackerman's on the basis of a normative political theory. Ackerman, however, has not elaborated such foundations for his constitutional theory, notwithstanding his title (*We the People: Foundations*). Indeed, Ackerman has stated—in terms of Ronald Dworkin's formulation of the two dimensions of best interpretation, fit and justification, see Ronald Dworkin, *Law's Empire* (Cambridge, MA: Belknap Press, 1986), p. 239; Ronald Dworkin, *Taking Rights Seriously* (Cambridge, MA: Harvard University Press, 1977), p. 107—that "fit is everything." Remarks at New York University School of Law Colloquium on Constitutional Theory. For suggestions that Ackerman's theory at bottom is a form of authoritarianism or formalism, see *infra* n. 59.

28. Cf. Oliver Wendell Holmes, *The Path of the Law*, in *Collected Legal Papers* (New York: Peter Smith, 1952), pp. 167, 171 ("If you want to know the law and nothing else, you must look at it as a bad man, who cares only for the material consequences which such knowledge enables him to predict, not as a good one, who finds his reasons for conduct, whether inside the law or outside of it, in the vaguer sanctions of conscience").

29. On one interpretation, which I offer below, these provisos in Article V entrenched compromises with our constitutive principles. See *infra* text accompanying notes 30–33. On another interpretation, which underscores the injustice of the original Constitution, these provisos entrenched two of our constitutive principles: the fundamental right of slaveholders to property in slaves and structural protections of states' rights. John Finn suggested the latter interpretation to me (without endorsing it).

30. For a suggestion that both the protection of slavery in the original Constitution and the provision for equal representation of each state in the Senate—the two matters that Article V entrenched against amendment—are inconsistent with the principles of "democratic reason" or "constitutional democracy," see Freeman, "Original Meaning," p. 35.

31. See Richard B. Morris, *The Forging of the Union: 1781–1789* (New York: Harper & Row, 1987), pp. 281–87. See also Richard B. Bernstein (with Jerome Agel), *Amending America: If We Love the Constitution So Much, Why Do We Keep Trying to Change It?* (New York: Times Books, 1993), pp. 20–22. Akhil Amar has observed that Article V's proviso regarding the equal representation of states in the Senate was not itself part of the famous "Connecticut Compromise" between the small and large states, noting that the proviso "was not even men-

108   JAMES E. FLEMING

tioned until the penultimate day of the convention, and was voted on with virtually no discussion or analysis of its implications." Akhil Reed Amar, "Philadelphia Revisited: Amending the Constitution Outside Article V," *U. Chi. L. Rev.*
55 (1988): 1043, 1070–71, n. 97.

32. See, e.g., Finn, *Constitutions in Crisis,* pp. 179–93; Kommers, *The Constitutional Jurisprudence of the Federal Republic of Germany,* pp. 36–39, 52–55.

33. Ackerman might concede this point yet still contend that it cuts in favor of
dualism that the American founders did not entrench unalienable rights. One
response is that they did, for example, in the Preamble, the First Amendment, the
Ninth Amendment, the Declaration of Independence, and the structural implications of the constitutional order. See, e.g., Harris, *The Interpretable Constitution,*
pp. 164–68, 191–201 (analyzing "the limits of textual amendability" and "a
hierarchy of amendment sequences" that distinguishes between the limits on
amendability through Article V and the greater revisability of the polity through
Article VII); Akhil Reed Amar, "The Consent of the Governed: Constitutional
Amendment Outside Article V," *Colum. L. Rev.* 94 (1994): 457, 504–5 (emphasizing the Declaration of Independence, the Preamble, and the logic of a system
of republican self-government in suggesting that "not everything is properly
amendable," for certain higher law principles, including popular sovereignty and
perhaps liberty of conscience, frame Article V itself); Amar, "Philadelphia Revisited," pp. 1044–45, n. 1 (arguing that "the First Amendment may itself be a
seemingly paradoxical exception to the general rule that amendments must not
be unamendable"); Walter F. Murphy, "The Art of Constitutional Interpretation:
A Preliminary Showing," in M. Judd Harmon, ed., *Essays on the Constitution of
the United States* (Port Washington, NY: Kennikat Press, 1978), pp. 130, 150–51
(suggesting that the First Amendment may be an "unamendable constitutional
provision"); Jeff Rosen, "Note, Was the Flag Burning Amendment Unconstitutional?" *Yale L. J.* 100 (1991): 1084–89 (arguing that there are natural rights
limitations on the amending power, derived from the history and structure of the
Constitution as a whole, that are expressed in the Declaration of Independence
and the Ninth Amendment). Below, I shall raise the possibility of a theory of
implicit or "structural entrenchments" of fundamental rights as distinguished
from explicit entrenchments of them in Article V. See *infra* text accompanying
notes 66–73.

Another response is that the American founders did not need explicitly to entrench unalienable rights. See, e.g., Freeman, "Original Meaning," p. 41. Here, I
shall emphasize the latter response. It is well to recall that the original Constitution did not include a Bill of Rights, much less an entrenched one. As Hamilton
wrote in *Federalist* No. 84, "the Constitution is itself, in every rational sense, and
to every useful purpose, A BILL OF RIGHTS." *The Federalist* No. 84, p. 515
(Alexander Hamilton). The arguments in favor of adopting a Bill of Rights ultimately prevailed, but against this background perhaps it would have been too
much to ask for an entrenched Bill of Rights. Moreover, in the historical circumstances surrounding the American founding, as contrasted with those surrounding the German reconstruction, explicit entrenchment of unalienable rights
would have been unnecessary.

34. See H.L.A. Hart, "1776–1976: Law in the Perspective of Philosophy," pp. 145–52, in Hart, *Essays in Jurisprudence and Philosophy* (Oxford: Clarendon Press, 1983) (discussing Bentham's famous attack on the Declaration of Independence); Hart, "The United States of America," pp. 53–65, in Hart, *Essays on Bentham* (Oxford: Clarendon Press, 1982) (same); see also Hart, "American Jurisprudence through English Eyes: The Nightmare and the Noble Dream," pp. 123, 123–25, 132–42, in Hart, *Essays in Jurisprudence and Philosophy* (discussing American jurisprudence's anti-positivist concentration on rights and moral principles in the judicial decisionmaking process).

35. Finn, *Constitutions in Crisis*, p. 188. See also Kommers, *The Constitutional Jurisprudence of the Federal Republic of Germany*, pp. 37–38.

36. Finn, *Constitutions in Crisis*, p. 179 (quoting *The Federalist* No. 1, p. 33 [Alexander Hamilton]).

37. *The Federalist* No. 14, p. 104 (James Madison).

38. I do not mean to overstate this point—for example, by implying that Americans actively participated in the drafting of the German Basic Law, that the American influence upon it was the only influence, or that the German Basic Law (and the Constitutional Court's interpretation of it) do not carry some "American" ideas further than the American Constitution, tradition, and practice have taken them. I simply mean to emphasize that the influence of American ideas upon the Basic Law was considerable, and that the contrast between these two constitutional orders is not as great as Ackerman's analysis suggests. Walter Murphy has written: "Not only did Britain, France, and the United States set the basic guidelines for the new order [the German Basic Law], but their military governors were also frequent, if seldom effective, kibitzers in the drafting process." Murphy, "Excluding Political Parties," p. 173. (He also has observed that the Japanese document was known for several decades as "the MacArthur Constitution." Murphy, "Constitutions, Constitutionalism, and Democracy," p. 22, n. 27.) For discussions of the impact of American ideas on the German Basic Law, see, e.g., Peter H. Merkl, *The Origin of the West German Republic* (New York: Oxford University Press, 1963); John Ford Golay, *The Founding of the Federal Republic of Germany* (Chicago: University of Chicago Press, 1958).

39. See Murphy, "An Ordering of Constitutional Values," pp. 751–53. Nonetheless, there are important differences between the American Constitution and the German Basic Law, most notably with respect to the latter's provisions regarding duties and responsibilities in addition to rights. See ibid., and Kommers, *The Constitutional Jurisprudence of the Federal Republic of Germany*, pp. 36–37, 41–42, 56. See also Mary Ann Glendon, *Rights Talk: The Impoverishment of Political Discourse* (New York: The Free Press, 1991), pp. 61–75 (observing differences between the American conception of the person as a "lone rights-bearer" and the German image of the person as having not only rights but also responsibilities and duties to others); but see Linda C. McClain, "Rights and Irresponsibility," *Duke L. J.* 43 (1994): 989 (criticizing Glendon's account of the relationship between rights and responsibilities in American jurisprudence).

40. See Freeman, "Original Meaning," pp. 41–42 (quoting Ackerman, "Constitutional Politics/Constitutional Law," pp. 468, 469) (arguing, *contra* Acker-

man, that substantive fundamental rights such as liberty of conscience, along with procedural democratic rights like the right to vote, are constitutive of and inalienable in our constitutional democracy).

41. A caveat is in order here. I am drawing an analogy by paraphrasing the Ninth Amendment, not offering an interpretation of that provision. The controversies surrounding the interpretation of the Ninth Amendment are beyond the scope of this chapter. See, e.g., Randy E. Barnett, ed., *The Rights Retained by the People*, vol. 1 (Fairfax, VA: George Mason University Press, 1989); Randy E. Barnett, ed., *The Rights Retained by the People*, vol. 2 (Fairfax, VA: George Mason University Press, 1993); "Symposium on Interpreting the Ninth Amendment," *Chi.-Kent L. Rev.* 64 (Randy E. Barnett, ed., 1988):1.

42. Ackerman, *We the People* 1:14.

43. Ibid., pp. 14–15.

44. Ibid., pp. 14–15 and 15–16 n.

45. Ibid., p. 15 and note. Ackerman states: "I doubt, moreover, that one may find many American lawyers who seriously disagree—even among those who presently wrap themselves up in foundationalist rhetoric" (pp. 14–15). He does, however, mention Walter Murphy as "a constitutionalist who may have the courage of his foundationalist convictions." See Ackerman, "Constitutional Politics/ Constitutional Law," p. 470, n. 28 (citing Walter F. Murphy, "Slaughter-House, Civil Rights, and the Limits on Constitutional Change," *Am. J. Juris.* 32 [1987]: 1). For analyses of the German constitutional order and judicial practice in this respect, see, e.g., Murphy, "An Ordering of Constitutional Values," pp. 754–57, and Finn, *Constitutions in Crisis*, p. 186 (discussing The Southwest Case, 1 BVerfGE 14 [1951]). See also *supra* n. 33 (citing arguments that the American Constitution entrenches certain unalienable rights against repeal).

46. Ackerman, *We the People* 1:321; see also p. 16.

47. Bruce A. Ackerman, *Social Justice in the Liberal State* (New Haven: Yale University Press, 1980).

48. Ackerman, *We the People* 1:11 (referring to John Rawls, "Kantian Constructivism in Moral Theory," *J. Phil.* 77 [1980]: 515; Dworkin, *Taking Rights Seriously*, and Dworkin, *Law's Empire*). But see Ackerman, *We the People* 1:30, 327–28, n. 49 (noting that his own work in political philosophy builds on the liberal tradition that includes Rawls); Bruce Ackerman, "Political Liberalisms," *J. Phil.* 91 (1994): 364 (criticizing Rawls, *Political Liberalism*, while also acknowledging similarities between Rawls's political philosophy and his own).

49. Michael J. Klarman, "Constitutional Fact/Constitutional Fiction: A Critique of Bruce Ackerman's Theory of Constitutional Moments," *Stan. L. Rev.* 44 (1992): 763–64, n. 37. Ackerman presumably would contend that there is no "glaring contradiction" between being a dualist constitutional theorist and being a rights foundationalist political philosopher. See Ackerman, *We the People* 1:16, 319–22.

50. See Henry P. Monaghan, "Our Perfect Constitution," *N.Y.U. L. Rev.* 56 (1981): 395.

51. See Christopher L. Eisgruber, "Justice and the Text: Rethinking the Constitutional Relation between Principle and Prudence," *Duke L. J.* 43 (1993): 7 (referring to Monaghan, "Our Perfect Constitution"). But liberal rights founda-

tionalists should not despair. On the evidence of Ackerman's *We the People*, they should rest assured that his constitutional theory will legitimate almost anything that they believe the Constitution protects, although in the name of We the People, not unalienable fundamental rights. See also Bruce Ackerman, "Liberating Abstraction," 59 *U. Chi. L. Rev.* 59 (1992): 317.

52. For the idea of a "Constitution-perfecting" theory, as distinguished from a "process-perfecting" theory, see Fleming, "Constructing the Substantive Constitution" (advancing a Constitution-perfecting theory of judicial review of ordinary lawmaking without taking up the issue of judicial review of higher lawmaking). I mean "perfecting" in the sense of interpreting the Constitution with integrity so as to render it as a coherent whole, not in Monaghan's caricatured sense of "Our Perfect Constitution" as a perfect liberal utopia or an "ideal object" of political morality. See Monaghan, "Our Perfect Constitution," p. 356. Cf. Frank I. Michelman, "Constancy to an Ideal Object," *N.Y.U. L. Rev.* 56 (1981): 406–7 (distinguishing "weak-sense perfectionism" or "constitutional rationalism" from "strong-sense perfectionism"). For the idea of amendments to the Constitution as responding to imperfection, see Sanford Levinson, ed., *Responding to Imperfection* (Princeton: Princeton University Press, 1995).

53. Ackerman, *We the People* 1:16, 319–22. For the notion of "temptation," see Robert H. Bork, *The Tempting of America: The Political Seduction of the Law* (New York: The Free Press, 1990).

54. Ackerman, *We the People* 1:15–16.

55. See Bork, *The Tempting of America*. (For Bork's discussion of Ackerman's theory, see pp. 214–16; for Ackerman's critique of Bork's theory, see Bruce Ackerman, "Robert Bork's Grand Inquisition," *Yale L. J.* 99 (1990): 1419 (reviewing Bork's book.) For discussion of the sort of *coup de grace* to be expected from someone with commitments like Bork's, see Stephen Macedo, *Liberal Virtues: Citizenship, Virtue, and Community in Liberal Constitutionalism* (New York: Oxford University Press, 1990), p. 182.

56. Macedo, *Liberal Virtues*, p. 182.

57. See, e.g., Ackerman, *We the People* 1:266–94; Bruce A. Ackerman, "Discovering the Constitution," *Yale L. J.* 92 (1984): 1051–57; Ackerman, "Constitutional Politics," pp. 486–515. Ackerman is not the only constitutional theorist who rejects the exclusivity of Article V's formal amending procedures. See also Amar, "Philadelphia Revisited"; Amar, "Consent of the Governed."

58. See, e.g., Ackerman, *We the People* 1:15, 15 n. (appealing to what "almost all lawyers" would think was "absurd" or "preposterous"). In remarks at the New York University School of Law Colloquium on Constitutional Theory, November 16, 1993, Ackerman made repeated recourse to "lawyerly criteria of fit," which he linked to his concern in his writings for "the possibility of interpretation." See, e.g., Ackerman, *We the People* 1:131–62; Ackerman, "Discovering the Constitution," pp. 1070–72; Ackerman, "Constitutional Politics," pp. 515–45.

59. See Sherry, "The Ghost of Liberalism Past," pp. 933–34 (suggesting that Ackerman's "originalism" reveals "the sad state of American liberalism" and that "[t]here is genuine pathos in seeing what was once the most optimistic and forward-looking of the American political philosophies reduced in this appeal to the authority of the past"). See also Frank Michelman, "Law's Republic," *Yale L. J.*

97 (1988): 1521–23 (interpreting Ackerman's dualism as a form of authoritarianism); Cass R. Sunstein, *The Partial Constitution* (Cambridge: Harvard University Press, 1993) p. 370, n. 21 (suggesting that Ackerman's theory is formalist).

60. David R. Dow, "When Words Mean What We Believe They Say: The Case of Article V," *Iowa L. Rev.* 76 (1990):1.

61. Klarman, "Constitutional Fact/Constitutional Fiction," p. 766.

62. See *supra* text accompanying n. 20.

63. Ackerman, *We the People* 1:14. For Ackerman's argument for a "regime perspective," or for conceiving our constitutional history in terms of three regimes or republics (those inaugurated by the Founding, Reconstruction, and the New Deal), see pp. 58–67.

64. Ibid., pp. 15–16 n. Ackerman's implicit distinction between "deep transformations" within dualist democracy and a "repeal of dualist democracy itself" bears a resemblance to Murphy's distinction between amending a constitutional order (correcting, adjusting, or modifying it) and repudiating it (destroying it and creating another one). See, e.g., Murphy, "Constitutions, Constitutionalism, and Democracy," p. 14; Murphy, "An Ordering of Constitutional Values," p. 757. The Supreme Court of California, drawing a distinction between "amendment" and "revision," struck down a state constitutional amendment, adopted by referendum, that would have required state judges, when interpreting the state constitution, to follow the United States Supreme Court's interpretations of similarly worded clauses in the national constitutional document. See Murphy, "Merlin's Memory" (discussing *Raven v. Deukmejian*, 801 P.2d 1077 [Cal. 1990]). The Court reasoned that such a change "would so fundamentally transform California's status as a member of a federal union as to effect a constitutional revision; and the [constitutional] text provided that 'revisions' could be accomplished only by special conventions."

65. See *infra* text accompanying n. 71.

66. See Ackerman, *We the People* 1:15–16 n.; see also *supra* n. 33 (citing arguments that the American Constitution entrenches certain unalienable rights against repeal).

67. See *supra* text accompanying n. 57.

68. See Ackerman, *We the People* 1:11–13. For the idea of "pre-constitutional principles" that bind even framers and ratifiers, see Finn, *Constitutions in Crisis*, pp. 7, 186, 188.

69. Let us say "moderately successful," so as not to seem Panglossian about our constitutional tradition and practice, which have been marred by many injustices.

70. Rawls, *Political Liberalism*, pp. 238–39. See also Macedo, *Liberal Virtues*, pp. 182–835.

71. Rawls, *Political Liberalism*, p. 239; Freeman, "Original Meaning," pp. 41–42.

72. For arguments that neither amendment nor entrenchment is purely positivist and confined to the formal procedures of Article V, see, e.g., Amar, "The Consent of the Governed," p. 457; Amar, "Philadelphia Revisited," p. 1043.

73. Ackerman presumably would deny that there is any real incongruity in this respect. He might advance a ratchet theory concerning We the People, contending that it is one thing to expand popular sovereignty through a theory of amend-

ing the Constitution outside Article V, but quite another to contract it through a theory of entrenching the Constitution outside Article V.

74. See Rawls, *Political Liberalism*, p. 233 (discussed *supra* text accompanying notes 25–26).

75. For the distinction between theory of the Constitution and theory of judicial review (and between the interrogatives what is the Constitution and who may authoritatively interpret it), see, e.g., Murphy, Fleming, and Barber, *American Constitutional Interpretation*, pp. 16–19; Sotirios A. Barber, *On What the Constitution Means* (Baltimore: Johns Hopkins University Press, 1984), pp. 196–99; Sotirios A. Barber, *The Constitution of Judicial Power* (Baltimore: Johns Hopkins University Press, 1993), pp. 40–43. See also Sanford Levinson, *Constitutional Faith* (Princeton: Princeton University Press, 1988), pp. 9–52.

76. See Ackerman, *We the People* 1: 15, 15 n. See also *supra* text accompanying n. 45. In referring to German judicial practice, Ackerman cites no cases but presumably is alluding to cases like the Southwest Case, 1 BVerfGE 14 (1951), and Privacy of Communications Case, 30 BVerfGE 1 (1970). These two cases are edited and translated in Murphy and Tanenhaus, *Comparative Constitutional Law*, pp. 208–12, 659–66. Murphy has observed that the Supreme Court in India has voided amendments, as has the Supreme Court of California. Murphy, "Constitutions, Constitutionalism, and Democracy," pp. 11, 23 notes 39–40.

77. I cannot pursue these complex matters here. For sophisticated discussions of such issues, see, e.g., Harris, *The Interpretable Constitution*, pp. 164–204; Barber, *On What the Constitution Means*, pp. 199–202; Hart, *The Concept of Law*, pp. 144–50; H.L.A. Hart, "Self-Referring Laws," p. 170 in Hart, *Essays in Jurisprudence and Philosophy*.

78. For a distinction between amending a constitutional order and repudiating it, see *supra* n. 64.

79. See *Colegrove v. Green*, 328 U.S. 549, 556 (1946) (arguing that courts ought to stay out of that "political thicket"). By "representation-reinforcing" judicial review, I refer to the type of theory epitomized by John Hart Ely, *Democracy and Distrust: A Theory of Judicial Review* (Cambridge: Harvard University Press, 1980) ("Democracy and Distrust").

80. See Charles L. Black, Jr., "Further Reflections on the Constitutional Justice of Livelihood," *Colum. L. Rev.* 86 (1986): 1116.

81. For Ackerman's discussion of FDR's choices between launching a court-packing plan and fighting for constitutional amendments through the formal procedures of Article V, see Bruce Ackerman, *We the People, vol. 2: Transformations*, ch. 11.

82. See Richard A. Epstein, *Takings: Private Property and the Power of Eminent Domain* (Cambridge, MA: Harvard University Press, 1985).

83. Indeed, Ackerman rejects a common interpretation of *Coleman v. Miller*, 307 U.S. 433 (1939), which some scholars read as precluding judicial review of the amending process on the ground that such matters are nonjusticiable political questions. See Ackerman, "Constitutional Politics/Constitutional Law," pp. 492–99. He argues that Coleman expressly repudiates the formalist view that "all constitutional change must be governed in strict accord with the rules of Article Five" (p. 492).

84. The cases are discussed in Harris, *The Interpretable Constitution*, pp. 187–201.

85. National Prohibition Cases, 253 U.S. 350 (1920). See also *United States v. Sprague*, 282 U.S. 716 (1931).

86. *Leser v. Garnett*, 258 U.S. 130 (1922).

87. For the idea of "sovereignty-reinforcing" judicial review of amendments to the Constitution, by analogy to Ely's notion of "representation-reinforcing" judicial review of legislation and administration, see Harris, *The Interpretable Constitution*, p. 195 (referring to Ely, *Democracy and Distrust*). I am aware that footnote 4 of *United States v. Carolene Products Co.*, 304 U.S. 144, 152–53, n. 4 (1938), cites precedents from the 1920s (and 1930s) for what we now would call "representation-reinforcing" judicial review. But it took Justice Stone's footnote to pull together and systematize these precedents into the intimations of such an approach, and only later were these precedents fully comprehended as applying (or anticipating) it.

88. See Hart, *The Concept of Law*, pp. 144–50.

89. Ibid., pp. 149, 150.

90. In describing the judiciary as the branch of government that is "the least dangerous to the political rights of the Constitution," Alexander Hamilton wrote: "It may truly be said to have neither FORCE nor WILL but merely judgment; and must ultimately depend upon the aid of the executive arm even for the efficacy of its judgments." *The Federalist* No. 78, p. 465 (Alexander Hamilton).

91. In response to *Worcester v. Georgia*, 31 U.S. (6 Pet.) 515 (1832), in which the Supreme Court per Chief Justice Marshall held that Georgia's anti-Cherokee laws were unconstitutional, President Jackson supposedly said: "Well, John Marshall has made his decision, now let him enforce it!" Edward S. Corwin, *The President: Office and Powers*, 4th ed. (New York: New York University Press, 1957), p. 64. This legend, however, has been disputed (ibid., pp. 350–51, n. 61).

92. James B. Thayer, "The Origin and Scope of the American Doctrine of Constitutional Law," *Harv. L. Rev.* 7 (1893): 156 ("Under no system can the power of courts go far to save a people from ruin; our chief protection lies elsewhere"). For a new interpretation of this passage from Thayer, see Mark Tushnet, "Thayer's Target: Judicial Review or Democracy?" *Nw. U. L. Rev.* 88 (1993): 9.

93. Learned Hand, "The Spirit of Liberty," pp. 189, 190 in Irving Dilliard ed., *The Spirit of Liberty*, 3rd ed (New York: Alfred A. Knopf, 1960) ("Liberty lies in the hearts of men and women; when it dies there, no constitution, no law, no court can save it. . . . While it lies there it needs no constitution, no law, no court to save it.").

94. Ely, *Democracy and Distrust*, p. 107 ("courts will tend to be swept along by the same sorts of fears" that moved legislatures, executives, and, for that matter, citizens). The fear of "futility" thesis often goes hand in hand with the fear of "destruction" thesis (ibid., pp. 47–48). For another contemporary version of the "futility" thesis, see Gerald N. Rosenberg, *The Hollow Hope: Can Courts Bring About Social Change?* (Chicago: University of Chicago Press, 1991).

95. Any calls for judicial civil disobedience must come to terms with the fact that abolitionist judges yielded to unjust positive laws supporting slavery. See Robert Cover, *Justice Accused: Antislavery and the Judicial Process* (New Haven:

Yale University Press, 1975); Ronald Dworkin, "The Law of the Slave-Catchers," *London Times Literary Supplement*, Dec. 5, 1975, p. 1437 (reviewing Cover). See also Barber, *On What the Constitution Means*, pp. 199–202; Christopher L. Eisgruber, "Dred Again: Originalism's Forgotten Past," *Const. Comm.* 10 (1993): 37; Christopher L. Eisgruber, "Note, Justice Story, Slavery, and the Natural Law Foundations of American Constitutionalism," *U. Chi. L. Rev.* 55 (1988): 273.

96. 418 U.S. 683 (1974).

97. See John Hart Ely, *War and Responsibility: Constitutional Lessons of Vietnam and Its Aftermath* (Princeton: Princeton University Press, 1993), p. 56. Ely also states: "That the president will disobey an order of the Supreme Court seems less likely in 1993 than it might have 100 years ago." Our long and moderately successful constitutional tradition and practice are what makes it seem less likely today. See *supra* text accompanying n. 69.

98. Hart, *The Concept of Law*, p. 149.

99. Cf. Ackerman, *We the People* 1: 272–80 (discussing signaling concerning higher lawmaking in constitutional moments).

100. Harris, *The Interpretable Constitution*, p. 1. Harris explains that he means the word "preposterousness" in "both its original and derived senses: (a) inverted in time, the 'later' coming before, and the 'before' coming later, and (b) 'contrary to nature, reason, or common sense.'"

101. Cf. *Marbury v. Madison*, 5 U.S. (1 Cranch) 137, 177 (1803) (discussed *supra* text accompanying n. 24).

102. I mean to echo Hart's notion of an "external" versus an "internal" point of view toward a legal system. See, e.g., Hart, *The Concept of Law*, pp. 86–88, 99–100, 112, 114.

103. See *supra* text accompanying notes 25–27.

104. *The Federalist* No. 14, p. 104 (James Madison).

105. See Ackerman, *The Future of Liberal Revolution*. Ackerman also considers "the meaning of 1989" and the revolutions of Eastern Europe for South Africa and Latin America, not to mention the United States (ibid., pp. 113–23).

106. See *supra* text accompanying notes 18–27.

5

Constitution and Revolution

JEFFREY K. TULIS

"THE FABRIC of American empire," Alexander Hamilton wrote, "ought to rest on the solid basis of THE CONSENT OF THE PEOPLE. The streams of national power ought to flow immediately from that pure, original foundation of all legitimate authority."[1] In its invocation of popular sovereignty, American constitutionalism seeks to preserve a place for revolution within its conception of an ordered polity. The legitimacy of the Constitution requires the intelligibility of revolution but, I shall argue, the political order established by the Constitution makes this theoretical necessity a theoretical impossibility. The Constitution rests on a fundamental incoherence.

To make this case, I need to sketch the understanding of revolution that the Constitution seeks to preserve and the rudimentary elements of the political order that subverts this predicate of legitimacy. One can see these various understandings by reconsidering the relation of the Declaration of Independence to the Constitution. This is a venerable topic. Dispute upon it began with the Federalists against the Antifederalists,[2] continued in the debate over slavery that preceded the Civil War, in debates engendered by progressive critiques of American politics at the beginning of the twentieth century, and in current arguments among "neoconservatives" and between neoconservatives and radical democrats. Let me try to indicate the oblique angle I wish to take on this relation by reminding you of some of what has been said before by others. Traditionally, the relation of the Declaration and Constitution has been raised in the context of attempts to ascertain how democratic American politics is. Critics of the Constitution, beginning with some Antifederalists, argued that various constitutional provisions designed to separate public from private, to turn over day-to-day matters of governance to representatives, to vastly enlarge the polity, to centralize and bureaucratize government, and generally, to depoliticize the citizenry represent an abandonment of democratic ideals acted upon in the Revolution and articulated in the Declaration. On this view, the Declaration contained a vision of citizenship that recapitulates the qualities of the revolutionary who seeks to establish a new political order. In suggesting that a people may dissolve ties that govern it and define new political arrangements, the Declaration seemed to privilege active citizen participation and institutional devices that approximate "direct democracy" as most consistent with the revolutionary charter. Calls for initiatives, referenda, and recall are parts of the familiar litany of reforms intermittently proposed to restore America's democratic origins.

Some critics of the Constitution go much further than this. Because the familiar litany of *reforms* presupposes our Constitution, such progressive changes fail to fully capture the understanding of politics that undergirds the Declaration. The people as makers of a constitution choose not just to make laws or hire and fire representatives, but to constitute their form of governance, their collective identity, their way of life. To embody that conception of democratic politics in a constitution would be tantamount to making revolution a regular and continual fact of political existence, not the exceptional state it is presumed to be by conservatives and progressives alike. Recovery of the perspective of the Declaration, on this view, requires progressives and conservatives to get over an aversion to revolution, perhaps born of the Constitution they seek to reform or defend. As one astute critic put it, "The Declaration envisaged a being who would not just participate in politics, but would join in actually creating a new political identity, to 'institute,' 'alter,' or 'abolish' governments, to lay a 'foundation' and to organize power."[3]

The Federalist and recent neoconservatives defend a Constitution that is very much opposed to the understandings of democratic politics that I have just alluded to. *The Federalist* attempts to show that the antidemocratic features of the Constitution are consistent with the democracy of the Declaration. It does this by distinguishing the activities of revolution and founding, by emphasizing the instrumental status of democracy within the Declaration, and by reserving a place of last resort for popular sovereignty.

The Declaration provides grounds and declares reasons for rejecting a government, but it does not specify the particular arrangements that should constitute a new one. Precisely because it is so democratic, it grants considerable latitude to its people "to institute new government, laying its foundation on such principles and organizing its powers in such form, as to them shall seem most likely to effect their Safety and Happiness." The Declaration suggests a range of possible governmental forms, extending from monarchy, which was legitimate until it engaged in a "long series of abuses" that signified that it had degenerated into tyranny, to democracy itself. It would be a strange form of democracy, indeed, that specified its legitimate forms in such detail that there remained no point to choice.

However, as the example of tyranny indicates, the people can not choose all forms of regime according to the Declaration and *The Federalist*. They are limited to those regimes that secure their liberties. Neoconservatives emphasize that the Declaration needs to be read "within the horizon of liberty."[4] From human equality derive "certain inalienable rights, that among these rights are life, liberty and the pursuit of happiness. That to secure these rights Governments are instituted among Men, deriving their just power from the consent of the governed." So while consent is a necessary condition for legitimate government, it is bounded and constrained by another necessary condition, that government secures liberty.

Critics of the Constitution tend to emphasize consent to the detriment of rights as they attempt to regularize democratic choice. *The Federalist* (like the Constitution) emphasizes liberty to the detriment of consent, as it seeks to bracket the concern for consent and enlarge that for liberty. Democracy is but one means to secure rights, according to *The Federalist*, and it must be compared to other means, including new forms contrived for the first time and lacking clear appellations and established histories.

According to *The Federalist*, democracy contains its own characteristic vices which tend toward the abrogation of rights. Principal among these is the problem of majority tyranny. The Constitution is structured so as to make the formation of majorities complicated and difficult. Government is insulated from the citizenry through representation. Thousands of factions are encouraged to flourish yet prevented by their very profusion from coalescing to legally oppress minorities. *The Federalist* and its contemporary exemplars actually point to the features of the Constitution designed to mitigate the vices of democracy as evidence of the democratic core of the Constitution. This is because such remedies are only necessary if the regime is, in some sense, fundamentally democratic. So while democracy generally is discussed in *The Federalist* as an inadequate instrument to secure rights, the persistent claim that the regime is "wholly popular" suggests an ambivalence: democracy is desirable itself *and* a means that needs to be modified to make it effectual to secure rights.

In this ambivalence, one may discover the place of revolution in the Constitution. Clearly, the Constitution represents a response to the fear of rebellion, political instability, social disharmony, and legal mutability. Its institutions and its conceptions of citizenship, and of politics more generally, are designed to make revolution unlikely. At the same time, this inhospitability to revolution in the normal course of affairs is joined to an insistence that these antidemocratic features are legitimate because they are the conscious political choice of a revolutionary generation, and it is clearly implied that if things get bad enough, the people may legitimately resort to revolution again. Although revolution is not welcomed by the Constitution, the fundamental insistence that the Constitution represents the collective will of the people requires that it be possible for its citizens to become revolutionaries once again, if only to reaffirm the desirability of the Constitution.[5]

In this brief sketch of *The Federalist*'s defense of the Constitution, I mean to emphasize the notion that the Declaration and the Constitution represent aspects of the same regime, each appropriate to a different time and a different task. On this view, revolution, as understood in the Declaration, continually provides democratic legitimacy because it remains *a last resort*. I should note that it is a last resort always, not just a last resort in the last resort!

It is this "last resort" theory of revolution that I wish to explore and question. To do this, it is necessary to take a fresh look at the Declaration's and the Constitution's polity and to ask the following questions: What sort of being is the Declaration's revolutionary? What sort of being is the Constitution's citizen? And finally, could the citizen become the revolutionary once again? As I indicated at the outset, my answer to this final question will be no.

The Declaration

The Declaration does not simply announce a revolution. That was done two days previous to it. The Declaration offers reasons for the revolution and therewith a theory of revolution. One might call the Declaration's view the "liberal theory" of revolution, not only because liberty is featured in it but more because revolution is defended as the product of collective, deliberate choice.

The Declaration begins not with a statement of historical necessity, as might Marx, but with a choice by "one people" to regard a pattern of events as making necessary their collective action. Many have noted the conservative cast to this decision. The theory is presented out of deference to "a decent respect to the opinions of mankind." The decision seems to be concluded reluctantly. "Prudence, indeed, will dictate that Governments long established should not be changed for light and transient causes; and accordingly all experience hath shown, that mankind are more disposed to suffer, while evils are sufferable, than to right themselves by abolishing the forms to which they are accustomed."

The Declaration presents itself as a result of considered judgment, deliberate choice. Because it does so, one can glimpse the radical core beneath the conservative package. At first glance, it appears that tyranny presents itself as a material fact and is rebuffed. The people face "a long train of abuses" and decide they have had enough. But the people also define the abuses, or more accurately, divine and describe a pattern to them. "But when a long train of abuses and usurpations, pursuing invariably the same object evinces a design to reduce them under absolute Despotism, it is their right, it is there duty, to throw off such government, and to provide new Guards for their future security." Tocqueville has clearly shown the political significance of the fact that no abuses appear to people unmediated by intellection. Thus, for example, although material conditions were objectively worse and inequality more severe in Germany than in France in the eighteenth century, the French were disposed to revolt because of changes that had taken place in the meaning they ascribed to their condition.[6] In a legitimate revolution, according to the Declaration, recognition of abuse seems to require a collective act of defensible political interpretation, not merely the political equivalent of a visceral response. The Declaration's revolutionary is not depicted simply as a political animal who interprets but as one who is called upon to publicly articulate and defend the interpretation.[7]

The pattern of alleged abuses is interpreted to evince a design of tyranny according to standards drawn from "the laws of nature and Nature's God" (which is to say, not the God of Abraham). From this appeal to nature is gleaned several "self-evident" truths:

> that all men are created equal, that they are endowed by their Creator with certain unalienable Rights, that among these are Life, Liberty and the pursuit of Happiness.—That to secure these rights, governments are instituted among them, deriving their just powers from the consent of the governed,—That whenever any form of government becomes destructive of these ends, it is the right of the people to alter or abolish it, and to institute new Government . . .

Looking back upon these principles from within the Constitution, they too appear conservative. This is not only because fashionable intellectuals today have reinterpreted appeals to nature or to self-evident truths as bespeaking an easily debunked "foundationalism." More importantly, these propositions look conservative because we have inherited them as conclusions. In a very real sense they have become conservative by becoming a creed. By contrast, for the potential revolutionary deciding whether to revolt they are invitations to thoughtful allegiance.

The Declaration reads, "We hold these truths to be self-evident." Who is the "we" that so holds? One might think that there exists an easily described "people," a collection of individuals, a nation, that replaces old governors with new ones. In fact, the people can not be easily identified before the Declaration. Too casual a reading of "We hold" conceals the extent to which the principles of the Declaration itself define the people who enunciate them. On this view the people create themselves by articulating and subscribing to a set of principles that define their collective identity. The Declaration thus invites the potential revolutionary to ask herself whether the principles are good, whether they ought to be her principles. The revolutionary is asked to consider the alternatives—the biggest alternatives (ranging from alternative regimes to alternative principles of justification)—and to ally with conclusions of the Declaration. Behind the conclusions of the Declaration (that all men are equal, for example) are implied principles regarding the reach of reason and the intelligibility of a whole animated and interpreted by humans. As conclusions of reason, the Declaration invites the challenges of reason.

This is a radical document indeed. My point in highlighting these features is to ask what qualities are presupposed of the Declaration's revolutionary. I do not mean to suggest that all followers of the Declaration need be philosophers. But I do wish to suggest that the potential revolutionary need be disposed to think about and compare large alternatives, and that the distillations of more philosophic leaders (like Jefferson) must make sense to them. The issue here is attitude, disposition, and experience, not formal education. Jefferson did not claim to repeat the views of the man on the street; the Declaration is not the result of a survey, even an open-ended survey that allows the respondent to speak. No, Jefferson claimed to restate and interpret common sentiment. For this to be true, it must be possible for a revolutionary generation to acquire intimations of the meaning of large political alternatives, and it must be possible for them to recognize the refined restatement of their own views in a document such as the Declaration. The Declaration's revolutionary respects reason in its broadest sense, and is disposed to listen to it. In this sense, even more than in the fact that the revolutionary is prepared to die (all revolutionaries are prepared to die), the Declaration's revolutionary truly participates in political life.

The Constitution

Two broad features distinguish the Constitution from the Declaration. In the Declaration the public life of the polity embraces the people in their collective capacity, and it invites reflection upon the broad and variegated conspectus of possible political regimes. The Constitution considerably narrows the concerns of public life, on the one hand, and insulates the people from even these restricted public concerns, on the other.

The Constitution is not an invitation to political debate but rather the solemn *settlement* of a debate in the past. This is an overstatement, of course, but I hope a useful one. Political debate after the Constitution is confined to tensions among its terms. It is no longer a debate about those terms and their fundamental alternatives. Once the Constitution is adopted the merits of aristocracy or monarchy, for example, are no longer live political questions. However undemocratic the Constitution, it is not a mixed regime. There are no permanent spokesmen for alternatives to its version of republicanism built into its design. Because the fundamental political questions are settled in a practical sense, one may say that the regime has been depoliticized. Hamilton regarded this feature of the Constitution as one of its great merits. It was a mark of praiseworthy distinction for him and other leading founders that politics would be replaced by "administration" and that government would mediate interests rather than be the arena for competing claims to rule.[8] The business of administration is conducted by representatives of the people rather than by the people themselves. *The Federalist* indicates that the conception of representation in the Constitution and the geographic extent of the regime combine to remove "the people" from political life in normal times, and that this marks the distinctive development of modern republicanism. Says *The Federalist*:

> it is clear that the principle of representation was neither unknown to the ancients nor wholly overlooked in their political constitutions. The true distinction between these and the American governments lies *in the total exclusion of the people in their collective capacity*, from any share in the *latter* [American governments].[9]

Because the Constitution promotes liberty by granting considerable scope for individuals to pursue their own endeavors, it is sometimes thought that the theory that informs the Constitution has little to say about private life. This is not so. As *The Federalist* demonstrates, the Constitution implies a political theory that privileges certain virtues, dispositions, and ways of life in and out of the "private" sphere. It does so intentionally. For example, in order to remedy the problem of majority faction, it is necessary not only to proliferate the factions, but to encourage certain kinds and discourage others. In *Federalist* No. 10, it is argued that a large commercial republic will produce factions whose disputes may be easily compromised and whose profits might seduce and temper men of towering ambition or fanatical devotion, redirecting their energies to the tasks of manufacture and trade.[10]

I need not elaborate the familiar story that culminates in the Lockean individual, nor do I wish to evaluate its prescriptive merits here. It is important to note, rather, how the allegiance of this kind of citizen is secured under the Constitution, how it is that citizen "affection" and "esteem" for the regime is defined and elicited once the people are dissolved into individuals.[11]

Although the Constitution narrows considerably the legitimate province of any government, it greatly enlarges the scope of federal (as against state) authority and power. It is in this context that *The Federalist* addresses the problem of allegiance. "The great and radical vice in the construction of the existing Confederation," says Publius, "is in the principle of legislation for states or governments, in their corporate or collective capacities, and as contradistinguished from the individuals of whom they consist."[12] The new Constitution establishes a direct coercive relation between the central government and the individual and it assumes daily responsibility for, in principle, almost all the matters of administration.[13] Antifederalists wondered what would replace the "republican sentiments" that animated the affection and esteem citizens felt for small republics.

According to *The Federalist*, allegiance would be achieved by virtue of the national government's manifestly greater administrative efficiency (as compared to the states) and, closely related, through *habituation* of citizens to its operations and laws. One especially revealing passage on this theme is worth quoting at length:

> I will, in this place, . . . hazard an observation which will not be the less just because to some it may appear new; which is, that the more the operations of the national authority are intermingled in the ordinary exercise of government, the more the citizens are accustomed to meet with it in the common occurrences of their political life, the more it is familiarized to their sight and to their feelings, the further it enters into those objects which touch the most sensible chords and put in motion the most active springs of the human heart, the greater will be the probability that it will conciliate the respect and attachment of the community. Man is very much a creature of habit. . . . A government continually at a distance and out of sight can hardly be expected to interest the sensations of a people. The inference is that the authority of the Union and the affections of the citizens toward it will be strengthened, rather than weakened, by its extension to what are called matters of internal concern.[14]

This perspective is extended beyond the day-to-day operations of government to the issues of reform. Precisely because reform through amendment of the Constitution might raise the possibility of revolution, procedures are established to make amendment infrequent and difficult. "As every appeal to the people would carry an implication of some defect in the government, frequent appeals would, in great measure, deprive the government of that veneration which time bestows on everything, and without which perhaps the wisest and freest governments would not possess the requisite stability. . . . Notwithstanding the success which has attended the revisions of our established forms of government and which does so much honor to the virtue and intelligence of the people of America, it must be confessed that the experiments are of too ticklish a nature to be unnecessarily multiplied."[15] Moreover, the processes of amendment in Article V do not recapitulate the process of constitutional creation, but through devices designed to make amendment infrequent and unusual, the Constitution produces an ironic result: it makes amendment a species of its normal politics. The Constitution allows for refinement of its terms, and elaboration or extension of its core principles, not abolition of them.[16]

When politics is transformed into administration, when the people in their collective capacity are dismembered, when individuals are encouraged to pursue private endeavor, when citizens are habituated to veneration, it is difficult to see what psychic or intellectual resources the Constitution's citizen could still possess that would enable him to assume the revolutionary posture of the Declaration.

I do not mean to suggest that revolution would be impossible under and against the Constitution. Rather, it is difficult to see how the Constitution's prescribed sort of revolution, namely the liberal revolution of the Declaration, would be possible. I do not mean to suggest, either, that no individuals could manifest the capacities of the Declaration's revolutionary—but I wish to ask the American reader to ponder what it means if you are such an individual. Does your existence reveal the inadequacy of the Constitution to fully constitute in the way its theory of itself suggests?

Let me state this conclusion again in several more ways to draw attention to a few more of its implications.

If the Declaration's revolutionary is shielded from the full reality and human cost of violent revolution in an effort to spur legitimate collective action, the Constitution shields its citizens from the full meaning of popular sovereignty in an effort in behalf of stability and tranquility. It is ironic that in making revolution in general difficult in order to make the Constitution safe for a liberal revolution, the Constitution by its own lights probably makes it likely that if there were to be any revolution it would be a non-liberal one. This is because it creates a regime that is permeable to fashionable currents of thought at the same time that it is relatively closed to the revolutionary thought that its legitimacy requires.[17]

If one distinguishes the activity of the Declaration from the Lockean principles that are its conclusion, one can say that the movement from revolutionary practice to our constitutional practice is something like a movement from Rousseau to Locke. It is easy to see how the Rousseauean citizen and the Rousseauean polity could choose to become Lockean, but it is hard to see how the Lockean could choose to be Rousseau.[18] It is essential to the Constitution's theory of itself that it was ratified and could be ratified again by consent. The force of consent stems from the fact that it is the actual or potential activity of human beings.[19]

By its own terms, the Constitution can not be legitimated by transforming the real revolution into a hypothetical one reconstructed in our minds so that it necessarily generates the political order we know as our constitution. Popular sovereignty is not a version of Rawls's original position. It would be nonsense on several levels, therefore, to say that we would choose the same constitution *if* we possessed qualities that we no longer have as a people. Yet this is precisely what is said all the time when one invokes the revolutionary generation as authority for the democratic legitimacy of the Constitution.

The normative legitimacy of the Constitution depends upon the possibility of a people publicly defining itself and consenting once again. But the same Constitution constitutes a people that would not be able to do so. This incoherent normative theory of legitimacy may be distinguished from a sociological theory that might account for the American public's belief that the Constitution is legitimate despite the fact that the Constitution's people lack the wherewithal to say so. Without speculating upon the details of a persuasive sociological theory, one can say this: founded with an unprecedented appeal to reason, the Constitution is preserved by faith.

Notes

1. *The Federalist*, Clinton Rossiter, ed. (New York: New American Library, 1961), No. 22, p. 152. All page references are to this edition.

2. "Thus, fellow citizens, have I pointed out what I thought necessary to be amended in our federal constitution. I beg you to call to mind our glorious declaration of independence, read it, and compare it with the federal constitution; what a degree of apostasy will you not there discover." Essay by a Georgian, in *The Complete Antifederalist*, Herbert Storing, ed. (Chicago: University of Chicago Press, 1979), 5.9.16.

3. Sheldon Wolin, "The People's Two Bodies," *Democracy* (January 1981): 12. See also Wolin, *The Presence of the Past: Essays on the State and Constitution* (Baltimore: Johns Hopkins University Press, 1989).

4. See, for example, Martin Diamond, "The Declaration and the Constitution: Liberty, Democracy, and the Founders," *Public Interest* (Fall 1975): 39–55, and Walter Berns, *Taking the Constitution Seriously* (New York: Simon and Schuster, 1987).

5. "If the American liberal democracy now established as the eventual result of the Declaration of Independence is still worth conserving, it must be because, if given the opportunity, Americans would choose it again." Harvey C. Mansfield, Jr., *The Spirit of Liberalism* (Cambridge: Harvard University Press, 1978), p. 88.

6. Alexis de Tocqueville, *The Old Regime and the Revolution*, trans. Stuart Gilbert (New York: Doubleday, 1955), pp. 22–32. See also Anne Norton, *Alternative Americas: A Reading of American Political Culture* (Chicago: University of Chicago Press, 1986), introduction; Pierre Manent, *Tocqueville and the Nature of Democracy* (Lanham, MD: Rowman and Littlefield, 1996); François Furet, *Interpreting the French Revolution* (New York: Cambridge University Press, 1981).

7. In addition, "the people must be made to see oppression before they feel it," because if feeling were the sole reliance, the revolution might come too late. Mansfield, *The Spirit of Liberalism*, p. 80. However, as I note below, the people can only be "made" to see things for which they have the capacity and disposition to see.

8. See Harvey Flaumenhaft, "Hamilton's Administrative Republic and the American Presidency," in *The Presidency in the Constitutional Order*, eds. Joseph M. Bessette and Jeffrey Tulis (Baton Rouge and London: Louisiana State Univ. Press, 1981), pp. 65–112.

9. *The Federalist* No. 63, p. 387.

10. For a more subtle account of the logic of Federalist 10, see David Epstein, *The Political Theory of The Federalist* (Chicago: University of Chicago Press, 1984). See also Martin Diamond, "Ethics and Politics: The American Way," in *The Moral Foundations of the American Republic*, ed. Robert Horwitz (Charlottesville, VA: University Press of Virginia, 1986).

11. See also John P. Diggins, *The Lost Soul of American Politics* (Chicago: University of Chicago Press, 1985).

12. *The Federalist* No. 15, p. 108.

13. Some of the most insightful works on the relation of the Constitution to American political development mark the New Deal as a constitutional revolution. They thus raise an especially important question: do we live under the same Constitution that was ratified in 1789? See for examples, Bruce Ackerman, "The Storrs Lectures: Discovering the Constitution," *Yale Law Journal* 93 (1984); and Theodore Lowi, *The Personal President* (Ithaca: Cornell University Press, 1985).

In contrast to such well-known arguments, I assume here a continuous regime. Constitutional commitments to rights, to a commercial economy, to a large republic, and to an unmediated coercive relation between the national state and individual citizens combine to generate a logic of political development that anticipates, indeed causes and conditions, the New Deal. I develop this argument in "The Constitution of American Political Development and the Modern Presidency" in Martin Fausold and Alan Shank, eds., *The Presidency and the Constitution* (Albany: SUNY Press, 1991). See also Herbert Storing, *Toward a More Perfect Union* (Washington, DC: AEI Press, 1995), ch. 14. Similar arguments could be made (though I have not yet made them) regarding the significance of the Civil War amendments as alleged fundamental alterations of the regime.

14. *The Federalist* No. 27, p. 176.

15. *The Federalist* No. 49, pp. 314–15. In this number, Madison also makes clear the proposition that the Constitution's legitimacy requires a kind of tyranny of the majority: "If it be true that all governments rest on opinion, it is no less true that the strength of opinion in each individual, and its practical influence on his conduct, depend much on the number which he supposes to have entertained the same opinion. . . . A reverence for the laws would be sufficiently inculcated by the voice of an enlightened reason. But a nation of philosophers is as little to be expected as the philosophical race of kings wished for by Plato. And in every other nation, the most rational government will not find it a superfluous advantage to have the prejudices of the community on its side."

16. Cf. William F. Harris II, *The Interpretable Constitution* (Baltimore: Johns Hopkins University Press, 1993).

17. On the permeability of the American political order to fashionable currents of thought, see Joseph Cropsey, *Political Philosophy and the Issues of Politics* (Chicago: University of Chicago Press, 1977), introduction. However, to my knowledge no one has yet joined the insights of cultural anthropology with those of students of the history of political thought to analytically explore the processes of vulgarization.

18. Of course, I don't mean to suggest that the Rousseauean could coherently or consistently conjoin Locke's principles to his own. Rather, I simply mean to suggest that the Rousseauean soul has more choices psychologically available than the Lockean individual, including the choice to abandon his Rousseauean commitments. Similarly, the Declaration's revolutionary has more choices psychologically available than does the Constitution's citizen.

19. See Harvey C. Mansfield, Jr., *America's Constitutional Soul* (Baltimore: Johns Hopkins University Press, 1991), ch. 10.

6

What Did They Think They Were Doing When They Wrote the U.S. Constitution, and Why Should We Care?

SUZETTE HEMBERGER

IN DEBATING ratification of the U.S. Constitution, both Federalists and Antifederalists offered implicit accounts of constitution making as an enterprise. At its starkest, the contrast between the two models centered on whether constitutions should empower governments or limit them. Federalists portrayed constitution making as the construction of a government powerful enough to represent its citizens' interests in international society. Antifederalists described constitution making as an exercise in the articulation of shared values—values that would not only constitute the community but limit what the government could do in its name. Each account reflected aspects of the States' constitutional experience during the colonial and revolutionary periods, and each embodies a broader truth about constitution making generally.[1] Yet there is irony in the fact that most constitutional scholarship today proceeds as if the Antifederalist model of constitution making offers the best description of the very constitution it opposed. My premise here is not that we cannot or should not interpret the U.S. Constitution as a limitation on national government,[2] but that by ignoring the Federalists' understanding of what their constitution would do, we systematically overlook crucial aspects of its character. I also want to suggest that by assimilating the Antifederalist model of constitution making to the Federalist text, we misapprehend the radically different vision of constitutional practice that Antifederalists promulgated. This essay, then, is primarily a work of reconstruction which attempts both to recapture the alternative conceptions of constitution making that inspired post-Revolutionary Americans and to see what light each sheds on the constitution they ultimately adopted.

The Philadelphia Convention was called by those who believed that it was necessary to strengthen the national government; those who did not share this belief stayed home. Debates within the Convention were, for the most part, debates among nationalists. As Madison remarked in the Convention, "According to the views of every member, the Genl. Govt.

will have powers far beyond those exercised by the British Parliament when the States were part of the British Empire."[3]

The principal disagreement among the delegates was whether the national government needed to be reconstructed before it could be more fully empowered. Edmund Randolph's resolutions, which were introduced in the first week of the Convention and served as its agenda, proposed major changes in the institutional structures of the national government. After weeks of debate over the Randolph plan, William Paterson of New Jersey introduced an alternative proposal: a series of amendments to the Articles of Confederation that would preserve the structure of the Continental Congress but endow it with additional powers.

The recorded debate over the Paterson and Randolph plans had less to do with the scope of national power than with the terms on which representatives from the smaller states would share in the exercise of that power. That the delegates from the small states were not primarily concerned with protecting the prerogatives of their particular governments is suggested by the fact that, at a number of points during the deliberations, they argued that the simplest way to resolve the conflict between the large and small states would be to dissolve the states or to redraw their boundaries so that each would have approximately the same population.[4] Once the concession was made that each state would receive equal representation in the Senate, representatives from the smaller states no longer objected to the expansion of national prerogatives.[5] Alexander Hamilton appears to have been right when he contended, in one of the Convention's more heated moments, that "the truth is it [the schism between the large and small states] is a contest for power, not for liberty."[6]

The public debates that followed the Convention implicitly acknowledged that the proposed constitution was the work of nationalists. Both Federalists and Antifederalists agreed that the constitution would significantly increase the power of the national government; they disagreed whether a more powerful and centralized government was desirable. Federalists urged the proposed constitution because it would restore "energy," "strength," and "vigor" to American government; they condemned government under the Articles of Confederation as "weak" and "imbecilic." Antifederalists argued that the virtually unlimited power of the new national government posed a threat to American liberty, and reminded their fellow citizens that Americans had just overthrown a powerful, distant, and oppressive government.

In championing the proposed constitution, Federalists faced the challenge of transforming the understanding of the relationship between liberty and government that had prevailed during the Revolution.[7] The key to this transformation was the adoption of an international perspective on state-building.[8] Employing this perspective, Federalist rhetoric did three things: it externalized the threat to individual liberties, it urged citizens to identify their interests with those of the national government, and it asked them to entrust that government with virtually unlimited power. These three moves—externalization, identification, and empowerment— served both to justify the construction of a national government with extensive powers and to recast such a government as the guarantor of, rather than a threat to, America's liberty.

Externalization

Federalist rhetoric cultivated a sense of insecurity. Publius reminded his readers that the United States were literally surrounded by hostile forces and cautioned "against an excess of confidence or security":

> On one side of us and stretching far into our rear are growing settlements subject to the dominion of Britain. On the other side and extending to meet the British settlements are colonies and establishments subject to the dominion of Spain. This situation and the vicinity of the West-India islands belonging to these two powers create between them, in respect to their American posses- sions, and in relation to us, a common interest. The savage tribes on our West- ern frontier ought to be regarded as our natural enemies their natural allies; because they have most to fear from us and most to hope from them.[9]

Americans had won their war against the British, but their indepen- dence was increasingly insecure. British re-conquest was an ever-present possibility, and because the States were now outside the realm of Britain's control and protection, they had become prizes that other European powers might reasonably aspire to win. The United States were essen- tially defenseless against the depredations of these foreign powers who threatened them with everything from economic ruin[10] to invasion,[11] par- tition,[12] and enslavement.[13] To begin with, the States were militarily vul- nerable. Indeed, one Federalist went so far as to suggest that

> There is hardly a circumstance remaining; hardly one external mark by which you can deserve to be called a nation. You are not in a condition to resist the most contemptible enemy. What is there to prevent an Algerine Pirate from landing on your coast, and carrying your citizens into slavery? You have not a single sloop of war.[14]

But military power alone would not secure American independence. After all, military defeat had not ended Britain's economic domination of her former colonies, leading one anonymous writer to ask:

Have we fought and bled, have we conquered and loaded ourselves with the trophies of this potent king, and yet shall we be by him condemned to beg our bread; while his subjects in full sail, are entering every port, choosing their own market and carrying away the fat of the land? . . . Are those that conquer accustomed to bear the yoke?[15]

Other nations treated the United States with contempt.[16] If Americans hoped to assume their rightful place in world affairs, they must adopt a proper constitution.[17]

According to the Federalists, the weakness of the national government was at the root of all of America's current problems. James Wilson portrayed the United States' economic distress as a consequence of her lack of political power:

Devoid of national power, we could not prohibit the extravagance of our importations, nor could we derive a revenue from their excess; devoid of national importance, we could not procure, for our exports, a tolerable sale in foreign markets; devoid of national credit, we saw our public securities melt in the hands of the holders, like snow before the sun; devoid of national dignity, we could not, in some instances, perform our treaties on our parts; and, in other instances we could neither obtain nor compel the performance of them on the parts of others. Devoid of national energy, we could not carry into execution our own resolutions, decisions, or laws.[18]

Wilson's speech identified two general defects in the nation's government: it was less powerful than the foreign powers with whom it would trade and negotiate, and it did not command the obedience of its own citizens. On Wilson's analysis, the two deficiencies were related: unless the United States' government was firmly in control at home, it would not be effective abroad. His goal was a government that could bring the full weight of "national power" to bear in its dealings with other countries. Although Wilson portrayed the threat to liberty as foreign, he anticipated that the power to meet that threat would first be exercised domestically.

Wilson thus tapped into a recurrent theme in Federalist writings: the constitution must organize force within the nation so that it can be projected outward. Oliver Ellsworth, writing as A Landholder, provided the most explicit articulation of this argument when he wrote:

A government capable of controling the whole, and bringing its force to a point is one of the prerequisites of national liberty. . . . If we mean to have our natural rights and properties protected, we must first create a power which is able to do it, and in our case there is no want of resources, but only of a civil constitution which may draw them out and point their force.[19]

National unification thus became a primary function both of the constitution and of the government it would create. In Federalist discourse, "disunity" was a symptom of the weakness of the national government,[20] conflict and persistent regional differences were represented as signs of impending anarchy, and economic competition among the states became a major source of American vulnerability to foreign conquest. A Landholder identified political unrest within the New England states as yet another threat to national unity:

> The rebellion of Shays and the present measures of Rhode-Island ought to convince us that a national legislature, judiciary and executive must be united, or the whole is but a name; and that we must have these or soon be hewers of wood and drawers of water for all other people.[21]

As these passages suggest, though Federalists typically represented the danger to American liberty as coming from abroad, they quickly assimilated internal dissension to such foreign threats. Sometimes the connection between foreign and domestic subversion was made directly. Those who disturb the domestic peace were said to be either in the pay of foreign masters or likely to turn to (or be turned to by) foreign governments with designs on the United States.[22] In other Federalist writings, an analogy between foreign and domestic threats was forged by invoking the logic of the social contract. Without Leviathan, the argument went, the war of all against all would continue to be waged at home as well as in the international sphere:

> [A]n internal government of strength is the only means of repressing external violence, and preserving the national rights of the people against the injustice of their own brethren. Even the common duties of humanity will gradually go out of use, when the constitution and laws of a country, do not insure justice from the public and between individuals.[23]

Finally, internal dissension was indirectly related to foreign subversion in the argument that unity at home was a prerequisite to successful action abroad.[24]

Implicit in each of these arguments was the suggestion that enemies of the national government are, presumptively, enemies of the American people. With the U.S. government cast as the guarantor of popular liberty, any threat to governmental power was a threat to liberty. Because the threat to American liberty was represented as essentially foreign, resistance to the central government or its nationalizing project could border on treason. Dissent (and even the valorization of difference) were thus implicitly rendered un-American. Moreover, the national government and popular liberty were so closely identified that there was little space in

Federalist discourse for conceptualizing resistance to the power of the
national government as a defense of liberty.

Identification

This asserted identity of interests between citizens and government was
not unproblematic in a nation where government had very recently been
seen as a source of oppression. The Federalists sought to redirect citizens'
distrust of government toward foreign regimes, dismissing fears of one's
own government as paranoia or even cowardice. Popular jealousy toward
state power may have been a virtue under a monarchical, aristocratic, or
colonial government, they acknowledged, but it made no sense in a republic.[25] Alexander Hamilton suggested that the Revolutionary experience had distorted America's political priorities:

> In the commencement of a revolution which received its birth from the usurpa-
> tions of tyranny, nothing was more natural than that the public mind should be
> influenced by an extreme spirit of jealousy. To resist these encroachments, and
> to nourish this spirit, was the great object of all our public and private institu-
> tions. The zeal for liberty became predominant and excessive.[26]

Unless Americans turned their attention from the question of liberty to
the question of power, Marcus argued, they would create a situation in
which "for want of a little rational confidence in our own government,
we might be obliged to submit to a master in an enemy."[27] Distrust of
government, rather than a republican virtue, became a hallmark of those
who were, in spirit, still subjects rather than citizens.

Federalists argued that the American people could safely entrust power
to the national government because it would be a republican government
that exercised its power on their behalf. The government represented the
citizens—its power would be *their* power:

> Who are Congress then? They are ourselves: The men of our own choice, in
> whom we can confide; whose interest is inseparably connected with our own.
> Why is it then, that gentlemen speak of Congress as some foreign body: as a set
> of men who will seek every opportunity to enslave us?[28]

Noah Webster made the argument more emphatically:

> The only barrier against tyranny, that is necessary in any State, is *the election of
> Legislators* by the yeomanry of that State. Preserve *that*, and every privilege is
> safe. The Legislators thus chosen to represent the people, should have all the
> power that the people would have, were they assembled in one body to deliber-
> ate upon public measures. The distinction between the powers of the *people*

and of their *Representatives* in the Legislature, is as absurd in *theory*, as it proves pernicious in *practice*.[29]

By endowing the national government with power, citizens would institutionalize their own power so that it could be used more effectively. Thus the more power the government was given, the more power the people would have. As one federalist argued, "[t]he stronger we make our government, the greater protection it can afford us, and the greater will our safety be under it."[30]

While striving to allay popular suspicion of government, the Federalists did not want to create a fearless citizenry. Citizens who did not perceive the existence of serious threats to their way of life or those who were confident of their own ability to resist oppression were equally unsuited to the Federalist agenda. The Federalists had to impress upon their audience the myriad dangers that would continually confront an independent America. Without such threats, there would be no need to create a powerful state. The success of the Federalist project thus depended on fostering a measure of insecurity among the citizenry.

Empowerment

To survive as an independent nation in an international system, the United States must have a government that possesses all of the powers that every other government possesses. As the Federalists saw it, three such powers were crucial—the power to make law, the power to deploy military force (against both foreign and domestic threats), and the power to raise revenue.[31] Under the Articles of Confederation, they contended, the U.S. government lacked all three. The Continental Congress could assign quotas of contribution, and requisition men or money from the States, but ultimately, it had no power to enforce compliance with its demands. Thus, the national legislature had to rely on the cooperation and the agency of the States in order to get anything done. As a result, Publius claimed, the Union had "neither troops, nor treasury, nor government."[32]

Of the three powers, law-making was the most important. Federalists considered the power to coerce obedience to law a basic attribute of sovereignty:

Government implies the power of making laws. It is essential to the idea of a law, that it be attended with a sanction; or, in other words, a penalty or punishment for disobedience. . . . This penalty, whatever it may be, can only be inflicted in two ways; by the agency of the Courts and Ministers of Justice, or by military force; by the COERTION of the magistracy, or by the COERTION of arms. The first kind can evidently apply only to men —the last kind must of necessity be employed against bodies politic, or communities or States.[33]

This required that "the authority of the union [extend] to the persons of the citizens,—the only proper objects of government."[34] To give the national government direct access to individuals meant abandoning what Publius referred to as one of the "first principles" of the Confederation:

> The great and radical vice in the construction of the existing Confederation is in the principle of LEGISLATION for STATES or GOVERNMENTS in their CORPORATE or COLLECTIVE CAPACITIES and as contradistinguished from the INDIVIDUALS of whom they consist. . . . The consequence of this is, that though in theory their [the Continental Congress's] resolutions . . . are laws, constitutionally binding on the members of the Union, yet in practice they are mere recommendations, which the States observe or disregard at their option.[35]

As the passages just quoted suggest, Federalists conceived the power to employ military force as the complement of the power to make law. Both were aspects of the power to coerce, which was the essence of government. Federalists believed that, like the power to make law, the power to employ military force must be institutionalized. Americans must not rely upon militias; they needed a more permanent military establishment:

> [A]ll government is restraint, and founded in force. We are the first nation who have ever held a contrary opinion, or even attempted to maintain one without it. The experiment has been made, and . . . there would hereafter be few men weak enough to suppose that some regular force ought not to be kept up, or that the militia ever can be depended upon as the support or protection of the Union.[36]

Finally, to perform its functions, the national government would need money—money to provide salaries for its officers, to provision its troops, and to pay off the nation's debts. Federalists argued that the power to tax, like the power to employ military force, was a basic attribute of national sovereignty:

> Every government must be empowered to raise a sufficient revenue; but I believe it will be allowed, on all hands, that Congress has been hitherto altogether destitute of that power so essential to every government. . . . [T]he United States wish to be established and known among other nations. This will be a matter of great utility to them. We might then form advantageous connections. When it is once known among foreign nations that our general government and our finances are upon a respectable footing, should emergencies happen, we can borrow money of them without any disadvantage. . . . We can borrow

money with ease, and on advantageous terms, when it shall be known that Congress will have that power which all governments ought to have.[37]

Federalists insisted that the national government must possess "the power of creating new funds upon new objects of taxation."[38] Any limits on its powers of taxation would jeopardize its ability to secure credit.[39]

In the case of taxation, the Federalist argument against the limitation of the national government's power was a pragmatic one. Nevertheless, throughout the ratification debates, a number of prominent Federalists— among them Alexander Hamilton, Oliver Ellsworth, James Wilson, James Iredell, and Noah Webster—asserted that the powers of the national government should, *in principle*, be unlimited.[40] Their argument consisted of three maxims:

> 1. "A constitution cannot set bounds to a nation's wants; it ought not, therefore, to set bounds to its resources."[41]
>
> 2. Power must not be withheld from the national government for fear that it might be abused. The potential for abuse is always present, since "a power of doing good always implies a power to do evil if the person or party be disposed."[42]
>
> 3. The way to prevent government from becoming oppressive is to structure it wisely—not to deny it power for which it might have a legitimate need. "The true principle of government is this—make the system complete in its structure, give a perfect proportion and balance to its parts, and the powers you give it will never affect your security."[43]

Ultimately, these Federalists wanted to establish a national government whose capacity for action was unconstrained.[44] They endowed that government with the powers of legislation, taxation, and the use of military force. What attracted Federalists to these forms of power was their plasticity: such powers could meet every unforeseeable contingency. The Antifederalists, on the other hand, thought there was something sinister in the very versatility of such powers. They championed powers, practices, and institutions which they believed had natural limits—preferring militias to standing armies, imposts to excises, and juries to judges.

Lawyers, Guns, and Money

The ratification debates brought to the surface a contest between two rival economies of power. The Federalists saw state building as a top-down process in which the powers of a government are largely determined by the requirements of the international system in which it will participate. The Antifederalists' goal was a constitution built upon local institutions, practices, and understandings—a constitution suited to preserve the genius of the American people—rather than a constitution produced in response to the imperatives of foreign policy. This difference in perspective surfaced as Antifederalists contested Federalist attempts to shift the center of constitutional discourse from questions of liberty to questions of power. In one of his first speeches to the Virginia ratifying convention, Patrick Henry addressed the issue explicitly: "You are not to inquire how your trade may be increased," he informed his fellow delegates, "nor how you are to become a great and powerful people, but how your liberties can be secured; for liberty ought to be the direct end of your Government."[45] An Antifederalist pamphleteer dramatized the trade-off he believed Americans were being urged to make in this parody of Federalist rhetoric:

> The congress having thus disentangled themselves from all popular checks and choices; and being supported by a well disciplined army and active militia, will certainly command dread and respect abroad, obedience and submission at home; they will then look down with awful dignity and tremendous majesty from the pinnacle of glory, to which fortune has raised them upon the insignificant creatures, their subjects, whom they have reduced to that state of vassalage and servile submission, for which they were primarily destined by nature. America will then be great amongst nations and princess amongst the provinces. . . . [F]or such a state who would not part with ideal blessings of liberty? who would not chearfully resign the nominal advantages of freedom? the dazzling splendour of Assyrian, Persian, Macedonian and Roman greatness will then be totally eclipsed by the radient blaze of this glorious western luminary![46]

Antifederalists also rejected the Federalists' claim that constitution makers should be guided by considerations of foreign policy. Thus Richard Henry Lee wrote that

> foreigners have no business with the nature of our government. Payment of their debts they are entitled to, but no possible reason can be assigned, why these debts may not as well be paid if the proposed constitution was to be so amended, as to secure the just rights and liberties of the people from violation, by a proper bill of rights; to retain the trial by jury in all cases, civil as well as criminal, as directed by the common law; to secure the rights of conscience, and freedom of the press. Will France, Holland, or Spain, be disturbed at our retaining these valuable privileges?[47]

Brutus conceded that the national government must be able to "provide for the protection and defence of [the] country against external enemies," but argued that "this is not the most important, much less the only object of their care":

> The European governments are almost all of them framed, and administered with a view to arms, and war, as that in which their chief glory consists; they

mistake the end of government—it was designed to save mens lives, not to destroy them. We ought to furnish the world with an example of a great people, who in their civil institutions hold chiefly in view, the attainment of virtue, and happiness among ourselves.[48]

This difference in emphasis between international and local perspectives corresponded to a disagreement over whether government would be based on force or on persuasion. The Federalists, in keeping with their international orientation, believed that "to pretend to exist as a nation without possessing those powers of coerce, which are necessarily incident to the national Character, would prove a fatal solecism in politicks."[49] The Antifederalists acknowledged the novelty of creating a free republic in a world of monarchical nation-states, but insisted that

> our Government must be a Government of confidence, it must be a Government Supported by affection arising from an apprehension of mutual interest, and Security, and not of fear and apprehension.[50]

The different emphases on force and persuasion, in turn, reflected different conceptions of political knowledge. The Antifederalists tended to see political knowledge as local, experiential, and historical, while the Federalists saw government as involving a science of politics whose truths were objective and universal. Federalists therefore argued for a political system in which expertise was relatively insulated from popular pressures, while Antifederalists championed institutions that would embed government in the political life of communities. The divergent assumptions about the nature of governmental power and the knowledge requisite for effective political action surface most clearly in Federalist and Antifederalist discussions of the national government's powers to make law, to employ military force, and to collect revenue.

Guns

In harmony with their arguments for a strong and professionalized central government, Federalists extolled the efficiency of a professionalized military. As Publius pointed out, the existence of Indians on the western frontier, the British to the north, and the Spanish to the south meant that garrisons would have to be maintained at all times, and it would be cheaper and less disruptive to staff them with professional soldiers than with militiamen who must return periodically to civilian pursuits.[51] By entrusting a small group of people with the job of national defense, the great majority of citizens could go about their business uninterrupted by calls to military service. Francis Corbin, a representative to the Virginia

Convention, made the case for specialization as part of a defense of standing armies:

> If some of the community are exclusively inured to its defence, and the rest attend to agriculture, the consequence will be, that the arts of war and defence, and of cultivating the soil, will be understood. Agriculture will flourish, and military discipline will be perfect. If, on the contrary, our defence be solely intrusted to militia, ignorance of arms and negligence of farming will ensue: the former plan is, in every respect, more to the interest of the state. By it we shall have good farmers and soldiers; by the latter we shall have neither.[52]

Publius added that the United States could not hope to protect itself against the professional armies of Europe unless it developed a professional army of its own:

> The steady operations of war against a regular and disciplined army can only be successfully conducted by a force of the same kind. . . . War, like most other things, is a science to be acquired and perfected by diligence, by perseverance, by time, and by practice.[53]

Federalists contended that an effective military force must be uniformly equipped and administered and that only the national government was capable of providing this sort of coordination. Once again, diversity within the United States figured as an obstacle to power in the international sphere. As James Wilson argued during Pennsylvania's ratifying convention:

> any gentleman who possesses military experience will inform you, that men without an uniformity of arms, accoutrements, and discipline are no more than a mob in a camp; that in the field, instead of assisting, they interfere with one another. If a soldier drops his musket, and his companion, unfurnished with one, takes it up, it is of no service because his cartridges do not fit it. By means of this system, a uniformity of arms and discipline will prevail throughout the United States.[54]

The hallmark of a well-trained military was that it would do what it was told to do. Impersonality was one aspect of such reliability—soldiers, like their weapons, should be interchangeable.

Antifederalist opposition to standing armies (and to the nationalization of the militia) proceeded from the premise that government's dependence on popular consent was a bulwark against oppression. The Antifederalists objected to the creation of a standing army partly because they believed that the national government would be unable to govern through persuasion. The alternative to persuasion was rule by force, and a standing army would make force a real threat.[55] Antifederalists refused the identification between the people and their government that the Federalists had urged. They contested the Federalists' emphasis on foreign threats by attempting to bring the consequences of such an orientation home. Thus an anonymous editorialist in the Philadelphia paper remarked that

> [Publius's] attempts to prove the expedience of supporting a *standing army* in time of peace have been so futile, that even the friends of the new plan are offended with them. His barefaced assertions, that our existence as a nation depends upon our keeping up a large military, to defend us on the north from the British, on the west from the Indians, on the south from the Spaniards, and on the Atlantic side from the invasions of a maritime enemy, have alarmed the people exceedingly. The common talk is, *Well, what do you think of being surrounded with a standing army?*[56]

While Federalists extolled the virtues of an army whose soldiers would be as undifferentiated as their weapons, Antifederalists championed militias precisely because they lacked such fungibility. According to the Antifederalists, militias were not equally adaptable to good or evil ends. They could be trusted to act in the public interest because they were, quite literally, the public. In theory, American militias in this period included every able-bodied adult (white) man in the community.[57] They were organized by township or county and elected their own commanders. Militias were self-governing bodies of men who knew each other and who were organized to defend their own community. Standing armies, of course, were another story. Because they had to be continuously available, they were typically staffed by professional soldiers. They lived in barracks, not communities, and their loyalties would be exclusively to their paymasters—in this case, the national government.

Because the logic of the militia was perverted whenever it ceased to embody community understandings, federal regulation of the militia raised fears similar to those engendered by the prospect of a standing army. There were two obvious ways to pervert the militia: the national government could either create select militias or it could employ militias outside of the communities from which they were drawn. A "select" militia was one created from a body of people—usually young men without property—who were unrepresentative of the community as a whole and whose political wisdom could not be trusted. As John Smilie argued in the course of the Pennsylvania Convention, a militia ceased to be a militia once it no longer required universal participation:

> The last resource of a free people is taken away; for Congress are to have the command of the militia. . . . The militia officers will be obliged by oath to support the general government against that of their own state. . . . Congress may give us a select militia which will, in fact, be a standing army—or Con-

gress, afraid of a general militia, may say there shall be no militia at all. . . .
When a select militia is formed; the people in general may be disarmed.[58]

Antifederalists believed that a militia employed outside of its own community raised the same problems as a select militia or a standing army. In short, it would lack the political judgment necessary to determine which side it should take. Thus William Findley worried that

the militia will be taken from home; and when the militia of one state has quelled insurrections and destroyed the liberties, the militia of the last state may, at another time, be employed in retaliating on the first.[59]

Put to such use, Centinel claimed, the militia could "be made as meer machines as Prussian soldiers."[60]

Antifederalists believed that the citizen's power over his government stemmed as much from his role as soldier as from his status as voter. Universal service in the militia affected the relationship between government and citizenry in three ways. First, because the government had to mobilize citizen-soldiers rather than rely on a professional army to do its bidding, it could use force only in situations where public opinion supported governmental policy. Second, where citizens were the soldiers, the army could not be used to coerce the populace at large. Finally, citizens who were armed and organized for service in the militia had the power to resist government that became oppressive. Federal Farmer argued that a select militia would simultaneously free the government from its dependence on the common people and sap the peoples' capacity to resist the government:

[T]he yeomanry of the country possess the lands, the weight of property, possess arms, and are too strong a body of men to be openly offended—and, therefore, it is urged, they will take care of themselves, that men who shall govern will not dare pay any disrespect to their opinions. It is easily perceived, that if they have not their proper negative upon passing laws in congress, or on the passage of laws relative to taxes and armies, they may in twenty or thirty years be by means imperceptible to them, totally deprived of that boasted weight and strength: This may be done in a great measure by congress, if disposed to do it, by modelling the militia. Should one fifth or one eighth part of the men capable of bearing arms, be made a select militia, as has been proposed, and those the young and ardent part of the community, possessed of but little or no property, and all the others put upon a plan that will render them of no importance, the former will answer all the purposes of an army, while the latter will be defenseless.[61]

For the Antifederalists, then, much more was at stake in debates over the militia than the question of who would go to war. Militia musters, even more than elections, were the occasions on which white men experi-

enced their status as republican citizens. In coming together at routine
intervals, as a community, citizens were reminded of their power—and
government was too. Thus when the Federalists held out the possibility
of relief from this admittedly burdensome obligation, the Antifederalists
foresaw the destruction of a vital civic institution and of one of the few
checks the people had on government.

Money

For the Federalists, the salient constitutional issue with regard to taxation
was ensuring that the national government would always be able to secure the revenue it needed. For Antifederalists, however, the taxing
power raised important questions about the size, reach, and impartiality
of the national government. Because there were numerous ways in which
the power of taxation could become oppressive, Antifederalists were concerned with how much the government would tax its citizens, how it
would collect revenue, and how it would distribute the burden of taxation. Some Antifederalists argued that the national government's power
of taxation should be limited to the assessment of import duties (or "imposts"). Brutus contended that imposts were safe because they placed
inherent limits both on the amount of the tax and on the method of its
collection:

> They may be collected in few places, and from few hands with certainty and
> expedition. But few officers are necessary to be imployed in collecting them,
> and there is no danger of oppression in laying them, because, if they are laid
> higher than trade will bear, the merchants will cease importing, or smuggle
> their goods. We have therefore sufficient security, arising from the nature of the
> thing, against burdensome, and intolerable impositions from this kind of tax.[62]

Conversely, excise taxes—taxes on sale, consumption, or production of
domestic goods—were prone to abuse. Such taxes provided the occasion
for diffusion of national power throughout the most remote (and most
private) corners of the republic:

> This power [of the federal government to pass excise taxes], exercised without
> limitation, will introduce itself into every corner of the city, and country—It
> will wait upon the ladies at their toilett, and will not leave them in any of their
> domestic concerns; it will accompany them to the ball, the play, and the assem-
> bly; it will go with them when they visit, and will, on all occasions, sit beside
> them in their carriages, nor will it desert them even at church; it will enter the
> house of every gentleman, watch over his cellar, wait upon his cook in the
> kitchen, follow the servants into the parlour, preside over the table, and note
> down all he eats or drinks; it will attend him to his bed-chamber, and watch

him while he sleeps; it will take cognizance of the merchant in the counting-house, or in his store; it will follow the mechanic to his shop, and in his work, and will haunt him in his family and in his bed; it will be a constant companion of the industrious farmer in all his labour, it will be with him in the house, and in the field, observe the toil of his hands, and the sweat of his brow; it will penetrate into the most obscure cottage; and finally, it will light upon the head of every person in the United States. To all these different classes of people, and in all these circumstances, in which it will attend them, the language in which it will address them will be GIVE! GIVE![63]

While Brutus asserted that extensive powers of taxation would render the national government too intrusive, George Mason opposed granting such powers because he felt that the national government would be too remote to exercise them justly. Mason argued that the House of Representatives was too small to possess enough information to tax equitably:

Sixty-five members cannot possibly know the situation and circumstances of all the inhabitants of this immense continent. When a certain sum comes to be taxed and the mode of levying to be fixed, they will lay the tax on that article which will be most productive and easiest in the collection, without consulting the real circumstances or convenience of a country, with which, in fact, they cannot be sufficiently acquainted.

The mode of levying taxes is of the utmost consequence; and yet here it is to be determined by those who have neither the knowledge of our situation, nor a common interest with us, nor a fellow-feeling for us.[64]

Federalists responded to arguments like Mason's by insisting that even a handful of people could possess all the information the federal government needed to make good policy. As Alexander Hamilton explained,

What are the objects of the government? Commerce, taxation, & c. . . . The information necessary for these purposes is that which is open to every intelligent inquirer, and of which five men may be as perfectly possessed as fifty. In royal governments, there are usually particular men to whom the business of taxation is committed. These men have the forming of systems of finance, and the regulation of revenue. I do not mean to commend this practice. It proves, however, this point—that a few individuals may be competent to these objects, and that large numbers are not necessary to perfection in the science of taxation.[65]

Hamilton's response must have done little to reassure Antifederalists. The common concern that united Brutus's and Mason's critique of the federal taxing power was that the national government would come to see its citizens primarily as sources of revenue. The difference between the question Hamilton answered—"What kind of resources does the state need to extract revenue from the citizens effectively?"—and the question Antifederalists asked—"How many representatives do citizens need to make sure their interests are taken into account when decisions about taxation are made?"—suggests that the Antifederalist fear that citizens would become objects of, rather than participants in, government was not far-fetched. When the Federalists argued that "the laws should be carried home to individuals themselves,"[66] Antifederalists envisioned tax collectors invading their bedrooms.

Even the apparent inconsistency between Brutus's distrust of proximity and Mason's concern about distance dissolves when, taken together, these two Antifederalist arguments highlight problems attendant upon the uneven development of the apparatus of national government. Tax collectors would soon be everywhere; but legislators would be hard to find. In essence, Antifederalists feared that, because of its constitutional structure, the national government's capacity for enforcing its will would outpace its capacity for informing its will. As subsequent developments would demonstrate, when excise officers preceded federal courts to the frontier, the Whiskey Rebellion ensued and the Antifederalist prophecy that the national government would rule through force rather than persuasion was, in that instance, fulfilled.[67]

Law

Antifederalists predicted that the national government would rule through force because the institutional structure of the government would not facilitate the communication necessary to ensure consent. The Antifederalists believed that the government must know its citizens, and that citizens must know their government and each other. A government that knew the circumstances and the desires of the people could fashion workable and just policies. A people able to see their representatives in action and hear them justify their policies would be more likely to trust their government and voluntarily comply with its dictates. And citizens who knew each other's minds could coordinate their opposition to unjust or oppressive policies. Conversely, where the circulation of political knowledge was inhibited, bad policies would be imposed upon a hostile and suspicious population. Government would ultimately have no choice but to rely on force to implement its programs, and a disorganized citizenry would have little capacity to resist. Antifederalists argued that the Federalist constitution would create such a regime.[68]

If the free flow of knowledge was the key to ensuring government based on consent, the national government faced an uphill battle. The Antifederalists feared that information and opinion would not circulate in a nation as large as that contemplated by the constitution; the development of common knowledge and common sentiments would be inhibited both by distance and by regional differences. Thus Antifederalists expressed a concern for bolstering those institutions and practices that would contribute local knowledge to national government and that would produce shared understandings among people in different parts of the nation. Three strategies emerge from these discussions: local administration; the frequent exchange of people between the center and the periphery; and the coordination of popular opinion through the authoritative articulation of shared political beliefs.

The Antifederalists sought to strengthen juries for the same reasons that they urged reliance on militias: both were institutions in which ordinary citizens would exercise power, and both provided opportunities for local knowledge to be brought to bear in the implementation of national policies.[69] The fact that the original Constitution guaranteed the right to a jury trial in criminal but not in civil cases may indicate an awareness of the class-based character of the institution of the jury. Federal Farmer addressed the issue explicitly when he argued:

> The trial by jury is very important in another point of view. It is essential in every free country, that common people should have a part and share of influence, in the judicial as well as in the legislative department. To hold open to them the offices of senators, judges, and officers to fill which an expensive education is required, cannot answer any valuable purposes for them; they are not in a situation to be brought forward and to fill those offices; these, and most other offices of any considerable importance, will be occupied by the few. The few, the well born, &c. as Mr. Adams calls them, in judicial decisions as well as in legislation, are generally disposed, and very naturally too, to favor those of their own description.[70]

The Antifederalists saw professional politics as a kind of class rule that must be tempered by a reliance upon the people. Thus, An Old Whig cautioned his readers to distinguish between what was necessary to strengthen the state and what would secure the elite's control of government:

> [H]ow could the stripping people of the right of trial by jury conduce to the strength of the state? . . . [T]hese things which merely tend to oppress the people without conducing at all to the strength of the state, are the last which aristocratic rulers would consent to restore to the people; because they increase the personal power and importance of the rulers. Judges, unincumbered by juries, have been ever found much better friends to government than to the people.[71]

Juries, then, were to function as a check on the national government's power. But just as militias marched outside their state could be put to any use, so, too, could juries be rendered manipulable if they tried cases whose parties and circumstances were beyond their ken. Antifederalists claimed that the guarantee of jury trials would be rendered meaningless unless jurors were drawn from the vicinity in which the crime was committed. Abraham Holmes, a delegate to the Massachusetts convention, argued that the proposed constitution did not adequately protect the rights of the accused because

> in a criminal process a person shall not have a right to insist on a trial in the vicinity where the fact was committed, where a jury of the peers would, from their local situation, have an opportunity to form a judgment of the *character* of the person charged with the crime, and also to judge of the *credibility* of the witnesses. There a person must be tried by a jury of strangers.[72]

In the North Carolina Convention, Joseph M'Dowall went even further, suggesting that the right to a jury trial would be eviscerated if jurors were not chosen from the local area: "They ought to be tried by the people of the vicinage; for when the trial is at such an immense distance, the principal privilege attending the trial by jury is taken away."[73]

Arguments in favor of juries of the vicinage brought forth the response that strangers might be fairer judges of lawsuits than neighbors. In Massachusetts, Christopher Gore argued that

> the idea that the jury coming from the neighbourhood, and knowing the character and circumstances of the party in trial, is promotive of justice, on reflection will appear not founded in truth—if the jury judge from any other circumstances, but what are part of the cause in question, they are not impartial—The great object is to determine on the real merits of the cause uninfluenced by any personal considerations—if therefore the jury could be perfectly ignorant of the person in trial, a just decision would be more probable.[74]

North Carolina's Governor Johnston adopted a similar approach, rejecting the claims of local knowledge in favor of a more distant objectivity.[75]

The question whether jurors should be neighbors of, or strangers to, the accused was, in essence, a controversy over the kind of knowledge appropriate to (or required for) judgment. Characteristically, Antifederalists stressed the importance of experience and knowledge of context, while Federalists treated such perspectives as inherently parochial.[76] While Federalists attempted to recruit and retain officials with specialized knowledge of the science of government, they sought ignorant juries. Thus civic incompetence was fostered not only by professionalization within government, but by the assertion that the knowledge that ordinary citizens *do* possess is an inappropriate basis for political judgment.

The controversy over the importance of local knowledge resurfaced when the state ratifying conventions debated the appropriate length of legislative terms. In Massachusetts, Fisher Ames justified the two-year term length for members of the House of Representatives by arguing that

> It is admitted that annual elections may be highly fit for the state legislature. Every citizen grows up with a knowledge of the local circumstances of the state. But the business of the federal government will be very different. The objects of their power are few and national. At least two years in office will be necessary to enable a man to judge of the trade and interests of states which he never saw. The time I hope, will come, when this excellent country will furnish food, and freedom (which is better than food, which is the food of the soul) for fifty millions of happy people. Will any man say that the national business can be understood in one year?[77]

General Heath responded by pointing out that

> It is a novel idea, that representatives should be chosen for a considerable time, in order that they may learn their duty; the representative is one who appears in behalf of, and acts for others, he ought therefore to be fully acquainted with the feelings, circumstances and interests of the persons whom he represents, and this is learnt among them, not at a distant Court.[78]

Although they believed that the primary function of a representative was to inform the national legislature of the interests and desires of his constituents, and although they were undoubtedly unnerved by the prospect that each congressman would routinely be judging "the interests of states which he never saw," Antifederalists didn't deny that a certain kind of knowledge would be acquired in the capital. In fact, their support for rotation in office was, at least in part, predicated on the idea that those who served time at the capital should be forced to bring that knowledge home at regular intervals. Thus Gilbert Livingston supported rotation in office not only because it would reacquaint representatives with their constituents, but because it would acquaint citizens with the operations of the national government:

> The senators . . . should not only return, and be obliged to live with the people, but return to their former rank of citizenship, both to revive their sense of dependence, and to gain a knowledge of the country. This will afford opportunity to bring forward the genius and information of the states, and will be a stimulus to acquire political abilities. It will be a means of diffusing a more general knowledge of the measures and spirit of the administration. These things will confirm the people's confidence in government. When they see those who have been high in office residing among them as private citizens, they will feel more forcibly that the government is of their own choice. The members of this branch having the idea impressed on their minds, that they are soon to return to the level whence the suffrages of the people raised them,—

this good effect will follow: they will consider their interests as the same with those of their constituents, and that they legislate for themselves as well as others. They will not conceive themselves made to receive, enjoy, and rule, nor the people solely to earn, pay, and submit.[79]

Antifederalists recognized that the success of the national government might depend on having, scattered throughout the country, people who had served in Congress and who could explain the wisdom of its policies. Without the influence of such people, suspicion of the national government could lead either to the subversion of its policies or to the use military force to implement them.

While their discussions of juries and legislative term lengths were concerned with bringing local knowledge to bear on the formulation of the national government's policies, Antifederalist support for a bill of rights involved a recognition of the need to organize popular opinion on a national basis outside of government. Antifederalists demanded a bill of rights because they wanted Americans to have a shared understanding of the appropriate limits on governmental power. They did not, as Federalists charged, put their faith in mere "parchment barriers." In fact, Antifederalists shared the Federalists' belief that governmental structure could minimize official abuses of power, but they also thought that it was important to organize the citizenry. Antifederalists believed that, in the final analysis, the people would be responsible for enforcing the constitution. To identify when the national government had exceeded the bounds of its legitimate authority, citizens needed a "plain, strong, and accurate criterion"[80] and a "permanent landmark."[81]

By providing a uniform standard for identifying transgressions, the Bill of Rights would contribute to the coordination of resistance. Thus, Thomas Jefferson argued that

> The jealousy of subordinate governments is a precious reliance. But observe that those governments are only agents. They must have principles furnished them whereon to found their opposition. The declaration of rights will be the text whereby they will try all the acts of the federal government.[82]

A divided citizenry would prove incapable of keeping the power of the national government within limits. Thus John Smilie argued that, without a bill of rights,

> it will be impracticable to stop the progress of tyranny, for there will be no check but the people, and their exertions must be futile and uncertain; since it will be difficult indeed, to communicate to them the violation that has been committed, and their proceedings will be neither systematical nor unanimous.[83]

From an Antifederalist perspective, then, the efficacy of the Bill of Rights would not depend on government voluntarily respecting rights. Instead, the Bill of Rights would alert citizens to abuses of governmental power and enable them to reach a consensus on when resistance was legitimate.[84] Moreover, a bill of rights could give opposition to government constitutional status. The same document that authorized the national government to exercise power would authorize the people to defend their rights against the government, if necessary.[85] Without a bill of rights, Antifederalists feared that the people would either be unaware that their rights had been violated or would become aware only when that situation had gotten so severe that nothing short of revolution was required. As Samuel Spencer, a delegate to the North Carolina Convention, put it:

> [Officials] might exceed the proper boundary without being taken notice of. When there is no rule but a vague doctrine, they might make great strides, and get possession of so much power that a general insurrection of the people would be necessary to bring an alteration about. But if a boundary were set up, when the boundary is passed, the people would take notice of it immediately.[86]

The "consequence of ambiguity," as Joseph M'Dowall explained to the North Carolina Convention, was that "[i]t may raise animosity and revolutions, and involve us in bloodshed."[87]

When Federalists responded to calls for a bill of rights, they either overlooked or misread what the Antifederalists were asking for. Federalists made three kinds of arguments against a bill of rights in the Constitution. The first was that it would be impossible for the states to agree on a bill of rights. The second was that because the national government was a government of limited powers, specifying the rights retained by the people and the states would be not only unnecessary but potentially counterproductive. Finally, Federalists argued that the inclusion of unenforceable rights in the Constitution would undermine the authority of the document. All three arguments highlight the differences in Federalist and Antifederalist conceptions of what a constitutional culture should be. Antifederalists drew precisely the opposite conclusion from the scenario which underlay the first of the Federalist arguments, and they flatly rejected the premise upon which the second two were based.

Federalists contended that, because practices varied from state to state, it would be impossible to construct a bill of rights that would satisfy all Americans, and unfair for the federal constitution to impose uniform rules regarding such things as the use of juries and the eligibility of voters.[88] In effect, federalism was offered as a justification for the Constitution's failure to protect individual rights. Far from obviating the Antifederalists' argument for a bill of rights, this analysis reinforced it. Antifederalists frequently quoted Montesquieu's argument that

> In a large republic, the public good is sacrificed to a thousand views; it is subordinate to exceptions, and depends on accidents. In a small one, the inter-

est of the public is easier perceived, better understood, and more within the reach of every citizen; abuses are of less extent, and of course are less protected.[89]

Diversity *was* an issue—that was why coordination was so important. The national government could easily oppress a large group of citizens incapable of acting in concert, especially if their opinions were sufficiently different from one another to enable officials to convince the rest of the nation that any particular group was simply shirking its obligations rather than resisting tyranny.

Most Antifederalists believed that Americans could agree on a bill of rights. In fact, An Old Whig suggested that the process of attempting to draft such a bill was itself an important step in national development:

> in very different parts of the continent, the very same objections have been made, and the very same alterations proposed by different writers, who I verily believe, know nothing at all of each other, and were very far from acting a premeditated concert. . . . It would be a most delightful surprize to find ourselves all of one opinion at last; and I cannot forbear hoping that when we come fairly to compare our sentiments, we shall find ourselves much more nearly agreed than in the hurry and surprize in which we have been involved on this subject, than we ever suffered ourselves to imagine.[90]

From an Antifederalist point of view, the failure to reach an agreement over which rights must be protected was an argument against national government, not an argument against a bill of rights. Thus Federal Farmer argued that if the understanding of politics in the thirteen states was so divergent that a consensus could not be reached on such basic issues, then they should not share the same national government:

> There are certain unalienable and fundamental rights, which in forming a social compact, ought to be explicitly ascertained and fixed—a free and enlightened people . . . will fix limits to their legislators and rulers, which will soon be plainly seen by those who are governed, as well as by those who govern: and the latter will know they cannot be passed unperceived by the former, and without giving a general alarm—These rights should be made the basis of every constitution and if a people be so situated or have such different opinions that they cannot agree in ascertaining and fixing them, it is a very strong argument against their attempting to form one entire society, to live under one system of laws only.—I confess, I never thought the people of these states differed essentially in these respects; they having derived all these rights, from one common source, the British systems; and having in the formation of their state constitutions, discovered that their ideas relative to these rights are very similar.[91]

The other two arguments Federalists offered against the inclusion of a bill of rights in the national constitution were largely unresponsive to Antifederalist concerns, because both were premised on the assumption that constitutions were, primarily, laws. The first of these legal arguments differentiated state and national constitutions. James Wilson (and, later, Publius) argued that, unlike the state constitutions, the U.S. Constitution represented a limited grant of power to government. The national government would possess only those powers that had been granted, and these did not include the power to regulate speech, religious freedom, and the like. Because a bill of rights would contain exceptions to powers, it would imply that the new government possessed all powers not withheld. Rather than limit power under the new constitution, a bill of rights could actually expand the government's power.

The second argument against a bill of rights was more directly critical of the concept of constitutionalism embodied in the state constitutions. It argued that the precepts contained in bills of rights "would sound much better in a treatise of ethics than in a constitution of government."[92] The suggestion seems to be that what makes these "aphorisms" inappropriate for inclusion in the constitution is that they are unenforceable. The constitution is to be a law. Law must be judicially enforceable. For every legal right there should be a legal remedy. If law includes provisions that cannot be enforced, it encourages breach of other provisions as well. Wilson and Hamilton gave reasons why a bill of rights wasn't legally necessary, but the opponents of the constitution weren't asking for a law. They wanted a set of political principles. More specifically, they wanted a constitution whose meaning was accessible to ordinary citizens and whose interpretation would not be monopolized by lawyers who, as one Antifederalist put it, are apt to "entangle the plainest rights in their net of sophistry:"[93]

> if the people are jealous of their rights, where will be the harm in declaring them? If they be meant as they certainly are to be reserved to the people, what injury can arise from a positive declaration of it? . . . I am well acquainted with the logical reason, that is general given for it. . . .
>
> To have the rights of the people declared to them, would imply, that they had previously given them up, or were not in possession of them.
>
> This indeed is a distinction of which the votaries of scholastic philosophy might be proud—but in the political world, where reason is not cultivated independently of action and experience, such futile distinctions ought not to be agitated.[94]

The Antifederalists were proposing a very different kind of constitutional practice—one in which the constitution was not a law whose authoritative interpretation would be in the hands of the national government, but a political creed that would unite American citizens. Hints of such a practice emerged in the North Carolina ratifying convention, whose proceedings began with readings of the Declaration of Independence, the state constitution, and the Articles of Confederation. On this model, the function of a constitution is to recall legislators to their duties and people to their rights.

From their discussions of militias, taxes, juries, and bills of rights, two Antifederalist strategies—dependence and resistance—emerge as mechanisms for protecting liberty from strong government. Both strategies have implications for constitutional design. Antifederalists believed not only that government should have no power that does not come immediately from the people, but also that the people should have ways of organizing their collective power outside the national government. In essence, the Antifederalists argued that the national government should be structured in such a way that the success of its initiatives would depend on its ability to mobilize ordinary citizens. At the same time, Antifederalists wanted to preserve and empower institutions that would enable the people to confront the national government. They opposed what would later be called the relative autonomy of the state. The community should loan, but never surrender, its power to the state. Thus Cincinnatus claimed that

> While the people have something to give, they will be respected by their rulers. When with Cappadocian baseness, they resign all at once, they will be deemed fit only to be hewers of wood and drawers of water.[95]

As long as force was a power that inhered in the community, it was a power that could not be used against the community.

In effect, the Antifederalists believed that the capacity for resistance must keep pace with the development of governmental power.[96] The Federalists, of course, could never agree to such an analysis, given that their first premise was that, to become a credible force on the international scene, the United States had to create a government that was indisputably in control of the nation. Ultimately, the Federalists carried the day, and, in their desire to create a government strong enough to command respect from the one they had just overthrown, Americans replaced one centralizing state with another.

So what do we learn from taking both the Federalist and the Antifederalist perspectives on constitution making more seriously? The Federalists, I think, challenge us to analyze the relationships between the national government and its citizens in terms of power as well as rights. If, as Linda Kerber has recently argued, there is a "disjunction between rights and obligations that characterizes the liberal state," then we should expect that any account of American citizenship that focuses solely on the questions of who is a citizen and what prerogatives citizenship confers misses important aspects of our constitutional experience.[97] The Antifederalists, on the other hand, may help radicalize our understandings of popular constitutionalism and clarify what is at stake, both politically and intellectually, in rejecting the court-centeredness that has characterized constitutional theory in both American law schools and political science departments.[98] Thus, the discussions between Federalists and Antifederalists over what it means to make a constitution represent an important reference point, not just for those who subscribe to an intentionalist jurisprudence, but for any scholar interested in addressing questions of citizenship and governmental power in the context of American constitutional practice.

Notes

1. That constitution making involves empowering governments is particularly apparent when we witness a constitution's creation, especially in cases that involve dramatic changes of regime. See, for example, Stephen Holmes's essay "Constitutionalism, Democracy, and State Decay," on constitution making in contemporary Eastern Europe and the former Soviet Union. In Harold Hongju Koh and Ronald C. Slye, eds., *Deliberative Democracy and Human Rights* (New Haven, CT: Yale University Press, 1999), pp. 116–35. John Lauritz Larson's recent work, *Internal Improvement: National Public Works and the Promise of Popular Government in the Early United States* (Chapel Hill: University of North Carolina Press, 2001), provides a powerful reminder that eighteenth-century Americans constructed a new national government because they wanted that government to be able to do things—even though they often disagreed about just what it should do.

2. I don't believe that the correct interpretation of the Constitution is the one that hews most closely to the ways in which those who drafted and/or ratified it understood its meaning at the time. I do, however, believe that one important way of understanding the Constitution is to study the historical context in which it was promulgated and, in particular, to pay attention both to what it replaced and to why it was controversial.

3. Speech of 29 June 1787, Max Farrand, ed. *The Records of the Federal Convention of 1787* (revised ed. in four volumes, New Haven, CT: Yale University Press, 1966; hereafter cited as Farrand), vol. I, 464.

4. Farrand I:136, 463 (Read of DE), I:177 (Brearly of NJ), I:178, 251 (Paterson of NJ). For other (usually critical) allusions to these proposals, see Farrand I:85, 133, 180, 199, 321, 446, 462. While working on the New Jersey plan, Paterson apparently drafted a resolution providing for the consolidation of the states, but this provision was not included in the plan he presented to the Convention. Farrand III:613.

5. Robert Yates and John Lansing, who *were* concerned with protecting the prerogatives of the state governments from the encroachments of national power, left the Convention at this point.

6. Speech of 29 June 1787, Farrand I:466.

7. Bernard Bailyn's *Ideological Origins of the American Revolution* (Cam-

bridge, MA: Harvard University Press, 1967) reconstructs this understanding through an analysis of revolutionary pamphlets. See, especially, ch. III's discussion of "Power and Liberty."

8. In *The Creation of the American Republic* (New York: W.W. Norton & Co., 1969), Gordon S. Wood offers a different account of this transformation. He treats the distance between Federalist thought and the political tenets of the Revolution as an indication of the extent to which American understandings of republicanism had evolved over the course of the Revolution. (See, especially, ch. XIII, "The Federalist Persuasion.") I think that Wood's explanation of Federalist thought is, at best, partial. In focusing on the republican character of the Revolution, he ignores the ways in which the post-colonial situation of the United States shaped constitutional thought. By contrast, I argue that the Federalists' understanding of constitution making was as much a response to what they saw as the imperatives of independence and of participation in a system of nation-states as it was a consolidation of lessons learned from the practical and theoretical shortcomings of the revolutionary state constitutions.

9. [Alexander Hamilton], Publius: *The Federalist* No. 24, *New York Independent Journal,* 19 December 1787, John P. Kaminski and Gaspare J. Saladino, *The Documentary History of the Ratification of the Constitution* (Madison, WI: The State Historical Society of Wisconsin, 1976– ; hereafter cited as *DHRC*), vol. XV, 41–42.

10. [James Iredell], Marcus V, *Norfolk and Portsmouth Journal,* 19 March 1788, *DHRC* XVI:429; One of the People, *Massachusetts Centinel,* 17 October 1787, *DHRC* XIII:395.

11. [Alexander Hamilton], Publius: *The Federalist* No. 25, *New York Packet,* 21 December 1787, *DHRC* XV:62; Extract of a letter from a gentleman . . . dated in England, 15 October 1787, *Connecticut Courant,* 11 February 1788, *DHRC* XVI:514.

12. Oliver Ellsworth, speech to the Connecticut ratifying convention, 4 January 1788, *DHRC* XV:247; Hugh Williamson, speech at Edenton, NC, *New York Daily Advertiser,* 26 February 1788, *DHRC* XV:206.

13. [Oliver Ellsworth], The Landholder X, *Connecticut Courant,* 3 March 1788, *DHRC* XVI:306; [James Iredell], Marcus III, *Norfolk and Portsmouth Journal,* 5 March 1788, *DHRC* XVI:325.

14. Hugh Williamson, speech at Edenton, NC, *New York Daily Advertiser,* 26 February 1788, *DHRC* XV:206.

15. Social Compact, *New Haven Gazette,* 4 October 1787, *DHRC* XIII:311.

16. *Virginia Herald,* 11 October 1787, *DHRC* XIII:372 (Congressional legislation and American ministers both held in "contempt," the former at home, the latter abroad); Social Compact, *New Haven Gazette,* 4 October 1787, *DHRC* XIII:310–11 ("totally destitute of rights," "indigent and begging").

17. *New York Daily Advertiser,* 24 September 1787, *DHRC* XIII:224 (adoption of the Constitution will "snatch us from impending ruin" and wipe away the "opprobrium" in which the country is currently held).

18. James Wilson, speech to the Pennsylvania ratifying convention, 24 November 1787, *DHRC* II:360.

19. [Oliver Ellsworth], A Landholder III, *Connecticut Courant*, 19 November 1787, *DHRC* XIV:139–40.

20. See, e.g., "Extract of a letter from a gentleman . . . dated in England, 15 October 1787," *Connecticut Courant*, 11 February 1788, *DHRC* XVI:514 ("The hopes of your enemies are not unreasonably grounded, on your follies—your disunion—your disaffection to government, and a reverse of system is your only security. . . . [Y]our present conduct is eagerly watched—your future security depends on unanimity and energy.")

21. [Oliver Ellsworth], A Landholder V, *Connecticut Courant*, 3 December 1787, *DHRC* XIV:338.

22. [Oliver Ellsworth], The Landholder VIII, *Connecticut Courant*, 24 December 1787, *DHRC* XV:78 (associating enemies of America with enemies of the Constitution, and Shays with the British); [James Madison], Publius: *The Federalist* No. 43, *New York Independent Journal*, 23 January 1788, *DHRC* XV:443 (claiming that "alien residents" and "adventurers" may swell the ranks of insurgents, providing them with a numerical advantage over loyal citizens); [Benjamin Rush?], Spurious Centinel XV, *Pennsylvania Mercury*, 16 February 1788, *DHRC* XVI:135 (associating Shaysites, Tories, and Antifederalists); J. Galba, *Philadelphia Independent Gazetteer*, 31 October 1787, *DHRC* XIII:319 (alleging that Antifederalist writers are "enemies and traitors to their country").

23. [Oliver Ellsworth], A Landholder III, *Connecticut Courant*, 19 November 1787, *DHRC* XIV:139.

24. [James Iredell], Marcus V, *Norfolk and Portsmouth Journal*, 19 March 1788, *DHRC* XVI:429 ("[I]f we continue as we now are, wrangling about every trifle, listening to the opinion of a small minority in preference to a large and most respectable majority of the first men in our country, and among them some of the first in the world; if our minds in short, are bent rather on indulging a captious discontent, than bestowing a generous and well-placed confidence in those who we have every reason to believe are entirely worthy of it, we shall too probably present a spectacle for malicious exultation to our enemies, and melancholy dejection to our friends; and the honor, glory and prosperity which were just within our reach, will, perhaps be snatched from us for ever").

25. See James Iredell, speech to the North Carolina ratifying convention, 26 July 1788, Jonathan Elliot, *The Debates of the Several State Conventions* (Philadelphia, PA: Lippincott, 1881; hereafter cited as Elliot), vol. IV, 97, and Marcus IV, *Norfolk and Portsmouth Journal*, 12 March 1788, *DHRC* XVI:384.

26. Alexander Hamilton, speech to the New York ratifying convention, 24 June 1788, Elliot II:301.

27. [James Iredell], Marcus III, *Norfolk and Portsmouth Journal*, 5 March 1788, *DHRC* XVI:325.

28. Samuel Stillman, speech to the Massachusetts ratifying convention, 6 February 1788, *DHRC* VI:1458.

29. [Noah Webster], America, *New York Daily Advertiser*, 31 December 1787, *DHRC* XV:196.

30. [Pelatiah Webster], A Citizen of Philadelphia: Remarks on the Address of the Sixteen Members, 18 October 1787, *DHRC* XIII:301.

31. Federalists also argued that the national government must be given the power to regulate commerce. I do not explore the commerce power in this article for two reasons. First, it did not enter into the Federalist theory of the necessary attributes of government. The commerce power raises the question of the national government's jurisdiction rather than its capacity for action; for this reason, the power to regulate commerce can be subsumed under the powers to legislate and to tax. Second, except for a few complaints that the constitution did not forbid the national government from granting monopolies, Antifederalists do not seem to have objected to the commerce power. Since I'm concentrating here on the differences between Federalist and Antifederalist visions of the national government, it makes sense to focus on areas of disagreement.

32. [Alexander Hamilton], Publius: *The Federalist* No. 15, *New York Independent Journal*, 1 December 1787, *DHRC* XIV:326.

33. Ibid., XIV:328.

34. Ibid., XIV:328.

35. Ibid., XIV:327.

36. Charles Pinckney, speech to the South Carolina legislature, 16 January 1788, Elliot IV:261.

37. Witmill Hill, speech to the North Carolina ratifying convention, 26 July 1788, Elliot IV:83–86.

38. [Alexander Hamilton], Publius: *The Federalist* No. 30, *DHRC* XV:164.

39. Governor Johnston, speech to the North Carolina ratifying convention, 26 July 1788, Elliot IV:78 ("[N]or can it be supposed that our credit will enable us to procure any loans, if our government is limited in the means of procuring money").

40. Not all Federalists took this extravagant a view of the necessary prerogatives of the national government, but the argument in favor of unlimited power was well circulated, both in the press and in the debates of the various state ratifying conventions. Brutus, The Federal Farmer, An Old Whig, and other Antifederalists further publicized this strain of Federalist thought as they warned their fellow citizens that tyranny would ensue if the constitution were adopted.

41. Alexander Hamilton, speech to the New York ratifying convention, 27 June 1788, Elliot II:351. See also [Alexander Hamilton], Publius: *The Federalist* No. 23, *New York Packet*, 18 December 1787, *DHRC* XV:4 (military power); [Alexander Hamilton], Publius: *The Federalist* No. 34, *New York Packet*, 4 January 1788, *DHRC* XV:259–60 (taxation); James Iredell, speech to the North Carolina ratifying convention, 26 July 1788, Elliot IV:95.

42. [Oliver Ellsworth], A Landholder III, *Connecticut Courant*, 19 November 1787, *DHRC* XIV:140. See also Thomas McKean, speech to the Pennsylvania ratifying convention, 28 November 1787, *DHRC* II:414–15; James Iredell, speech to the North Carolina ratifying convention, 26 July 1788, Elliot IV:95; [James Iredell], Marcus IV, *Norfolk and Portsmouth Journal*, 12 March 1788, *DHRC* XVI:385; [John Jay], A Citizen of New-York: An Address to the People of the State of New York, 15 April 1788, *DHRC* XVII:119; and Samuel Holden Parsons, letter to William Cushing, Middletown, CT, 11 January 1788, *DHRC* III:571.

43. Alexander Hamilton, speech to the New York ratifying convention, 27 June 1788, Elliot II:350. See also William Davie, speech to the North Carolina ratifying convention, 24 July 1788, Elliot IV:20–21; Samuel Huntington, speech to the Connecticut ratifying convention, 9 January 1788, *DHRC* III:556; [Roger Sherman], A Countryman II, *New Haven Gazette*, 22 November 1787, *DHRC* III:471–73.

44. There would, of course, be countervailing forces *within* the national government. But, as Brutus's analysis of the federal judiciary suggests, the common interest of all three branches in expanding the power of the national government can be expected to supersede differences of opinion about who will exercise that power once it has been acquired.

I have purposely avoided addressing the question of whether and how this account of what effective national government requires can be reconciled with federalism. At the end of the ratification debates, I think this remained a very real question and one that many observers believed would be resolved only over time and in practice.

45. Speech in the Virginia ratifying convention, 5 June 1788, *DHRC* IX:951–52.

46. Aristocrotis, The Government of Nature Delineated or An Exact Picture of the New Federal Constitution, Carlisle, [March or April] 1788, Storing III:208–9.

47. Richard Henry Lee, letter to James Gordon, Jr., Chantilly, VA, 26 February 1788, *DHRC* XVI:211.

48. Brutus VII, *New York Journal*, 3 January 1788, *DHRC* XV:236.

49. John Hancock, speech to the General Court, *Boston Independent Chronicle*, 28 February 1788, *DHRC* XVI:225.

50. William Findley, letter to William Irvine, Philadelphia, 23 March 1788, *DHRC* XVI:373.

51. [Alexander Hamilton], Publius: *The Federalist* No. 25, *New York Packet*, 21 December 1787, *DHRC* XV:60–62. See also [Alexander Hamilton], Publius: *The Federalist* No. 24, *New York Independent Journal*, 19 December 1787, *DHRC* XV:41–42; Thomas McKean, speech to the Pennsylvania ratifying convention, 28 November 1787, *DHRC* II:415.

52. Francis Corbin, speech to the Virginia ratifying convention, 7 June 1788, *DHRC* IX:1014–15. See also Edmund Randolph, letter to M. Smith, Charles M. Thurston, John H. Briggs, and Mann Page, dated 10 October 1787, Richmond, VA, published 27 December 1787, *DHRC* XV:124–25.

53. [Alexander Hamilton], Publius: *The Federalist* No. 25, *New York Packet*, 21 December 1787, *DHRC* XV:62.

54. James Wilson, speech to the Pennsylvania ratifying convention, 11 December 1787, *DHRC* II: 577–78. See also Timothy Pickering, letter to Charles Tillinghast, 24 December 1787, Philadelphia, *DHRC* XIV:202.

55. See Luther Martin, speech to the Maryland House of Delegates, 29 November 1787, *DHRC* XIV:290–91.

56. *Philadelphia Freeman's Journal*, 2 January 1788, *DHRC* XV:230.

57. For purposes of this argument, which focuses on alternative ideals of how military force should be organized, the question of whether the Antifederalist

account of militias represents myth or reality is largely irrelevant. But readers interested in that question should see Saul Cornell's article "Commonplace or Anachronism: The Standard Model, the Second Amendment, and the Problem of History in Contemporary Constitutional Theory," *Constitutional Commentary* 16 (1999): 221–46 (which calls for more scrutiny of the claim that militias were inclusive institutions) and Michael Bellesiles's *Arming America: The Origins of National Gun Culture* (New York: Alfred A. Knopf, 2000) (which questions how widespread gun ownership was in early America).

58. John Smilie, speech to the Pennsylvania ratifying convention, 6 December 1787, *DHRC* II:508–9.

59. William Findley, speech to the Pennsylvania ratifying convention, 6 December 1787, *DHRC* II:509. See also A Son of Liberty, *New York Journal*, 8 November 1787, *DHRC* XIII:482 ("The militia of New-Hampshire, or Massachusetts, dragged to Georgia or South-Carolina, to assist in quelling an insurrection of Negroes in those states; and those of Georgia, to another distant quarter, to subdue their fellow citizens, who dare to rise against the despotism of government").

60. [Samuel Bryan], Centinel III, *Philadelphia Independent Gazetteer*, 8 November 1787, *DHRC* XIV:60.

61. Federal Farmer: Letters to the Republican III, 8 November 1787, *DHRC* XIV:39. See also Dissent of the Minority of the Pennsylvania Convention, 18 December 1787, *Pennsylvania Packet*, *DHRC* II:638, and John Smilie, speech to the Pennsylvania ratifying convention, 6 December 1787, *DHRC* II:508–9.

62. Brutus V, *New York Journal*, 13 December 1787, *DHRC* XIV:427.

63. Brutus VI, *New York Journal*, 27 December 1787, *DHRC* XV:113–14. See also A Democratic Federalist, *Pennsylvania Herald*, 17 October 1787, *DHRC* XIII:390; A Son of Liberty, *New York Journal*, 8 November 1787, *DHRC* XIII:481; Luther Martin, Genuine Information VI, *Baltimore Maryland Gazette*, 15 January 1788, *DHRC* XV:377.

64. George Mason, speech to the Virginia ratifying convention, 4 June 1788, *DHRC* IX:937.

65. Alexander Hamilton, speech to the New York ratifying convention, 21 June 1788, Elliot II:255.

66. William Davie, speech to the North Carolina ratifying convention, 25 July 1788, Elliot IV:21–22.

67. For my analysis of this episode, see Hemberger, "A Government Based on Representations," *Studies in American Political Development* (Fall 1996): 289–332.

68. See, e.g., Brutus I, *New York Journal*, 18 October 1787, *DHRC* XIII: 419–20.

69. Localism and ordinary citizens were also associated in Federalist rhetoric. The local was recast as the parochial, just as the common people were portrayed as incapable of seeing beyond their own petty grievances. By contrast, members of the national government and the rich were characterized as groups whose outlook was sufficiently broad to encompass all interests. This juxtaposition of place and class is nicely captured in Jackson Turner Main's description of "cosmopolitans"—that is, of those merchants whose interests crossed state boundaries—

whom he contends were the principal supporters of the Federalist constitution. See *The Antifederalists: Critics of the Constitution, 1781–88* (Chicago: Quadrangle Books, 1961). Main's analysis enables us to reread what the Federalists portray as an enlightened sensibility—characterized by "impartiality," and "enlarged sympathies" as the worldview of a discrete group of men who traveled in circles that didn't correspond with existing political boundaries. Seen in this light, impartiality represents not neutrality or objectivity, but indifference to (even disdain for) the claims of local communities. Local attachments, on this model, are portrayed as obstacles to, rather than the building blocks of, national government.

70. Federal Farmer: Letters to the Republican IV, 8 November 1787, *DHRC* XIV:46–47.

71. [George Bryan, James Hutchinson, John Smilie?], An Old Whig VIII, *Philadelphia Independent Gazette*, 6 February 1788, XVI:55.

72. Abraham Holmes, speech to the Massachusetts ratifying convention, 30 January 1788, *DHRC* VI:1366.

73. Joseph M'Dowall, speech to the North Carolina ratifying convention, 28 July 1788, Elliot IV:150.

74. Christopher Gore, speech to the Massachusetts ratifying convention, 30 January 1788, *DHRC* VI:1369.

75. Governor Johnston, speech to the North Carolina ratifying convention, 28 July 1788, Elliot IV:150.

76. Though he argued in favor of professionalism in military affairs, James Wilson sided with the Antifederalists on the question of juries:

Where jurors can be acquainted with the characters of the parties, and the witnesses, where the whole cause can be brought within their knowledge and their view, I know no mode of investigation equal to that by a jury; they hear everything that is alleged; they not only hear the words, but they see and mark the features of the countenance; they can judge of [the] weight due to such testimony; and moreover, it is a cheap and expeditious manner of distributing justice. There is another advantage annexed to the trial by jury; the jurors may indeed return a mistaken, or ill-founded verdict, but their errors cannot be systematical.

DHRC II:573.

77. Fisher Ames, speech to the Massachusetts ratifying convention, 15 January 1788, *DHRC* VI:1192.

78. General Heath, speech to the Massachusetts ratifying convention, 15 January 1788, *DHRC* VI:1194. For a similar exchange in the Virginia convention, see George Nicholas's defense of the two-year term and George Mason's response, speeches to the Virginia ratifying convention, 4 June 1788, *DHRC* IX:924, 937.

79. Gilbert Livingston, speech to the New York ratifying convention, 24 June 1788, Elliot II:287–88.

80. John Smilie, speech to the Pennsylvania ratifying convention, 28 November 1787, *DHRC* II:392.

81. Robert Whitehill, speech to the Pennsylvania ratifying convention, 28 November 1787, *DHRC* II:393.

82. Thomas Jefferson, letter to James Madison, 15 March 1789, in *The Portable Thomas Jefferson* (New York: Penguin, 1975), p. 439.

83. John Smilie, speech to the Pennsylvania ratifying convention, 28 November 1787, *DHRC* II:392.

84. The idea that citizens have a role to play in constitutional interpretation and enforcement is a recurrent theme in African-American political discourse. See, for example, Frederick Douglass, "July Fourth and the Negro" and "The Dred Scott Decision," in Foner, ed., *The Life and Writings of Frederick Douglass* (New York: International Publishers, 1950), II:181–204, 407–24, esp. 202, 424; Martin Luther King, Jr., "An Address before the National Press Club," *Testament of Hope* (San Francisco: HarperCollins, 1986), pp. 99–105; Bayard Rustin, "We Challenged Jim Crow," *Down the Line* (Chicago: Quadrangle Books, 1971), pp. 113–25.

85. See A True Friend, Richmond, 6 December 1787, *DHRC* XIV:376–77.

86. Samuel Spencer, speech to the North Carolina ratifying convention, 29 July 1788, Elliot IV:168.

87. Joseph M'Dowall, speech to the North Carolina ratifying convention, 29 July 1788, Elliot IV:189.

88. See, for example, James Wilson, speech to the Pennsylvania ratifying convention, 7 December 1787, *DHRC* II:516 (jury trials); James Iredell, speech to the North Carolina ratifying convention, 28 July 1788, Elliot IV:144–45 (jury trials); [James Madison], Publius: *The Federalist* No. 52, *New York Packet*, 8 February 1788, *DHRC* XVI:84 (electoral qualifications).

89. Brutus I, *New York Journal*, 18 October 1787, *DHRC* XIII:417. See also [George Clinton?], Cato III, *New York Journal*, 25 October 1787, *DHRC* XIII:474.

90. [George Bryan, James Hutchinson, John Smilie?], An Old Whig VII, *Philadelphia Independent Gazetteer*, 28 November 1787, *DHRC* XIV:250.

91. Federal Farmer: Letters to the Republican II, 8 November 1787, *DHRC* XIV:27. See also Timothy Bloodworth, speech to the North Carolina ratifying convention, 28 July 1788, Elliot IV:151 ("[I]f the genius of the people of the United States is so dissimilar that our liberties cannot be secured, we can never hang long together").

92. Publius: *The Federalist* No. 84, New York, 28 May 1788, *DHRC* XVIII:130.

93. A True Friend, Richmond, 6 December 1787, *DHRC* XIV:376–77.

94. A Federal Republican, A Review of the Constitution, 28 November 1787, *DHRC* XIV:274–75.

95. Cincinnatus III, *New York Journal*, 15 November 1787, *DHRC* XIV:125.

96. "My great objection to this Government," said Patrick Henry, "is, that it does not leave us the means of defending our rights; or, of waging war against tyrants." Speech in the Virginia ratifying convention, 5 June 1788, *DHRC* IX:954.

97. See Linda K. Kerber, "H-LAW Comment: Kerber Responds to Thomas, Smith, and Gordon," 14 July 1999, archived at http://www.h-net.msu.edu/logs/showlog.cgi?list=h-law&file=h-law.log9907b/41&ent=0. Kerber's *No Constitutional Right to Be Ladies: Women and the Obligations of Citizenship* (New York: Hill and Wang, 1998) represents an important first step in producing this more complicated account of American citizenship.

98. This project, too, is already underway. See Wayne D. Moore, *Constitutional Rights and Powers of the People* (Princeton, NJ: Princeton University Press, 1996); John J. Dinan, *Keeping the People's Liberties: Legislators, Citizens, and Judges as Guardians of Rights* (Lawrence: University Press of Kansas, 1998); Daniel Lessard Levin, *Representing Popular Sovereignty: The Constitution in American Political Culture* (Albany: State University of New York Press, 1999); Mark Tushnet, *Taking the Constitution Away from the Courts* (Princeton, NJ: Princeton University Press, 1999).

7

Notes on Constitutional Maintenance

SOTIRIOS A. BARBER

IF OUR BEST understanding of the American Constitution (the document) should hold that it charters a government to pursue goods like national security and the general welfare,[1] and if the field of constitutional studies were impressed by that fact, constitutional theorists would face an agenda far beyond the court-centered concerns (doctrinal and behavioral) of mainstream constitutional commentary. Constitutional theorists would have to renew the old attempt to reconcile an instrumental constitution to the requirement of fidelity to established law. On affirming applicable philosophic assumptions, or neutralizing their contraries, theorists would have to debate different conceptions of substantive constitutional ends, like the general welfare.

Needed also would be theories of constitution making, constitutional maintenance, and deliberate constitutional change (via amendment, revolution, or other means). Theorists would have to decide what distinguishes these types of action and how they are related to each other and to other forms of political action. Theorists would have to reconceive the category "constitutional limitations" to include not only exemptions from state power (rights), but also the conditions, formal and substantive, in which it would be rational to reaffirm the Constitution's authority. Theories of this last kind would converge on theories of constitutional maintenance and include theories of constitutional emergencies (when constitutional means are inadequate to any defensible conception of constitutional ends?) and the principles (constitutionalist if not constitutional) for addressing them.

Nonlitigational and systemic issues of this sort have preoccupied American constitutional thought on a number of occasions, like the founding, nullification, progressive, and early New Deal periods. Though no generation has seen the absence of these concerns, the postwar constitutional consensus shifted most of legal academe to a court-centeredness that took the Constitution's authority and goodness more or less for granted and concentrated either on what the Court had to say and should say about constitutional meaning (academic law) or on the extralegal determinants of judicial behavior and decision (political science). The postwar consensus didn't last long, however, and as it crumbled in the 1960s and '70s, groups of constitutional theorists began to revisit larger questions, like the nature of constitutional interpretation and the scope of judicial power in a democracy, though not without a continuing court-centeredness.

Among American political scientists, three groups of scholars moved to another perspective. Loosely organized and with partially overlapping memberships, they are associated chiefly with Herbert Storing, late of the University of Chicago, Stephen Elkin and Karol Soltan of the University of Maryland, and Princeton's Walter Murphy. Elkin and Soltan speak for all when they describe their ambition as theory from "a designer's point of view" in a constitution-making tradition that stretches from the Greeks to Madison and beyond.[2] Murphy and some of his colleagues express the same ambition in terms of the categories of "constitutional politics." I submit here some reflections on one of these categories, "constitutional maintenance."

1.

When Aristotle advises democrats and oligarchs to moderate their demands against each other, he does so partly because he believes it difficult to maintain pure constitutions of either sort. He suggests that a maintainable constitution is one that pursues moderate or compromised ends (Politics, 1302a). When Aristotle proposes a specific division of power between oligarchs and democrats, he assumes each wants to be honored for its distinctive contributions and virtues, especially its wisdom, and he has the democrats moderating their political ambitions to fit a role in which their claim to wisdom has some plausibility to all parties. He assumes democrats possessing a modicum of virtue can come to accept a constitution in which they control only the assembly and its several functions (1281a–1282b).

Aristotle's most maintainable constitution (1302a) thus pursues compromised oligarchic and democratic ends (liberty, equality, private wealth) blended by a formula that reflects an aristocratic end (virtue, especially wisdom), without admitting aristocrats to power. Harry Jaffa describes this strategy as one that "compound[s] the simulacra of virtue in the nonvirtuous, as a device rendered necessary by the withdrawal of the virtuous from active contention."[3] Publius might describe Aristotle's strategy as he describes his own: arranging matters in ways that "supply the defect of better motives," motives strong enough to decide matters only during revolutionary times (Federalist 49, 51).

2.

Publius's scheme for maintaining the Constitution is neither clear nor simple. He says in *Federalist* No. 51 that the nation can maintain the constitutional separation of powers by relying not on "better motives" but on countervailing ambitions in a system of "balances and checks." This system itself relies largely on representative institutions that work best in a pluralist and commercial society whose many groups will readily enter into shifting political coalitions. Accepting these parts of Publius's theory, modern commentators of the left and the right (mostly the right) oppose a strong judicial role in constitutional maintenance.

Yet *Federalist* No. 49 prefigures *Federalist* No. 78 by suggesting that constitutional disagreements should be decided by judges who are "too far removed from the people to share much in their prepossessions," to the end that "*the reason,*" not the "passions . . . of the public, would sit in judgment" of conflicting constitutional claims. Not that Publius regards all "passion" as dysfunctional. When, in No. 49, he cautions against submitting constitutional conflicts to the public, he does so to prevent weakening the public's "reverence for the laws" and depriving institutions of the support they derive from the favorable "prejudices" and "veneration" which attach to old and relatively undisturbed institutions. A role for the judiciary, and therewith "reason," in constitutional maintenance is evidently one of the ways to build the public's veneration for the Constitution. One reason for trying to institutionalize a role for reason when relying on prejudice is that prejudice presupposes truth. Prejudice is a predisposition to believe without weighing the available evidence that some belief is true or that some person or other thing is truly good or right or successful.

Another sign that Publius can't want everyone to venerate what was after all originally no more than an instrumental proposal is his praise for an experimental spirit in America that respects "the opinions of former times" without permitting "a blind veneration" for antiquity and custom "to overrule" the people's "own good sense, the knowledge of their own situation, and the lessons of their own experience" (No. 14). Blind veneration of the Constitution would hardly nourish the virtues of intellect and spirit needed when timely change is necessary to avert disaster. Nor would blind veneration foster even informed preservation of the Constitution, for veneration precludes a willingness to criticize that is integral to rational reaffirmations of the Constitution.[4]

All of this suggests that the judiciary should play a role in constitutional maintenance greater than that of mere auxiliary to the representative institutions of a pluralist culture, which of course also have a role.

3.

Viewing his project as a stage of the revolution (No. 49), Publius acts the part by explicitly treating all governmental institutions as answerable to instrumental concerns, notwithstanding preambulatory solemnities about "perpetual Union" and the like. On the other hand, Publius claims (No. 40) that the Philadelphia Convention was on balance faithful to Congress's charge to revise the Articles of Confederation to make them adequate to the exigencies of government and the preservation of the Union. In response to critics, he suggests that when the relationship between a legal instrument and its end unravels beyond interpretive repair, the law is incoherent and therefore can't function as law; fidelity to a law in such cases would be fidelity to the end it envisions. Accordingly, fidelity to Congress demands a new national government because the old confederation can't do what Congress wants government to do.

Federalist No. 40 thus indicates that sometimes the distinction between making and maintaining a constitution isn't clear. Nor is it clear that preserving institutions no longer "adequate to the exigencies" should count as constitutional maintenance. But if the exigencies are ultimately beyond control (if history doesn't really end, if people remain attracted to a reality beyond moral and scientific conventions), constitutional maintenance must be more than a matter of institutional maintenance.

4.

What then can constitutional maintenance be?

Lincoln's answer (Address of January 27, 1838) is inculcating popular reverence for law. But this answer needs amendment in view of Lincoln's own example of irreverence for unjust and ineffective laws. Inculcating lawfulness, perhaps. Lawfulness, let us say, as a virtue that exhibits commitments to principles of equality and government by consent, reason-giving, and public and private restraint when no plausible reason can be given. If so, an important policy for maintaining the Constitution would be providing everyone with opportunities for a liberalizing education. On a hypothesis of need for positive provision of any sort, the elected branches and therewith the electorate become key institutions. Taxpayers and their representatives must somehow come to appreciate either genuine lawfulness or its probable rewards, either Lockean or Socratic.[5] If lawfulness is as I have sketched it, modern legislatures must concern themselves with more than systems of formal education. Taking seriously the practices of questing for, exchanging, and acting on what all responsible elements of society can recognize as reasons means fighting the attitudes and socioeconomic conditions in conflict with this broad commitment. At this time in our history, this means government committed more to the values of the American Left (*sans* an illusory neutrality and an untenable skepticism about the good[6]) than the American Right. Racism, sexism, zealotry, greed, and economic disfranchisement either deny or corrode the aspiration to act on what all can recognize as reasons.

5.

Even if sound, these reflections could bring constitutional theorists and their allies only to the threshold of daunting questions of philosophic principle and public policy, like how best to conceive and promote the general welfare. We would have been prepared for these inquiries by the knowledge that constitutional maintenance has less to do with formal institutions than with the attitudes, skills, and material conditions for reaffirming the Constitution as an effective means to the good society.

Object that reaffirming the Constitution is a question of policy and that constitutional studies should study the Constitution as law—revert, in other words, to a view that takes the Constitution's authority and goodness for granted—and I'll recall *Federalist* No. 40 and point out that the conditions for reaffirming the Constitution are the same as those for recognizing the Constitution as the law it claims to be.

Notes

1. For a defense of this assumption see Sotirios A. Barber, *On What the Constitution Means* (Baltimore: Johns Hopkins Press, 1984) pp. 40–61.

2. Stephen L. Elkin and Karol Edward Soltan, *A New Constitutionalism: Designing Political Institutions for a Good Society* (Chicago: The University of Chicago Press, 1993), pp. vii, 1.

3. Harry V. Jaffa, "Aristotle," in Leo Strauss and Joseph Cropsey, eds., *The History of Political Philosophy* (Chicago: University of Chicago Press, 2nd edition, 1973), pp. 106–7.

4. Barber, *On What the Constitution Means*, pp. 59–62, 118–20.

5. See Thomas L. Pangle, *The Spirit of Modern Republicanism* (Chicago: The University of Chicago Press, 1988) ch. 21; see also Sotirios A. Barber, *The Constitution of Judicial Power* (Baltimore: Johns Hopkins University Press, 1993), pp. 187–97, 215–18.

6. See generally George Sher, *Beyond Neutrality: Perfectionism and Politics* (Cambridge: Cambridge University Press, 1997), esp. chs. 5, 6.

8

Transformative Constitutionalism and the Case of Religion: Defending the Moderate Hegemony of Liberalism

STEPHEN MACEDO

Liberalism and Normative Diversity

What is the relation between a liberal constitutional order, understood as a normative structure, and the other normative structures that exist within a polity? What is the aim of a liberal constitution—such as the United States'—with respect to normative diversity, especially religious diversity?[1]

I begin by sketching a simple and straightforward view of liberalism's aims with respect to normative diversity. This simple picture sees the role of a liberal legal system as that of providing an ordering framework to allow individuals to pursue their freely chosen—and extra-politically defined—purposes. This simple picture might be thought of as the classical liberal conception of the rule of law.

Familiar as it is, the simple and straightforward conception of the normative aims of a liberal constitutional order's purposes is radically deficient.[2] A far more adequate view is provided by Walter F. Murphy, who insists that

> the goal of a constitutional text must . . . be not simply to structure a government, but to construct a political system, one that can guide the formation of a larger constitution, a "way of life" that is conducive to constitutional democracy. If constitutional democracy is to flourish, its ideals must reach beyond formal governmental arrangements and help configure, though not necessarily in the same way or to the same extent, most aspects of its people's lives.[3]

My aim here will be to emphasize just how much is missed by the simplistic "rule of law" conception of the normative aims of a liberal legal system. It wholly misses the radically transformative dimension of liberal constitutionalism, and is liable to obscure the extent to which a liberal constitutional order is a pervasively educative order. It contributes to the misconception that liberalism is based on a pre-social conception of persons, with interests that somehow preexist the constitutive effects of social practices and political institutions. I will explore the shortcomings of the simple view by looking at the tension between civic education and religion in America. I will defend an alternative view of liberal democratic constitutionalism that is much more thoroughgoing and radical in its transformative ambitions with respect to normative diversity.

The Simple View

> Law as hedges "set, not to stop Travellers, but
> to keep them in the way."
> —Hobbes, *Leviathan*, ch. 30[4]

The simple picture of liberal legalism is familiar enough. It is the view that law, properly understood, is a system of impartial rules that serves as a framework within which individuals and groups may pursue their own divergent and independently defined conceptions of what constitutes the good life. The law furnishes a set of "baselines" for individual conduct, as Lon Fuller put it, but otherwise should be "non-instrumental" or "purposeless," in the sense that it does not seek to impose purposes or ends on free citizens.[5] Hobbes prefigured such a view, and so too did Locke ("that ill deserves the Name of Confinement which hedges us in only from Bogs and Precipices"[6]).

Of course, government is necessary to enforce the law and regulate freedom. It will be very important, on this view, to ensure that political power is limited to the right sorts of objects (to our "civil interests," as Locke put it), and is justified on the basis of reasons that we can share (as the social contract tradition hopes). So a vital task of constitutional law is to strike reasonable balances between private freedom and public power: to draw lines demarcating the proper spheres of conscience and religious association on the one side, and political authority on the other.

At a certain level, these images are useful: law does help secure ordered liberty, and it does help let individuals and groups know how they may go about pursuing their purposes under the law's protection. Thinking of the role of law in these terms alone, however, misses much of what is really interesting and important. Indeed, taking this view of law as the centerpiece of one's political philosophy—as some classical liberals and libertarians are apt to do—covers over some of the deepest ambitions of a liberal constitutional order. I want to emphasize, therefore, just how inadequate, even potentially misleading, is this simple picture of the social functions of law.

Liberal constitutional institutions have a more deeply constitutive role, which is to work at shaping or constituting all forms of diversity over the course of time, so that people are *satisfied* leading lives of bounded individual freedom. Successful constitutional institutions must do more than help order the freedom of individuals prefabricated for life in a liberal political order: they must shape the way that people use their freedom, and shape *people* to help ensure that freedom is what they want. If a constitutional regime is to succeed and thrive, it must constitute the private realm in its image, and it must form citizens willing to observe its limits and able to pursue its aspirations.

The simple picture of law's purposes misses the transformative dimension of liberalism. There is no reason to think that liberal citizens come about naturally, though some people seem to think otherwise. Let us consider an example of how the formation of citizens is taken for granted. By taking this discussion from recent discussions of public school reform I do not mean to suggest that the most direct educative mechanisms of civic education are the ones of most interest or importance. Indeed, I shall argue that the contrary may be true. The point of the discussion that follows is to suggest how easy it is to overlook the radically educative dimension of liberalism, even when discussing public education policy.

Taking Constitutional Citizens for Granted

Stephen Arons decries the intellectual homogenization that public schools, on his account, often attempt to impose on families and local communities who disagree about their religious and moral convictions. Arons describes harrowing incidents of censorship and community conflict provoked by struggles to control public school curricula, libraries, and ideology. He argues that because public schools are educational institutions that, by political fiat, must serve families with radically different values and ideals, they inevitably furnish many occasions for deep and irresolvable normative conflicts. We should get rid of these conflicts by eliminating public schools as we know them, says Arons, putting in their places a much more diverse range of publicly supported educational institutions.[7]

Arons insists that the First Amendment should be understood to protect not only the expression of beliefs and opinions but their formation.[8] Arons would eliminate public control over schools (beyond banning racial discrimination) and provide public support to poorer families, so that all will be equally free to determine their own beliefs and pass these along to their children by choosing among competing schools.[9] We could, thus, both avoid passionate conflicts and respect "individual political sovereignty."[10]

I want to note only one thing about this libertarian stance, which is its cramped view of the proper educative ambitions in a liberal democracy.[11] Arons is so opposed to the notion of government-imposed orthodoxy that he ignores all other causes of concern. Most obviously, religious communities may be deeply illiberal and anti-individualistic, so simply curbing government control will not necessarily promote freedom—at least the freedom of the children involved.

Arons also ignores the potential conflicts between particular normative communities—religious and otherwise—and the liberal community as a whole: the great society of many communities. He expresses solicitude about the "search for community" among Protestant Fundamentalists, and speaks of their desire to create a moral "cohesiveness or sense of shared belief" through Christian schooling.[12] But the children of Fundamentalists are also future citizens, so we also need to give some thought to the cohesiveness of our *political* community. Whether we merely tolerate religious schooling or join Arons in seeking to subsidize it, some account needs to be provided of how future citizens acquire the character traits, habits, and virtues they must have if the liberal political project is to survive and thrive.

Arons simply assumes that if only public schools can be gotten rid of—if only the proper lines can be drawn between private freedom and public power—then people will disagree peacefully. He provides no account of where this good temper comes from. He takes for granted a mutually respectful desire to live in peace with those one believes to be damned. This desire is, however, a political achievement and not an assumption to be taken for granted. We need to avoid the mistake of assuming that liberal citizens—self-restrained, moderate, and reasonable—spring full-blown from the soil of private freedom.

It is one thing to disagree with particular means to the end of a shared citizenship, it is quite another to neglect the importance of that basic end. Arons may or may not be right to suggest the need for fundamental revision of public school policy, but no adequate judgment can be made on this score until we take account of the need to constitute citizens.

Arons at least has the sense to look at the religious and political conflicts that surround school policy. Other proponents of reform, such as John E. Chubb and Terry M. Moe, write as though the only thing we should want out of schools is what people call academic achievement: high test scores, low dropout rates, and so on.[13] In a way, of course, the very fact that these indices of success are taken for granted is enormously revealing. Taking for granted that worldly achievement is the overriding educational goal of parents and local communities may implicitly attest to the *success* of civic education in America. Not mentioning the most basic civic *ends* might imply that these are, after all, really quite unproblematic, so that all we need to think about are the best *means*.

Still, one would like to know how this successful convergence on ends was brought about, and what must be done to preserve it. Did public schools as an institution have a role bringing about Arons's assumed peaceful coexistence, or the emphasis on success that Chubb and Moe assume? What is the libertarian plan for keeping America's families happily occupied with these sober and regime-supporting interests?

Of course, as Arons's account indicates, any analysis of our political interests in the education of future generations that takes no account of passionate conflict is part fantasy. Those who think that Americans care only about academic achievement are far too complacent: the work of constituting diversity is far from complete.[14]

Both the simple picture of law as hedges and the more general neglect of the need to shape and create liberal citizens might be taken to be part and parcel of the intellectual poverty of the liberal political tradition. This seems to me wrong. There are ample resources in the liberal tradition, but one must be prepared to look for them. The fault is not in the tradition so much as in the simplicity of much contemporary political thinking.

Transformative Liberalism: The Direct Approach

Public schooling may not be the preferred way to exert political influence over the formation of liberal citizens. Constitutionalists may well prefer more indirect and subtle means for realizing their educative ends. But a brief discussion of certain conflicts around public schooling helps make vivid both what needs to be done and the deep partisanship of the task.

The ideal of the common school in America, which was articulated and began to be widely disseminated in the second quarter of the nineteenth century, entailed concentrating public moneys in publicly controlled educational institutions designed to educate under one roof all the children in a certain geographical area. In some places, the new common schools supplanted systems of public subsidy not entirely unlike the voucher systems proposed in recent years: prior to the emergence of common schools in New York City and elsewhere, public subsidies were channeled to a diverse array of charity schools, private academies, and religious schools. The new institutional pattern of common schooling was a very direct way of exercising greater political leverage over the intellectual development and moral character of future citizens.[15]

The agenda of the common school was to forge an identity capable of unifying a diverse polity. Free public schools for all would, it was hoped, include children from all social, religious, and ethnic backgrounds, in an institution that represented and would help promote their capacities as future citizens. And so the trustees of the New York City Public (formerly "Free") School Society urged in 1828 that common schools "should be supported from the public revenue, should be public property, and should be open to all, not as charity, but as a matter of common right."[16]

The schools sought to accomplish their civic task by reinforcing those basic beliefs and commitments that, it was believed, could and should come to be shared by all citizens. Among these shared commitments were certain religious beliefs and practices, and so one important aim of the common schools was to reshape or supplant more particular cultural and religious identities. Horace Mann and many other school reformers advocated staying to the middle, stressing the beliefs shared by all—or at least *most* citizens—and avoiding "sectarianism" (or the beliefs and practices that distinguished one religious sect from another).[17] The problem was that what Mann saw as an effort to enlighten and elevate democracy others saw as public partisanship on behalf of a wishy-washy version of Protestantism.

Religious exercises in public schools were not declared unconstitutional until the 1960s, and in nineteenth-century America virtually no one supported excluding religion altogether from the common schools.[18] Religion was understood to be the foundation of morality. The common school religion tended to consist of the tenets common to a wide range of Protestants. (Bible reading without commentary was the primary method of moral instruction.) A central tenet of the common school religion was that charity toward others should take precedence over different and more particular claims to religious truth. Horace Mann furnished a creed for the public school religion in 1843, in an anonymous article in his *Common School Journal*, entitled, "What Shall Be My Sabbath Reading?":

> Is there not a danger of my becoming proud even of my religious opinions? . . . I must, therefore, not read anything that diminishes my charity for my fellow-creatures,—for their character, their purposes, or their opinions. Whatever is written in an uncharitable spirit, no matter what name it has, I will endeavor to avoid . . . [no less if it is] under the cloak of a sermon or a religious tract. . . . Whatever renders me uncharitable must be wanting in that Christian spirit.[19]

The common school creed held that concern with particular truths—truths that divide rather than unite different religions—is positively unchristian.[20] Religion properly understood is ecumenical: charity toward others should take precedence over different and more particular claims to religious truth. The aim was civic: to undergird public morality and promote cross-sect cooperation.

The public schools were, then, thought to be an appropriate public instrument for promoting the reasonableness and cooperation that a healthy liberal political order depends upon. Concentrating public funds in schools with a relatively ecumenical, "nonsectarian" religious content was bound to have the result of favoring tolerant and ecumenical beliefs and practices, and thereby, of reforming religion to suit the political project of liberal democracy. Even if the religious content of the public school curriculum was low—and even if it had been *nonexistent*—its mission with respect to religion and other "private" normative systems was crucial: that mission was the creation of liberalized, ecumenical, tolerant, and "charitable" forms of religious and ethical belief.

Now all this will sound to many like the height of illiberality. If liberalism stands for anything, after all, it is the separation of church and state: the conviction that politics should respect religious freedom. This is, of course, true (and I certainly do not mean to defend every aspect of the nineteenth-century public school agenda), but it is neither the whole truth nor the most interesting part of the truth. The fact is that many "private" communities in mid-nineteenth-century America—including some religious ones—needed to be transformed in light of liberal democratic principles.

Even if the public schools had left religious instruction to parents and private communities, religious objections would not have been avoided. The very idea of a formal education lacking in religious content would itself have been seen as depreciating the importance of religion. Indeed, so it was seen by Catholic bishop John Hughes of New York City, who in 1840 objected to an education that excluded religion:

> To make an infidel, what is it necessary to do? Cage him up in a room, give him a secular education from the age of five years to twenty-one, and I ask you what will he come out, if not an infidel? . . . They say that their instruction is not sectarianism; but it is; and of what kind? The sectarianism of infidelity in its every feature.[21]

The question of religious partisanship does not, therefore, turn solely on the explicit religious content of the curriculum. There is also what is nowadays called a "hidden" or "silent" curriculum (though these terms are misnomers here, for the issue of religious partisanship has been a source of intense controversy from the beginning). Public schools that (as Mann advised) promoted only those religious beliefs common to all and necessary to support public morality were charged with fostering watered-down religiosity. Public schools lacking in religious instruction will be interpreted by many as downplaying the importance of religion in people's lives (as per Hughes's sect of infidelity). Schools that present all religious beliefs in an even-handed way have been charged with treating religion as a mere choice, like styles of dress, thus implicitly denying the truth of any particular religious view.[22]

The transformative ambitions of the early American common schools with respect to religious diversity was fairly straightforward. The question is: To what extent did Mann and the common school idea go beyond the proper aims of a liberal constitutional order? Perhaps not as far as it may at first appear. To consider this question, let us recall the argument of a founding document of the liberal tradition: Locke's *Letter on Toleration*.

The most memorable part of Locke's important argument is his strident insistence on the separation of religion and politics. This insistence recalls the simple view of liberal law, discussed above. Politics is not about religious ends, only certain defined "civil interests": the rule of law, the preservation of the peace, and the protection of the "just possession of the things of this life."[23] And that's it. The whole political jurisdiction is contained in these civil interests, which are not our highest goods, but the most basic: things of the body, not the soul. Civil magistrates have no expertise in matters of religion, no authority in its realm. Political and religious authority are entirely different and so, Locke said, the church is

> absolutely separate and distinct from the Commonwealth. The boundaries on both sides are fixed and immovable. He jumbles heaven and earth together, the things most remote and opposite, who mixes these two societies; which are in their original end, business, and every thing, perfectly distinct and infinitely different from each other.[24]

This is conclusive language: a hard liberal line for the separation of church and state. If liberalism stands for anything, one is tempted to say, it stands for this Lockeian separation of the spheres. And if these claims do indeed ring true, then surely the transformative ambitions of the American common school are beyond the just powers of the liberal state.

But this is far from all that Locke says on the relations between religion and politics. He also makes the equally important if less noted point that the sustainability of a liberal political order depends upon the religious beliefs that citizens form and act upon. This is most dramatically apparent in his insistence that Catholics and atheists could not be good citizens, but that is not the end of it.[25]

Locke recognized that a political order in which church and state occupied separate spheres was itself a constructive achievement, requiring the reform of political authority *and* religious belief and practice. Liberal politics cannot in fact leave religion to one side: it cannot altogether leave the soul alone and care only for the body, for the soul and religion need to be shaped in accordance with political imperatives. This is clear right from the start of the *Letter*, for Locke does not begin with an account of rights or an appeal to political values; he begins rather with an account of our religious duties: of what is *right* as a religious matter.

The very first sentence of the *Letter* insists that toleration is "the chief characteristical mark of the true church." So toleration (the basic liberal virtue) is in the first instance defended *as a religious mandate*. And thus Locke can appeal soon thereafter to the conscience of those that persecute.[26] Strikingly, the principle theme of much of the *Letter* is that Christ and the Gospels command toleration. All this signals the dependence of Locke's liberalism on the prevalence of religious sensibilities that support toleration: liberalism needs the support of private beliefs and practices that are at least congruent with liberal politics. Liberalism depends on a certain ordering of the soul.

The boundaries between politics and religion are therefore not as sharp and "immovable" as Locke sometimes asserts. Consider how Locke himself describes the duties of Christian preachers:

> It is not enough that Ecclesiastical men abstain from Violence and Rapine, and all manner of Persecution. He that pretends to be a Successor of the Apostles, and takes upon him the Office of Teaching, is obliged also to admonish his Hearers of the Duties of Peace, and Good-will toward all men; as well as toward the Erroneous as the Orthodox; towards those that differ from them in Faith and Worship, as well as towards those that agree with them therein: And he ought industriously to exhort all men, whether private Persons or Magistrates, (if any such there be in his church) to Charity, Meekness, and Toleration; and diligently endeavor to allay and temper all that Heat, and unreasonable averseness of mind, which either any man's fiery Zeal for his own Sect, or the Craft of others, has kindled against Dissenters.[27]

Note that Locke's account of our religious duties is virtually identical to the creed that Mann prescribes for the common schools. Whereas Locke is exhorting private preachers to teach the Christianity of "charity, meekness, and toleration," Mann sees the common school as the fit instrument of this purpose: a fit instrument, presumably, because if public ends are important, then adequate public means should be found. Lockeian politics cannot, any more than our own, leave private convictions altogether aside: for a good deal of moral and political education occurs in the private sphere.

The American common schools were intended to represent to all the public morality that it was hoped would come to be shared by all. For that morality to be widely shared, let alone shared by all, takes a good deal of political work, work that remains far from complete, for this morality—even if conceived and presented in more strictly political terms than was the case in seventeenth-century England or nineteenth-century America—is far from equally appealing to all religious communities. It was, is, and will be regarded with suspicion and hostility by those who reject Locke's liberal Christianity, or liberalized versions of other religions or philosophies. The task of liberal constitutionalism at the deepest level is not to avoid this deep partisanship—for that would mean abandoning liberal public morality itself—the task is rather to promote in reasonable ways the right sort of liberal partisanships in all spheres of life.[28]

My interest here is primarily with ends and not means. I want to argue that any tolerably complete account of our disposition toward diversity needs to take account of the dependence of our political order on the habits, values, and interests formed in "private" communities, including but not only religious communities. The degree of support that these communities provide for our shared political project is a vital public concern; indeed, there is ample reason to think that a modern mass liberal democracy cannot survive—or at least thrive—without the support of certain patterns and kinds of intermediate associations. Modern liberal democracy needs the right sort of civic culture, and religious communities *of the right sort* are an important part of this culture.[29] Once we take account of this observation we will have moved very far indeed from the simple view elaborated at the outset.

American Catholicism and the Triumph of Transformative Liberalism: The Indirect Approach

Creating a certain religious homogeneity—to the extent at least of favoring conditions in which religions and other nonpublic moral communities will come to support basic constitutional values—is crucial and legitimate political work that liberals must hope is performed somehow. Public schools have been a direct instrument for bringing about this convergence, but there are other less direct mechanisms that may be more important, and more appealing to political founders and constitutional designers. Let us consider the striking case of the Catholic Church in America.

There was without question in the nineteenth and early twentieth centuries much xenophobia and ethnic bigotry bound up in the nativist Protestant suspicion of Catholics. There was also, however, a worry about the compatibility of liberal democracy and the Church's structure of authority. Prejudice against Catholics should be distinguished from not unreasonable fears that those educated in relatively authoritarian religious doctrines may be more prone than others to reject liberal democratic political norms and institutions.

Of course, the American Catholic Church made important contributions to the well-being of masses of Catholic immigrants. The Church provided an intermediate refuge for immigrants and important forms of social assistance.[30] The American Catholic Church has always been relatively flexible and open to the values of the larger liberal democratic society. The nineteenth-century "trusteeship" movement among American Catholics included calls for congregational authority over parish property and the selection of priests. It reflected the sense of many ordinary American Catholics that something was amiss with the structure of authority within the Catholic Church, a sense that was surely related to their embrace of republican citizenship. The American Church also accommodated the rise of labor unions more freely than did its European counterparts, which probably helped moderate the American labor movement, according to John Tracy Ellis.[31] We should not forget, however, that Rome bitterly resisted this Catholic embrace of liberal democratic values, and characterized as the "heresy of Americanism" this tendency that was especially characteristic of the American Church.[32]

But the question remains, did the fears and suspicions of the "Americanizers" stem from religious prejudice, xenophobia, and an exaggerated sense of political and moral fragility? In part, of course, but not altogether. Recent research supports the view that institutionalized Catholicism in its traditional form, with its "vertical" patterns of authority, discourages the formation of an associative civic culture supportive of liberal democracy. Robert Putnam, for example, provides evidence showing that in those areas of contemporary Italy in which traditional Catholicism is strong (especially the South), patterns of civic community and political engagement are weak. In the north of Italy, the church itself is characterized by a greater degree of the sort of trusteeship that manifested itself in nineteenth-century America—with active lay control and relatively "horizontal" patterns of authority. Only where the Catholic Church itself adopts the sort of leveling of authority that is associated with Protestantism does it appear to promote a social order supportive of active citizenship and healthy liberal democracy.[33]

Consider an even more striking finding. Students of democratization movements around the world have argued that up until the mid-1960s (pre-Vatican II) "the greater the proportion of the population that is Protestant, the higher the level of democracy."[34] Having surveyed much of the evidence, Samuel P. Huntington concludes that "The social scientists of the 1950s were right: Catholicism then was an obstacle to democracy. After 1970, however, Catholicism was a force for democracy because of changes within the Catholic Church."[35] An historic transformation was apparently brought about in the 1960s.

After centuries of often quite effective opposition to liberal democracy, the Catholic Church reversed its position and became a positive force for democracy around the world. Those changes within Catholicism were, in important respects, concessions to liberal democratic political values, and were also in part the consequence of the Catholic experience in America. Of the factors that made the Catholic Church more supportive of democratic reform around the world, "particularly important," according to George Weigel, was the influence of the United States and the American bishops. Their influence culminated in Vatican II and its Declaration on Religious Freedom, which was "a child of the American experience and experiment," and especially of the American theologian, John Courtney Murray.[36]

The importance of this story can hardly be overestimated. The suggestion here is that the Catholic encounter with America helped lead to the eventual liberalization of the Catholic Church itself, making that institution a positive and in many instances decisive force for liberalization around the world. The indirect, educative effects of American liberal democracy may have altered, in this way, not only the beliefs of American Catholics, but the official doctrine of the Roman Catholic Church itself, and thereby the beliefs of Catholics around the world. This story suggests the importance of transformative constitutionalism.

It may also represent a triumph of indirect educative mechanisms. American Catholics rejected public schooling: not uniformly, but in impressive numbers, Catholic communities educated their own children. The causes of Catholicism's transformation are thus likely to be outside the public schools. (The causes are bound to be complex, and I do not mean to fully describe them here.)

One significant instrument of religious liberalization—a crucial if indirect liberal transformative device—may be precisely what many interpret as the separation of religious and political spheres. Decades ago, Will Herberg went so far as to argue that the "segmentation" of religious and political spheres lies at the very root of the American civil religion. The price of assimilation into the American way of life, he argued, is that religious people must be prepared to regard their religious views as politically irrelevant. All three of the great American religions share this view, Herberg argued (in 1960, a bit prematurely perhaps): all three have cooperated in establishing their own political irrelevance, and have thereby promoted the moral supremacy of the belief system of "Americanism" (on which the three great religions have become mere variations).[37]

We might almost say that American Catholics (though perhaps not Fundamentalists as yet) have come to accept the American rather than the Catholic position on the separation of church and state. To be American is to have a religion (we have very few village atheists these days), but any religion at all will do. As President Eisenhower put it: "Our government makes no sense unless it is founded in a deeply felt religious faith—and I don't care what it is."[38] This is an odd view of religion, when one thinks about it.

Consider the *Ladies Home Journal* poll conducted in 1948. In it, Americans were asked to "look within [themselves] and state honestly whether [they] thought [they] really obeyed the law of love under certain special conditions." As Herberg reports,

> 90 percent said yes and 5 percent said no when the one to be "loved" was a person belonging to a different religion; 80 percent said yes and 12 percent no when it was the case of a member of a different race; 78 percent said yes and 10 percent no when it concerned a business competitor—but only 27 percent said yes and 57 percent no in the case of "a member of a political party that you think is dangerous," while 25 percent said yes and 63 percent said no when it concerned an enemy of the nation.[39]

A number of things are incredible about these findings. For one thing, as Herberg says, "no people on earth ever loved their neighbors as themselves as much as the American people say they do."[40] More to present purposes, Americans apparently feel that

> they *ought* to love their fellow men despite differences of race or creed or business interest; that is what the American Way of Life emphatically prescribes. But the American Way of Life also explicitly sanctions hating a member of a "dangerous" political party . . . or an enemy of one's country. . . . while the Jewish-Christian law of love is formally acknowledged, the truly operative factor is the value system embodied in the American Way of Life.[41]

Mr. Dooley famously remarked that the Supreme Court follows the election returns. On Herberg's account, the three great religions of America have also followed, if not the election returns, at least the basic imperatives of political liberalism in America. And most importantly, it may be the apparent segmentation of religion and politics that has helped indirectly to establish the practical supremacy of shared liberal democratic values.[42]

Consider as well the ritual which Catholic judges and candidates for President have had to pass through in their quest for high office. As Sanford Levinson observes, Catholics have effectively "been forced to proclaim the practical meaninglessness" of their religious convictions as a condition of being allowed to serve.[43] Jewish judges such as Frankfurter have often not had to make similar public professions, Levinson argues, but only because their secularism seemed indisputable.

Such rituals are bound to be educative, and they reflect a deeper mindset played out in innumerable public institutions, practices, and in less formal expectations and norms. They express our commitment to ensuring that political power will be exercised on grounds of reasons that we can share, and for purposes we can hold and justify in common. One consequence of these public rituals may be to diminish the importance of some religious convictions in people's lives—especially religious convictions that exist in some tension with liberal democratic values. Here, then, is the "hidden" or "silent" curriculum writ large: an educative agenda inscribed in the value patterns of liberal democratic institutions and practices as a whole.

None of this necessarily calls for regret, apologies, or adjustment, or so it seems to me. The natural course of things in a healthy liberal democracy will be that beliefs in tension with fundamental liberal democratic commitments will be diminished in importance. Transformative constitutionalism makes use, I would suggest, of many mechanisms and practices and expectations which have the effect of shaping our commitments and habits very deeply, without exactly announcing that purpose on their face.

It is hard for me to see why any of this is to be regretted, though there are many who seem to disagree. Perhaps because the range of diversity is diminished? But why is diversity as such (let alone "difference") a value? What we want are predominantly civic forms of diversity: and from a liberal standpoint that must mean forms of diversity that support basic principles of justice and equal freedom for all.

All of this will, nevertheless, seem deeply illiberal to some. It all depends, of course, on how one understands liberalism. The liberalism I want to defend is one that has a central place for individual liberty. Putting liberty at the center of our politics does not mean that liberty must be the whole of our politics. Liberals need not and should not neglect the quality of our shared civic life, or ignore the need to educate people for liberal citizenship.[44]

It is also worth remembering that the point of transformative mechanisms (as I want to endorse them) is *political*. They are deployed in liberal politics, and their effects are welcomed insofar as they help secure a system of political liberty, and other basic political goods and liberal civic virtues. The political aim is to secure our civil interests, not to promote Protestantism over Catholicism *per se*, little less to promote Atheism. From a political standpoint the religious dimensions of these changes does not need to be denied or affirmed: it is enough to emphasize that there are adequate political reasons for what we seek.[45]

The operation of these institutional tendencies and biases is also *gentle* rather than oppressive, influencing the deeply held beliefs of vast numbers of people without coercion or force. A range of religious ways continues to thrive within liberal political arrangements, and of course people remain free to practice whatever religion they choose within the bounds of legality (and I am all in favor of the bounds of legality being considerably broader than the bounds of what we would ideally like from an educative standpoint). That the system as a whole tilts in a certain self-supporting direction, and that extra-political communities of all sorts tend to adjust to the tilt in their distinctive ways, is perfectly legitimate and often politically quite helpful (as I have said). No one has a right to a level playing field.[46]

Not everyone agrees that the transformation of extra-political normative systems is to be applauded. There are those who argue for greater "fairness" toward religious people in our public life, which would be manifested in a greater solicitude for the ways that public policies impose unequal burdens on people with peculiar religious beliefs and practices. My worry, as I will explain in what follows, is that the proponents of greater solicitude for religious minorities could cripple the subtle and indirect means of turning religious and other systems of private belief in directions that support the regime.[47]

Transformation as Oppression?

Few charges are more popular these days than that liberalism—especially its insistence on the political authority of public reasons—effectively silences or marginalizes some people. Levinson worries that in a host of ways, religious identities, reasons, and deep convictions are "excluded" from the public realm. Some of the excluded will be those who refuse to accept the segmentation of religion and politics. The price of public office for Catholics or Jews has, Levinson suggests, been the modulation or suppression of what distinguishes their respective religious cultures from the larger American culture which, for the most part, has an easier time with the privatization of religious identities.[48] To be more precise, high costs are born by all those whose religious or philosophical convictions are in tension with liberal democratic public values, including those whose religious or moral beliefs tend toward the totalistic, and this includes some Protestant Fundamentalists.

Levinson suggests that it is "gratuitously censorial" to exclude religious reasons and sensibilities from political argument.[49] He would allow more religious speech in politics, and he would allow public moneys to flow to religiously affiliated schools and day care programs, as a way of ensuring that parents of modest means can exercise their "right" to "maintain particular ways of life into future generations."[50] All this to help those "relegated to the margins" by "modernists."[51]

Levinson's is a fairly qualified solicitude for the politically marginalized: he would allow religious arguments to be advanced in politics, but only for "non-prohibited" ends. He limits his call for greater religious accommodationism to the American pluralist context in which it is "simply unthinkable" that religious sectarians could "capture national political institutions."[52] So Levinson would let religious zealots talk but not win. When push comes to shove, he would keep the marginalized close enough to the margins to guarantee that they do not prevail.

Levinson is not alone. Stephen Carter complains that contemporary liberals will not be happy until religion is rendered a mere "hobby" in people's lives: something for the weekends but not otherwise to be taken seriously in the important affairs of life, especially politics. But Levinson himself has observed that when religious arguments are made in politics, it is far from obvious "where the conversation might go next."[53] Wherever the conversation might go, the issue is not really talk but power. The fault of those who seek to shape the coercive powers of the state on the basis of reasons that can only be appreciated from within a particular religious community is not that this cuts off conversation. It is rather that this violates our duty as citizens to offer one another reasons that we can publicly share for the ways we seek to shape coercive political power.[54]

Both Levinson and Carter obscure another point. No liberal advocates *censoring* religious speech: no liberal seeks to deny First Amendment protection to those who advocate theocracy, or to those who would use the criminal law to punish heresy or apostasy. The liberal claim is that it is wrong to seek to coerce people on grounds that they cannot share without converting to one's faith. One is free to advocate theocracy, but doing so (liberals say) is a poor use of one's freedom. The liberal hope is that politicians who violate these liberal norms will be punished, not by the government, but by commentators and voters. If, in response to these judgments about appropriate political argument, people feel "censored" or marginalized, they have nothing but their own hypersensitivity to blame.[55]

But perhaps the point of Carter, Levinson, and others has less to do with the logical extension of our rights in a liberal order, than with what is psychologically easy and sociologically likely as political institutions become settled over the course of time. To ask some religious people— some will be tempted to say "seriously religious people"—to "divide their lives" in the way that I have said liberalism does is psychologically demanding. Unless, of course, one's religious views are tolerant and ecumenical: the psychological demands are minimal if one accepts Locke's Protestantism in which charity toward dissenters is a prime *religious* virtue. Then the inappropriateness of invoking religious reasons in politics rests on religious as well as political grounds. The psychological demands were also rather minimal for Horace Mann with his Unitarianism. But if one really believes that those who dissent from the rather demanding creed of one's church have gone badly wrong and are doomed to roast in hell for eternity, then the compartmentalization of one's political and religious views may come at a decided cost, and the requisite attitude may indeed be difficult to sustain over the course of time. It is in this sense that liberalism might be said to "silence" the "religious voice": not through direct censorship and the heavy hand of state oppression, but rather through a wide array of sometimes subtle expectations about appropriate forms of speech and reasoning which amount to a system of unequal psychological taxation sufficient to drive out certain patterns of deeply held belief and practice, not all at once but over the course of generations.[56]

All of this is true. Carter, Levinson, and others *do* have a point (if this is it). *My point* is that what will be seen by some as "oppressive" (incorrectly), seems to me to be legitimate, indeed crucial, political work. Diversity does not harmonize automatically (or if it does, let's hear how; whatever that magic process is, some people will find *it* oppressive). If parents want their children always to be guided solely by sectarian religions teachings—both in politics and elsewhere—then their view of good citizenship is at odds with the liberal one (which we have good reason to see as the best conception available). If these children are one day nominated to the Supreme Court, they will have no grounds for complaint if senators have concerns about whether their political views can be defended independently of their religious convictions. We have good public reasons to wish all these conflicts to be resolved in favor of liberal principles. We have good reason to hope that there will be fewer families raising such children in the future.

We should, therefore, preserve liberal institutions, practices, rituals, and norms that psychologically tax people unequally, for if that has the effect of turning people's lives—including their most "private" beliefs—in directions that are congruent with and supportive of liberalism, thank goodness it does. This is what transformative constitutionalism is all about.

This is not to say that we should never accommodate religious dissenters. When heavy religious burdens are imposed on people for the sake of trivial public purposes, fairness demands that we should take the project of accommodation seriously. But we should do so from a perspective that recognizes the political importance of constituting diversity for liberal ends. We should not aim to create a level playing field in which no special burdens are placed on some religious people.[57] We should not be concerned to make it equally easy for Fundamentalist Protestants and modernist Protestants to pass along their beliefs to their children.

Transformative constitutionalism itself suggests certain principles of accommodation, for it is not simply a set of limits on political power, but an aspiration toward a certain kind of civil society: one in which people share a public moral order, and respect one another as free and equal citizens. Since a liberal public morality is always (more or less) in a state of coming-into-being, we should accommodate dissenters when doing so helps draw them into the public moral order: when it helps transform a *modus vivendi* into a deeper set of shared principled commitments. Will the refusal to accommodate religious complaints about public schooling drive religious families out of public schools and into Christian schools? If so (and assuming that public schools are important agents of liberal socialization, at least by virtue of mixing people of different backgrounds), then we have a powerful pragmatic argument for accommodation.

I might also note, in this regard, that Chief Justice Burger's opinion in the Amish high school case of *Wisconsin v. Yoder* is frequently criticized, with reason. Burger lauds the Amish for their law-abidingness and old-fashioned bourgeois virtue: they "reject public welfare in any of its usual modern forms," they are not a "group claiming to have recently discovered some 'progressive' or more enlightened process for rearing children for modern life."[58] No doubt, Burger's basis for accommodating dissenters is rather cramped and even illiberal. Are only those communities that zealously promote "family values" to be accommodated? What about communities of Thoreauian individualists, or others?

At one level, however, Burger is not all wrong. Part of his point seems to be that small religious communities may help enrich the polity as a whole by furnishing especially intense examples of what it means to live up to some of our very own values. It is perfectly legitimate to ask whether accommodation promotes any of *our* liberal civic values, so long as they are not *merely* our values but also grounded in good public reasons. The important point is that the political system must decide which communities are accommodated, and there is nothing wrong with deciding—so far as we can—on the basis of the best public reasons that are available, and with due confidence in the worth of preserving and protecting liberal institutions. Of course, we should not accommodate only those conscientious communities that espouse right-wing values.

The case for accommodating pacifistic Quakers in cases of military service is similar in structure to Burger's argument. As Rawls suggests (in a discussion that is a left-leaning version of Burger's *Yoder* opinion), the pacifism of the Quakers presents us with an intense version of some of our own values. Quakers may keep us alert to some of our values (reminding citizens, as Rawls says, that governments are apt to commit serious wrongs in the people's name), and so having Quakers around may well improve the moral quality of our society on the whole, and that is an important part of the case for accommodating them. All this in spite of the fact that we believe the Quaker position on military service to be deeply mistaken.[59]

We find, finally, suggestions along similar lines in Ronald Dworkin's defense of lenient treatment of civil disobedients who, it turns out, are not justified in their disobedience. Lenient treatment of even unjustified conscientious disobedience may help promote public, principled challenges to political authority and counteract political apathy.[60] There is, then, nothing eccentric about the structure of Burger's argument in *Yoder*: one good ground for accommodating dissenters is that doing so improves our polity overall.

There are, therefore, various public grounds for accommodating dissenters by making exceptions to general, publicly justified rules, but there is no general *right* of conscientious exemption. Liberal constitutionalism properly understood holds that laws must be based on reasonable public grounds. When faced with dissenters who refuse to recognize the weight or authority of those grounds, we must not cast aside our public standards. We may sometimes accommodate or exempt dissenters, but we cannot, at the stage of exception-making, discover or construct some new or higher ground that promises necessarily to *reconcile* religious or other conscientious dissenters to the political order. We must listen to dissenters, engage them in political conversation, and ensure that their interests are not unfairly discounted, but we must, in the end, be prepared to acknowledge and defend our own partisanships. It is hard to see why we should do more.

It may nevertheless be true that, from a public perspective, something is lost when religious beliefs in tension with liberalism are diminished. Daniel Boorstin suggested, in 1953, that

> an especially valuable role may be reserved to those religions, like Judaism, Catholicism, and the intransigent Protestant sects which remain in a sense "un-American" because they have not yet completely taken on the color of their environment. Such sects, while accepting the moral premises of the community, can still try to judge the community by some standard outside its own history.

Though Boorstin went on to note that "even these religions often take on a peculiar American complexion and tend toward validating themselves by their accord with things as they are."[61] The tendency of our public order, then, might not only be indirectly to promote "liberal" forms of religious faith, but also to undermine radical perspectives on our own deepest commitments, and so to promote a certain forgetfulness about what we stand for.

While the liberal order in America is well justified, not all of its consequences are happy. When the consequences are unhappy, we may have grounds for accommodation. Nevertheless, it is likely that no political order, including our own, can be a home to all good things. It would indeed be unfortunate and a cause for public concern if the educative or transformative effects of our political institutions were so thoroughgoing that no lived community in our midst offered a critical alternative to, for example, the materialism of mainstream culture. We should, however, assess worries such as these at retail, not wholesale. The extinction of many of the communities that pose truly radical alternatives to liberal democratic political principles is to be welcomed. If and when we achieve a world in which we have to resort to history books, literature, and film to remind ourselves of the radical alternatives to liberalism posed by the Communist and Fascist tyrannies of this century, that will not be a cause for regret.

Conclusion

The "separation of church and state," as it plays itself out in practice, is undoubtedly an important component of liberal constitutionalism in America. This separation serves to protect our politics from sectarian religious interventions, and also to protect religion from the worldly influence of politics. But as noted in the beginning, this simple and familiar account leaves out what may be the most interesting and, in the long run, important part of the story, which is how this happy coincidence of worldly and transcendent purposes is brought about. The separation of church and state, and the liberal insistence on the political authority of public reasons, may themselves have important transformative dimensions.

I have tried to suggest just how deficient is the view of law as boundaries and, relatedly, how inadequate is any view of the ambitions of constitutionalism that does not account for the transformative dimension. My aim has not been to undercut the value or reality of liberty, but to clarify what it takes to make a stable and decent system of liberty possible. Drawing lines in the right places, demarcating the spheres of individual rights and legitimate political power, is one significant component of system maintenance, but it is far from the only one. When demarcating private liberties and public powers, we want to make sure to keep the transformative ambitions of liberalism in mind.

While racism and narrow-mindedness have often characterized anxieties about "Americanization" as well as other experiences of national loyalty-building, this should not lead us to ignore the partisanship of our regime, and the fact that it depends upon the existence of character traits that cannot be taken for granted. Tolerance and respect for individual rights must be watchwords in a liberal political order, but nothing about those ideals bars us from taking measures to promote citizen virtues and convergence on a harmonious and liberal pattern of diversities. We need to pay more attention, as well, to the indirect means of civic education furnished by various constitutional structures and political practices. These would include choices among representative institutions (will groups be represented as such?), the size and nature of electoral districts, the structure of parties and interest groups, the distribution of power among centralized and localized institutions, the degree to which commercial activity is encouraged, and so on. Virtually all large institutional questions will have important educative dimensions that should be attended to. Liberals have sometimes pushed these matters too far into the background.[62]

We have every right and plenty of reason, in the end, to aim at a "moderate hegemony" of liberal public values. "Hegemony," because we should not shirk from accepting the pervasive effects and influences of liberal political practices. "Moderate," because transformative constitutionalism confines itself to political virtues, seeks to respect freedom, and takes advantage, where possible, of indirect and non-oppressive means.

Notes

1. These questions were originally posed to me by Sotirios A. Barber, who helped organize a conference on constitutionalism at Princeton University in the spring of 1995. That meeting was held in part to honor Walter F. Murphy, the McCormick Professor of Jurisprudence at Princeton, on the occasion of his retirement from that post. With esteem and gratitude to a great scholar and teacher, I dedicate this essay to Walter Murphy. My thanks, as well, to the other participants in that conference: Mark Brandon, Chris Eisgruber, Judy Failer, John Finn, James E. Fleming, Robert George, William F. Harris III, Suzette Hemberger, H. N. Hirsch, Sanford Levinson, Jeffrey Tulis, and Wayne Moore. I have expanded on the themes of this essay, both the historical and institutional developments and the principled conflicts, at much greater length in *Diversity and Distrust: Civic Education in a Multicultural Democracy* (Cambridge: Harvard University Press, 2000).

2. I should emphasize at the outset that I am using the phrase "liberal consti-

tutionalism" in the contemporary sense as it would apply to the basic elements of the American political system. I do not mean to exclude democratic values, even if I regard them as secondary to the protection of individual liberty. In some instances here, "political" might do as well as "constitutional," but I favor the latter word because it seems to me that the transformative ambition of a liberal democratic polity such as ours is especially liable to be missed by legalistic understandings of liberalism.

3. "Civil Law, Common Law, and Constitutional Democracy," the 19th Tucker Lecture, *Louisiana Law Review* 52:1 (1991): 91–136, 129.

4. Thomas Hobbes, *Leviathan*, C. B. Macpherson, ed. (Harmondsworth, UK: Penguin, 1981), p. 388.

5. I explored the views of Fuller, Hayek, and Oakeshott and this conception of law, with far more sympathy, in "The Public Morality of the Rule of Law: A Critique of Ronald Dworkin," *Harvard Journal of Law and Public Policy* 8:1 (1985).

6. John Locke, *Two Treatises of Government: Second Treatise*, ed. Peter Laslett (New York: Mentor, 1963), p. 348, par. 57.

7. Stephen Arons, *Compelling Belief: The Culture of American Schooling* (New York: McGraw Hill, 1983).

8. Ibid., p. 205.

9. Ibid., pp. 214–21.

10. Ibid., p. 207.

11. Arons is an egalitarian libertarian: he wants some equalization of educational resources to make equal opportunity possible, but otherwise he wants political institutions to remain neutral about educational ideals and purposes.

12. Arons, *Compelling Belief*, p. 153.

13. John E. Chubb and Terry M. Moe, *Politics, Markets, and America's Schools* (Washington, DC: Brookings, 1990).

14. See, for example, Arthur Schlesinger, Jr., *The Disuniting of America: Reflections on a Multicultural Society* (New York: Norton, 1992).

15. For a more detailed account, see Macedo, *Diversity and Distrust*.

16. "1828 Appeal from Trustees of the Public School Society," reprinted in William Oland Bourne, *History of the Public School Society of the City of New York* (New York: William Wood, 1870), pp. 114–15; and see the excellent discussion, from which I have learned much, in Diane Ravitch, *The Great School Wars: A History of the New York City Public Schools* (New York: Basic Books, 1988). It is interesting to see the language of positive rights used so early here.

17. See the Mann's Twelfth Annual Report, *Annual Reports of the Secretary of the Board of Education* (Boston: Lee and Shepard, 1891).

18. Public school prayer and Bible reading were declared unconstitutional establishments of religion in *Engel v. Vitale*, 370 U.S. 421 (1962), and *Abington School District v. Schempp*, 374 U.S. 203 (1963).

19. *Common School Journal*, August 15, 1843, quoted in Charles Leslie Glenn, Jr., *The Myth of the Common School* (Amherst: University of Massachusetts Press, 1988), 143–44.

20. As Glenn suggests, ibid., and *passim*. There is an important distinction between religious and civil doctrines of toleration: a religious doctrine of tolera-

tion, such as the one advanced by Mann here, would say that all religions are the same in the eyes of God; a civil doctrine would say they are the same in the eyes of the state. Liberal states should, I will argue, confine themselves to civil doctrines of toleration; see "Liberal Civic Education and Religious Fundamentalism: The Case of God v. John Rawls?," *Ethics*, 105 (April 1995): 468–96.

21. Speech of Bishop Hughes in the Debate on the Claim of Catholics to a Portion of the Common School Fund, in Bourne, *History of the Public School Society*, p. 220.

22. I discuss an example of this latter charge in "Liberal Civic Education and Religious Fundamentalism."

23. *A Letter Concerning Toleration*, ed. J. H. Tully (Indianapolis: Hackett, 1985; originally pub. 1689), p. 26.

24. Ibid., p. 33.

25. For civil reasons: Catholics insofar as they professed allegiance to a foreign prince, atheists insofar as they could not be trusted to keep their oaths; ibid.

26. Ibid., p. 23.

27. Ibid., pp. 33–34.

28. Although not every liberal democrat agrees, for two notable examples see George Kateb, *The Inner Ocean* (Ithaca: Cornell, 1994), and Richard E. Flathman, *Willful Liberalism: Voluntarism and Individuality in Political Theory and Practice* (Ithaca: Cornell, 1992).

29. I try to provide an account of this dependence in "Community, Diversity, and Civic Education: Toward a Liberal Political Science of Group Life," *Social Philosophy and Policy* 13:1 (Winter 1996), and in "The Constitution, Civic Virtue, and Civil Society: Social Capital as Substantive Morality," forthcoming, *Fordham Law Review* April 2001.

30. See John Tracy Ellis, *American Catholicism*, 2nd ed. (Chicago: University of Chicago, 1969), p. 105, to whom I am indebted in this paragraph generally.

31. Ibid., pp. 107–8.

32. Ibid. Papal Encyclicals issued in 1832, 1834, 1864, contained fulsome denunciations of core republican commitments, and the spirit of American freedom more broadly. As Pope Gregory XVI nicely put it in "Singulari Nos": "We greatly deplore the fact that, where the ravings of human reason extend, there is somebody who studies new things and strives to know more than is necessary, against the advice of the apostle. There you will find someone who is overconfident in seeking the truth outside the Catholic Church, in which it can be found without even a light tarnish of error." *The Papal Encyclicals, 1740–1878*, ed. Claudia Carlen Ihm (Raleigh, NC: McGrath Publishing Co., 1981), p. 251.

33. Robert D. Putnam, *Making Democracy Work: Civic Traditions in Modern Italy* (Princeton: Princeton University Press, 1993), pp. 100, 107, 126, 172, 175–76. Consider Putnam's remark: "Organized religion, at least in Catholic Italy, is an alternative to the civic community, not a part of it. . . . In today's Italy, as in the Italy of Machiavelli's civic humanists, the civic community is a secular community" (ibid., p. 109). See also Robert D. Putnam, *Bowling Alone: The Collapse and Revival of American Community* (New York: Simon and Schuster, 2000), where similar themes can be found, as I argue in "The Constitution, Civic Virtue, and Civil Society."

34. Kenneth A. Bollen, "Political Democracy and the Timing of Development," *American Sociological Review*, 44:4 (1979): 572–87, 583; and see the discussion in Samuel P. Huntington, *The Third Wave: Democratization in the Late Twentieth Century* (Norman: University of Oklahoma Press, 1991), p. 75.

35. Huntington, *Third Wave*, p. 77.

36. George Weigel, "Catholicism and Democracy: The Other Twentieth-Century Revolution," in *The New Democrats: Global Change and U.S. Policy*, ed. Brad Roberts (Cambridge: MIT Press, 1990), pp. 20–25. Developments in Europe were also extremely important, of course; see Gene Burns, "The Politics of Ideology: The Papal Struggle with Liberalism," *American Journal of Sociology*, 95:5 (1990): 1123–52.

37. See Will Herberg, *Protestant, Catholic, and Jew: An Essay in American Religious Sociology* (Garden City, NY: Anchor, 1960), esp. ch. 5. It may go too far to say that people must regard their religious views as politically irrelevant. What is required is that they have public grounds for their political views, but of course their political convictions will also typically gain support from religious and other non-public views.

38. *The New York Times*, December 23, 1952, quoted in ibid., p. 84. And in 1948, Eisenhower said, "I am the most intensely religious man I know. Nobody goes through six years of war without faith. That doesn't mean I adhere to any sect. A democracy cannot exist without a religious base. I believe in democracy." *New York Times*, May 4, 1948, quoted in Ellis, *American Catholicism*, p. 155.

39. Barnett, "God and the American People," *Ladies Home Journal*, November 1948, pp. 235–36, quoted in Herberg, *Protestant, Catholic, and Jew*, p. 76.

40. Ibid., p. 76.

41. Ibid.

42. See also the discussions of religion in America in Daniel J. Boorstin, *The Genius of American Politics* (University of Chicago, 1953), discussed below.

43. Sanford Levinson, "The Confrontation of Religious Faith and Civil Religion: Catholics Becoming Justices," *DePaul Law Review* 39 (1990): 1047–81, 1049.

44. For a fuller account see my *Liberal Virtues: Citizenship, Virtue, and Community in Liberal Constitutionalism* (Oxford: Clarendon Press, 1992).

45. I have elsewhere argued in favor of Rawls's account of political justification, as he elaborates it in *Political Liberalism* (New York: Columbia University Press, 1993); see my "Liberal Civic Education and Religious Fundamentalism," and *Diversity and Distrust*, part III. It is not my aim, as should be clear, to defend a version of liberalism that accommodates the widest social diversity. Political liberalism accommodates a greater philosophical diversity at the foundational level than comprehensive versions of liberalism which assert the truth of one comprehensive philosophical or religious view.

46. For a provocative alternative view, see John Tomasi, *Liberalism beyond Justice: Citizens, Society and the Boundaries of Political Theory* (Princeton: Princeton University Press, 2001).

47. I should emphasize that just because transformative mechanisms are subtle and indirect does not mean that they cannot be publicly defended; see Macedo, *Diversity and Distrust*.

48. Levinson, "Catholics Becoming Justices," pp. 1058–59.

49. Sanford Levinson, "Religious Language and the Public Square (Review of Michael Perry: *Love and Power: The Role of Religion and Morality in American Politics*)," *Harvard Law Review*, 105 (1992): 2076–77.

50. Ibid., p. 2078, text and fn. 72.

51. Ibid., p. 2079.

52. Ibid., pp. 2077–79. Levinson says we need not bar religious speech or religious purposes, "especially in a country as remarkably pluralistic as the United States, where it is simply unthinkable that the members of a particularistic religion could ever capture national political institutions" (p. 2077). Which seems to mean that he would be prepared to be censorial if religious types could win. He also speaks of allowing people to advance religious claims in politics so long as they are on "behalf of non-prohibited legislative ends"; he would retain bars on "the use of state apparatus to declare theological positions or otherwise infuse an overtly religious sensibility into public life" (ibid., pp. 2077–78). Levinson accuses Michael Perry of "relegating to the margins" those who are not modernists, but since Levinson would allow those with totalistic (pre-modernist?) religious views to talk but not to win, he seems guilty of the same thing; see pp. 2078–79. Where Levinson goes wrong (to my mind) is in thinking that there is something necessarily wrong with practices that in effect marginalize those who reject liberalism.

53. Sanford Levinson, "Review of Stephen Carter's Culture of Disbelief," *Michigan Law Review* (May 1994): 1879, quoting Mark Tushnet.

54. The point of liberal "public reason" is to attempt to define the appropriate grounds for shaping the most basic principles of justice, which will limit and direct, after all, the fearsome coercive powers of the modern state. Rawls argues that the fair and appropriate grounds for determining the constitutional basics are grounds that reasonable fellow citizens can share; see *Political Liberalism*, and my discussion, *Diversity and Distrust*, part III. Our fellow citizens disagree permanently and reasonably about their ultimate religious commitments as well as their deepest philosophical commitments, so these grounds should not be invoked to justify constitutional basics. Rawls's conviction—which I share—is that we should not expect the constitutional basics to embody our comprehensive conceptions of the truth as a whole insofar as these are subject to permanent and reasonable disagreement. To fairly shape the constitutional basics let us focus, liberal contractualists say, on values and reasons that we can publicly share with our reasonable fellow citizens. These will be reasons that support basic human rights of the sorts familiar from many bills of rights—including the right to democratic participation—along with some guarantee of material security.

55. In fact, much of Stephen Carter's argument (see *Culture of Disbelief: How American Law and Politics Trivialize Religious Devotion* [New York: Basic, 1993]) depends on giving far too much weight to the sensitivities of people in the face of disagreement, or so I argue in "Multiculturalism for the Religious Right? Defending Liberal Civic Education," *Journal of the Philosophy of Education*, 29:2 (1995): 223–38.

56. See John Murray Cuddihy, *No Offense: Civil Religion and Protestant Taste* (New York: Seabury, 1978); and Tomasi, *Liberalism Beyond Justice*.

57. I consider the problem of accommodation at greater length in *Diversity and Distrust*.

58. *Wisconsin v. Yoder* 406 U.S. 205, 222, 235.

59. See John Rawls, *Theory of Justice* (Cambridge: Harvard University Press, 1971), sec. 56.

60. See Ronald Dworkin, *Taking Rights Seriously* (Cambridge: Harvard University Press, 1977), ch. 8.

61. Boorstin, *Genius*, p. 148.

62. Liberal political thinking often pushes these educative, formative questions into the background, but not entirely out of the picture. An example would be the political science of the *Federalist Papers*, which clearly, though often implicitly, counts on the ability of the new Constitution to reorder citizens' basic values and identities in deep and pervasive respects, creating a national, commercial, liberal, democratic people out of a people that, as Barry Shain has recently argued, was strongly attached to a Protestant, small communitarian outlook; see *The Myth of American Individualism* (Princeton: Princeton University Press, 1995). Shain's account makes clear just how far the constitutional order has transformed the American polity, though where I would largely applaud this transformation, he seems disposed to bemoan it.

9

Promoting Diversity in the Public Schools (Or, To What Extent Does the Establishment Clause of the First Amendment Hinder the Establishment of More Genuinely Multicultural Schools?)

SANFORD LEVINSON

Some Introductory Autobiography

I was born and grew up in Hendersonville, North Carolina, a small town of about 6,000 people in the western part of the state. There were about 30 Jewish families in Hendersonville, and I knew from a very early age that I was Jewish and, consequently, that I was different in an important way from almost all of my neighbors and classmates. The most evident way, especially to a child, involved dietary prohibitions against eating pork. I also knew that I was allowed absences from school (Rosh Hashanah and Yom Kippur) while other children were not. Inevitably, my Jewishness accounts for many of the memories—most of them, it is important to say at the outset, quite pleasant—I have of growing up in Hendersonville, and I begin this essay with two of them.

Thesis: Learning Bible and Singing Carols

As a third-grader, I won a "Bible certificate" from the State of North Carolina for memorizing a number of Bible verses, including John 3:16, which I can summon up in my mind to this very day: "For God so loved the world that he sent his only begotten Son, and whosoever believeth in him shall be granted everlasting life."[1] From the vantage point of fifty years later, I think that I recall, as a Jewish youngster, finding something at least odd, if not objectionable, about saying the verse aloud in front of my class (which is how we got credit for memorizing the verse of the week). After all, most Jewish children, at least in the United States, are initially taught about Judaism in terms of what it is *not*, i.e., Christianity, and John 3:16 is perhaps the quintessential summary of Christian belief, not to mention its being one of the central sources of the no-salvation-other-than-through-Jesus view that has been so disastrous for Jews throughout history. However difficult it may be to determine the theological tenets of traditional Judaism, it is clear that none of them recognizes Jesus as divine or as the carrier of salvation.[2] Although I cannot be sure, I strongly suspect that I already knew by the third grade that, at least so far as Jews are concerned, what John was stating *I* could not affirm as the truth even as I proclaimed it aloud. But the challenge of winning the certificate (and, I suspect in retrospect, of proving myself not *so* different from my biblically proficient classmates) prevailed over any other considerations that might have come to my very young mind.

Far more vivid in my memory are my reactions to marching each December with other public school students to the First Methodist Church for our annual concert of Christmas carols (which, needless to say, we had rehearsed at school). This provoked a sharper conflict in regard to my own sense of Jewish identity; though once again, I did little to set myself apart from the hegemonic majority. In retrospect, I have no idea if the concert was "compulsory." I doubt that it was; had I, or my parents, insisted on non-participation, I am quite sure that would have been acceptable. The community as a whole was quite tolerant, in its own way. Jews were well integrated into the fabric of community life and were often called on to explain Passover and other Jewish holidays. So why did I march? One answer is that, if truth be known, I rather enjoyed (and enjoy to this day) the tunes of most of the various carols.

Still, I recall feeling certain tensions about some of the lyrics we were called upon to sing. My personal resolution of any such tensions that I felt was simply to avoid singing those lines that included reference to Jesus or, even more to the point, "Christ our Lord." Thus I joined happily in calling on all of the faithful, joyful and triumphant, to come to Bethlehem to adore an unnamed "him." I maintained a stony silence, however, at the last line, which seemed to suggest that I did indeed recognize "him" as "Christ our Lord." Similarly, I always enjoyed the lovely Moravian hymn, "I Wonder as I Wander," but I never joined in the words "Jesus our Savior." Again, as with John 3:16, I recall most of the words of most of the standard Christmas carols to this day.

I also believe that the elementary school day began with the Lord's Prayer. I know its text, and I remember saying it repeatedly while I was growing up. I cannot imagine where I might have learned or recited it other than the public schools. None of its overt language, of course, is offensive to a Jew—how could it be, given Jesus' own status as a Jew?—and I recall little hesitation in joining in.

Later, at Hendersonville High School, I had the opportunity to take an elective course in Bible. The class was taught, I believe, by volunteers supplied by local churches. It was, most definitely, *not* a course on the Bible in Western literature or the like. I did not enroll in that course. Instead, I happily took typing, perhaps the most useful course I ever had in high school. I am not aware that *any* Jewish student ever took the Bible course, though the low number of Jewish students—I was one of two in my class of 70—limits the force of any generalization on this point.

As I got further along in school, I did begin to wonder about the legitimacy of all of this interaction between school and church. Certainly by the time I graduated from college (I attended Duke, a Methodist school that required two semesters of religion courses in order to graduate) I had come to the firm opinion that North Carolina had behaved not simply questionably, but unconstitutionally. I had discovered the First Amendment in political science courses and, more to the point, the "separationist" perspective identified especially with Hugo Black, Felix Frankfurter, and Robert Jackson.[3] I am quite confident that I agreed with the latter two justices that even the limited state aid accepted by Black in *Everson v. New Jersey*[4] was constitutionally illegitimate. There should indeed be a "wall of separation" between church and state that would basically cordon off the institutions of the latter from any real contact with, or encouragement of, the former. Not a penny of public funds should go to, or otherwise indirectly help out, a religious institution. The aid upheld in *Everson* was of the latter variety inasmuch as it provided public transportation to students attending parochial schools, and four justices vigorously dissented from even that level of aid.

During my senior year of college (1962), school prayer was found constitutionally illegitimate by the Supreme Court.[5] I rejoiced. Indeed, I can recall quite vividly the fantasy of becoming a lawyer, returning to Hendersonville, and using my skills as a constitutional lawyer to eliminate any reference to God from the school day.

Antithesis: Religious Pluralism in Hendersonville

There are, however, other memories of religion connected with the important aspects of my growing up in Hendersonville. Some of them have to do with the local synagogue. The synagogue was too small to afford a rabbi, which meant that services were conducted by the lay members of the community (including myself). I have little doubt that this emphasis on lay participation was extraordinarily important in developing some of my views about the dispensability of certain hierarchical roles, including "supreme" courts, that we too often take for granted.[6]

In relation to this particular essay, however, the most important memo-

ries, and certainly among my fondest, involve what through the haze of
years appear to have been "endless" discussions with a group of friends
about religion. A fairly typical evening, especially in summers, would be
to drink beer or play poker while at the same time energetically debate
the basic questions of religion, especially those involving theodicy and
the existence of an afterlife. Though, as children of the 1950s, we were
thoroughly segregated racially—I did not have non-white classmates until I went to graduate school at Harvard in 1962—we were otherwise
wonderfully pluralistic. My friends included a Catholic (a Massachusetts
native whose father had come South when General Electric moved one
of its plants to Hendersonville), several Southern Baptists, a Methodist, a
Presbyterian, and myself. We argued with the particular intensity of teen-
agers, though never, so far as I recall, acrimoniously. (The parents of the
two Southern Baptists, however, did express concern to their sons about
the heretical views to which they were being exposed.)

I particularly remember my Southern Baptist friends expressing seemingly genuine regret that my failure to acknowledge Jesus as my personal
Savior condemned me to eternal torment in hell. They would have preferred knowing that I would join them in heaven. This was said by them,
and perceived by me, without the slightest personal hostility. My non-
saved fate was, from their perspective, simply a statement of theological
fact, and their attempt to save me from what was quite literally a fate
worse than death was, consequently, an act of friendship. Imagine, for
example, a friend observing someone close to her driving while intoxi-
cated. Surely we would not expect the friend to remain silent and accept
as dispositive, following a fatal accident, the statement: "Well, it was her
life, and friends don't interfere with one another." Friends *ought* to warn
one another about perceived dangers facing them.

My Baptist friends were engaged in an act of such warning, even
though I chose to ignore it. I do not censure them for their concern,
especially given their general courtesy and willingness to tolerate my response to their entreaties that, as a Jew, I just did not see any reason to
accept Jesus as divine, though I always took care to describe him as a
great man eminently worth respecting even if not worshipping. Moreover, I added that I did not believe that a God worth worshipping (or
even respecting) would condemn anyone to the torments of eternal punishment. My Christian friends were scarcely monolithic on any of these
points, and, among other things, I got to know the differences among
Christian denominations.

In looking back and trying to determine, for better or worse, what
might help to account for the development of my particular persona, I
often think of those friends and of our discussions. I am convinced that
they had far more to do with my becoming an academic intellectual than

anything that took place during the generally dreary school days, during which my primary achievement was getting so many C's in "cooperation" that I was ineligible for the National Honor Society. It was with John, Jim, Benny Cole, and Gar that I became comfortable exploring some basic issues of life. I remain forever grateful to them.

In many ways the rest of this chapter is an exploration of whether it is possible to synthesize these two sets of memories, not simply in accounting for autobiographical development, but, far more importantly, in terms of general social and legal analysis. My own life was immeasurably aided by friendships, the result, with one exception, of mutual attendance at the local public school with other youngsters who, from a variety of perspectives, unabashedly took religious questions seriously. Less happily, my life was also affected by state-encouraged feelings of marginality and difference connected to such phenomena as the Bible memorization and Christmas carols. Is there a way of putting together these memories— and, concomitantly, engaging in cogent analysis of the issues raised by them—in some way that makes sense?

On the Difference between Pluralism and Separatism

What I have celebrated, in the second set of memories, is the actuality of a certain model of *pluralism*; the ability of persons from a variety of subcultures to come together and encounter one another without negating those aspects that indeed make them different from each other. To use a term that was blessedly absent from the language of my youth, a kind of *multiculturalism* was present in Hendersonville, with enormous benefit. There are, of course, many definitions of "multiculturalism," and they tend to differ depending on whether the definer is, broadly speaking, favorably or unfavorably disposed to the concept under discussion. That being said, I find one of the most useful definitions that offered by the art and social critic Robert Hughes. Multiculturalism is

> [the] assert[ion] that people with different roots can coexist, that they can learn to read the image banks of others, that they can and should look across the frontiers of race, language, gender and age [and, presumably, religion] without prejudice or illusion, and learn to think against the background of a hybridized society.[7]

Whatever the obvious limits of my small North Carolina town's multiculturalism—the most notable certainly was a racial segregation that deprived me of any real contact with African-American students—it was also a powerful reality in at least the dimension of religion, with enduring importance for my life. And what allowed these encounters across culture to take place was, in substantial part, the fact that most of us attended the same public school. (There was a Catholic elementary school, however, and some Catholic students attended a Catholic school in Asheville, 20 miles away. My friend Gar attended a local private boys' school, but very few other local students attended it.)

I hope my friends believed (and believe now in retrospect) that they benefited from having a Jewish friend. We too often automatically sneer at the phrase "some of my best friends are Jewish" (or any other given religion or race), but surely it would be a profound social good if all of us could in fact say, with conviction, that some of our best friends *are* from groups other than those with which we most centrally identify. No heterogeneous society can long survive if it becomes truly exceptional to develop the particular intimacies of friendship with anyone other than those who are exactly like oneself in most important aspects. I know that I think differently, and better, of Southern Baptists because some of my best childhood friends were members of that denomination. I would hope that the same is true for them in regard to Jews.

My life in the elite legal academy has, however, been basically devoid of contact with committed Christians, especially evangelical Protestants. One can count literally on the fingers of one hand the number of publicly visible Protestant evangelicals who hold tenured positions at America's "leading" law schools. In this respect (and, undoubtedly, many others), no elite law school even remotely "looks like America," at least if that is meant to suggest that members of the various subcultures of American society should actively participate in each of the institutional structures that comprise that society. And, as I have written elsewhere, it is noteworthy "that almost none of the contemporary demands for greater diversity of voices within the academy include a call for a greater presence of the almost totally absent sound of a strong religious sensibility."[8]

It should be clear that the creation of a public school system that truly brings together, in a context of mutual respect and concern, persons of different backgrounds is a high social good. Concomitantly, the adoption of policies that discourage such multicultural encounters and, instead, lead to withdrawal into separate enclaves of homogeneity is, if not an unequivocal social bad, then at least something that should scarcely be applauded without grave reservations. It is in thinking about public schools that we most directly confront the questions of social reproduction and the inculcation of values that constitute us as a distinctive social order. As the Supreme Court once put it, quoting two historians: "The role and purpose of the American public school system [is to] 'prepare pupils for citizenship in the Republic.'"[9] This, one hopes, includes development of a stance of "tolerance of divergent political and religious views" and the taking into account "of the sensibilities of others."[10] My very citation of the Court's opinion in *Bethel* signifies the fact that in the United States, for better *and* worse, the kinds of questions I am raising are not merely ones of "social policy" or even political theory. Instead, what Justice Cardozo once called "[t]he great generalities of the constitution"[11] are thought to speak with sometimes surprising specificity, let the consequences be what they may. Two strands of cases are particularly important in the context of my reminiscences and subsequent reflections. The first involves the constitutionality of state aid to religious schools. The second deals with what might be termed the secularization of the public school system and consequent withdrawal of at least some Christians (and, no doubt, other sectarians as well, including Orthodox Jews) from the public schools.

There are many fine articles detailing the specific doctrinal twists and turns within these areas,[12] and this essay is not intended to compete with any of them. Instead, I want to offer some modest reflections about the interplay between current doctrinal developments and the achievement of a multicultural society whose members are nonetheless bonded by mutual respect and, if this is not too completely utopian, affection.

Aid to Parochial Schools

As already suggested, I initially had little trouble supporting the stance of "hard-core separationists" that public monies should be used little, if at all, to "support" or "subsidize" religion. People certainly had a right to be religious, but let them do so on their own time and spending their own money. They were just as certainly not entitled to even a penny of my taxes to spend in ways that furthered their religious aims. The key word in this sentence is "furthered," since, as economists teach, state provision of *any* goods, including police and fire protection, frees up funds that can now be used for other purposes, including religious indoctrination.

Though few persons are so relentlessly anticlerical as to deny police and fire protection to a church, it is not altogether clear what distinguishes such permitted aid from other, unpermitted benefits other than the fact that we as a culture have become used to the former (as, perhaps, is the case with the presence of "In God We Trust" on the coinage), whereas the latter appear "new" and (therefore?) indefensible. In any event, these issues were not to be settled through ordinary political debate and votes. Instead, I believed that the Court should militantly use the Establishment Clause of the First Amendment as a sword against any legislative decisions to expend public monies in ways that aided religious schools.[13] "[T]axpayers have a right," enforceable by the courts, "not to

subsidize religion."[14] Religious parents *do* apparently have a constitutional right, thanks to the 1925 case *Pierce v. Society of Sisters*,[15] to withdraw their children from public schools and educate them privately. They
should not, however, expect public aid in financing this private education. Indeed, they should realize that it is illegitimate even to ask for such
aid.

I have been persuaded[16] by Michael McConnell,[17] however, that this
interpretation of the Constitution is profoundly wrong,[18] especially if one
believes that the principle of "equal concern and respect" is a foundational predicate of our constitutional order.[19] The key here is the attitude
one adopts with regard to *Pierce*. On one hand, *Pierce*'s support of a
constitutional right to opt out of public education could be viewed simply as the unfortunate positive law of our Constitution, to be submitted
to so long as it is not formally repealed or overruled, but not to be ad-
mired. Conversely, *Pierce* could be read as a constitutional principle
which should be supported and perhaps even venerated. This is the view
of Mark Yudof, who has interpreted *Pierce* as standing for the proposition
that governments, while "free to establish their own public schools and
to make education compulsory for certain age groups," cannot use state
power "to eliminate competing, private-sector educational institutions
that may serve to create heterogeneity and to counter the state's dominance over the education of the young."[20]

From this perspective, *Pierce* is a powerful barrier to totalitarianism
through its recognition of the legitimacy of multiculturalism. The state
cannot reinforce the hegemony of the dominant culture by prohibiting
parents from engaging in at least partial "secession" from that culture as a
means of cultivating within their children alternative ways of looking at
the world.[21] *Pierce* seemingly calls for a measure of "equal concern and
respect"[22] for these alternatives, certainly if parents are willing to pay the
costs of the education at issue even as they pay taxes to support a public
school system that they reject.

One of the key questions raised by this last sentence is what happens if
parents are formally willing, but in fact basically unable, to pay the costs
of private education.[23] In other words, should the putative benefits of
private education, well articulated by Yudof, be limited only to the relatively affluent or to those who receive voluntary contributions from people of greater means? It is hard, at least for those of us who profess to be
egalitarian in our political sympathies, to figure out how the answer to
this question might be "yes."

McConnell, for example, makes very effective use of the point that
most contemporary liberals support state subsidy of abortions for poor
women on the ground that their formal right to enjoy reproductive freedom, labeled "fundamental" by the Court,[24] is hollow if it is rationed by

a price mechanism that effectively denies indigent women access to abortions. If we secular liberals are so solicitous about ensuring the practical right of poor women to enjoy their right of reproductive choice, why then are we not equally concerned, at least as a political matter, about the equally constitutionally protected fundamental right of less affluent parents to choose religious education for their children? Attempting to defend one's lack of equal concern by reference to the Establishment Clause simply begs the central issue of how in fact the clause should be interpreted.

McConnell argues, and I (now) agree, that arguments like Professor Kathleen Sullivan's, with their blithe reference to unacceptable "subsidies" of religious education, depend on a baseline that in effect presumes the classically liberal "night-watchman" state which leaves the provision of important services, including education, to the operation of the market.[25] It is reference to this baseline that justifies the provision of publicly funded police and fire protection to religious schools. It had simply become an accepted practice even of a relatively minimal state to provide such protection to the general public, and it would have truly appeared (and would have been) discriminatory had the state declared, in effect, that every building *except* for churches would be protected against fire or theft. Concomitantly, if the state had declared that it would provide some special protection *only* for churches, then I, and I think most analysts, would interpret this as clearly aiding religion in violation of any plausible interpretation of the Establishment Clause. Over the past half-century, the majority of the Supreme Court has tended to interpret aid to parochial schools (in the context of some general scheme of aid to private schools, for no one has ever defended providing aid only to religious schools) as in effect something very special, a deviation from a baseline of no aid.

Education, however, has for at least 140 years been an important aspect of governmental budgets, especially (and until the 1960s, almost exclusively) at the local level. Even the classic westerns featured the "schoolmarm" whose state-funded task was to maintain civilization on the frontier. Like fire and police protection, education has been viewed as something the state provides, even if, from a contemporary perspective, much of the past provision was minimal. In any event, as McConnell notes, we have moved very far from the minimal state and entered the world of the contemporary welfare state. That type of state features extensive and, some would say, pervasive expenditures by the state in order to provide goods and services at less than market cost to those who could not otherwise afford them.[26] The baseline is now that of the modern welfare state, whose most substantial expenditures, particularly at the state and local levels of government, are for educating the young.

For McConnell, then, the contemporary situation is more akin to the police and fire protection example. To offer extensive aid *only* to those who will send their children to public schools or to non-religiously affiliated private schools is, in effect, to exhibit a gross lack of equal concern and respect for the non-well-off religious (and, of course, the non-well-off who desire private education for other reasons as well). Moreover, there is the reality that some parents cannot afford nonpublic education in part because taxes for public education continue to mount.

The question then becomes whether legislatures can vote to return some of this tax money through support for nonpublic education, which would, as a practical matter, be used primarily in religiously based schools.[27] I am no longer persuaded by the argument that the Constitution deprives legislatures of the freedom to exercise such judgment. Although I generally oppose, and am often appalled by, the rightward drift of the contemporary Supreme Court, I confess to supporting the willingness of its conservative majority to reconsider what I now regard as one of the most dubious legacies of the Warren Court era—the hostility to aid to religious schools.[28]

Although there are advances in this direction,[29] it is noteworthy that the majority has been rather cautious in rewriting doctrine. Cases upholding aid have often been intensely fact specific, as seen, for example, in *Zobrest v. Catalina Foothills School District*.[30] There Chief Justice Rehnquist, speaking for a five-justice majority, reversed a decision of the Court of Appeals for the Ninth Circuit that had held that Arizona could not provide an interpreter to James Zobrest, a deaf student who depended on the use of sign language, so that he could attend a Catholic high school that would not otherwise have been able to accommodate him. Instead, said the Supreme Court, the state-financed interpreter was able to surmount the barriers erected by the Establishment Clause. No one, however, could accuse Rehnquist of cutting a wide swath.[31] He defined Arizona's payment of the interpreter's salary as "part of a general governmental program that distributes benefits neutrally to any child qualifying as 'handicapped.'"[32] He emphasized as well that the Catholic school in question was "not relieved of an expense that it otherwise would have assumed in educating its students,"[33] inasmuch as it presumably did not generally provide interpreters to deaf students. Moreover, Rehnquist found it significant that "the task of a sign-language interpreter seems to be quite different from that of a teacher or guidance counselor," for the interpreter ostensibly exercises no discretion in communicating with his or her charge.[34] "[E]thical guidelines," Rehnquist pointed out, "require interpreters to transmit everything that is said in exactly the same way it was intended."[35] Although Rehnquist would almost certainly allow far more expansive distribution of state funds to religious schools, his opinion, given its specificity, leaves other members of the Court free to rein in any given program that they believe goes too far.

Given the limited reach of Rehnquist's opinion, it is noteworthy that Justices Blackmun and Souter dissented on the merits.[36] They rejected the claim that Arizona should be able to provide funds to Salpointe High School so that James Zobrest could enjoy, as a practical matter, his constitutional right to attend a religiously based school. Instead, they accused the majority of "authoriz[ing] a public employee to participate directly in religious indoctrination," presumably by signing material with religious content that the deaf child could therefore understand.[37]

For me, especially as tutored by McConnell, this conclusion seems to tread dangerously close to an "unconstitutional condition"—that is, the forced waiver of a constitutional right as consideration for some valuable governmental benefit.[38] Here, the availability of the valuable benefit of a state-funded interpreter, making it possible for a deaf child to be "mainstreamed" in regard to receiving an education, requires the waiver of the student's right to attend a religious school. Although such conditions can be imposed on any citizen, it is obvious that the poor are especially vulnerable to the blandishments held out by the welfare state, whose "safety net" may be the only thing between the recipient and a hard fall.

It is, of course, a rich irony that in other cases the chief justice had been generally unsympathetic either to the plight of the poor or to the more general "unconstitutional condition" analysis,[39] while Justice Blackmun had proved himself quite sensitive both to the general needs of the poor and to the potential for abuse of governmental largesse.[40] In *Zobrest*, though, Blackmun seemed sublimely uninterested in the fact that the Zobrest family paid $7,000 a year to hire an interpreter for their son following the decision of the Ninth Circuit Court of Appeals invalidating Arizona's provision of aid.[41] But what if another family in the same position as the Zobrests, but unable to afford the extra $28,000 over four years to send their child to a religious school, had in effect been compelled to send her to a public school (or to a nonsectarian private school) in order to receive the necessary services of a state-funded interpreter? Why should we complacently accept this as "required" by the Establishment Clause? I (now) see no good reason for such acceptance. As should be obvious, I see good reason to be more understanding of the plight of families like the Zobrests.

It is possible, though, that the cracks in the classical "no-aid" view of the Establishment Clause, articulated most clearly in the current Court by Justice Souter,[42] are threatening a doctrinal dam-burst, as seen in two more recent cases. The first, *Rosenberger v. University of Virginia*,[43] involved not aid to parochial schools, but, rather, a policy of the university that, while generally funding student publications, explicitly denied fund-

ing to a Christian journal, *Wide Awake*, on the grounds that its publication was in fact a "religious activity" insofar as it "promote[d] . . . a
particular belie[f] in or about a deity or an ultimate reality." A bitterly
divided Court held that Virginia's policy in effect was an invidious discrimination against a particular way of viewing the world. Although the
Court held that this violated the students' First Amendment interests, it
is more sensible to view the case as a mixed free speech–equal protection
case insofar as the heart of the decision (and the reason for my support of
the majority) was the unequal respect displayed by the state for religious
perspectives, even as it offered generous subsidies to a wide variety of
other views. Still, Justice O'Connor, who formally joined the majority
opinion, also took care to write a separate concurrence describing the
case as lying "at the intersection of the principle of governmental neutrality and the prohibition of state funding of religious activities."[44]

The far more important case is *Mitchell v. Helms*, in which six justices
upheld a program whereby Louisiana made a variety of resources—including "slide projectors, movie projectors, overhead projects, television
sets, tape recorders, projection screens, maps, globes, filmstrips, cassettes,
[and] computers"[45]—available to nonpublic, including religious, schools.
As already noted, there was no majority opinion, though Justice Thomas
garnered three other votes for an extremely wide-ranging opinion that
suggested that the state is free to distribute any such resources to private
schools, whether secular or religious, so long as the aid is evenhandedly
distributed and does not in itself contain any content that overtly en-
dorses religion. That such aid could be "diverted" to religious uses was
irrelevant for the plurality. It was this casualness about "diversion" that
evoked Justice O'Connor's concurring opinion. Instead, she argued,
rather implausibly, that there was little evidence of actual diversion in
Louisiana and, even more implausibly, that one should trust the assur-
ances of local school officials that they would not in fact make use of such
materials for religious purposes.

By the time this chapter is published, of course, we may know who is
to replace the justices who are almost sure to retire in the next several
years. One of them is John Paul Stevens, with Justice Souter the most
active adherent of the "no-aid" view, and his replacement by a Bush
appointee will almost certainly mean the arrival of a fifth vote for the
plurality position. Had a President Gore been able to replace Chief Justice Rehnquist, the most likely retirement from the conservative side,
then we might look back on *Mitchell* as the "high point" (or "low
point," depending on one's own position) of the Court's willingness to
rewrite our understanding of the Establishment Clause with regard to
religious schools in the modern welfare state.

It is ever more difficult for me to understand how anyone at all supportive of one or another of the contemporary defenses of "multicultural-ism" could oppose on principle the kind of legislative discretion at issue in the contemporary parochial school funding cases. It is a deep irony that at least some of the Christian supporters of nonpublic education are vehemently opposed to "multiculturalism," which, by ostensibly promot-ing a kind of relativism, in their opinion attacks the one true view of the world.[46] Yet surely the strongest arguments likely to persuade secularists to tolerate (and perhaps even to support) the various Christian academies and other religious schools that dot the landscape are precisely those that emphasize the importance of nurturing a vibrant and, therefore, con-tentious cultural pluralism. This means, almost by definition, that we ex-hibit a measure of concern and respect for cultural perspectives that we may not only not identify with, but even find abhorrent in significant aspects.[47]

All of this being said, though, I find myself lamenting the retreat from public education by groups who increasingly feel alienated from the cul-ture of the public schools. That I have been persuaded by McConnell's arguments as to what the Constitution allows (and what a serious com-mitment to egalitarianism may require, at least as a matter of political theory) is not the same thing as saying that it is an affirmative social good that children be educated in homogeneous environments free from the taint of contact with children who may be quite different. Indeed, I have no hesitation in counting it as an overall social evil that the challenge of coming to terms with our multicultural reality is increasingly taking on a frankly separatist dimension.[48]

To this extent, I disagree with McConnell when he argues that "[t]he common school movement has run its course and no longer can establish a coherent position in the face of the conflicting demands of a diverse nation."[49] For McConnell, the American public school has in effect be-come estopped, because of constitutional interpretations of the Supreme Court or, simply, acquiescence to the fragmented nature of American society, from "teach[ing] any god because it would have to teach all gods; it cannot teach any culture because it would have to teach all cul-tures. . . . The common school movement now teaches our children, un-intentionally, to be value-less, culture-less, root-less, and religion-less."[50] Thus, he says, "it can no longer achieve its crowning purpose of provid-ing a unifying moral culture in the face of our many differences."[51] For McConnell, the answer is to adopt educational financing systems that would maximize the "freedom of choice" of the parents by providing them with vouchers, even if the likely consequence is the flourishing of individually homogeneous schools.[52]

At some point, the nurturance of "pluralism" requires the toleration of "separatism." This is exemplified most clearly in our constitutional law by

Wisconsin v. Yoder,[53] where the state was required to subordinate its general educational policy of compulsory education to the interests of a minority community in maintaining its own distinctive way of life apart from the surrounding society. In Amy Gutmann's terms, the "family state," predicated on emphasizing a common membership in an overarching political community, was subordinated to a "state of families," in which the primary unit is the particularistic community and the wider polity more a confederation of these communities than a genuine community in its own right.[54]

All of this being said, and conceding the importance of nurturing pluralism, I think it important that we try, as much as is reasonably possible, to resist the development of the separatism to which it can too easily lead. The "resistance," it is important to say, should be based on force of argument rather than force of law. I trust I have made clear the extent to which I support the rewriting of our received doctrines interpreting the Establishment Clause in order to allow more state funding of nonpublic, including religiously based, schools. But one can also, at the very same time, support strengthening public schools in ways designed to encourage (even if not to *require*) persons from all sorts of backgrounds, and with all sorts of views, to attend them and to interact with one another.

On School Prayer and Similar Matters

How might one go about the task of bringing about what seems to be the increasingly utopian dream[55] outlined in the last paragraph? To answer this question adequately would obviously require a book. My goals here are considerably more modest. I want to address the question of what types of "concessions" (if this is the proper word) I am willing to make in order to allow self-consciously religious parents to feel more comfortable in sending their children to public schools. I am assuming, of course, that my own sensibility is not unique and that I can speak to, even if not for, others who share my own self-definition as a secularist in at least two somewhat different senses. First, I possess no "religious" beliefs, as conventionally defined. Though I continue strongly to identify myself as Jewish, this has little, if anything, to do with embracing any theological propositions myself. Secondly, I reject the propriety of the states' overtly articulating any theological propositions. I read the Establishment Clause as prohibiting "In God We Trust" from the coinage. I thus remain militantly opposed (as do many non-secularists) to any endorsement, direct or indirect, of the United States as a "Christian" (or even "Judeo-Christian") nation.

It should be no surprise, then, that my initial delight with *Engel v.*

Vitale,[56] the first Supreme Court decision striking down state-sponsored school prayer, has never entirely dissipated. Officially composed prayers, even with an opt-out provision for those who wish not to participate, easily count as a violation of my version of the Establishment Clause. I was pleased when a slender majority struck down, in *Wallace v. Jaffree,*[57] an Alabama "moment of silence" law that was passed at the behest of religious groups and involved teachers overtly informing their students that one (presumably preferred) use of the moment of silence would be "prayer." Similarly, I rejoiced when the Court, to many analysts' surprise, struck down in *Lee v. Weisman*[58] the Rhode Island school district's practice of inviting members of the clergy to deliver prayers (albeit "nonsectarian") at the official baccalaureate ceremonies that are part of graduation from high school. Again, it seemed to me that the state was in effect trying to extract an "unconstitutional condition"—the waiver of one's right not to be subjected to official state-organized prayer in order to attend the public baccalaureate ceremonies of graduation week.

On reflection, though, I am reminded of the curse of being granted what (one thinks) one wishes. Has this triumvirate of cases in fact made this a better society overall? I would like to think so, but I suspect these cases have made their own contribution to the perception of a *kulturkampf*—a cultural war—between secularism and sectarianism and, concomitantly, to the further fraying of any remaining social bonds that might once have linked these elements of society.[59] Not the least contributor to the fraying is precisely the treatment of the issue of prayer in the public schools as one of high legal principle, and subject, therefore, to resolution only by the analytical techniques ostensibly mastered by constitutional lawyers.

As Stephen Carter wrote in a review of Ronald Dworkin's *Life's Dominion,*[60] which purported to settle the questions of abortion and euthanasia by reference to consistent principles, society sometimes (perhaps often) is far more in need of compromise than of rigorous adherence to principles. As Carter points out, "Compromises, by their nature, possess the internal inconsistencies and contradictions that scholars, by their nature, abhor. Scholars want arguments to *make sense*; but politicians know that arguments have to *work*—which means, in the long run, that they must form the basis for a stable consensus."[61] Therefore, what I offer now is not a refinement of the doctrinal arguments so ably made by others. Instead, I am interested in exploring what kinds of compromises might work to still some of the cannon- (and canon-) fire in the *kulturkampf.*

I begin with the set of issues raised in *Mozert v. Hawkins County Board of Education,*[62] in which several fundamentalist "born-again Christian"[63] parents claimed a constitutional right to have their children exempted from certain reading assignments in the local public schools because these assignments purportedly encouraged beliefs that ran contrary to the version of biblical literalism embraced by the parents. Two parents testified, in the language of the court, that they "objected to passages that expose their children to other forms of religion and to the feelings, attitudes and values of other students that contradict the plaintiffs' religious views without a statement that the other views are incorrect and that the plaintiffs' views are the correct ones."[64]

To put it mildly, I do not share the worldview of these parents. Taken seriously, it represents nothing less than an attack on the very notions of independent analysis and self-reflection to which I would like to think I have dedicated my own life.[65] Moreover, one notes that the readings at issue ostensibly were chosen by Tennessee to carry out the statutory duty of public schools "to help each student develop positive values and to improve student conduct as students learn to act in harmony with their positive values and learn to become good citizens in their school, community, and society."[66] For ease of argument, let it be stipulated that the readings in fact did these desirable things. Does this combination of desirable readings and questionable, perhaps even appalling parental values conclude the discussion?

To answer this question requires returning to *Pierce* and its protection of private education. For all of the emphasis placed by the court on the importance of public schools as the molder of democratic citizens, it readily embraces the legitimacy of fleeing from the public school and the presumed inculcation of quite different values. Judge Lively, for the majority in *Mozert*, sets out his view of the choices facing the parents:

> The parents in the present case want their children to acquire all the skills required to live in modern society. They also want to have them excused from exposure to some ideas they find offensive. Tennessee offers two options to accommodate this latter desire. *The plaintiff parents can either send their children to church schools or private schools, as many of them have done, or teach them at home. Tennessee law prohibits any state interference in the education process of church schools.*[67]

So the choice is (deceptively) clear: One can attend the public schools on the state's terms, or place one's children in church or home schools, which can apparently be operated entirely on the parents' (or a religious school's) terms. Are we stuck with these two alternatives?

I think not, precisely because *Pierce*, at least as interpreted by the court and substantiated by Tennessee law, seems sublimely indifferent to the universal inculcation of "positive" values. That is, once the state tolerates, either out of constitutional necessity or political ideology, what might be termed counter-hegemonic schools, then its seems hard, if not impossible, for the very same state to say that it has a "compelling state interest" justifying the burden placed on religious students by disallowing them from opting out of certain aspects of the public school curriculum. If the interest is truly "compelling," then one would think that the state would act aggressively to make sure that no child is denied its enjoyment.

However, if the state allows parents to withdraw their children entirely from the public schools and to inculcate views and values that might be quite antagonistic to the interests of the liberal democratic state, then why not in addition allow these parents to enjoy the public schools on at least some of their own terms, including the opting out from offensive curricular requirements? There is an easy answer to this question that involves the potentially high administrative costs attached to tolerating the opting out and, for example, preparing tests on reading material different from that read by most of the students. I do not in the least deny the reality of these and other costs that undoubtedly make the already hard work of the public school teacher more burdensome. I do offer two observations, though. First, there is no indication in the *Mozert* opinion of precisely what these costs, as a practical matter, would be. Secondly, there is a whole body of constitutional law, most of it admittedly from the Warren Court days, denigrating administrative ease and low costs as counterweights to "fundamental" constitutional interests. It seems hard to gainsay, for example, that protection of religious free exercise is at least equal in fundamentality as a constitutional value to the "right to travel" of indigents so vigorously protected by the majority in *Shapiro v. Thompson* against Connecticut's attempt to impose a one-year residency requirement, justified by reference to administrative and fiscal convenience, prior to the receipt of welfare.[68]

Moreover, liberals who often are properly quick to label as an "unconstitutional condition" the state's attempts to "buy up" important constitutional rights through the provision of public assistance, seem all too acquiescent here.[69] Surely, at least if one is even modestly egalitarian, *Pierce* cannot stand for the proposition that the state can exact any requirement it wishes from those who attend publicly financed schools so long as individuals with enough money or ideological zeal are free to withdraw and attend nonpublic schools. It should be chastening, at the least, to realize that Justice Frankfurter, in his (in)famous dissent in *West Virginia State Board of Education v. Barnette*,[70] based his argument on the propriety of forcing children, including Jehovah's Witnesses, to begin the school day with a salute to the American flag on the proposition that, after all, the parents of the Witnesses could withdraw their children and send them to private schools if they did not want their children to commit what they viewed as idolatry by saluting the flag. "As to its public schools, West Virginia imposes conditions which it deems necessary in the development of future citizens,"[71] and, for Frankfurter, that con-

cludes the discussion. If liberals properly reject Frankfurter's argument in
Barnette, it is not clear what makes it so much more attractive in a case
like *Mozert.*

Whatever else might be said about these parents, they were willing to
reject the option of separatism that the Constitution, and the laws of
Tennessee, granted them. For this, they should be praised rather than
discouraged and made to feel ever more marginal. For better or worse,
one cannot compel these students to attend public and multicultural
schools; that is the meaning of *Pierce*. By definition, this means that they
must be lured, and this requires offering them at least some of what it
will take to keep them within the public schools. As a practical matter,
only attending public (or what used to be called "common") schools will
offer the possibility of contact being made with persons significantly different from themselves. Although one certainly should not overestimate
the importance of such contact—Catholics, Eastern Orthodox, and Muslims, after all, used to live next door to one another in Bosnia—it seems
to me better than the alternative of ever-more separatism.

Candor compels me to state that I am considerably less willing to compromise in terms of the curriculum foisted on *nonreligious* students. For
example, I am certainly disinclined to support the entry into the general
curriculum of "creation science." That is easy (at least for me). What is
harder is deciding whether the Constitution is best interpreted as fore-
closing a state legislature or local school board from requiring that "creation science" be taught as an alternative account of the origins of life to
evolution.[72] I personally doubt that exposure to "creation science" arguments is all that important, and it is even possible that a gifted teacher
could use the conflict between such accounts and those of more traditional evolutionary biology to teach students, including religious students, something about the way that scientific arguments are actually
conducted in terms of evidence, hypotheses, the handling of anomalous
data, and the like.

I suspect that the conflict, like so much legal strife, is of primarily
symbolic importance. It has to do precisely with the determination of religious parents that the public school system pay them some formal respect
by acknowledging the "thinkability" of some of their cherished views
about the creation of life. To say that it is primarily a symbolic issue is not
meant to denigrate it; after all, as Justice Holmes once pointed out,
"[w]e live by symbols."[73] No one who has drunk from the (post)modern
well of semiotics can be blind to the importance of symbolism. It is in the
very nature of a *kulturkampf* that the issues of maximum strife will have
far less to do with the division of material resources—the basic issue of
class warfare—than with the valence to be placed on certain cherished
myths and symbols by which the cultural combatants give meaning to

their otherwise literally meaningless lives. No less than the Godfather do most human beings yearn for "respect," and woe to the society that systematically denies respect to any large (and mobilizable) subset of its population.

The universal desire for respect, incidentally, suggests why it is important that offers of compromise be two-way, including the acceptance by the "religious right" of a substantially more secular, culturally pluralistic school system than they might otherwise prefer. There is certainly reason for secularists to believe that they are fundamentally disrespected by many of the so-called "new religious right." As with tangos, it takes two to engage in a *kulturkampf*. If there is no alternative to a *kulturkampf*, then I have no hesitation in lining up with the opponents of religious orthodoxy. The question, though, is whether there is indeed an alternative to such a grim prospect.

All of these issues come together with regard to prayer in the public schools. To the extent that religious students continue to attend public schools, school prayer will undoubtedly continue to be a minefield. What am I willing to offer here? From one perspective, undoubtedly, the answer is, not much. I still unequivocally applaud both *Engel* and *Lee*; the state has no business either composing or arranging for the offering of prayers in public events. I also have no trouble supporting the most recent decision of the Court invalidating a school district policy that allowed student-led, student-initiated prayer before football games.[74] On the other hand, I find myself much less enamored of *Wallace*, even conceding that the purpose of the Alabama legislators who passed the statute was to sneak prayer, at least somewhat, back into the schoolroom, and that the teacher would state the magic word in calling the class to silence. Is it worth it, even from a secularist perspective, to prohibit such a law if the cost—and one must, of course, see this as a cost and not a benefit— is to alienate yet more religious parents (and possibly their children) from the public schools and, in some cases, to drive them from the public schools into one or another religious "academy?"

My answer, as one can readily gather, is no. The loss of such students, should it be occurring, deprives the public school of an important "different voice" that enhances the diversity so important to education. If one can keep some students simply by allowing a moment of silence, and allowing a teacher to say that at least some students might use this moment for prayer while others contemplate the meaning of life, last night's date, or whatever, it is a cheap price to pay. To insist on stamping out such moments in the name of the "wall of separation" is to fall victim to an ideological zeal that is little better, I am now convinced, than the zealotry exhibited by those who would wish to absorb the state as an ally in endorsing or enforcing a specific theological program. It is, therefore,

my hope that *Wallace*, if not flatly overruled, will in the future be restricted to its specific facts. State-imposed moments of silence and con-
templation, unaccompanied by state-composed prayers or entreaties from
the teacher to engage in prayer, ought not to be viewed as presenting
threats to the values underlying the Establishment Clause.

I conclude this section by trying to answer a series of questions directly
posed to me by Professor McConnell. They both capture the kinds of
controversies increasingly being litigated and, more importantly, present
just the kinds of questions that anyone concerned with the practice (and
not simply the theory) of multiculturalism must grapple with. The challenge offered by McConnell was as follows:

> [W]hat would you do if the graduating class is allowed to vote on whom to
> invite to give the graduation address, and the class votes for a person whose
> principal appeal is religious (the local bishop, perhaps—or a religious writer)?
> Would you allow a separate, voluntary baccalaureate service, organized by the
> school (or, better yet, a committee of the student government)? Would it be
> permissible for the student government to allow a representative sampling of
> the viewpoints in the class each to speak for five minutes at the graduation
> ceremony—and include an evangelical type? And what about non-school set-
> tings? Presumably, for the President to include prayers at his inauguration is
> permissible on the ground that it is done in his "private" capacity; presumably
> the same would be true of a joint swearing-in of a group of congressmen; why
> isn't the same principle applicable to graduating seniors from high school?[75]

Would I allow the graduating class to pick the speaker, even if the basis
of the selection is presumably the (likely) religious content of the address? I distinguish this, incidentally, from a class vote to have a student-
led prayer, which I would strike down in an instant.[76] As to selecting the
speaker, one might want to know the background history that provides a
"baseline" for consideration. *If* students traditionally chose the speaker,
and *if*, over many years, speakers had been drawn from a variety of places
on the intellectual spectrum, and *if* speakers had taken advantage of the
opportunity offered them to make controversial speeches challenging
conventional views (conditions that I would be absolutely astonished to
find met in more than a handful of high schools), *then* I would be inclined to describe as "censorship" the refusal by a school to honor a
class's choice to hear, as in McConnell's example, the local bishop and
the likely invocation of religious themes.

I would analogize the example to the situation presented before the
Supreme Court in *Lamb's Chapel v. Center Moriches Union Free School
District*,[77] where a unanimous Court struck down the refusal of a New
York school board to grant permission to Lamb's Chapel, an evangelical
church in the local community, to present a film series concerning the

family and encouraging the return to "traditional, Christian family values." The board was applying its rule prohibiting the use of public school facilities, even after school hours, for "religious purposes," even though other rules allowed access to a multitude of nonreligious groups. The Court properly found this content-based distinction in violation of the First Amendment.

An obvious distinction is that the Lamb's Chapel program is not formally sponsored or otherwise endorsed by the school board, whereas the graduation ceremony, even if not compulsory, is a central public ritual, and it would be unfortunate indeed if a member of the non-hegemonic minority was reluctant to attend such an important occasion because of the anticipatory discomfort produced by the prospect of a religiously oriented speech. But, of course, the discomfort could well be produced by inviting the local member of Congress or anyone else identified with any controversial stance on public issues.[78] Under these circumstances, then, I would support the students' choice. If, however, as I suspect is almost certainly going to be the case, student selection of the speaker is a brand-new option, adopted at least in part to evade the strictures of *Weisman* and other similar decisions, then I have little hesitancy in striking down McConnell's first example.[79]

Would I permit a separate, voluntary baccalaureate service, organized by the school (or, better yet, a committee of the student government) at which prayer(s) would be offered? No, to the school-organized service. After all, the "official" baccalaureate service is "voluntary," and that properly made no difference to the *Weisman* majority. The school system should not be in the business of organizing "separate-but-equal" services, regardless of the basis of the separation. I am inclined to give the same answer for the service organized by the student government.

Far different is a separate ceremony organized by a group of students, including, for example, the president of the student council and the captain of the football team, and held "off-campus," perhaps at a local church. I can see no argument for enjoining students from announcing their desire to offer thanks to God upon completion of their high school careers and inviting their classmates to join them. What if the "supplementary" ceremony in fact became the principal one, so that most of the students and parents showed up at the local church and relatively few bothered to come to the high school auditorium? (I assume, for ease of argument, that the two services are not scheduled at the same time.) I would regard this as most unfortunate, but again I cannot imagine any reading of the First Amendment that would bar students and parents from organizing a religious service to which the public is invited. Only if the organizing committee included school officials might there be a genuine dilemma, though even here one should be wary of forcing public employees to waive their own rights of free expression as a condition of accepting public employment.

Could the student government allow a representative sampling of the viewpoints in the class to speak for five minutes each at the graduation ceremony, and include an evangelical type? This strikes me as an easy case: The answer is yes. It becomes especially easy if the "representative sampling" includes students expressing nonreligious views likely to get under the skin of many of those in attendance, such as endorsements of gay and lesbian rights, attacks on welfare recipients, support (or denunciation) of capital punishment, and the like. *Weisman* properly bars the state from asking students to "join in" a prayer, even if they have the option of refusing the invitation. Hearing an evangelical student, one among many other students, witness his or her faith in Jesus, is simply not the same thing.

Indeed, the evangelical student need not necessarily be "balanced" with nonreligious counterparts. If, for example, the valedictorian is evangelical and wishes to begin her speech with thanks to God, then that is acceptable. She earned her right to speak on grounds wholly separate from her religious identity, and, generally speaking, the state ought not be able to extract a "bleaching out"[80] of her religious identity as a condition for enjoying what all valedictorians have enjoyed before her—the right to speak to her classmates and parents. Things get far trickier, of course, if, as is common, valedictory speeches are in effect subject to censorship via submission to the principal for review. However, I confess that I find the idea of review itself to be far more constitutionally suspect than the prospect of the speaker "slipping in" some prayer. The valedictorian should have the same freedom as the President of the United States to include religious references in her speech.[81]

Conclusion: Toward Synthesis?

I have tried in this essay to offer reflections on some implications of the reality of religious multiculturalism within America. I have also tried, quite self-consciously, to present myself as a wonderfully tolerant person who genuinely wishes to reach out to persons of decidedly different sensibility from my own. Yet candor requires me to admit that one reason I would prefer the children at issue in *Mozert* to attend the public schools is precisely to increase the likelihood that they might be lured away from the views—some of them only foolish, others, alas, quite pernicious—of their parents. Perhaps *they* will meet and begin talking with, and learning from, more secular students.

Here we see the underside of terms like "tolerance," for, generally speaking, one who self-consciously "tolerates" opposing views or ways of life is unlikely to offer them "equal concern and respect." Instead, the tolerator only holds back from exercising certain kinds of force that would make the lives of the tolerated even worse. I do not mean to denigrate "toleration." There can be no doubt that the move from a society in which one is actively suppressed to one in which one is tolerated is an important gain, and most of the world would be better off if toleration were more widespread. Still, no one should confuse this with full and complete acceptance. It is this difference that is at the heart, I believe, of the contemporary debate about the public stance regarding gays and lesbians. Many straight Americans are far more willing to "tolerate" gays and lesbians than to acknowledge that there is really nothing at all objectionable about gay and lesbian behavior. Similar tensions are present when sectarians are asked to grant full legitimacy to secular perspectives and, of course, vice versa.

In any event, I find myself far more in a "tolerationist" than a genuinely "accepting" posture vis-à-vis persons like Vicki Frost. Thus I confess my hope that her children, by attending public schools, will in fact meet and begin talking with (and learning from) more secular students. My anger at the Hawkins County School Board is derived as much from their driving the children away, and thus, from my perspective, contributing, albeit indirectly, to the reinforcement of their parents' worldview, as it is from the board's exhibiting antagonism to the worldview itself. To push these students from the public schools, by refusing to make the kinds of concessions their parents demanded—which, after all, went only to *their* education and not to the materials assigned all of the other children— will assure that they will in fact be educated within institutions that are, from my perspective at least, far more limiting and, indeed, "totalitarian" than anything likely to be found within a decent public school. My desire to "lure" religious parents back to the public schools thus has at least a trace of the spider's web about it.

I recognize, of course, that in a genuinely religiously multicultural school some secular students will be led to accept the students' religious understanding. Isn't this what education is all about—to present alternative views of the world and thus potentially transform the lives of individuals who had not heretofore dreamt of these possibilities? But, as already indicated, I am, perhaps optimistically, assuming that the transformation is far more likely to run from the religious to the secular than vice versa, and I cannot honestly say I know what I would be arguing if I were persuaded that the likelihood, as a practical matter, ran in the opposite direction.

Do the last several paragraphs undercut the professed aim of this essay and thus deny the possibility of a synthesis of the initial thesis and anti-

thesis presented at the beginning? Or, to adopt a question posed by
James Boyd White,[82] do I reveal myself to be fundamentally uninterested
in truly encountering the Others who do not share my own secular sensibility? And if that is the case, then why should they trust me truly to
adjudicate their claims, anymore than I would be inclined to trust one of
them to adjudicate my own?

My professed aim is to call upon fellow secularists to think of possible
grounds of compromise with religious sectarians, especially in regard to
the extraordinarily complex issue of education. I would like to think that
is my real aim as well. But it is altogether possible that what this essay
ultimately reveals is the difficulty, if not outright impossibility, of finding
a common ground on which secularists and the religiously orthodox can
walk together. After all, as the prophet Amos asked more than two mil-
lennia ago, "Do two people travel together unless they have agreed to do
so?"[83] Perhaps I simply have not taken sufficient account of, and I may
even illustrate, the deep chasm separating these two parts of the American social community. But we will not know this for a fact unless we at
least make good faith attempts to understand the positions of the combatants in America's *kulturkampf* and to see if there are indeed ways to
prevent the conflicts from becoming ever more deadly to the hope of
achieving some kind of *unum* among the *pluribus* of American society.

Notes

An earlier version of this chapter appeared under the title "Some Reflections on
Multiculturalism, 'Equal Concern and Respect,' and the Establishment clause of
the First Amendment," in 27 University of Richmond Law Review 27 (1993):
989–1021.

1. I have purposely left in the text what I remembered the text saying, prior to
"looking it up." One "official" version is "For God so loved the world that he
gave his only Son, that whoever believes in him should not perish but have eternal life" John 3:16 (Revised Standard Version). It is this version that is quoted in
Michael McConnell, "Christ, Culture, and Courts: A Niebuhrian Examination of
First Amendment Jurisprudence," Depaul L. Rev. 42 (1992): 191, 215 n. 136
(quoting H. Richard Niebuhr, *Christ and Culture* [New York: Harper, 1951], p.
197).

2. It is important to recognize, though, the existence of self-described "Jews
for Jesus," or "completed Jews," who proclaim the coexistence of Jewish identity
and acceptance of Jesus as their Lord and Savior. Their claims, however, have not
been accepted by anyone within the "mainstream" Jewish community. See Sanford Levinson, "Identifying the Jewish Lawyer: Reflections on the Construction
of Professional Identity," *Cardozo L. Rev.* 14 (1993): 1585, n. 20.

3. See especially the opinions of these justices in *Illinois* ex rel. *McCollum v. Board of Educ.*, 333 U.S. 203 (1947) (invalidating in-school "released time" programs).

4. 330 U.S. 1 (1947) (upholding the provision of bus service for parochial school students).

5. *Engel v. Vitale*, 370 U.S. 421 (1962). See also *Abington Sch. Dist. v. Schempp*, 347 U.S. 203 (1963).

6. See Sanford Levinson, *Constitutional Faith* (Princeton: Princeton University Press, 1988), ch. 1.

7. Robert Hughes, *The Culture of Complaint* (New York: Oxford University Press, 1993), pp. 83–84.

8. Sanford Levinson, "Religious Language and the Public Square," *Harv. L. Rev.* 105 (1992): 2062, n. 2 (book review). See also Levinson, "Diversity," U. of Penn. J. of Const'l L. 2 (2000): 603–5.

9. Bethel Sch. Dis. No. 403 v. Fraser, 478 U.S. 675, 681 (1986) (quoting C. Beard and M. Beard, *New Basic History of the United States* [1968], p. 228). This "civic education" aspect of education is scarcely uncomplicated. See, e.g., Meira Levinson, *The Demands of Liberal Education* (New York: Oxford University Press, 1999), ch. 4 ("Culture, Choice, and Citizenship: Schooling Private Citizens in the Public Square), pp. 100–131. It is safe to say, though, that no society that wishes to endure can be indifferent to the problem of socializing successor generations into the central values of the existing political order. See also Sanford Levinson, "Is Liberal Nationalism an Oxymoron? An Essay for Judith Shklar," 105 *Ethics* 626–45 (1996) (review of Yael Tamir, *Liberal Nationalism* [Princeton: Princeton U. Press, 1993]).

10. *Bethel Sch. Dis. No. 403 v. Fraser*, 478 U.S. 673, 681 (1986).

11. Benjamin Cardozo, *The Nature of the Judicial Process* (New Haven: Yale University Press, 1921), 17.

12. I have consistently benefited from the work of my colleague Douglas Laycock, among whose more important work is "The Remnants of Free Exercise," *Sup. Ct. Rev.* 1990: 1; "A Survey of Religious Liberty in the United States," *Ohio St. L. Rev.* 47 (1986): 409; "Towards a General Theory of the Religion Clauses: The Case of Church Labor Relations and the Right to Church Autonomy," *Col. L. Rev.* 81 (1981): 1373.

13. For a forthright presentation of this view, see Kathleen Sullivan, "Religion and Liberal Democracy," in *The Bill of Rights in the Modern State* (Geoffrey R. Stone et al., eds., Chicago: Chicago University Press, 1992), p. 196.

14. Ibid., p. 211.

15. 268 U.S. 510 (1925).

16. An earlier, far briefer version of this discussion can be found in my contribution to *American Jews and the Separationist Faith: The New Debate on Religion in Public Life*, ed. David G. Dalin, (Washington, DC: Ethnics and Policy Center, 1993), pp. 74–75.

17. My colleague Douglas Laycock, who is unusual in his ability to take with utmost seriousness the claims of the religious without, so far as I know, being religious himself, also provided a great deal of help.

18. For an especially brilliant article, see Michael W. McConnell, "The Selective Funding Problem: Abortions and Religious Schools," *Harv. L. Rev.* 104 (1991): 989.

19. The term "equal concern and respect" is probably most identified with Ronald Dworkin. See, e.g., Dworkin, *Taking Rights Seriously*, (Cambridge: Harvard University Press, 1977), 180–83. However, Dworkin builds on the earlier work of John Rawls; See Rawls, *A Theory of Justice* (Cambridge: Harvard University Press, 1971), p. 511. See also John Hart Ely, *Democracy and Distrust* (Cambridge: Harvard University Press, 1980), where the notion of "equal concern and respect" also plays a central role.

20. Mark G. Yudof, *When Government Speaks* (Berkeley: University of California Press, 1983), p. 229.

21. The "secession" image is developed by Professor Toni Marie Massaro in *Constitutional Literacy: A Core Curriculum for a Multicultural Nation* (Durham, NC: Duke University Press, 1993), pp. 99–100. The "at least partial" in the text comes from the fact that not even Pierce places absolute control in the hands of parents, for the state retains the right to make sure that some "minimal" educational goods, as defined by the state, are transmitted to children. See Mark G. Yudof et al., *Educational Policy and the Law*, 3rd ed. (St. Paul, MN: West Publishing Co., 1992), pp. 43–77. Whether these requirements actually apply to home schooling, for example, is doubtful, but as a formal question of constitutional power, there is little doubt that courts will reject a claim of sovereign right by parents to disregard any and all state commands with regard to the education of their children.

22. See Dworkin, *Taking Rights Seriously*, pp. 180–83.

23. I put to one side the equally important question of whether it is legitimate to make parents pay for both public education they do not use and private schools they patronize. My answer is that the general public benefits of (or, in the language of economics, the "externalities" generated by) public education are sufficient to support coerced taxation for public education. I offer a similar analysis with regard to taxing the childless, who make no direct use of public schools. The religious parent sending children to nonpublic schools is no different, positionally, from the childless person who is deprived of some important want because of the duty to pay education taxes.

24. *Roe v. Wade*, 410 U.S. 113, 152 (1973).

25. See Michael McConnell, "Religious Freedom at a Crossroads," in Geoffrey R. Stone et al., eds., *The Bill of Rights in the Modern State* (Chicago: University of Chicago Press, 1993), pp. 184–85. McConnell's former colleague, Cass Sunstein, emphasizes the importance of baselines and their ostensible (and false) "neutrality" in setting the terms of constitutional argument in Sunstein, *The Partial Constitution* (Cambridge: Harvard University Press, 1993). See Sanford Levinson, "Unnatural Law," *The New Republic*, July 19 and 26, 1993, p. 40 (reviewing Sunstein).

26. See McConnell, "Religious Freedom at a Crossroads."

27. A second important question, well beyond the scope of this informal essay, is whether the state has not just permission, but a duty, to return such money. I am decidedly more uncomfortable with this argument than with the more mod-

est, though scarcely less controversial, view that the Constitution, correctly interpreted, does not deprive the state of the ability to aid private schools, including religious ones.

28. As I have said elsewhere, "I would . . . gladly overrule Committee for Educ. v. Nyquist, 413 U.S. 756 (1973)," one of the most important barriers standing in the way of state aid to religious schools. Sanford Levinson, "Religious Language and the Public Square," *Harv. L. Rev.* 105 (1992): 2078, n. 72.

29. See, e.g., *Agostini v. Felton*, 521 U.S. 203 (1997); *Zobrest v. Catalina Foothills Sch. Dist.*, 509 U.S. 1 (1993); *Witters v. Washington Dept. of Servs. for the Blind*, 474 U.S. 481 (1986). *Mitchell v. Helms*, 120 S.Ct. 2530 (2000), which will be discussed below, is an unusually interesting case, perhaps portending a far more drastic shift in doctrine. Still, given the failure of the Court to coalesce around a single opinion—there was a plurality opinion for four justices, written by Justice Thomas, and an opinion concurring in the result by Justice O'Connor, joined by Justice Breyer—the statement in the text remains accurate at least until the arrival of one or more new justices who will provide the votes for a stable majority.

30. 509 U.S. 1 (1993).

31. Interestingly enough, Justice Thomas's plurality opinion in *Mitchell v. Helms*, for himself and three other justices, including Chief Justice Rehnquist, offered a significantly more capacious reading of Zobrest, which brought forth complaint from Justice O'Connor, who, as a result, joined only in the result and not the Thomas opinion. See 120 S.Ct. 2545 (Thomas); 2558 (O'Connor).

32. 509 U.S., p. 10.

33. Ibid., p. 12.

34. Ibid.

35. Ibid. Were this an essay on theories of interpretation and postmodernism, one could certainly debate whether this guideline, in fact, is capable of being complied with (and how one might conceivably know of this). Fortunately, this is not such an essay, and I am assuming that most of us agree with Rehnquist that it is indeed cogent to view the interpreter as being in a different position from the overtly choice-making teacher.

36. Justices Blackmun, Stevens, O'Connor, and Souter joined in a procedural dissent protesting the Court's deciding the substantive issue at all in this particular case.

37. 509 U.S., p. 18.

38. See, e.g., Richard Epstein, "The Supreme Court, 1987 Term—Foreword: Unconstitutional Conditions, State Power, and the Limits of Consent," *Harv. L. Rev.* 102 (1988): 4; Kathleen Sullivan, "Unconstitutional Conditions," 102 *Harv. L. Rev.* 102 (1989): 1413. See generally Paul Brest et al., *Processes of Constitutional Decisionmaking*, 4th ed. (New York: Aspen Publishers, 2000), pp. 1415–92.

39. See, e.g., *Rust v. Sullivan*, 500 U.S. 173 (1991); *Federal Communications Comm'n v. League of Women Voters of California*, 468 U.S. 364 (1984); *Regan v. Taxation With Representation of Wash.*, 461 U.S. 540 (1983).

40. Justice Blackmun dissented, for example, in the abortion funding cases, *Harris v. McRae*, 448 U.S. 297 (1980) and *Maher v. Roe*, 432 U.S. 464 (1977), as well as in Rust.

41. See Linda Greenhouse, "Court Says Government May Pay for Interpreter in Religious School," *N.Y. Times*, June 19, 1993, pp. 1, 8. One assumes that, as a result of the Supreme Court's decision, they were remunerated for their expenditures.

42. See, e.g., his dissent in *Mitchell v. Helms*, 120 S.Ct. 2572.

43. 515 U.S. 819 (1995).

44. Ibid., p. 847.

45. 120 S.Ct. 2592 (Souter, J., dissenting).

46. See, e.g., the description of Vicki Frost's views in *Mozert v. Hawkins County Bd. of Educ.*, 827 F.2d 1058, 1060–62 (6th Cir. 1987), discussed below in the section on school prayer

47. No doubt there are limits to the tolerance due truly pernicious subcultures, especially if, as a matter of social fact, they potentially threaten the maintenance of liberal democracy itself. Fortunately, that is a topic beyond the scope of this particular essay. See Stanley Fish, *The Trouble with Principle* (Cambridge: Harvard University Press, 1999), particularly chs. 4 ("Boutique Multiculturalism") and 11 ("Mission Impossible"). I note also that Stephen Macedo has written a recent book that is obviously relevant to the central themes of this chapter, *Diversity and Distrust: Civic Education in a Multicultural Democracy* (Cambridge: Harvard University Press, 1999), but I have not had the time fully to integrate it into this discussion.

48. See Hughes, *The Culture of Complaint*, for an eloquent polemic on this point.

49. Michael McConnell, "Multiculturalism, Majoritarianism, and Educational Choice: What Does Our Constitutional Tradition Have to Say?" *U. Chi. Legal F.* 1991: 149.

50. Ibid., pp. 148–50.

51. Ibid.

52. Ibid., p. 126.

53. 406 U.S. 205 (1972).

54. See Amy Gutmann, *Democratic Education* (Princeton: Princeton University Press, 1987), pp. 19–41.

55. As one reader suggested, some persons (including, presumably, the parents who brought the Mozert litigation discussed below) might well regard this as a dystopian nightmare instead.

56. 370 U.S. 421 (1962).

57. 472 U.S. 38 (1985).

58. 505 U.S. 577 (1992).

59. See, e.g., James D. Hunter, *Culture Wars: The Struggle to Define America* (New York: Basic Books, 1991). The most famous judicial invocation of the term is surely Justice Scalia's angry dissent in *Romer v. Evans*, 517 U.S. 620 (1996), in which the Court struck down an amendment added by popular referendum to the Colorado Constitution that seemingly denied gays and lesbians a host of legal protections. According to Scalia, "The court has mistaken a Kulturkampf for a fit of spite" (ibid., p. 636), and he left no doubt that he saw no constitutional problem in the use of the state to engage in the culture war involving the place of homosexuality in American culture.

60. Stephen L. Carter, "Strife's Dominion," *New Yorker*, August 9, 1993, p. 86.

61. Ibid., p. 92.

62. 827 F.2d 1058 (6th Cir. 1987). See generally the important article by Nomi Maya Stolzenberg, "'He Drew a Circle that Shut Me Out': Assimilation, Indoctrination, and the Paradox of a Liberal Education," *Harv. L. Rev.* 106 (1993): 581. Also essential for any student of Mozert is Stephen Bates, *Battleground: One Mother's Crusade, the Religious Right, and the Struggle for Control of Our Classrooms* (New York: Poseidon Press, 1993).

63. By no means are all "born-again Christians" either "fundamentalists" or committed to the kinds of views articulated by the plaintiffs in this case.

64. 827 F.2d, p. 1062.

65. In these postmodernist times, it is necessary to note that "independence" and "self-reflection" are highly problematic notions, for we are always embedded within the presuppositions of a given culture, and our "self" is substantially a creation of that culture. One can, therefore, never gain a leverage point of "independence" from culture per se, nor, obviously, can one engage in out-of-self experiences in order to reflect in a thoroughly detached way on the object that goes under one's name. All of this can be conceded, I believe, without giving up all allegiance to the Enlightenment value of "thinking for oneself" that remains the core of a liberal education.

66. 827 F.2d, p. 1060 (quoting *Tenn. Code Ann.* 49-6-1007 [Supp. 1968]).

67. Ibid., p. 1067 (emphasis added). Judge Lively quotes Tennessee Code Annotated § 49-50-801(b) (Supp. 1968): "The state board of education and local boards of education are prohibited from regulating the selection of faculty or textbooks or the establishment of a curriculum in church-related schools." If this statute means what it appears to say on the surface, then the state does indeed seem to have ceded sovereignty to the parents (or at least to the administrators of a church school).

68. 394 U.S. 618 (1969).

69. See Justice Douglas's dissent in *Wyman v. James*, 400 U.S. 309, 327 (1971) ("[T]he central question is whether the government by force of its largesse has the power to 'buy up' rights guaranteed by the Constitution.").

70. 319 U.S. 624 (1943).

71. Ibid., p. 656.

72. See *Edwards v. Aguillard*, 482 U.S. 578 (1987) (striking down a Louisiana law that required the teaching of "creation science" together with evolution, because passage of the law was motivated by the illegitimate purpose of aiding religion).

73. Oliver Wendell Holmes, *Collected Legal Papers* (New York: Harcourt, Brace and Co., 1920), 270.

74. *Santa Fe Independent School District v. Doe*, 120 S.Ct. 2266 (2000).

75. Letter from Michael W. McConnell to Sanford Levinson (July 7, 1993).

76. Cf. *Jones v. Clear Creek Ind. Sch. Dist.*, 977 F.2d 963 (5th Cir. 1992), cert. denied, 113 S. Ct. 2950 (1993) (holding student-initiated prayers in graduation ceremonies acceptable). Although the Court denied review in Jones, the Fifth Circuit later confined its reach to graduation exercises when striking down pre-

football student-delivered prayer in *Doe v. Duncanville Ind. School Dist.*, 70 F.3d 402 (1995). It is impossible to believe that the majority that struck down the similar process of student-initiated prayer in the recent *Santa Fe* case would not apply its analysis to graduation events, though it remains open to unsympathetic courts below to argue that *Santa Fe* is merely a "football" (or, more broadly, "athletic events") case and has no application to graduations.

77. 508 U.S. 384 (1993).

78. Consider, for example, the demonstrations mounted in June 1993 at Harvard in protest of the selection as graduation speaker of General Colin Powell, who opposed proposals by President Clinton to integrate gays and lesbians fully into the armed forces.

79. A reader for the Princeton University Press objected that I am biased against "new" empowerment of students insofar as I am relying on a baseline of past events in order to allow students in a given month or year to invite a religious speaker. That is probably true. One reason for my suspicion of "new" empowerment is that it often appears to occur as a fairly obvious pretext to allow (and, indeed, subtly encourage) students to do what the school district no longer can do, i.e., require prayer before school events. See, for example, the background of the student-empowerment policy adopted in Santa Fe. As Justice Stevens wrote for the majority, "We refuse to turn a blind eye to the context in which this policy arose, and that context quells any doubt that this policy was implemented with the purpose of endorsing school prayer" (120 S.Ct. 2282). I would be more receptive to "new" empowerment were there no such evidence, but, alas, I doubt that such situations will often, if ever, arise.

80. See Sanford Levinson, "Identifying the Jewish Lawyer: Reflections on the Construction of Professional Identity," *Cardozo L. Rev.* 14 (1993): 1577, 1578, 1601.

81. This being said, I must note my own personal wish that presidents would in fact choose to omit opening and closing benedictions at inaugurations. Indeed, I believe that these should come under the "unconstitutional conditions" strictures announced in Weisman, though I scarcely expect any court to enjoin the President from inviting ministers, priests, and rabbis—and, in the near future, Islamic and Buddhist prelates—to take part in inaugural rituals. Whatever else one might think of the selection of Joseph Lieberman to be Al Gore's running mate in the 2000 presidential election, I suspect that it set back the cause of secularism at least a decade. More than ever, it seems impossible for a major American politician to declare forthrightly that he or she has no religious beliefs and/or wishes to secularize public ceremonies by omitting religious benedictions.

82. "I think it less important," he wrote in a very thoughtful letter commenting on an earlier draft, "how a particular judge or scholar comes out than who he manages to make himself—and his audience, and the law—in the way in which he thinks and talks about the case." Letter from White to Levinson (October 13, 1993). I am not at all sure that this conclusion, rewritten as a result of White's letter, fully meets his point, but I am grateful to him for pushing me to think more deeply about what I hope to do (and to reveal) by writing this article.

83. Amos 3:3. Of course, much of the major political theory of our time is structured by the obvious reality that society has become radically pluralistic, which by definition means there is substantial disagreement about basic issues.

10

Second Thoughts on the First Amendment

H. N. HIRSCH

I.

It has become quite common and even fashionable to have second thoughts about the First Amendment. In the academy, in the civil liberties and civil rights communities, and in constitutional law, the liberal orthodoxy that governed decades of thinking about the First Amendment has disintegrated.

In terms of First–Amendment theory, the most prominent of the many challenges to free speech have come from two separate but broadly similar fronts: the anti-pornography, feminist jurisprudence of Catharine MacKinnon, and the school of thought coming to be known as Critical Race Theory, the proponents of which argue for restrictions on hate speech when it is directed against historically disadvantaged minorities. Both of these schools of thought have garnered voluminous attention, and deserve to be treated seriously. They are dead wrong, but they are not frivolous theories, and must be met head on.

At the same time, an impressive body of new First Amendment theory has been generated by legal scholar Cass Sunstein, who argues for a "new deal" for speech that would, much like the New Deal of the 1930s, address many of the most egregious problems in the free speech marketplace. Where MacKinnon and Critical Race theorists are radicals, we might say, Sunstein is our leading reformer.

In terms of First Amendment practice, the most serious challenge has come from civil rights attorneys who have turned to civil suits, and a novel theory of civil liability, to prosecute white racists.

This paper will examine these challenges to the First Amendment. The view of the amendment put forward here promises the liberty to criticize and even advocate fundamental reform of any and all political establishments. This is the perspective both of the would-be framers of new constitutions and of those who would conserve a capacity for making and remaking constitutions as both a good in itself and an essential of liberalism. This is the perspective of a very strong First Amendment. From this perspective, second thoughts about the First Amendment may well be appropriate, but not for the reasons these current critics think.

II.

Let us begin with the case of the new theory of civil liability being put forward to combat white racist organizations. The most prominent of these trials involved the prosecution of two neo-Nazis, Tom and John Metzger, father and son, of Fallbrook, California, in connection with the beating death of Mulugeta Seraw, an Ethiopian student, in Portland, Oregon in 1988. The civil suit was filed on behalf of Seraw's family by Morris Dees, one of the country's most prominent civil rights attorneys, a founder of the Southern Poverty Law Center.[1] The case was even the subject of an approving Bill Moyers documentary aired on PBS.[2]

Dees's star witness at the trial was one Dave Mazzella. According to Dees, Mazzella, who had been a skinhead since the age of 16, was sent by the Metzgers to Portland with the explicit purpose of organizing skinheads there to commit violent acts. According to Dees, Mazella was the Metzgers' agent, and his action on behalf of his principals directly caused the death of Mr. Seraw. In Dees's words, the baseball bat that killed Seraw "started in Fallbrook, California."[3]

There is no question that the Metzgers urged Mazzella to go to Portland; he carried with him a letter of introduction from John Metzger, addressed to one of the Portland skinheads who eventually pled guilty to the murder. In his opening exchange on the witness stand with Dees, Mazzella admitted being the vice president of WAR—the White Aryan Resistance, the Metzgers' primary organization—at the time of the murder:

DEES: In that capacity, did Tom and John Metzger instruct you to teach skinhead recruits to commit violent acts against blacks and Jews and other minorities?

ANSWER: Yes, they did.

DEES: Did these instructions include the commission of physical violence?

ANSWER: Yes, they did.

DEES: Were you sent to Portland by Tom and John Metzger in October 1988 to organize East Side White Pride . . . ?

ANSWER: Yes, I was.

DEES: Now, David, while you were in Portland, did you teach and direct East Side White Pride members to commit violent acts against blacks and other minorities in the Portland area?

ANSWER: Yes, I did—several times, as a matter of fact.[4]

From testimony such as this, and despite the fact that no criminal charges were ever filed against the Metzgers, Dees attempts to establish the Metzgers' liability for the death of Mr. Seraw.

So: what's the problem? Mazella has turned against the Metzgers, and seemingly presents damning evidence.

The problem is that Tom and John Metzger have First Amendment rights, and those rights include the right to advocate violence. They do not have the right to commit violent acts, or to incite immediate violence, or to conspire to commit specific crimes, but they have the right, under hard-won Supreme Court precedent, to believe racial violence is necessary, to promulgate that view, and to urge others to adopt that view and to act upon it.

If we look again at the verbs in Dees's questioning—did the Metzgers teach you, did they instruct you, did they help organize—we see that these are all activities protected by the First Amendment; all these activities involve not the commission of violent acts, or the preparation for specific violent acts, but rather the type of political advocacy central to the First Amendment.

What is so startling about the Metzger trial transcript is the parallel between the activities of the Metzgers—teaching, instructing, organizing, directing—and the activity of American Communists from the 1920s to the 1950s, many of whom were sent to jail for doing nothing more than advocating an unpopular political perspective.[5] The persecution of these men and women was, in time, used to forge a liberal consensus about the First Amendment, culminating in a case in 1969 in which the Supreme Court finally held that the First Amendment protects even the advocacy of violence, so long as that advocacy does not include "incitement to imminent lawless action." (The case, of course, is *Brandenberg v. Ohio*.)[6] The word "imminent" is vital, for it means that if there is a passage of time between the act of teaching and the ultimate violent act, it is the perpetrator of the violence, and not the advocating teacher, who is legally responsible. Such a rule is necessary in any constitutional order based on notions of individual equality and autonomy.

Where is the mention of *Brandenberg* in the Metzger case? There is none; instead of First Amendment precedent, Dees puts forward the theory of vicarious liability, under which Dave Mazzella is the Metzgers' agent, and they are responsible for the violent acts he encourages.

From the point of view of the First Amendment, there are at least two problems with this. First, Mazzella can be characterized as a *convert* to the Metzgers' point of view, not as, or not merely as, their agent. There was no evidence that the Metzgers coerced, or paid, Mazzella in any way; the evidence instead demonstrated that Mazzella was a committed skinhead who believed in the need for racial violence, and willingly went to Portland to spread his own political message. In a letter Mazzella to the Metzgers soon after his arrival in Portland, he wrote, "I'm really glad I made the choice to come here."[7] The First Amendment protects the speech rights even of violence-prone neo-Nazis to seek converts to their cause.

Second, and more seriously, there was absolutely no evidence presented at the trial that the Metzgers in any way conspired to commit any specific crime at any specific time, nor that they taught people how to act violently. They advocated the need for racial violence as part of their overall ideology of racial superiority, just as American Communists advocated the need for class struggle. On cross-examination, Tom Metzger (who was acting as his own attorney) asked Mazzella:

> QUESTION: Now, tell me how I taught you to kill people.
> ANSWER: Through your literature. I passed out, you know, papers.
> Q: Passed out papers?
> A: Uh huh, and encouraged my friends around there to commit acts of violence.
> Q: You encouraged your friends to commit acts of violence?
> A: Through your papers, yes. . . .
> Q: Did I teach you how to use a gun in the living room?
> A: No.
> Q: Well, to your knowledge, do I have any skinhead boots?
> A: No.
> Q: Did you ever see any baseball bat in my living room?
> A: No.
> Q: Brass knuckles?
> A: No. . . .
> Q: Well, how did I teach you to kill people and hurt people in that living room?
> A: . . . It was what was said—things, not direct . . .[8]

"It was what was said"—and in fact, what was said in Tom Metzger's publications is enough to turn your stomach, but is no more connected to specific acts of violence than *Mein Kampf*, or even, say, the writings of Malcolm X.[9]

III.

Why is *Brandenberg* the appropriate standard upon which to decide questions concerning incendiary speech—that is, speech that could lead to violence? If we examine the facts of the *Brandenberg* case itself, we begin to find an answer to this crucial question.

In *Brandenberg*, the appellant was a leader of the Ohio Ku Klux Klan; on one particular occasion he arranged for a local television station to cover his speech at a Klan rally.[10] At this rally, he said: "We're not a revengent organization, but if our President, our Congress, our Supreme Court, continues to suppress the white, Caucasian race, it's possible that there might have to be some revengence taken."[11] He also made deprecating comments about Blacks and Jews.[12] On the basis of this speech, he was convicted under Ohio's criminal syndicalism statute.

It is clear from the tone of Brandenberg's speech, and the context in which it was uttered, that no immediate violence was likely on that day. Moreover, any violence committed by a member of his audience would occur, not because of what Brandenberg said, but because of what the particular audience member believed and chose to do. Brandenberg's speech might help crystallize someone's resolve to act, but the decision to act would be that person's. And there would, without a doubt, be a passage of time between Brandenberg's speech and the commission of a crime—a passage of time during which members of Brandenberg's audience would decide for themselves whether it was time to take "revengence" on the government.

There are two crucial moral judgments being made when we require that speech incite imminent lawlessness before we allow the state to suppress it. The first is that the state has the authority to punish breaches of the peace, but not states of mind that could, at some time in the future, produce such breaches of the peace—in other words, the state can suppress action, but not thought. The second is that adult citizens are morally independent beings who can make up their own minds concerning the course of action they will pursue. Both of these moral judgments are essential components of American constitutionalism and the liberal political theory from which American constitutionalism derives.

The requirement of "incitement" is as old as Thomas Jefferson—though, to be sure, it was ignored by a majority of the Supreme Court until the 1960s. In a discussion of religious freedom, Jefferson wrote:

> to suffer the civil magistrate to intrude his powers into the field of opinion and to restrain the profession or propagation of principles on supposition of their ill tendency is a dangerous falacy [*sic*], which at once destroys all religious liberty, because he being of course judge of that tendency will make his opinions the rule of judgment, and approve or condemn the sentiments of others only as they shall square with or differ from his own; . . . it is time enough for the rightful purposes of civil government for its officers to interfere when principles break out into overt act against peace and good order.[13]

In this passage we see both a strong suspicion of government's motive for the suppression of speech, and a firm distinction between speech and action[14]—a distinction that often gets lost in discussions of politically distasteful, provocative speech. For example, in a friend of the court brief submitted in the Metzger case, the ACLU of Oregon fudges this distinction between speech and action; the verb "encouraging" is used several times in place of "inciting."[15] But encouraging violence is not the same thing as inciting it; the difference, while subtle, is absolutely crucial. To allow the state to criminalize the "encouragement" of violence is to use a "bad tendency" test—a test specifically rejected by *Brandenberg*, on wholly sound liberal principles.

IV.

Let us turn from words to pictures and movies, and the theoretical argument against pornography. In her most recent book, *Only Words*, Catharine MacKinnon elaborates upon her well-known argument that pornography is a form of gender discrimination that directly causes harms the state should prevent. The first graphic paragraphs of this book read as follows:

> Imagine that for hundreds of years your most formative traumas, your daily suffering and pain, the abuse you live through, the terror you live with, are unspeakable. . . . You grow up with your father holding you down and covering your mouth so another man can make a horrible searing pain between your legs. When you are older, your husband ties you to the bed and drips hot wax on your nipples and brings in other men to watch and makes you smile through it. Your doctor will not give you drugs he has addicted you to unless you suck his penis.
>
> You cannot tell anyone. When you try to speak of these things, you are told it did not happen, you imagined it, you wanted it, you enjoyed it. Books say this. . . . Laws say this. No law imagines what happened to you, the way it happened. You live your whole life surrounded by this cultural echo of nothing where your screams and your words should be.
>
> In this thousand years of silence, the camera is invented and pictures are made of you while these things are being done. You hear the camera clicking or whirring as you are being hurt, keeping time to the rhythm of your pain. You always know that the pictures are out there somewhere, sold or traded or shown around or just kept in a drawer. In them, what was done to you is immortal.[16]

There are several remarkable things about these passages, including the fact that MacKinnon's prose could itself be termed pornographic. In terms of the law, MacKinnon makes a direct and unchallengeable connection between violence and pictures of sex, and it is this unchallengeable link that stands at the center of her thinking about pornography. Pornography isn't about sex, it isn't a representation of sex; it is sex, and it is, always, violent sex. She writes:

The more pornography invades the sexuality of a population, the more wide-spread this dynamic becomes. It is not so much that the sexual terms reference a reality as that they reaccess and restimulate body memory of it for both the aggressor and victim. The aggressor gets an erection; the victim screams and struggles and bleeds and blisters and becomes five years old. "Being offended" is the closest the First Amendment tradition comes to grasping this effect.[17]

Powerful words, but an equivalent argument would be that the *Communist Manifesto* isn't about revolution, it is revolution; or that a Nazi pamphlet of the type promulgated by the Metzgers (which often contains graphic cartoons and pictures) isn't about race hatred, it is itself racial genocide. An argument equivalent to MacKinnon's is that the *Communist Manifesto* or a Nazi pamphlet or the writings of Malcolm X don't stimulate thoughts about political violence or murder, they are themselves violent. Methodologically, the First Amendment commands us to make these sorts of hypothetical substitutions when censorship is being urged upon us. The fact that sexual ideas and images can cause physiological responses and trigger body memories does not really explain why speech about sex, or pictures of sex, is different. All sorts of speech can cause physiological responses, including traditional political speech of many kinds. (Consider Pat Buchanan's speech to the 1992 Republican National Convention, which, I would guess, produced profound physiological responses in many members of American minority groups.)

More importantly, "physiological response" is not the same thing as violent action. Even if we grant MacKinnon's premise about the effects of pornography on the individual viewer, she still has not demonstrated, nor has anyone been able to demonstrate, a direct and immediate link between viewing pornography and the commission of violent crime.[18] On what ground does MacKinnon make her argument for censorship? She makes it in the name of the equality mandated by the Fourteenth Amendment, and here she is on shakier ground still. "The law of equality and the law of freedom of speech are on a collision course in this country," she writes. "Both bodies of law," she continues, "show virtual total insensitivity to the damage done to social equality by expressive means and a substantial lack of recognition that some people get a lot more speech than others."[19]

But is *social* equality what the Fourteenth Amendment mandates? For MacKinnon the Fourteenth Amendment is no longer about state action, or equal access to public goods, but about two social groups, oppressed victims and oppressing victimizers, and the need to redress the imbalance of social power between them. For MacKinnon there is no longer a public sphere of legal equality and a private sphere of social freedom; there should be instead a unified world of legislated perfect social equality.

Along the same lines MacKinnon argues that the question of how much free speech any social group deserves is to be determined in large part by the litmus test of whether the group supports or rejects her particular version of equality. Criticizing the Supreme Court for decisions that consider the First Amendment rights of the KKK as equivalent to the speech of civil rights activists conducting a boycott of white merchants in the South, MacKinnon writes:

> Suppressed entirely in the piously evenhanded treatment of the Klan and the [civil rights] boycotters—the studied inability to tell the difference between oppressor and oppressed that passes for principled neutrality in this area as well as others—was the fact that the Klan was promoting inequality and the civil rights leaders were resisting it, in a country that is supposedly not constitutionally neutral on the subject.[20]

Praising the Canadian Supreme Court for rejecting the American concept of free speech neutrality, MacKinnon writes that equal protection ought to be interpreted to mean that "social inferiority cannot be imposed through any means, including expressive ones."[21]

There are several problems with MacKinnon's vision of equality. First and most important, there is utterly no historical evidence to suggest that the destruction of social inferiority of any kind was in any way remotely contemplated, even in the abstract, by the framers and ratifiers of the Fourteenth Amendment. As I have argued elsewhere,[22] legitimate constitutional interpretation does require some connection to the intentions of the framers, however abstractly conceptualized.

Second, her vision of a world neatly and forever divided into the oppressed and their oppressors belies a sometimes more complex reality. Imagine a confrontation, in a large midwestern or eastern city, between a white woman, newly arrived from Appalachia, on welfare, and a male African-American police officer. She calls him a fascist pig (or worse), he calls her a dumb honky bitch. Whose speech is to be valued, using MacKinnon's vision of social equality?

Third, MacKinnon's rejection of free-speech neutrality, her willingness to tear down the distinction between public and private, her substitution of a single, approved view of women and men, paradoxically requires a re-creation of the kind of patriarchial authority she means ultimately to challenge (here I am drawing on an important discussion of MacKinnon by Wendy Brown).[23] For MacKinnon the goal is not human liberation or freedom; it is the protection of victims. Who does the protecting? The monolithic state, acting through law, or at least the state when it has come to its senses and accepted the single ultimate truth as revealed through Catharine MacKinnon. The goal is not the encouragement of the free individual; the goal is the police state, rigid, unswerving, enforcing the truth; the state as Rambo, or, perhaps, more accurately, the Terminator. This police state will, when it wises up, act to protect gender equality.

Moreover (as Brown argues) for MacKinnon gender is "fully comprised by sexuality," and pornography is "the singular truth of male domination."[24] Pornography enacts gender subordination, taking away from women their sexuality, just as expropriated labor takes away from workers that which should be most their own, according to classical Marxism.[25]

But what if sexuality is more complex, more differentiated, more nuanced, less chronological than MacKinnon suggests? Where are lesbians in MacKinnon's world? They don't really exist; sexuality is about one single thing, the violent male exploitation of women. What of lesbian pornography? It can't exist; pornography is about men exploiting women. As Brown asks,

> what if sexuality is not a single social relation but is itself a complex non-schema of discourses and economies. . . . What if gender generally and woman's subordination in particular does not devolve on a single social relation but has manifold sites and sources of production and reproduction—for example in discourses organizing motherhood, race, philosophical truth, citizenship, class, heterosexuality, war, science, and so forth?[26]

These are important questions, and MacKinnon's simplistic vision of equality does not begin to address them.

V.

There is a similar problem with the vision of equality put forward by Critical Race theorists, who argue that the First Amendment should not be read as protecting "assaultive speech," that is, "words used as weapons to ambush, terrorize, wound, humiliate, and degrade" historically disadvantaged minorities.[27]

Critical Race theorists say that they "present a dissenting view" from First Amendment orthodoxy, one "grounded in our experience as people of color."[28] On this basis, they argue that college campuses (among other institutions) must restrict racist speech. Why? Because if racial minorities are forced to endure verbal harassment, they will choose to withdraw from the university; if they withdraw, they have been denied equal access to state facilities and the Fourteenth Amendment has been violated. Once again, this time in the words of Mari Matsuda, the "liberation" of "victims . . . must be the bottom line of any First Amendment analysis."[29] The First Amendment, Critical Race theorists write, should not be used as a trump to "nullify the only substantive meaning of the equal protection clause, that the Constitution mandates the disestablishment of the ideology of racism."[30]

But the Fourteenth Amendment was not written to disestablish the ideology of racism; it was written to disestablish the public embodiment and the public effects of the ideology of racism, the denial of civil and political rights that flow from the ideology of racism. The Fourteenth Amendment is about the abuse of state power and state action, not the opinions and feelings of private citizens.

And as for the argument that, if forced to endure verbal harassment, minorities will withdraw from the university, there is, first, absolutely no evidence of any kind presented in anything I have read to substantiate that empirical claim; second, even if it were true, it would not mean that equal access to state institutions was being denied under any plausible construction of the Fourteenth Amendment. At my university, many students must work 20 to 30 hours a week to support themselves, and life is far more difficult for them than for full-time students; a student without the financial resources to pay our fees might well choose to withdraw from the University of California and pursue an education elsewhere. Has the state illegally denied him equal access to its facilities by being expensive? The argument is no more or less absurd than the argument of critical race theorists about campus hate speech. Equal access to public goods does not require freedom from insult by private individuals. Both Critical Race theorists and Catharine MacKinnon simply concoct the state action element of their argument; they attempt to use the Fourteenth Amendment to limit the First Amendment, but these arguments don't stand up to even the briefest scrutiny.

VI.

A less radical vision of the First Amendment is put forward by Cass Sunstein. Seeking to reform rather than to revolutionize, Sunstein argues two central points: that the First Amendment is linked to the concept of popular sovereignty—that is, that the purpose of the First Amendment is to protect, enhance, and facilitate political deliberation;[31] and that government interventions in the supposedly free speech "marketplace" may be beneficial and necessary; that "what seems to be government regulation of speech might, in some circumstances, promote free speech, and should not be treated as an abridgment at all."[32] Sunstein is here reviving the jurisprudence of Alexander Meiklejohn, the theorist most identified with a "political" interpretation of the First Amendment.[33] His effort to do so is a bit bizarre, given a whole generation of criticism of Meiklejohn's theory; in the words of one commentator, "Sunstein's effort to revive Meiklejohn . . . strikes a rather tinny, anachronistic note, much like an appeal to the Beatles in the age of Snoop Doggy Dogg."[34] The central problem is with the concept of the "political." Surely "politics" extends beyond discussions of partisan electoral politics; and yet, once we extend our definition beyond that subject, where can principled lines be drawn? There is now an impressive body of theoretical literature arguing that "the personal"—most especially including sex—is political, and, following this logic, one would have to conclude that sexually explicit speech is, in some sense, "political"—a conclusion Sunstein might be reluctant to accept.[35] Similarly, one could argue that commercial advertising—another form of speech often considered "low value"—involves the availability and price of consumer goods—surely a matter not irrelevant to "politics," if politics is understood to involve who gets what, when, and how. Thus either the definition of politics must be expanded to include almost any conceivable form of supposedly low-value speech, or the effort to restrict the First Amendment to "political" purposes must be abandoned and a new first principle discovered.

Sunstein's second major argument—that governmental interventions in the marketplace of ideas may sometimes be justified—is closely tied to, and dependent upon, his first argument about the "political" goal of free speech, and thus is valid only to the extent that his first argument holds up as an all-inclusive theory of the First Amendment. His examples of justified government interventions mostly involve the conventional political process—air time for political candidates, campaign finance laws, and so on. Sunstein is surely right that CBS, a vast corporate body, is not the same constitutional entity as an individual speaker,[36] but this doesn't really tell you what to do about (for example) pornography, or libel, or hate speech, or criminal solicitation laws.

Moreover, his argument that it may serve ultimately acceptable "Madisonian" goals to allow governmental intervention in political campaigns is an argument with perhaps some chilling implications. Basically, he argues in favor of some allowable governmental redistribution of resources—air time, campaign money, and so on. But why stop there? Surely the abilities of a candidate's political handlers, or the quality of her advertising firm, is critical to the effectiveness of any serious political campaign. Should political handlers and advertising agencies be assigned randomly by the government in some sort of lottery? Absurd, we would say—but is the argument really that different from an argument for equal air time, or campaign finance restrictions?

VII.

Where does this all leave us in our thinking in more general terms about the First Amendment?

First, it is clear, as we begin the new century, that we need to reaffirm that part of the liberal orthodoxy on speech that suggests that the First Amendment is indivisible; or, to put it another way, that the First Amendment must be enforced in a content-neutral manner. One cannot argue to restrict the rights of bad guys, like pornographers or neo-Nazis, without setting traps that could ensnare good guys, traps involving highly speculative theories of causation, as in the case of the Metzgers, or traps involving the embodiment of one single Truth and the banishment of any dissenting voice, as in the arguments about pornography and racist speech. If the Metzgers are responsible for the death of Mr. Seraw in Portland, then is perhaps the Bible, with its vision of apocalypse, ultimately responsible for the deaths in Waco, Texas? Is the argument really so different? And if racist slurs can be banished from campuses because they are insulting and might (hypothetically) lead students to withdraw, why not ban the giving of low grades, which can also be highly insulting and which, almost certainly, force far more instances of withdrawal from campuses around the country? Again, is the argument really that different?

Thirty years ago it was very widely believed, and confirmed by the highest psychiatric authorities, that homosexuality was a disease, a perversion, a menace to society, a concrete harm society has every reason to suppress. Homosexual organizations met in secret, if at all; homosexual publications were ruthlessly persecuted. Few dared utter the words, "I am a homosexual." Learned men spoke of homosexuality as degrading and inevitably violent in the same way MacKinnon speaks of pornography and Critical Race theory speaks of hate speech. If nothing else, these facts should give us serious pause about unchallengable truths, and—make no mistake—it is unchallengable truth that Catharine MacKinnon and Critical Race Theory offer us. They claim their truth can be derived from the Fourteenth Amendment, but the Fourteenth Amendment can't even begin to bear the weight they assign it.

Second, we need to remind ourselves that even creeps have rights. An elementary truth, but one seemingly lost on an increasing number of law professors.

Third, and most fundamentally, we need to develop an argument for free speech that is not consequentialist. We need a theory of free speech that rejects the notion of a marketplace of ideas—even, as Sunstein suggests, a "corrected" marketplace—that will, in the long run, produce "truth." For we live in a world in which "truth"[37] is an elusive and always debatable entity, a world in which truly free speech will produce bad consequences as well as good ones. People with access to, and the right to engage in, truly free speech may become excited by this or that ideology and do crazy things, like move to a religious compound and listen to a crackpot. But until they break specific laws, they must be left alone. In Justice Holmes's famous words, "every idea is an incitement," and we censor the spread of any idea at our own peril.

We also live in a world in which the resources that make speech effective—eloquence, education, access to George W. Bush or Dick Cheney, money—are not distributed evenly. That is a fact of life, and, to at least some extent, will remain a fact of life in any society that protects private initiative and accomplishment. The "marketplace" of ideas will simply not produce a fair hearing for every point of view, or a just final result, as measured against any individual's or group's particular conception of justice.

Ultimately, we need an argument about free speech that recognizes that every appeal for censorship, every argument based on a "truth," assumes the existence of unanimous political agreement that simply does not exist.[38] In a postmodern world,[39] any restriction on free speech is arbitrary, or, at best, merely majoritarian.

A non-consequentialist argument for free speech would root itself, not in a theory of citizenship, but in a theory of liberty. It would recognize that thinking and speaking freely is an essential component of human freedom. It would do away with the notion of "low" value speech, for what is of low value to some, or to many, may be of great value to others. It would proclaim that free speech is necessary, not to produce truth, or for the good of society, but because thoughts, ideas, and feelings are an essential component of a free human being.

Notes

The author thanks Alan Houston, Gary Shiffman, Nancy Rosenblum, Shannon Stimson, Keith Bybee, and Mark Sniderman for comments on an early draft.

1. The case is described in Morris Dees and Steve Fifer, *Hate on Trial: The Case against America's Most Dangerous Neo-Nazi* (New York: Villard Books, 1993).

2. "Hate on Trial with Bill Moyers," air date February 5, 1992. A transcript of this program—which contains filmed excerpts from the Portland trial—can be obtained from Journal Graphics, Denver, CO (Transcript #BMSP-21). All quotations from the trial are taken from this transcript.

3. Transcript, p. 26.

4. Ibid., pp. 2–3.

5. Consider the following from the Court's majority opinion in *Gitlow v. New York*, 268 U.S. 652 (1925), sustaining the conviction of a leftist named Benjamin Gitlow:

The indictment . . . charged that the defendant had advocated, advised and taught the duty, necessity, and propriety of overthrowing and overturning organized government by force, violence, and other unlawful means, by certain writings . . . entitled "The Left Wing Manifesto." . . .

[The Manifesto] condemned the dominant "moderate Socialism" for its recognition of the necessity of the democratic parliamentary state; repudiated its policy of introducing Socialism by legislative measures; and advocated, in plain and unequivocal language, the necessity of accomplishing the "Communist Revolution" by a militant and "revolutionary Socialism," based on the "class struggle" and mobilizing the "power of the proletariat in action," through mass industrial revolts. . . .

The Manifesto, plainly, is neither the statement of abstract doctrine nor . . . mere prediction that industrial disturbances and revolutionary mass strikes will result spontaneously in an inevitable process of evolution in the economic system. It advocates and urges in fervent language mass action. . . .

Freedom of speech . . . does not protect publications or teachings which tend to subvert or imperil the government. . . . Such utterances, by their very nature, involve danger to the public peace and the security of the State.

6. 395 U.S. 444 (1969).

7. Transcript, p. 6.

8. Ibid., pp. 6–7.

9. Consider the following from *The Autobiography of Malcolm X* (New York: Grove Press, 1966), pp. 366–67 (emphasis in original):

when the law fails to protect Negroes from whites' attack, then those Negroes should use arms, if necessary, to defend themselves. . . . I believe it's a crime for anyone who is being brutalized to continue to accept that brutality without doing something to defend himself. . . . I *am* for violence if non-violence means we continue postponing a solution to the American black man's problem.

10. Martin H. Redish, *Freedom of Expression: A Critical Analysis* (Charlottesville, VA: Michie, 1984), p. 183.

11. Ibid., pp. 183–84.

12. Ibid.

13. Julian Boyd, ed., *The Papers of Thomas Jefferson, 1777–1799*, Vol. II (Princeton: Princeton University Press, 1950), p. 546, quoted in David A. J. Richards, *Toleration and the Constitution* (New York: Oxford University Press, 1986), p. 184.

14. Richards, *Toleration*, p. 184.

15. Trial brief of the American Civil Liberties Union of Oregon, pp. 1, 4, 8, 24.

16. Catharine A. MacKinnon, *Only Words* (Cambridge, MA: Harvard University Press, 1993), pp. 3–4.

17. Ibid., pp. 58–59.

18. See my discussion of this issue in *A Theory of Liberty: The Constitution and Minorities* (New York: Routledge, 1992), pp. 17–18, 100–104, 145.

19. MacKinnon, *Only Words*, op. cit., pp. 71–72.

20. Ibid., p. 86.

21. Ibid., p. 106.

22. *A Theory of Liberty*, see esp. ch. 1.

23. "The Mirror of Pornography," ch. 4 in *States of Injury: Power and Freedom in Late Modernity* (Princeton: Princeton University Press, 1995).

24. Ibid., p. xxx.

25. Ibid.

26. Ibid.

27. Mari J. Matsuda, Charles R. Lawrence III, Richard Delgado, and Kimberle Williams Crenshaw, *Words That Wound: Critical Race Theory, Assaultive Speech, and the First Amendment* (Boulder, CO: Westview Press, 1993), p. 1.

28. Ibid., p. 2.

29. Ibid., p. 9.

30. Ibid., p. 15.

31. See Sunstein, *The Partial Constitution* (Cambridge, MA: Harvard University Press, 1993), esp. ch. 8; *Democracy and the Problem of Free Speech* (New York: The Free Press, 1993); see also "Free Speech Now," *University of Chicago Law Review* 59 (1992): 255 and "Pornography and the First Amendment," *Duke Law Journal* 1986: 589.

32. Sunstein, *The Partial Constitution*, p. 204.

33. See esp. Meiklejohn, *Free Speech and Its Relation to Self-Government* (New York: Harper and Bros., 1948).

34. Jeffrey Rosen, "The Limit of Limits," *The New Republic*, February 7, 1994. For examples of criticism of Meiklejohn, see Martin H. Redish, *Freedom of Expression: A Critical Analysis* (Charlottesville, VA: Michie, 1984), pp. 14–15; Rodney A. Smolla, *Free Speech in an Open Society* (New York: Knopf, 1992), pp. 15–16; Mark A. Graber, *Transforming Free Speech: The Ambiguous Legacy of Civil Libertarianism* (Berkeley: University of California Press, 1991), pp. 169–76, 215; Frederick Schauer, *Free Speech: A Philosophical Enquiry* (Cambridge: Cambridge University Press, 1982), pp. 37–39.

35. See Sunstein, *Democracy and the Problem of Free Speech*, p. xviii.

36. Ibid., pp. 36–37.

37. See Shane Phelan, "(Be) Coming Out: Lesbian Identity and Politics," *Signs* (Summer 1993): 767.

38. On these grounds, even the interpretation of the First Amendment put forward here cannot be established as "true"—a conclusion from which we should not shrink. The interpretation put forward in this paper is just that—one interpretation among others. Whether it is a better or worse interpretation than others is a matter to be settled by the canons of constitutional interpretation, canons set forward in this volume and by other scholars.

39. Among many works discussing postmodernism, see: Phelan, "(Be) Coming Out"; Thomas L. Pangle, *The Ennobling of Democracy: The Challenge of the Postmodern Era* (Baltimore: The Johns Hopkins University Press, 1992); John McGowan, *Postmodernism and Its Critics* (Ithaca: Cornell University Press, 1991); Seyla Benhabib, "Epistemologies of Postmodernism," in Linda J. Nicholson, ed., *Feminism/Postmodernism* (New York: Routledge, 1990); Jane Flax, "Postmodernism and Gender Relations in Feminist Theory," in ibid.

11

Constitutional Citizenship

WAYNE D. MOORE

THE UNITED STATES Constitution presumes to rest on the foundational political authority of "the people of the United States." They are its purported authors. They continue to hold amending powers and other retained and reserved prerogatives. Constitutional structures empower public officials to act on behalf of the people and for their benefit. Yet relatively little attention has been devoted to their roles in creating and re-creating constitutional norms.

This essay focuses on popular participation in maintaining and changing constitutional norms through interpretive practices. Accordingly, I set aside two related sets of issues: those surrounding popular involvement in formally amending the constitutional text and other extraordinary forms of popular political activity. Instead, I deal with normal and ongoing processes of constitutional criticism and affirmation.

More specifically, I examine ways that Frederick Douglass exemplified forms of unofficial lawmaking. During the antebellum period, the former slave advocated radical reinterpretation of the Constitution; with other radicals, he denied that the Constitution tolerated or supported slavery.

Douglass's arguments are instructive precisely because they did not achieve prominence during the antebellum period. The realization of radical antislavery ideals came through a civil war, formal constitutional amendments, reconstruction, and other political developments—not primarily through reinterpretation of the existing Constitution. Douglass's example thus provides a context for examining the status of out-of-favor positions: their standing independently of formal amendments, judicial pronouncements, and other changes in the official law of the Constitution.

According to conceptions of constitutional meaning and authority that predominated during the antebellum period, including applicable judicial precedents, the former slave was not an American "citizen" and could not become part of "the people" upon whose authority the Constitution rested and for whom it existed.[1] In practice, however, Douglass exercised rights of citizenship, asserted constitutional power as a member of "the people," and otherwise participated actively in constitutional governance.

This discrepancy directs attention toward vital aspects of American constitutionalism that are obscured by official interpretative precedents. Popular commitments are at the heart of American constitutionalism, not at its margins; and ordinary people, along with judges and other governing officials, have directly and indirectly shaped the course of American constitutionalism.

Criticism and Affirmation

Although Douglass eventually argued that the American Constitution was incompatible with legally sanctioned slavery, he had earlier "denounce[d] the Constitution and government of the United States as a most foul and bloody conspiracy."[2] Before he advocated radical reinterpretation, Douglass treated the Constitution as "a compact demanding immediate disannulment, and one which, with our view of its wicked requirements, we can never enter."[3] These earlier views were not surprising, considering his status as a former slave and his identification with blacks still held in bondage. Douglass's reasons for initially opposing the Constitution remained important, moreover, since they informed his later analysis.

Opposition

Douglass repeatedly defied and otherwise opposed "official law," both as interpreted and as enforced. He was born in Maryland as a "slave" and treated as "property" until 1838, when, at the age of twenty-one, he escaped from bondage and remained a fugitive until 1847, when some of his friends purchased his freedom. Even while formally a fugitive, however, Douglass lived in Massachusetts as if he were a free person. After his formal emancipation from slavery, he continued to defy authoritative legal precedents by claiming to be a citizen of New York and of the United States and by exercising a wide range of rights and powers of state and federal citizenship. He voted in national and state elections, owned property, gave speeches, edited a newspaper, traveled among the states and abroad, advised President Abraham Lincoln, and otherwise expressed commitment to constitutional norms.[4]

Douglass's autobiography tells how he had initially been a "faithful disciple" of William Lloyd Garrison, "fully committed to his doctrine touching the pro-slavery character of the Constitution of the United States, also the non-voting principle of which he was the known and distinguished advocate." Opponents of slavery, not just its defenders, interpreted the Constitution as protecting slavery:

> Brought directly, when I escaped from slavery, into contact with abolitionists who regarded the Constitution as a slaveholding instrument, and finding their views supported by the united and entire history of every department of the government, it is not strange that I assumed the Constitution to be just what these friends made it seem to be.[5]

Thus he initially endorsed what William Wiecek has called the "federal consensus," whose correlative central tenets were that the Constitution allowed slavery within the states and that it precluded the federal government's abolishing slavery.[6]

In speeches, articles, and correspondence, Douglass criticized the Constitution as a pro-slavery compact. He pointed out that the constitutional text, "standing alone, and construed *only* in the light of its letter, without reference to the opinions of the men who framed and adopted it, or to the uniform, universal and undeviating practice of the nation under it, from the time of its adoption until now, is not a pro-slavery instrument." But he claimed that the Constitution, "having a terrestrial, and not a celestial origin," had to be "explained in the light of those maxims and principles which human beings have laid down as guides to the understanding of all written instruments, covenants, contracts and agreements emanating from human beings, and to which human beings are parties both on the first and second part." Interpreted in that light, Douglass argued, the Constitution was "a most cunningly-devised and wicked compact," one "made in view of the existence of slavery, and in a manner well calculated to aid and strengthen that heaven-daring crime." To support that conclusion, he referred to parts of the constitutional text that distorted representation in favor of slave states, gave Congress power to suppress insurrections, prohibited Congress from outlawing the slave trade until 1808, provided for the return of fugitive slaves to their alleged masters, and purportedly justified the use of national power to protect slaveholders from insurrection within the states.[7]

As did other Garrisonians, Douglass at first relied primarily on moral suasion, rather than representative institutions, for legal change. He rejected Gerrit Smith's argument for change through voting and official actions. According to moral perfectionists with whom Douglass associated, those who relied on corrupt governmental structures would become tainted by association, even if these persons' motives were good and their actions helped to bring about good results. Based on a premise that the Constitution was a pro-slavery pact, the Garrisonians also argued that federal officials would be acting illegally if they used their positions to abolish slavery. They repudiated both popular and governmental efforts to construe the Constitution as antislavery and regarded such efforts as forms of "do[ing] evil that good may come." Douglass claimed that "a man is lame, impotent, and worse than weak, when he ceases to regard the clear convictions of his understanding, to accomplish anything, no matter how desirable that thing may be."[8]

Thus Douglass initially argued against "mending old clothes with new cloth, or putting new wine into old bottles." Instead, he treated the Constitution as a "compact demanding immediate disannulment, and one which, with our view of its wicked requirements, we can never enter." He sought, in short, to expose the Constitution's wickedness as a way to "hasten the day of deliverance" from the present Union. He pledged that until then, he would not defile himself by engaging in unholy practices: "For my part I had rather that my right hand should wither by my side than cast a single ballot under the Constitution of the United States."[9]

Yet even as he criticized the Constitution and argued against seeking to eliminate slavery by relying on representative structures, Douglass held out the possibility of reinterpreting the document. Reflecting his confidence that truth would prevail in an unfettered environment, Douglass wrote in the *North Star* on March 16, 1849 that he was "prepared to hear all sides," including Smith's argument that the Constitution could be used as a "*rightful* instrument against slavery." Douglass initially commended Smith's moral position even though he was unpersuaded by Smith's analysis of what the Constitution meant. Though he eventually confessed to Smith that he was "sick and tired of arguing on the slaveholders' side of this question," he remained doubtful that it was possible to interpret the Constitution as other than a pro-slavery compact. Douglass questioned whether the antislavery movement could legitimately avail itself of "legal rules which enable us to defeat the wicked intentions of our Constitution makers." Douglass wanted to make *legal* arguments, not only *prudential* arguments, for interpreting the Constitution as an antislavery charter. He was especially concerned about whether it was "good morality to take advantage of a legal flaw and put a meaning upon a legal instrument the very opposite of what we have good reason to believe was the intention of the men who framed it."[10]

Thus Douglass considered himself bound by conventions of legal interpretation. He assumed that "law" had positive attributes, making it potentially divergent from norms of morality or principles of justice. In addition, he implicitly denied that he could claim that the "law" of the Constitution meant whatever he wanted it to mean. He sought to rely on legal meanings that transcended his own will, even as he searched for a conception of such meanings grounded in something other than the will of the Constitution's original makers.[11]

In May of 1851, Douglass announced a breakthrough in his thinking. He wrote to Smith that he was at that time "prepared to contend for those rules of interpretation which when applied to the Constitution make its details harmonize with its declared objects in the preamble." He also announced his break from the Garrisonians:

> [W]e had arrived at the firm conviction that the Constitution, construed in the light of well established rules of legal interpretation, might be made consistent in its details with the noble purposes avowed in its preamble; and that hereafter we should insist upon the application of such rules to that instrument, and demand that it be wielded in behalf of emancipation.[12]

Douglass did not deny what he had earlier argued: some "established rules of legal interpretation," including literal reading of particular provisions and/or analysis of framers' intentions, might lead to objectionable results. But he asserted the possibility of a different blend of literalism and purposive analysis, interpreting "the intentions of those who framed the Constitution *in the Constitution itself.*"[13]

Douglass's new approach used the preamble as the cornerstone for constitutional interpretation. The purposes set forth in the preamble supplied him with guides for analyzing constitutional purposes. The preamble's writtenness also enabled him to link ideals that he affirmed independently of the Constitution to the positive law of the constitutional text itself. Douglass claimed, moreover, that the Constitution's authority as "supreme law," as a matter of internal coherence, depended on reconciliation among it parts and its self-proclaimed ideals:

> [A] careful consideration of the subject convinced me that . . . the Constitution of the United States not only contained no guarantees in favor of slavery, but, on the contrary, was in its letter and spirit an antislavery instrument, demanding the abolition of slavery as a condition of its own existence as the supreme law of the land. . . . I was conducted to the conclusion that the Constitution of the United States—inaugurated to "form a more perfect union, establish justice, insure domestic tranquility, provide for the common defense, promote the general welfare, and secure the blessings of liberty"—could not well have been designed at the same time to maintain and perpetuate a system of rapine and murder like slavery, especially as not one word can be found in the Constitution to authorize such a belief. Then, again, if the declared purposes of an instrument are to govern the meaning of all its parts and details, as they clearly should, the Constitution of our country is our warrant for the abolition of slavery in every state of the Union.[14]

This interpretive approach—a hybrid of textualism and purposive analysis—enabled Douglass to reconcile his twin commitments to morality and the rule of law.

Radical Reinterpretation

Douglass's change of opinion on how to interpret the Constitution, and hence on what it meant, enabled him to endorse a wider range of political activity. Beginning in 1851, Douglass urged every American "to use his *political* as well as his *moral* power" to overthrow slavery.[15] Rather than advocating dissolution of the Union, he could now seek its preservation.

Douglass adhered to a Garrisonian premise that the North was responsible for slavery as long as it remained in a Union with slaveholding states. But he repudiated Garrison's argument that dissolving the Union would dissolve that responsibility. Douglass explained: "There now, clearly, is no freedom from responsibility for slavery, but in the Abolition of slavery." He pointed out that "[t]o dissolve the Union would be to withdraw the emancipating power from the field," thereby leaving no remedy for slaves left in bondage within slaveholding states.[16] In Robert Cover's terms, "Douglass' greatest need was for a vision of law that both validated his freedom and integrated norms with a future redemptive possibility for his people."[17]

Douglass recognized a profound truth: the Constitution could accommodate radical change, even without any formal amendment of the constitutional text. Douglass was aware that many of the text's original framers had designed some of its provisions to protect slavery and that those provisions had been *interpreted* since the founding generation in ways that provided support for that institution. But he denied that those interpretations were, or had to remain, parts of the law of the Constitution itself.

In a speech on July 5, 1852, shortly after his break with the Garrisonians, Douglass explained how the Constitution, as law, could realize its moral potential. He relied on the Declaration of Independence to highlight gaps between constitutive national ideals and actual political practices: "What, to the American slave, is your 4th of July? I answer; a day that reveals to him, more than all other days of the year, the gross injustice and cruelty to which he is the constant victim."[18] He repeatedly distanced himself from "the people" of the United States by referring to "*your* 'sovereign people,'" "*your* nation's history," "the birthday of *your* National Independence, and of *your* political freedom."[19] Not surprisingly, he denied that the "great principles of political freedom and of natural justice, embodied in that Declaration of Independence," had been extended to persons of color. Thus he refused to join in celebrating the nation's independence: "This Fourth of July is *yours*, not *mine*.[20]

Douglass did not, however, consider himself bound by past understandings of what the Constitution meant, including the scope of "the people" for whom it had been ordained and established. He sought to shift the focus of constitutional analysis from studying the past to bringing about a very different future: "My business, if I have any here to-day, is with the present. . . . We have to do with the past only as we can make it useful to the present and to the future."[21] Accordingly, Douglass sought to put the most favorable gloss possible on the constitutional document: a gloss that would bring interpretations of it into line with the ideals set forth in the Declaration of Independence and in the constitutional text's own preamble.

He suggested that persons of color would be able to celebrate the nation's independence and to affirm the Constitution as supreme law only if this sort of change in interpretive practices occurred—thus his willingness to affirm the Constitution was tentative and forward-looking rather than grounded in maintaining continuity with America's constitutional past. In short, he concentrated not on how the Constitution *had been* interpreted but on how it could "*become* the inheritance of all the inhabitants of this highly favoured country."[22]

Douglass emphasized, moreover, how all the land's inhabitants could regard the United States Constitution as "a glorious liberty document" and "not a sentence or syllable of the Constitution need be altered."[23] He later compared constitutional compromises and original understandings regarding slavery to artifices, or parts of an "unwritten constitution," that could be removed from the main structure: "If in its origin slavery had any relation to the government, it was only as the scaffolding to the magnificent structure, to be removed as soon as the building was complete."[24] In addition, he claimed that if the text were interpreted with reference to the goals set forth in the preamble rather than used to perpetuate historical compromises regarding slavery, "it will be found to contain principles and purposes, entirely hostile to the existence of slavery."[25] Accordingly, he exhorted all Americans to "live up to the Constitution, adopt its principles, imbibe its spirit, and enforce its provisions."[26]

These passages indicate how Douglass linked forms of constitutional criticism and affirmation. He recognized the organizing functions of the Constitution as a symbol of national ideals and as an instrument of collective power.[27] Rather than conceding those functions to his opponents, he sought to enlist them in the cause of radical change: eliminating slavery. As with revolutionaries preceding and following him, including leading members of the founding generation, he presented radical change as more faithful to past traditions and to existing ideals than were the practices of his day. Thus he claimed that affirming his conception of the Constitution, along with corresponding changes in federal and state laws and their enforcement, would be fundamentally preservative. In a manner both paradoxical and profound, he was advocating fundamental continuity through radical change.

Limitations of Official Law

The Supreme Court's decision in *Dred Scott v. Sandford* (1857) was, of course, a setback to those who sought to abolish legally sanctioned slavery.[28] Not surprisingly, Douglass criticized the majority decision and similar official pronouncements that upheld slavery.[29] But Douglass and others of like mind were relatively powerless to bring about change in the "official law" regarding slavery under the conditions that prevailed during the antebellum period.

Robert Cover has described how radical antislavery constitutionalism, like other "redemptive" movements of law, was vulnerable to failure. One of the principal aims of Douglass and his radical colleagues, as Cover explained, was to bring about "an alternative world in which the entire order of American slavery would be without foundation in law." Cover pointed out, moreover, that the radicals' vision "require[d] for its fulfillment the participation of the larger community that exercise[d] state power." Because a popular movement sought changes in official practices, members of the movement could not, by themselves, bring about the desired change. Thus Douglass and other abolitionists risked "the failure of the conversion of vision into reality."[30] As William Wiecek concluded, the radicals' efforts "to construe slavery out of the Constitution" did not achieve prominence, either within society at large or by governmental action, at least through the beginning of the Civil War.[31] In some respects, therefore, radical abolitionists failed to bring about the legal change they sought.

The radicals failed largely because of limitations imposed by representative structures. These structures precluded individuals and groups, acting separately, from preempting a range of authoritative choices that were entrusted by the Constitution and other laws to mechanisms of collective determination. The Constitution delegated legislative and executive powers to federal officials in ways that superseded other claims of lawmaking and enforcement authority, and therewith unofficial claims to interpretive authority. By definition, those who were not governmental officials could not make legally authoritative *official* decisions, including interpretive decisions on matters of constitutional meaning.

A variety of constitutional structures did, however, provide individuals and groups with means of influencing official choices. Then as now, individuals were able to rely separately and collectively on political processes such as writing, speaking, and voting to reinforce and/or oppose governmental choices and thereby promote continuity and/or change in the official law—including the law of the Constitution itself. Douglass recognized the potential of these structures. After breaking from the Garrisonians, he urged abolitionists to direct their efforts through established constitutional forms. He became active in partisan politics, voted, and exercised other rights and powers of political expression by writing, speaking, and using similar means to voice opposition to slavery.[32]

But Douglass recognized that the representational structures upon which he relied would not necessarily ensure governmental compliance with constitutional norms. On the contrary, his position was that public officials had acted inconsistently with the constitutional text's self-proclaimed ideals since its ratification. He was aware, moreover, that proponents of change faced substantial political obstacles.

During the antebellum period, political processes were distorted in at least two ways of immediate relevance to slavery. First, those in power within many of the states excluded blacks (among others) from voting and exercising other rights and powers of political participation. Persons held as slaves were, of course, denied these prerogatives. In addition, free blacks in the North and South were subjected, in varying degrees, to various forms of official and unofficial discrimination that deprived them of opportunities for political expression.[33]

The nation's representative structures also failed to count the votes of all voters equally. Article I enhanced the relative political power of voters in slave states, at the expense of voters in free states, for purposes of apportionment within the House of Representatives. In addition, electoral rules within states further diminished the relative power of voting blacks.[34]

The Constitution did not, of course, contemplate simple majoritarian decision making. Even if members of the House had been chosen through procedures that counted equally the votes of all residents of the United States (including slaves, free blacks, women, and others), and even if a majority of those persons supported federal efforts to abolish slavery,[35] other obstacles to simple marjoritarianism would have remained. The Constitution placed substantive limits on federal powers and established complex structures of popular representation that removed important collective choices from immediate majority control.

The people at large made legally authoritative decisions, but so did state officials, members of Congress, presidents, federal judges, and other governmental officials. The Constitution's complex configuration of political power had been designed to enable public officials to act *consistently* with constitutional norms even in the face of widespread popular opposition.[36] But these same structures, along with informal norms such as the functioning of political parties, also made it possible for those

CONSTITUTIONAL CITIZENSHIP

holding power to act independently of popular opinion in a manner *in-consistent* with constitutional imperatives. Changing electoral rules would not have eliminated that possibility.

Although Douglass might have argued that unconstitutional governmental actions were void, he treated them as legally authoritative. As would Lincoln, Douglass regarded governmental actions as legally preclusive for some purposes even as he argued that they went against constitutional ideals. For example, he did not deny that acts of Congress had authority as positive law, even though he criticized some such acts as unconstitutional. Again like Lincoln, he accepted *Dred Scott* as final for purposes of resolving the lawsuit, even though he argued that the decision was based on constitutional flaws.[37] He did not presume that persons other than governmental officials, whether citizens or not, had authority to exercise governmental powers. Many of his efforts, on the contrary, were directed toward influencing *who* would hold office and how *they* would exercise *their* powers.

Douglass's predicament thus highlights possibilities of constitutional failure, obstacles in the way of correcting official interpretive mistakes, and limitations on popular efforts to bring about legal change. Representative processes gave some persons means of influencing official choices, but these processes excluded many voices from important channels of public expression. Complex allocations of governing authority gave a variety of officials opportunities to block unofficial efforts to make or enforce unconstitutional laws, but representative structures did not ensure that all legally authoritative decisions measured up, in practice, to constitutional standards. Those seeking legal reform did not have the prerogative, based only on claims of constitutional error, to substitute their judgments for official decisions.

Unofficial Commitments

The fact that public officials continued to interpret the Constitution as consistent with (and supportive of) slavery during the antebellum period does not mean that the efforts of radical antislavery constitutionalists to change law failed entirely. Insofar as persons like Douglass called attention to discrepancies between basic legal ideals and actual political practices, the radicals contributed to analyzing problems of constitutional meaning and authority. Some of the tensions between ideals and practices were alleviated through civil war, formal amendments, and later interpretive changes. Certainly the radicals were not solely responsible for bringing about the ends they sought, but neither should their contributions be dismissed as insignificant.

The radicals also contributed to transforming law in a more immediate way: by acting consistently with their conceptions of the Constitution. In the process, these individuals expressed commitment to constitutional norms, as they understood them. It makes sense to regard the norms these persons articulated as important forms of unofficial law.[38] In some respects, these norms either were or have become cornerstones of the Constitution's own authority as "supreme law."

Creating Meanings and Enhancing Authority

There are good reasons to acknowledge the existence of legal norms, including constitutional norms, that go beyond "official law." Governmental decisions have preempted a range of unofficial lawmaking, law-interpreting, and law-enforcing claims, but such decisions have not preempted all important forms of popular constitutional activity. While the Constitution has entrusted certain types of decisions to governmental officials for authoritative determination, it has also reserved a variety of constitutional rights and powers to the people at large for their collective and/or separate exercise. I have already explained how persons could directly and indirectly influence official actions through voting and exercising other rights and powers of speech, the press, petitioning, assembly, and the like. By interpreting and exercising these prerogatives, individuals have also been able to create and reinforce unofficial constitutional norms that have been integral components of the law of the land.

It is important to distinguish individuals' exercising what they claim as *their* rights and powers from their seeking to exercise *other persons'* constitutional prerogatives, including those entrusted by the Constitution to governmental officials. Douglass did not presume that he had authority to adjudicate lawsuits or to act as a legislative or executive official. But he did claim to hold rights, as an individual, that he could exercise as he chose.

Among other things, Douglass asserted that he had authority to interpret the Constitution and other laws independently of governmental officials, at least for purposes of deciding what his legal prerogatives were and how to exercise them. In one of his most important speeches, on July 5, 1852, Douglass proclaimed: "I hold that every American citizen has a right to form an opinion of the constitution, and to propagate that opinion, and to use all honorable means to make his opinion the prevailing one."[39] By characterizing his position as a "holding," Douglass implicitly gave an official aura to his moral stance. Thus the form and substance of his comments were complementary: each expressed a conviction that the course of American constitutionalism could be shaped by ordinary persons, not just public officials.

Douglass adhered to this conviction even after the Supreme Court's decision in *Dred Scott*. As would Lincoln, Douglass denied that the case resolved the scope of Congress's power to prohibit slavery. He associated the Court's decision with previous and increasingly short-lived efforts to settle the slavery controversy. He alluded, moreover, to extrajudicial interpretive and enforcement powers by noting that "[t]he Supreme Court of the United States is not the only power in this world."[40]

Douglass's approach to voting epitomized his commitment to individuals' exercising their separately held rights and powers consistently with their conceptions of constitutional ideals. Because he relied on formal and informal electoral practices in New York, his ability to vote and express positions on candidates was not entirely independent of others' actions (including those of state officials). But within the range of discretion allowed by these practices, Douglass exercised a large measure of political autonomy.

Although he rejected Garrisonian arguments that voting was itself morally impermissible, Douglass remained concerned about moral dimensions of voting. He became associated with the Liberty Party, which was committed to the complete abolition of slavery. But as the Republican Party became stronger, Douglass and other abolitionists were encouraged to join its ranks. Writing in 1856, however, Douglass declined to support Republicans in the upcoming elections and urged fellow members of the Liberty Party to support its candidates even if they were unlikely to prevail.[41]

Douglass criticized the Republicans for moving away from commitment to complete abolition of slavery. For this reason, he argued that voting for Republicans would weaken the antislavery movement. He even expressed a willingness to sacrifice an end he sought, saving Kansas from slavery, in order to preserve the moral integrity of the antislavery movement. He recognized that supporting members of the Liberty Party rather than Republicans might "give the Government into the hands of the Democratic Party, and thereby establish Slavery in Kansas." But he claimed that "tenfold greater would be the misfortune, should Kansas be saved by means which must certainly demoralize the Anti-Slavery sentiment of the North, and render it weak and inefficient for the greater work of saving the entire country to Liberty." Emphasizing that "our aim is the entire abolition of Slavery," he argued that it was preferable to vote based on principle, even if it led to a short-term loss, rather than to sacrifice integrity by joining a party of compromise: "With Kansas saved, and our Anti-Slavery integrity gone, our cause is ruined."[42]

Convincing himself that it was reasonable to interpret the Constitution as consistent with efforts to abolish slavery was only one of several hurdles that Douglass confronted in seeking to reconcile his commitments to acting morally and relying on constitutional structures. Even after he became willing to endorse voting and other forms of constitutionally sanctioned political action, not just moral suasion, he remained unwilling to rely on those forms in ways that he thought would undercut claims of moral integrity. As he had been unwilling to advocate unconstitutional actions by governmental officials, he treated supporting Republicans as an impermissible means to accomplish a valid end. In both cases, he sought to avoid undercutting moral claims upon which he thought the antislavery cause depended.

Douglass eventually changed his position on whether to support the Republican Party, as he had changed his position on how to interpret the Constitution. Later in 1856 he defended acting within the Republican Party as most likely to promote the ultimate end of abolishing slavery.[43] It was possible for Douglass to reconcile each approach to principles of morality, though based on different premises regarding matters of instrumental rationality. He also seemed more willing to rely on prudential considerations and to accept compromise.[44]

For present purposes, the fact that Douglass changed his position on how he and others like him should have voted is less important than his conclusion that abolitionists should have voted at all. Rather than repudiate constitutional forms, he elected to act through representative structures, even when he predicted loss at the polls.[45] Thus he treated voting as valuable independently of its immediate success or failure.

Douglass did not articulate all the ways that he regarded voting as intrinsically significant, but several considerations may have informed his analysis. First, he might have been concerned about how votes could enhance or detract from the authority of particular governmental officials. Political authority is, in some respects, categorical in nature: a specific person either has, or does not have, formal authority to exercise a given power. But there are also gradations, or degrees, of governing authority. For those whose offices depend on electoral results, political power is a function, at least in part, of the depth and breadth of popular support. As a result, those who voted for a victorious candidate could enhance his authority, while those who voted otherwise could withhold their endorsement. These types of considerations may have informed Douglass's analysis of whether radical abolitionists should have voted for Republican candidates. His comments on the likely success of Republican candidates indicate, however, that his remarks were primarily driven by other concerns.

Douglass's reversal from opposing to supporting voting, as explained above, accompanied his shift from repudiating to endorsing structures of constitutional representation. He recognized that voting not only provided mechanisms through which the people chose governmental officials. It is clear that Douglass also considered voting to be a vehicle for endorsing constitutional norms of popular participation.

In addition, Douglass understood that voting was a means of expressing positions on broader issues of constitutional meaning and authority. He was committed in particular to voting for candidates who both opposed slavery and favored governmental efforts to eliminate it (or, in the case of Republicans, limit its spread). More generally, he suggested that voting and other forms of popular participation enabled individuals and groups to take positions on a variety of constitutional issues.[46]

Douglass's example indicates, moreover, that popular endorsement of constitutional norms could, in practice, be qualified. His willingness to support the Constitution was contingent on his ability to interpret the constitutional text as an antislavery rather than pro-slavery charter. In addition, his conceptions of constitutional meaning and authority were tentative and forward-looking rather than grounded primarily in historical practices. He was likewise willing to affirm some governmental decisions as consistent with constitutional ideals but criticized others.

For these reasons, there is a need to qualify conclusions regarding the failure of radical antislavery constitutionalism. Douglass and others may have failed to bring about a change in the *official* law, but they were effective in changing *unofficial* practices. It makes sense, moreover, to attribute the unofficial norms these persons created as forms of constitutional "law." The redemptive vision of radical abolitionists did not depend entirely on changes in official practices. Part of the radicals' vision was for abolitionists to conform *their* actions to *their* understandings of the law of the Constitution, even if in opposition to official positions. Ordinary citizens, or aspiring citizens, could bring about these changes in unofficial practices. In the process, Douglass and other abolitionists contributed to sustaining, reinforcing, and enhancing the Constitution's meaning and authority during their lives and suggested ways that others could later do likewise. During the antebellum period, as during earlier and subsequent periods, the Constitution's meaning and authority were in part constituted by popular commitments.

It would be a mistake not to treat those commitments as important components of the "law of the land" independently of whether they received official endorsement or became parts of a broader social consensus. Several parts of the constitutional text, along with general principles of American constitutionalism, indicate that the Constitution's meaning and authority have rested, at least in part, on the people's foundational commitment to constitutional norms. The preamble presumes that constitutional norms have been established by positive acts of the people at large and implies that "the people" have been able in some manner to withdraw support for such norms. Articles V and VII complement the preamble by providing for ratification and amendment of the constitutional text through conventions chosen by the people at large and from among their members. The Ninth and Tenth Amendments further reinforce premises regarding the people's original and continuing political authority. The electoral provisions of Articles I and II likewise attach normative significance to the people's continuing to endorse representative structures.

Many persons committed to abolishing slavery during the antebellum period, including radical constitutionalists, were doubtless formally "citizens" for purposes of the United States Constitution, or members of the American "people." If anyone could create constitutional norms through unofficial practices, these persons did. They created and supported antislavery norms through voting, signing petitions, writing in the media, giving speeches, participating in public dialogue, and otherwise expressing positions on constitutional issues. In short, some persons were not only formally "citizens"; they made themselves active, participating members of "the people" through their political practices.

The status of Douglass and others who were not formally "citizens" was more complex. It is less clear whether he or other black persons could, through their own actions, become "citizens" in the formal or participatory senses. At issue was more than whether governmental officials were obliged to treat him as a "citizen." The preceding analysis indicates that he had effective powers of citizenship that he could exercise on his own. By doing so, he effectively created, sustained, and changed the law of the Constitution through unofficial practices.[47]

Reconceiving Citizenship

Douglass claimed to be a "citizen" and a member of the American "people" despite the Supreme Court's decision in *Dred Scott* and similar official pronouncements. He conceded that some or all of "the people" who made the Constitution had designed it to secure "the blessings of liberty" to themselves and *their* posterity, not to "the colored persons of African descent."[48] But he claimed that the Constitution itself drew no such distinction:

> "We, the people"—not we, the white people—not we, the citizens, or the legal voters—not we, the privileged class, and excluding all other classes but we, the people; not we, the horses and cattle, but we the people—the men and women, the human inhabitants of the United States, do ordain and establish this Constitution, &c.[49]

In a later speech, he affirmed a corresponding conception of native-born, national citizenship: "There is in the Constitution no East, no West, no North, no South, no black, no white, no slave, no slaveholder, *but all are citizens who are of American birth.*"[50]

There are at least three ways to regard these claims. First, one may dismiss them as based on mistaken conceptions of constitutional meaning and authority. Douglass's position was eventually vindicated by the Fourteenth Amendment, but that amendment arguably changed the law rather than reinforcing preexisting norms.[51] Conversely, it is possible to endorse Douglass's interpretive claims as correct and to reject opposing positions as erroneous.[52] Extending such positions and relying on conventional conceptions of constitutional meaning and authority, one may claim that Douglass could not have been a "citizen" and at the same time not been a "citizen" as a matter of constitutional law.[53] Similarly, one may claim that logic compels a conclusion that Douglass either was a member of "the people" or was not a member of "the people." And if some forms of interpretive authority are only available to "citizens," then perhaps Douglass's authority to interpret the Constitution for some purposes may have depended on whether he was a citizen.

This type of categorical analysis is appropriate in many contexts. But dichotomies fail to account adequately for diversities of opinion on constitutional issues. The American "people" were deeply divided on basic constitutional issues during the antebellum period. These disagreements included the status of free blacks. Instead of (or in addition to) searching for a definitive answer to the question of whether or not persons like Frederick Douglass were "citizens" or members of "the people" as contemplated by the Constitution, much may be gained from attending to the problematic status of such persons. Rather than assuming that the law of the Constitution on this issue must have been fully coherent, it might be more appropriate to recognize the unsettled nature of the law on this subject and thus to allow for variations or gradations of constitutional meaning. The Constitution neither fully supported nor completely undercut Douglass's claims for himself and other blacks, free and enslaved.[54]

Allowing for degrees or variations of constitutional coherence is suitable for analyzing problems of political membership because the concepts of membership and participation are themselves variable and not simply dichotomous. Citizenship is not only simply present or absent; it is also something persons can be in the process of *obtaining* through their actions. Individuals do not simply act consistently or inconsistently with constitutional norms; they express commitment to the Constitution and abide by its imperatives in varying degrees.[55]

Douglass supported his claims of citizenship by exercising rights and powers of citizenship. He owned property, voted, wrote publicly, spoke at political gatherings, petitioned governmental officials, offered and affirmed theories of constitutional meaning and authority, criticized official and unofficial actions that he regarded as constitutionally flawed, and otherwise participated actively in political and extrapolitical life at the national and state levels. He supported his claim to be a "citizen" and a member of "the people" by bringing his acts into line with his conceptions of constitutional imperatives. In doing so, he invoked not only his own will but also the preamble's statement of foundational political ideals, and he claimed to be acting consistently with them even when opposing established power. He thus acted as a citizen long before public authorities recognized his citizenship.

Douglass, in short, exemplified a form of active self-constitution: becoming a member of the polity through one's actions and not just those of other persons. He was obviously not of the generation that originally formed—and were formed by—the Constitution.[56] And his race made it unclear to some that he was among that people's "posterity." Of greater importance to Douglass was gaining membership among "the people" who re-formed—and were re-formed by—the Constitution, a reformation necessary to sustain the Constitution's ongoing authority. The Constitution could embrace such persons, according to Douglass, even if they were not among the people who originally formed the Constitution or their posterity.

Douglass thus gained new identities as constitutional author and subject. By claiming membership among "the people," he presumed to be among those able to maintain (re-authorize) constitutional forms to represent the people's collective and separate political identities. He affirmed national institutions while gaining attributes of national citizenship. He likewise endorsed state mechanisms while acting as a citizen of New York. He was a member of religious organizations, antislavery associations, and other groups that also had distinct identities and corresponding constitutional prerogatives. As an individual, he asserted rights of speech, the press, conscience, property ownership, and the like.

My view that Douglass became both author and subject of the re-formed law of the Constitution resonates with Michael Warner's statement that "the people who give law [implicitly] vow that they will take their place as its subjects."[57] Douglass is also an example of someone William Harris would characterize as "domesticated" insofar as he redefined his identity as a subject of the existing order rather than remaining detached from it.[58] The former Garrisonian moved away from repudiating the Constitution and toward committing himself to obey its imperatives.

Yet even as he re-formed himself politically and assumed the status of "citizen," Douglass maintained a critical posture toward the Constitution. His endorsement of the Constitution was never more than tentative and qualified. Unwilling to accept disparities between constitutional ideals and political practices, he sought to bring about changes in the practices and thus to reconcile tensions within the constitutional terrain. He looked forward, not only backward, to identify constitutional possibilities.

Americans today occupy similar terrain and face similar prospects. Constitutional politics is a function of unofficial as well as official choices. Wide gaps remain between constitutional ideals and actual political practices. Membership in the polity continues to offer meaningful possibilities and impose serious constraints. Whether the U.S. Constitution can withstand critical scrutiny remains an open question. Those seeking to become citizens and to make the Constitution worthy of respect have good reasons to offer critical perspectives and commit themselves to change, not only to confine themselves to reinforcing existing norms.

Notes

This essay derives from chapter 2 of Wayne D. Moore, *Constitutional Rights and Powers of the People* (Princeton: Princeton University Press, 1996).

1. Remarkably, Douglass was ineligible for citizenship even after his formal emancipation, according to the reasoning of Justice Benjamin Curtis in his dissent as well as Chief Justice Roger B. Taney in his majority opinion for *Dred Scott v. Sandford*, 60 U.S. 393 (1857). See Moore, *Constitutional Rights and Powers of the People*, ch. 1.

2. Douglass, "Comments on Gerrit Smith's Address," from the *North Star*, March 30, 1849, reprinted by Philip S. Foner, ed., *The Life and Writings of Frederick Douglass*, 4 vols. (New York: International Publishers, 1950–55) (hereinafter "Foner, *Life and Writings*"), 1:374–79.

3. Douglass, "The Constitution and Slavery," from the *North Star*, March 16, 1849, in Foner, *Life and Writings* 1:366.

4. For accounts of Douglass's life, see his biography, *Life and Times of Frederick Douglass* (New York: The Macmillan Company, 1962, reprinted from the revised edition of 1892); and the editor's introductions to Foner, *Life and Writings*, vols. 1–4.

5. See Douglass, *Life and Times*, pp. 260–61.

6. See William M. Wiecek, *The Sources of Antislavery Constitutionalism in America, 1760–1848* (Ithaca: Cornell University Press, 1977), pp. 15–19 and *passim*.

7. See Douglass, "The Constitution and Slavery," reprinted by Foner, *Life and Writings* 1:361–67 (emphasis in original). See also p. 366 ("The parties that made the Constitution, aimed to cheat and defraud the slave, who was not himself a party to the compact or agreement. It was entered into understandingly on

both sides.") See also Douglass, "American Slavery," speech delivered in New York City on October 22, 1847, in Foner, *Life and Writings* 1:269, 274 ("The Constitution I hold to be radically and essentially slave-holding, in that it gives the physical and numerical power of the nation to keep the slave in his chains by promising that that power shall in any emergency be brought to bear upon the slave, to crush him in obedience."); Douglass, "The Revolution of 1848," speech delivered in Rochester, New York, on August 1, 1848, in Foner, *Life and Writings* 1:321, 328 ("The people of this country are held together by a Constitution. That Constitution contains certain compromises in favor of slavery, and which bind the citizens to uphold slavery."). See also Paul Finkelman, *An Imperfect Union: Slavery, Federalism, and Comity* (Chapel Hill: University of North Carolina Press, 1981); William M. Wiecek, *The Guarantee Clause of the U.S. Constitution* (Ithaca: Cornell University Press, 1972).

8. See John L. Thomas, *The Liberator: William Lloyd Garrison, A Biography* (Boston: Little, Brown and Company, 1963); Wiecek, *Sources Of Antislavery Constitutionalism*, ch. 10; Douglass, "Comments on Gerrit Smith's Address," from the *North Star*, March 30, 1849, in Foner, *Life and Writings* 1:374–79.

9. See Douglass, "Comments on Gerrit Smith's Address," in Foner, *Life and Writings* 1:375, 379; Douglass, "The Constitution and Slavery," in Foner, *Life and Writings* 1:366; Douglass, "American Slavery," in Foner, *Life and Writings* 1:269–70, 275.

10. Douglass, "The Constitution and Slavery," in Foner, *Life and Writings* 1:366 (emphasis on "rightful" added); Douglass, "Comments on Gerrit Smith's Address," in Foner, *Life and Writings* 1:374–79; Douglass, Letter to Gerrit Smith, Esq., January 21, 1851, in Foner, *Life and Writings* 2:149–50.

11. See, e.g., Douglass's criticism of "forced and latitudinarian construction[s] of the Constitution," in his "Comments on Gerrit Smith's Address," in Foner, *Life and Writings* 1:378.

12. See Douglass, "Change of Opinion Announced," from the *North Star*, May 23, 1851, in Foner, *Life and Writings* 2:155–56.

13. See Douglass's letter to Gerrit Smith, Esq., May 21, 1851, in Foner, *Life and Writings* 2:157 (emphasis in original).

14. See Douglass, *Life and Times*, pp. 260–62.

15. See Douglass, "Change of Opinion Announced," in Foner, *Life and Writings* 2:156 (emphasis in original).

16. Douglass, "The Dred Scott Decision," speech delivered before the American Anti-Slavery Society, New York, on May 11, 1857, in Foner, *Life and Writings* 2:407, 416–17.

17. Robert M. Cover, "Forward: *Nomos* and Narrative," *Harv. L. Rev.* 97 (1983): 4, 38.

18. Douglass, "The Meaning of July Fourth for the Negro," speech at Rochester, New York, on July 5, 1852, in Foner, *Life and Writings* 2:181, 192. See also 2:201 ("The existence of slavery in this country brands your republicanism as a sham, your humanity as a base pretense, and your Christianity as a lie").

19. Ibid., 2:182, 183, 185 (emphasis added).

20. Ibid., 2:188–89 (emphasis in original).

21. Ibid., 2:188.

22. Douglass, "The Dred Scott Decision," in Foner, *Life and Writings* 2:424 (emphasis added).

23. Ibid.; Douglass, "Address for the Promotion of Colored Enlistments," delivered at a mass meeting in Philadelphia, Pennsylvania, on July 6, 1863, in Foner, *Life and Writings* 3:365.

24. Douglass, "The Dred Scott Decision," in Foner, *Life and Writings* 2:419; Douglass, "Address for the Promotion of Colored Enlistments," in Foner, *Life and Writings* 3:365.

25. Douglass, "July Fourth and the Negro," in Foner, *Life and Writings* 2:202.

26. Douglass, "The Dred Scott Decision," in Foner, *Life and Writings* 2:424.

27. Compare generally Edward S. Corwin, "The Constitution as Instrument and as Symbol," *Am. Pol. Sci. Rev.* 30 (1936): 1071; Sanford Levinson, *Constitutional Faith* (Princeton: Princeton University Press, 1988).

28. I am not here ignoring (or dismissing) the possibility that *Dred Scott* provoked political responses that, along with other developments, ultimately culminated in the abolition of slavery. My comment here pertains to the more direct and immediate consequences of the Court's decision. For analysis of the decision's broader political ramifications, see Don E. Fehrenbacher, *The Dred Scott Case, Its Significance in American Law and Politics* (New York: Oxford University Press, 1978).

29. See Douglass, "The Dred Scott Decision," in Foner, *Life and Writings* 2:407–24.

30. See Cover, "*Nomos* and Narrative," p. 35 and *passim*.

31. Wiecek, *Sources of Antislavery Constitutionalism in America*, p. 274 ("In the short run, radical constitutionalism was a failure"). Cover quoted and endorsed Wiecek's conclusion in "*Nomos* and Narrative," pp. 38–39, although he challenged Wiecek's characterization of radical antislavery constitutionalism as a "sectarian" movement. For purposes of this essay, it is not necessary to evaluate the longer-term legacy of radical antislavery constitutionalism.

32. See Douglass, "The Suffrage Question," April 25, 1856, and "What is My Duty as an Anti-Slavery Voter," April 25, 1856, in Foner, *Life and Writings*, 2:389–95. See also Articles I and II of the New York Constitution of 1821, as reprinted in Francis N. Thorpe, ed., *The Federal and State Constitutions, Colonial Charters, and other Organic Laws of the States, Territories, and Colonies Now or Heretofore Forming the United States of America* (Washington, DC: Govt. Printing Office, 1909) 5:2653–56. Article II, section 1 limited the franchise to adult male "citizens," but contained additional requirements for "person[s] of color": a requirement of three years' citizenship and ownership of "a freehold estate of the value of two hundred and fifty dollars, over and above all debts and incumbrances charged thereon."

33. For historical overviews of restrictions on suffrage in the United States, see Kirk H. Porter, *A History of Suffrage in the United States* (New York: Greenwood Press, 1918); Chilton Williamson, *American Suffrage: From Property to Democracy, 1760–1860* (Princeton: Princeton University Press, 1960). See also James H. Kettner, *The Development of American Citizenship, 1608–1870* (Chapel Hill: University of North Carolina Press, 1978), esp. ch. 10; Paul Finkelman, "Prelude

to the Fourteenth Amendment: Black Legal Rights in the Antebellum North,"
Rut. L. Rev. 17 (1986): 415; Judith N. Shklar, *American Citizenship: The Quest for Inclusion* (Cambridge: Harvard University Press, 1991). These sources also identify obstacles confronting members of other racial and ethnic groups (not just blacks), women, and even white men who failed to meet property qualifications.

34. See generally Charles L. Black, Jr., "Representation in Law and Equity," in J. Roland Pennock and John W. Chapman, eds., *Representation* (Nomos X) (New York: Atherton Press, 1968), pp. 131–43; Paul Finkelman, "Slavery and the Constitutional Convention: Making a Covenant with Death," in Richard Beeman, Stephen Botein, and Edward C. Carter, eds., *Beyond Confederation: Origins of the Constitution and American National Identity* (Chapel Hill: University of North Carolina Press, 1987).

35. The opposite assumption is equally plausible: A majority of Americans (broadly conceived) may have opposed efforts by the federal government to abolish slavery throughout the United States. It is difficult to gauge public sentiment at such a high level of generality on such a complex issue, especially as it might have existed under imagined, counterfactual circumstances.

36. See, e.g., James Madison's treatment of this issue in *Federalist* No. 10.

37. See Douglass, "The Dred Scott Decision," in Foner, *Life and Writings* 2:407–24. Compare Abraham Lincoln's speech at Springfield, Illinois, on July 17, 1858 ("[I]n so far as [the Court's decision] decided in favor of Dred Scott's master and against Dred Scott and his family, I do not propose to disturb or resist the decision. . . . [Stephen Douglas] would have the citizen conform his vote to that decision; the member of Congress, his; the President, his use of the veto power. He would make it a rule of political action for the people and all the departments of government. I would not. By resisting it as a political rule, I disturb no right of property, create no disorder, excite no mobs."). The speech is reprinted by Roy P. Basler, ed., *The Collected Works of Abraham Lincoln* (New Brunswick: Rutgers University Press, 1953), 2:504–20. See also Lincoln's speech at Springfield, Illinois, on June 26, 1857, as reprinted by Basler, 2:398–410.

Some persons might dismiss as incoherent a position that governmental decisions have been legally authoritative even if they have been inconsistent with the law of the Constitution itself. One could rely, for example, on Chief Justice John Marshall's reasoning in *Marbury v. Madison*, 5 U.S. (1 Cranch) 137 (1803), to argue that governmental actions not in accord with the Constitution have been void, and hence not validly enforceable, even if officials have *regarded* them as valid. To be sure, it would be incoherent for the Constitution to sanction its own breach. But neither constitutional logic nor Marshall's reasoning in *Marbury* is inconsistent with the possibility, *in practice*, of legally authoritative but constitutionally erroneous decisions.

Marshall argued in *Marbury* that members of the Supreme Court had authority to decide for themselves whether an act of Congress was valid, at least for purposes of deciding how (or whether) to exercise their judicial powers in a case over which they presumably had some jurisdiction. But the chief justice did not suggest that other persons (including other officials) had discretion to disregard the Court's decision, based on their independent interpretations of applicable norms. On the contrary, his implicit premise was that other persons were obliged to accept the Court's decision as final, at least for purposes of resolving the case brought by Marbury to the Supreme Court. Although Marshall's reasoning suggested the possibility of judicial mistakes, as measured with reference to standards of the Constitution itself, he apparently did not think others had authority to disregard *judicial* orders as void. Marshall, like others since him, have presumed that judges have had preeminent interpretive powers in at least some contexts and for at least some purposes, even if not in all contexts and for all purposes.

38. For a complementary treatment of these issues, see Cover, "*Nomos* and Narrative," pp. 44–60 and *passim.*

39. Douglass, "July Fourth for the Negro," in Foner, *Life and Writings* 2:202.

40. Douglass, "The Dred Scott Decision," in Foner, *Life and Writings* 2:410–11. See the passage quoted in n. 37, above, for Lincoln's treatment of these issues.

41. See Douglass, "What Is My Duty as an Anti-Slavery Voter," in Foner, *Life and Writings*, 2:390–95.

42. Ibid.

43. See Douglass, "Freemont and Dayton," from the *North Star*, August 15, 1856, in Foner, *Life and Writings*, 2:396–401; see also 2:84–85.

44. Along with the sources cited in the previous note, see David W. Blight, *Frederick Douglass' Civil War: Keeping Faith in Jubilee* (Baton Rouge: Louisiana State University Press, 1989); pp. 50–58; Waldo E. Martin, Jr., *The Mind of Frederick Douglass* (Chapel Hill: University of North Carolina Press, 1984), pp. 182–85.

45. See n. 42, above, and the accompanying text.

46. But see Stanley Kelley, Jr., *Interpreting Elections* (Princeton: Princeton University Press, 1983), for analysis of problems associated with efforts to treat election results as evidence of popular support for (or opposition to) particular positions. The book's focus is policy positions, but there are analogous problems associated with efforts to construct popular positions on constitutional issues. Evidentiary problems are distinct, however, from the normative implications of persons' regarding their votes as means of expressing positions on constitutional issues.

47. I am not claiming here that the only way persons may reshape the law of the Constitution is by exercising rights and powers of citizenship as members of the constitutional "people." Others, such as foreigners and resident aliens (who may be constitutional citizens or members of "the people" for some purposes), may play similar roles—including through influencing other persons' commitments. My focus here is on ways that principles of popular sovereignty support attributing normative significance to a range of unofficial practices. Other lines of reasoning may support other types of claims.

48. See Douglass, "The Dred Scott Decision," in Foner, *Life and Writings* 2:424. See also notes 18–20, above, and the accompanying text.

49. Douglass, "The Dred Scott Decision," reprinted by Foner, *Life and Writings* 2:419. See also 2:424 ("The Constitution knows all the human inhabitants of this country as 'the people'"); Douglass, "The Constitution and Slavery," in Foner, *Life and Writings* 2:477 ("Its language is 'we the people;' not we the white people, not even we the citizens, not we the privileged class, not we the

high, not we the low, but we the people; not we the horses, sheep, and swine, and wheel-barrows, but we the people, we the human inhabitants; and, if Negroes are people, they are included in the benefits for which the Constitution of America was ordained and established.").

50. Douglass, "Address for the Promotion of Colored Enlistments," in Foner, *Life and Writings* 3:365 (emphasis added).

51. For arguments that blacks were not "citizens" before the Fourteenth Amendment became part of the Constitution, see, e.g., Edward S. Corwin, "The Dred Scott Decision in the Light of Contemporary Legal Doctrines," *Am. Hist. Rev.* 17 (1911): 52; Herbert J. Storing, "Slavery and the Moral Foundations of the American Republic," in Robert H. Horwitz, *The Moral Foundations of the American Republic*, 2nd ed. (Charlottesville: University Press of Virginia, 1982).

52. For arguments that free blacks, at least, had been "citizens" from the time of the Constitution's ratification, see, e.g., Fehrenbacher, *The Dred Scott Case*, esp. pp. 64–73, 337–64, 405–8, 575–76; Finkelman, *An Imperfect Union*, pp. 279–80.

53. But see Fehrenbacher, *The Dred Scott Case*, pp. 72 and 277, for the possibility of treating particular persons as "citizens" for some purposes but not others.

54. By acknowledging here problems of consistency among constitutional norms, I am not denying that normative coherence is a value for the polity as a whole or that individuals should strive for consistency among their interpretive commitments. On the contrary, I endorse and rely on ideals of normative coherence throughout this essay. My point here is that such ideals have not been achieved fully through the *practices* that have constituted norms of American constitutionalism.

55. See Shklar, *American Citizenship*, pp. 1–23 and passim, for a complementary treatment of citizenship. Her work identifies four conceptions of citizenship, at least three of which are variable rather than dichotomous: citizenship as standing, active participation, and republican virtue. The problematic status of blacks in the antebellum period indicates that even the idea of citizenship as nationality admits of gradations in meaning.

56. On the Constitution's mediation of these two functions, see William F. Harris II, *The Interpretable Constitution* (Baltimore: Johns Hopkins University Press, 1993), pp. 74; 115, n. 4; and passim.

57. Michael Warner, *The Letters of the Republic: Publication and the Public Sphere in Eighteenth-Century America* (Cambridge: Harvard University Press, 1990), esp. p. 110 ("with the Constitution, consent is to sovereignty as readership is to authorship").

58. See Harris, *The Interpretable Constitution*, p. 202 (he distinguished "[t]he Constitutional People [who] has been domesticated and civilized to the Constitution" and for whom the Constitution "supplies the political categories of their thought" from "[t]he popular sovereign [who] is a wild and natural people, a potentially new constitution maker outside the bounds of the constitutional order"). William Lloyd Garrison would qualify as someone not "domesticated" in this sense; he repudiated the Constitution and expressly disavowed forms of political participation that he viewed as attributes of membership *within* the existing order.

12

The Political Foundations of Judicial Supremacy

KEITH E. WHITTINGTON

AT LEAST in the United States, judicial supremacy is often regarded as essential to constitutionalism. In 1803, Chief Justice John Marshall declared that it was emphatically the duty of the Supreme Court "to say what the law is," and since the Constitution was a form of law, the Court had a primary responsibility for determining constitutional meaning.[1] Marshall himself tempered this strong claim for judicial authority, pointedly arguing only that the Constitution was intended to be "a rule for the government of courts, as well as of the legislature."[2] Nonetheless, since Marshall's time the claims on behalf of the Court have grown. By the mid-twentieth century, the Court itself interpreted Marshall's argument to mean that the judiciary was "supreme in the exposition of the law of the Constitution" and that judicial supremacy was "a permanent and indispensable feature of our constitutional system." Not only the Constitution, but also the Court's own interpretations of the Constitution were the "supreme law of the land."[3]

Constitutional maintenance, in this view, requires an independent judiciary with the authority to articulate the meaning of the Constitution and have all other political actors defer to those judicial interpretations. Without judicial supremacy, government officials would be free to ignore constitutional requirements with impunity. The Constitution cannot be maintained as a coherent law unless the Court serves as its "ultimate interpreter," whose understandings of the constitutional text supercede any others and which other government officials are required to adopt.[4] This claim on behalf of the Court's special interpretative authority is intimately linked with the countermajoritarian function that the judiciary is generally understood to serve.[5] In the name of constitutional values, an independent judiciary resists the pressures of democratic majorities conveyed through the elected branches of government. Whereas the other branches of government concern themselves with mere "policy" and the momentary "preferences" of electoral majorities, the Court is a "forum of principle," concerned only with interpreting the Constitution and applying its dictates without fear or favor.[6] If the Court fails in this task, or if other officials fail to defer to its judgments, then the success of constitutionalism itself is put in doubt.

But this strong vision of judicial supremacy raises a number of problems. Those who advocate judicial supremacy, including the Court itself, tend to treat it as a matter of normative directive and accomplished fact. The Court has claimed that judicial supremacy follows logically from the constitutional design and that since Marshall's declaration of judicial independence "that principle has ever since been respected by this Court and the Country."[7] But of course this was wishful thinking on the part of the justices. Their very assertion of the principle of judicial supremacy in this case came in response to Southern politicians denying that the Court had the authority to bind the states to its own controversial constitutional interpretations. American history is littered with debates over judicial authority and constitutional meaning. Although powerful federal officials have usually acceded to the Court's claims, judicial authority has often been contested by important segments of the populace, from abolitionists to labor unions to segregationists.

If judicial supremacy cannot simply be assumed to exist, then it must be politically constructed. Many scholars have argued that it cannot be, that judicial independence is in fact a myth. In reassuring nervous New Yorkers that the proposed Supreme Court would not be a threat, Alexander Hamilton indicated the problem, arguing that the judiciary "will always be the least dangerous" branch. In contrast to the other branches of government, the judiciary "has no influence over either the sword or the purse; no direction either of the strength or of the wealth of the society, and can take no active resolution whatever . . . and must ultimately depend upon the aid of the executive arm even for the efficacy of its judgments."[8] A Court too weak to threaten the people's liberties, however, may also be too weak to protect them.

Many have looked at the Court's formal powers and historical track record and concluded that the judiciary lacks the means to act independently. Faced with hostile political majorities, a "rational" Court is assumed to act "strategically" so as to avoid conflict with the elected branches.[9] Gerald Rosenberg, for example, has argued that the Court would rather switch than fight. His "findings suggest that judicial independence is least likely to be found when it is most necessary." The Court is in fact highly constrained, and "the hypothesis of judicial independence is wrong."[10] Robert Dahl argued that the Court's brief resistance to the New Deal was the exception that proved the rule. Given electoral stability and regular judicial nominations, the Supreme Court is usually under the firm control of the other branches. "Except for short-lived transitional periods . . . the Supreme Court is inevitably part of the dominant national alliance."[11] If, Dahl observed, the Court actually did function in an independent and countermajoritarian fashion, then "it would be an extremely anomalous institution from a democratic point of view."[12] Such anomalies are politically unsustainable. Despite the founders' best efforts, judicial independence would likely be short lived and ill fated. Politics would beat out constitutionalism.

Such pessimistic conclusions need to be challenged on two fronts. First, we need to question the normative starting point, that judicial supremacy is really essential to the maintenance of constitutionalism. If other institutions and political actors in addition to judges take the Constitution seriously, then the constitutional order itself might not be threatened by periodic challenges to the judicial authority to interpret the Constitution. Before we conclude that the political vulnerabilities of the judiciary render constitutionalism unstable, we need to examine more carefully the relationship between elected government officials and the Constitution. We cannot conclude that judicial independence fails us precisely "when we need it most," unless we have previously determined that we are best served by judicial intransigence in the historical periods in question. Second, we need to reconsider the political roots of judicial independence. The general presumption of empirical social scientists has been that the judiciary has little ability to sustain itself in the face of political criticism and that politicians have little incentive to defer to the judiciary when they disagree with its substantive conclusions. An "independent" judiciary is presumed to be one that can and does render decisions with which powerful political actors disagree. Since politicians such as Franklin Roosevelt have demonstrated that they will not defer to the Court when constitutional law gets in the way of policy desires, many social scientists have expected the Court to sink into quiescence. Of course, in practice the Court has not been so restrained. The question that needs to be answered is why the Court has seemingly become quite powerful when other government officials seemingly have the formal power to quash it. Why would politicians tolerate an independent judiciary?

Although the issues raised by those questions are more extensive than I can adequately address here, I want to consider an important piece of the puzzle, the problem of the political incentives underlying judicial supremacy. Specifically, in this chapter I will consider some of the political incentives facing American presidents and how they often lead presidents to value judicial independence and seek to bolster, or at least refrain from undermining, judicial authority over constitutional meaning. An examination of the political considerations of presidents sheds light on how constitutions are constructed and maintained in politically fractious environments. For constitutions and institutions like judicial review to exist in historical reality as more than imagined moral abstractions, powerful social actors must have political reasons to support them over time. Fortunately, there are such reasons.

I focus here on the president because the presidency is perhaps the most significant competitor with the Court for constitutional authority. The president is a highly visible institutional representative with numerous political and constitutional resources and functions that could easily lead him into conflicts with the judiciary. The president and the Court are, therefore, likely to compete for the right to authoritatively determine constitutional meaning. If the Court is to establish its authority as the ultimate interpreter of constitutional meaning, and thus secure judicial independence, it will have to contend with presidential challenges. Judicial success in this competition, I believe, depends crucially on the incentives facing the president.[13] The president has the formal tools to defeat the Court. The interesting question is whether he has the will or political support needed to successfully challenge the Court for constitutional leadership. Generally, he does not, creating a politically sustainable place for autonomous judicial action.

Presidential Leadership in Constitutional Regimes

My starting point for examining the president's relationship with the Court is to note that presidents inhabit distinctive strategic environments. Presidents face particular political tasks, reflecting their individual goals and political contexts. Although aspects of this presidential task are highly individualized, many of its features are shared among presidents who find themselves in similar historical circumstances. One important dimension of the presidential experience results from the relative stability of electoral and legislative coalitions, ideological assumptions, and policy agendas in American politics. As many scholars have observed, important political change in the United States tends to be punctuated with historically limited moments of turmoil and rapid reform followed by much longer periods of incremental adjustment and consolidation.[14] The four-year cycle of presidential politics takes place within this larger pattern of political development. An individual president's political task will be shaped by where his administration lies within this cycle. Stephen Skowronek has labeled this cyclical feature of presidential leadership, "political time."[15]

A president's authority to lead is partly determined by his relationship to the dominant political "regime" and the relative strength of that regime. The idea of a political regime incorporates not only electorally dominant partisan coalitions, but also a set of dominant policy concerns and legitimating ideologies. A regime in this sense overarches contending policy orientations at lower levels such that even electorally successful oppositional figures can be forced to sustain the commitments of the dominant regime. A strong regime transcends partisanship. The authority for a president to act is structured largely by the expectations of other political actors, which help define "what is appropriate for a given president to do." "A president's authority hinges on the warrants that can be drawn from the moment at hand to justify action and secure the legitimacy of the changes affected."[16] The president is both empowered and constrained by the set of partisan commitments and informal political resources that he brings with him to the office and builds during his term. Thus, although all presidents have quite a bit of power to effect political change, not every president can do so successfully, and the response to those changes is neither uniform across presidencies nor strictly a function of the political skill of individual presidents. All presidents disrupt the status quo and change their political environments to some extent. Not all presidents, however, have the authority to explain and legitimate those changes. Not all presidents have the ability to lead.

Presidents can be characterized in accord with four broad types, depending on their place within this cycle of authority. A president's location within political time does not completely determine either his behavior or his success in office, but it does help set the available resources and constraints. Successful presidents exploit that structure effectively, while building their own authority for further action. Unsuccessful presidents either fail to recognize or are forced to ignore their situations; their actions eventually outrun their political support, and they lose the authority to act. The "great" presidents tend to be *reconstructive*. They come to power by opposing collapsing regimes, and their presidencies are spent tearing down the remnants of the old order and laying the foundations for the new. This describes the presidencies of Thomas Jefferson, Andrew Jackson, Abraham Lincoln, Franklin Roosevelt, and, more controversially, Ronald Reagan. These presidents can also be loosely regarded as coming to power through critical elections, as supporters of the old regime fly to new leaders. Oppositional presidents can also come to power when the dominant regime is still vital, however. Such *preemptive* presidents are "accidental" in a larger sense, overcoming the electoral bias against them usually through some unusual characteristic or circumstance such as the splintering of the dominant party, a fortuitous economic downturn, or their own prior celebrity. Thus, presidents such as John Tyler, Zachary Taylor, Andrew Johnson, Grover Cleveland, Woodrow Wilson, Dwight Eisenhower, and Richard Nixon have interrupted otherwise stable electoral and political orders. Though such presidents inherit few preset commitments, they also have few resources and little authority to follow their partisan instincts. *Affiliated* presidents, by contrast, arise during a period of regime stability and are in concert with those dominant commitments. Their mandate is to extend and consolidate what they have inherited. Presidents such as James Polk, Theodore Roosevelt, Harry Truman, and Lyndon Johnson have substantial authority to act, but they also operate within a jungle of exuberant and potentially conflicting commitments. Other affiliated presidents are less fortunate; they inherit a weak regime that is vulnerable to outside pressure and fragile from internal tensions. Such *disjunctive* presidents have little authority to do anything, for any actions are likely to destabilize their fragile base of support. Historically weak and hapless presidents such as John Quincy Adams, James Buchanan, Herbert Hoover, and Jimmy Carter have encountered these problems.

Incorporating constitutional interpretation into our notion of the political regime makes room for developing the president's relationship with the Court. Most theories of American political development focus on parties and policies, not the Constitution. The Constitution is often regarded as a stable framework within which American politics is played out. But our understanding of the Constitution itself has also undergone substantial development over the course of American history, and much of this development has likewise been punctuated in character. The Constitution has been the subject of normal politics as well as a context within which normal politics takes place.[17] By creating a system of separated powers, the Constitution ensures that presidents will struggle with other actors for control of the government, just as the judiciary has asserted its dominance over other officials in defining constitutional meaning. As part of their struggle for control of the government, however, presidents will grapple with constitutional meaning as well. Most significantly, presidential efforts to recast the dominant regime are significant for our understanding of the constitutional order. As Skowronek briefly notes, reconstructive presidents "have reset the very terms and conditions of constitutional government" and their struggles "have penetrated to the deepest questions of governmental design and of the proper relations between state and society."[18] The political regime within which political time is played out is in part a constitutional regime, "the constitutional baseline in normal political life."[19]

Since political authority in America is often linked to constitutional meaning, the judiciary is unlikely to be detached from a president's efforts to draw authority unto himself. The Constitution can motivate and legitimate political action, and it provides an important grammar of American political discourse. Presidents must at least be prepared to refer to the Constitution to authorize the prerogatives of their office, from the scope of the veto power to the extent of the war power. More broadly, however, presidents and others refer to the Constitution as an aspirational ideal, a set of principles that help define the American political identity. The centrality of the Constitution to American governance ensures that these initially partisan regimes will be built in part on a particular vision of the Constitution. Presidents can be expected to tell a story about how their most fundamental commitments are consistent with, and perhaps necessary implications of, the most fundamental commitments of the nation as a whole.

The president is in part an interpreter of the national heritage, of which the Constitution is a prominent part. In this effort, the judiciary is both a potential competitor and a potential ally. The judiciary is not simply an institution with the power to veto legislation. It is also an institution that legitimizes legislation in constitutional terms and regularly articulates national ideals and commitments. The presidential struggle for political authority is likely to have implications for judicial authority. The judiciary's authority to act is likewise structured by the president's authority to act. Like presidential authority, judicial authority can be expected to fluctuate over time and to help determine the relative power and independence of the judiciary within the larger political system.

Constitutional meaning emerges from the interplay of multiple actors, rather than through the abstracted reasoning of an isolated judiciary.[20] Partly as a result of its dynamic origins, constitutional meaning is part of politics, not isolated from it. This is true in two senses. Political actors are concerned with the Constitution, and their understandings of it affects their behavior. They pursue goals and respect restraints that they understand to be required by the Constitution. In addition, constitutional meaning is often the product of politics. Not only do a variety of political actors contribute to final settlements over how the Constitution will be applied, but our understandings of the Constitution are dynamic, shaped by changing social conditions, practical experience, ideological commitments, and political calculation.[21] Understanding how judicial authority is constructed over time is both an end and a means in an effort to make sense of how constitutional politics develops.

A president has two overriding imperatives. He wishes to advance his agenda and to maintain his political coalition. Presidential agendas vary over time. Some presidents have broad and ambitious agendas. Others have narrow and modest agendas. Presidents would prefer to be able to define their own political agenda, and not merely advance a preset list of initiatives drawn from a party platform or the congressional calendar. That is, presidents want to lead. Few are content with the role of a mere clerk, and all hope to occupy the office in their own right and to leave their individual stamp on the nation.

The presidential office is unique in American politics; it invites its occupant to make expansive claims of authority to lead the nation. Moreover, part of the presidential agenda is likely to involve constitutional meaning. The Constitution is foundational in American politics, not only in the sense that it establishes the boundaries of legal action but also in the sense that it authorizes, invites, and structures political activity. An implicit or explicit constitutional discourse comes naturally to presidents, not because they are the special caretakers of our constitutional tradition but because their visions of political leadership lead them to push the boundaries of that tradition. The president "tells us stories about ourselves, and in so doing he tells us what sort of people we are, how we are constituted as a community. We take from him not only our policies but our national self-identity."[22] Because presidential ambitions are foundational, the Constitution becomes a basic resource and constraint.

In addition to defining and promoting an agenda, presidents are obliged to maintain their political coalition. This is in part an instrumental good: maintaining coalitional stability facilitates implementation of the presidential agenda. It is also a distinct presidential imperative. To a greater or lesser degree, presidents are representatives of a preexisting political coalition. That coalition places independent demands on the president, which the president will likely seek to meet both out of a sense of political obligation, in payment for earlier assistance rendered, and in expectation of future benefits. Whether for independent or instrumental reasons, however, presidents must expend resources nurturing political coalitions. The president will be required to pursue an agenda that is secondary to his own but favored by coalition members, and he will be expected to help build and avoid damaging coalitional strength.[23]

Presidents also face a variety of constraints that limit their ability to pursue those goals. The president has limited resources. The supply of such resources as time is finite, and this imposes opportunity costs and prevents presidents from pursuing every issue that they might favor. Presidents must pick their battles. Moreover, the institutional powers of the presidency are specific and limited. The president cannot, for example, govern by decree. He must usually win support for his policies from Congress and, ultimately, the Court.

The president is also constrained by the strength of his coalition. The presidential agenda may be hard to pursue if legislative support is weak or lacking, as when the opposition party controls one or both houses of Congress. Likewise, the presidential coalition may be relatively brittle, even if it retains control of crucial government institutions. The relative vulnerability or strength of the presidential coalition will alter calculations of whether and how to pursue individual agenda items, while also shifting the priority between the president's own positive agenda and his responsibility to maintain the coalition.

Finally, the president is constrained by the broader ideological and institutional context within which he must operate. The president cannot be idiosyncratic in defining his agenda. The credibility of the president's agenda depends in part on its fit within the larger ideological and institutional environment. An individual presidency is structured by a preexisting regime. The Eisenhower administration, for example, was partly prefigured by expectations that defined the modern presidency and government itself as the post–New Deal era. Despite Eisenhower's own preferences for congressional leadership and smaller government, he did not have the option of emulating Calvin Coolidge. Similarly, in the shadow of Ronald Reagan, Bill Clinton's political legacy will be shaped more by deficit reduction and welfare reform than by such activist proposals as health care reform that he might have otherwise favored.

The president's challenge is both to pursue his goals within these constraints and to attempt to loosen the constraints themselves. Others have examined a variety of ways in which American politics has been configured by the interaction of these several factors. My particular concern here is with how the Court plays into these presidential calculations. If these are the fundamental features determining presidential behavior, how do they structure the presidential relationship with the Court? More specifically, how do they structure the incentives for the president to either support or undermine the judicial authority to settle questions of constitutional meaning?

Three Presidential Contexts

The remainder of this chapter outlines three situations that reflect the president's relationship to the political regime. Each of these situations creates a different set of incentives facing the president and therewith a distinct set of strategic choices. In only one of these situations does the president have an incentive to challenge judicial authority. In two of the three possibilities, the president has incentives to support or attempt to strengthen judicial authority. This matrix of possibilities suggests that serious threats to judicial authority should be relatively rare, and that when those challenges arise they are likely to be limited. A better understanding of the reasons for presidential attacks on the Court will also clarify the scope of those attacks and the degree to which they represent challenges to fundamental constitutional values.

Analysis of these scenarios improves our understanding of the judicial role in normal politics. It also illuminates constitutional politics. Constitutional maintenance requires a political commitment to constitutional interpretation. Political actors must care what the Constitution means, and be willing to temper their immediate political desires accordingly. From early in the nation's history, this interpretive task has been portrayed as fundamentally legal, technical, and institutionally contained.

Constitutional maintenance was represented to be the special responsibility of the Court, and this construct helped secure the practice of
judicial review.[24] But American history reveals that constitutional maintenance has been a more politically vibrant task than this judicial mythol-
ogy would suggest, occasionally requiring renewed national debates over
the content of our most fundamental commitments. In such periods, the
authority to interpret constitutional meaning is often wrested away from
the Court. In more normal times, political actors are not unconcerned
with constitutional meaning, but they have less direct investment in taking a leadership role in specifying its requirements. Under such circumstances, the Court can carve out a constrained, but autonomous, role for
itself as the "ultimate interpreter" of constitutional meaning, with the
assistance and tolerance of other political actors.

Reconstructive Presidents and Departmentalism

Reconstructive presidents come to power opposed to a collapsing regime.
These presidencies are concerned with destroying the last vestiges of the
old regime and articulating the foundations of the new one. The president's political authority is maximized if he possesses the capacity to disrupt a status quo whose legitimacy is shaky. Because the key question
during these moments is who will set the future direction of the polity,
overpowering competing institutions and actors is a prerequisite for the
president's success.

The reconstruction of an American political regime will require the
reinterpretation of constitutional commitments. As a consequence, the
Court is a key competitor for political authority. A reconstructive leader
must shoulder aside the Court's claim to be the primary expositor of
constitutional meaning and must shift constitutional discourse more explicitly into the political arena. Dominant understandings of the Constitution must be formed on the president's own terms in order for his
reconstructive project to be successful, and this critical task is likely to be
too important to leave in the hands of isolated, holdover judges.[25]

The reconstructive task leads presidents to politicize constitutional
meaning. Reconstructive leaders come to power not only with a new set
of constituents and a new list of policy proposals, but also with a new
legitimating vision. Winning an election is not enough to establish the
warrants for the sort of actions that such leaders hope to pursue. In order
to reconstruct the inherited order, such presidents must redefine the
terms of debate and the basis for action. Such efforts to recast the terms
of legitimacy are substantively constitutional—reconstituting the accepted powers of government, the rights of individuals, and the standards

of political action. In the American context, reconstructive leaders are likely to echo the terms of the Constitution and reprise the role of the founders. The recurring trope is one of national renewal, but the substantive interpretation of what it means to recover inherited constitutional values will differ for each reconstructive president. We must recover what we have lost in the corrupted politics of the recent past, but it is the task of the reconstructive leader to articulate exactly what has been lost and what the constitutional regime is in the current historical context. For Thomas Jefferson, for example, the country had lost its revolutionary and democratic promise at the hands of the centralizing, monarchical Federalists.[26] For Franklin Roosevelt, the potential of the national government had been squandered by "economic royalists" who were willing to sacrifice the general welfare to their own private gain.[27]

Reconstructive presidents come to power with an ambitious agenda to reshape the foundational commitments of the regime. They are backed by a strong and coherent political coalition. They have access to a wide variety of resources for addressing and leading an ideological transition. The Court is a prime competitor of these presidents, and the Court is likely to be affiliated with the collapsing regime. As a consequence, reconstructive presidents are likely to deny judicial supremacy and reject the idea that the Court is the ultimate expositor of constitutional meaning.

Historically, reconstructive presidents are presidents who have asserted an authority to ignore the Court's constitutional reasoning and act upon their own independent constitutional judgments. This theory of coordinate constitutional interpretation is known as departmentalism, the doctrine that each branch of government has the authority to determine constitutional meaning independent of the judgments of the other branches.[28] Whether proposing legislation, exercising their veto power, or enforcing statutes, departmentalist presidents are guided by their own constitutional interpretations, regardless of prior judicial rulings relating to relevant aspects of the Constitution. By contrast, a model of judicial supremacy posits that the Court does not merely resolve particular disputes involving the litigants directly before it or elsewhere in the judicial system; it also authoritatively interprets constitutional meaning for the nation as a whole. For the judicial supremacist, other government officials are bound not only by the Court's disposition of a specific case but also by the Court's constitutional reasoning. Judicial supremacy requires deference by other government officials to the constitutional dictates of the Court, even when other government officials think that the Court is wrong about the Constitution and in circumstances that are not properly subject to judicial review. The departmentalist feels no such obligation to defer to judicial authority. For the departmentalist, the Court's rulings are binding only within its own legal context, on litigants and lower courts. Other constitutional actors, such as presidents, are free to follow their own constitutional understandings, whether that leads them into direct conflict with the Court or simply to narrow the scope of judicial reasoning.

Departmentalism is not the strongest possible challenge to judicial authority. Departmentalism does not, for example, challenge the existence of judicial review itself. A departmentalist president may well agree with John Marshall that in conducting its own duties the Court is not obliged to follow a law that it believes to be unconstitutional.[29] The departmentalist would simply claim a similar authority for the other branches, limiting the generative force of judicial pronouncements. The departmentalist does not deny the Court's authority to decide cases. But he does deny the Court's authority to articulate constitutional norms or to settle questions of constitutional meaning for everyone. The Court's constitutional reasoning can only guide its own actions; other political actors must act on their own best understandings of the Constitution, even if those lead them to different conclusions than those of the Court.

Because reconstructive presidents are likely to disagree with important aspects of existing judicial doctrine, and because reconstructive presidents must be able to elevate particular constitutional disagreements into a challenge to judicial authority, they must transform a legal debate into a political crisis. To the extent that the Court has been active in articulating the foundational commitments of the prior regime, advancing the agenda of the president and his supporting coalition will require altering constitutional doctrine. The Court may retaliate by striking down reconstructive policies as inconsistent with the Constitution and existing constitutional law. In such instances of judicial activism, the president must somehow overcome the judicial veto in order to realize his agenda. This was most obviously the case in the New Deal, when Roosevelt's reconstructive agenda pointed toward an activist national state that would offend established constitutional law. The Hughes Court struck down important components of Roosevelt's legislative program, prompting the president not only to criticize the Court's specific rulings but to attack the idea of judicial supremacy as well.[30] The president may find existing constitutional law a threat to his agenda not only because the Court presently stands ready to veto reconstructive legislation, but also because earlier judicial opinions articulated and formalized the ideological commitments of the regime that the president is attempting to overthrow. Constitutional law becomes a target not only because it serves as an indicator of future judicial action against the president, but also because it stands in and of itself as a challenge to the reconstructive constitutional vision. The Taney Court thus became an important foil for Abraham Lincoln, for the *Dred Scott* decision was not only a set of doctrines regarding matters of citizenship and Congress's power over the territories, it was also a symbol of the constitutional vision that the ascendant Republican Party wanted to overthrow.

But the judiciary is not always active in exercising the power of review. Through much of the nineteenth century, the Court was relatively inactive in reviewing national legislation, and thus it was not a significant part of Congress's calculations. Moreover, items of the president's agenda may not be readily reviewable by the judiciary. Andrew Jackson's veto of the National Bank, though integral to the Democrats' constitutional and policy programs, was not justiciable. Perhaps most importantly, since judicial review is primarily concerned with preventing government from exceeding its authority, judicial review is only likely to be triggered by a presidential program that expands the role of the state beyond previously recognized limits, as in the case of the New Deal. The reconstructive agenda need not be expansionistic in this fashion, however, as in the case of Jefferson, Jackson, and Reagan, all of whom sought primarily to reduce the responsibilities of the national government. Thus the judiciary may not challenge the president's agenda.

As the purveyor of constitutional norms, however, the Court is always relevant to regime reconstruction. Not only is the Court a standing challenge to the president's new constitutional vision, but the Court's earlier rulings are implicit rebukes to current presidential claims. The Court becomes relevant to the reconstructive project not because of what it might do, but because of what it has already done. The president has an interest in overcoming that implicit substantive challenge to his reconstructive project, whether by pushing the Court to reverse its previous rulings or by weakening the Court's hold on public opinion.[31]

In addition to incentives for criticizing the substance of judicial opinions, the reconstructive president also has incentive to attack judicial supremacy itself. The central task of the reconstructive president is to tear down the old regime and articulate the foundations for a new one. This presidential task is made possible by the weakness of the old regime, which no longer retains the intellectual coherence or political support necessary to make it compelling and authoritative. As Skowronek details, reconstructive presidents are actually strengthened through their encounters with the political opposition.[32] Each political conflict, and even setback, provides further public justification for increasing the strength of the president. Once the old regime loses its authority, its partisans come to seem like naked interests, obstructing the public good for the sake of themselves, or at best on behalf of discredited beliefs. The substantive collapse of the old regime is so complete as to undermine the institutional position of its defenders. Reconstructive politics elevates the im-

portance of substantive authority to such a degree that it largely eclipses
mere institutional authority. This dynamic redounds to the benefit of the
president, who sees his institutional authority expanded in the name of
his substantive vision. It works against other institutions, which are
pressed to embrace the new substantive order or see their institutional
authority delegitimated. The dilemma is particularly acute for the Court,
whose institutional authority largely rests on its relationship to the
Constitution.

The judiciary is supposed to speak not for itself but for the Constitution. In that voice, it can command other political actors who are otherwise empowered not only by the quality of their substantive goals but
also by such things as their electoral mandates. Americans have sufficient
respect for the ideal of law that they allow it to trump both favored
substantive goods and democracy. In the context of reconstructive politics, however, the Court's claims to speak on behalf of the law become
less persuasive. When the meaning of the Constitution itself becomes
politically contested, the judiciary seems politicized. Its claims to neutral
interpretations of law are subject to challenge. In times of constitutional
politics, the Court's articulation of past verities seems more contestable
and less authoritative. The president can then become the more reliable
oracle of the nation's constitutional faith.

Within the politics of reconstruction, the president's agenda dictates a
challenge to the Court without serious political or ideological constraints. Reconstructive presidents possess an extraordinary degree of political support to play the role of constitutional prophet. In these moments of constitutional flux, judicial authority is at its nadir. The judiciary
may well have the will to resist elected officials, but it lacks the popular
support to sustain its resistance. Judicial obstruction, in such circumstances, appears illegitimate, and as a consequence the political willingness to use available powers to curtail the judiciary is increased. During
such periods, it is the Court, not the president, which is most likely to be
perceived as unfaithful to the Constitution and having abandoned its interpretive responsibilities.

Judicial independence is unlikely to be taken as an independent political good during periods of reconstruction, not because constitutionalism
is no longer valued but because the judicial monopoly over constitutionalism has been broken. The reconstructive president has the incentive
and power to challenge judicial authority because he is now seen to have
the Constitution on his side.

There is general agreement as to which periods of American history are
"court-curbing," and which presidents have been departmentalists.[33]
Skowronek has identified five reconstructive presidents: Jefferson, Jackson, Lincoln, Roosevelt, and Reagan. Constitutional scholars have inde-

pendently identified the same five presidents as departmentalists. All five of these presidents were concerned with re-envisioning the foundations of the American constitutional order. All five not only criticized specific judicial rulings or constitutional doctrines, but also asserted that the judicial authority to bind the president was limited and that the president had an independent responsibility to act on his own constitutional judgments. All five used the Court as an important foil for developing their own constitutional visions and for building political support for themselves and their agenda. All five went out of their way to attack the Court. All five denounced the judiciary as politicized, partisan, and the tool of their discredited opposition. Only one of these presidents, however, was seriously hampered by the Court in implementing his primary policy agenda. For Roosevelt's New Deal, judicial review was a serious problem that had to be overcome. For the other four reconstructive presidents, active judicial review was less of the problem than was the judicial control over constitutional norms.

Each of these presidents believed and acted on the sentiment best expressed by Lincoln, that "if the policy of government, upon vital questions, affecting the whole people, is to be irrevocably fixed by the decisions of the Supreme Court . . . the people will have ceased to be their own rulers."[34] Lincoln did not simply urge the Court to change its mind, he denied its authority to fix constitutional meaning, at least on the issues that most concerned his own political movement. Few presidents have the expansive authority to make such sweeping claims, an authority not simply to criticize but to ignore the Court. Reconstructive presidents do have such an authority. During periods of reconstruction, institutional responsibility for the task of interpreting constitutional meaning tends to shift from the judiciary to the presidency. During such periods, judicial independence is weakened. But constitutionalism as such is not threatened. The constitutional regime is reinvigorated through a wider political debate over its content and its future.

Affiliated Presidents and Constitutional Partnership

Reconstructive presidents are relatively rare. Few presidents have the desire or authority to challenge inherited constitutional and ideological norms and to attempt construction of a new political regime. Far more common are affiliated leaders, who rise to power within an assumed framework of goals, possibilities, and resources.[35] Affiliated leaders are primarily concerned with continuing, extending, or more creatively reconceptualizing the fundamental commitments made by an earlier reconstructive leader. They are second-order interpreters. They interpret the inherited regime, not the constitutional order itself—that is, they interpret the interpretations of the previous reconstructive leader. They are the workaday practitioners of constitutional politics, concerned with clarifying what the constitutional regime is rather than with specifying what it should be.

Affiliated leaders are not weak presidents; they are simply limited. Their goals do not extend to the foundations of the regime. In fact, affiliated leaders have a powerful, if constrained, authority. They come to power as leaders of the dominant political coalition in a generally hospitable political and ideological environment. Their goals can necessarily therefore be quite ambitious, and the expectations placed on them by their supporting coalition can be quite high. They are expected to advance the coalition's inherited agenda in favorable circumstances. Within the context of their particular agenda and historical period, affiliated presidents are expected to be activists.

As affiliated leaders of an inherited partisan regime, these presidents can also expect to inherit an affiliated Court. As Robert Dahl pointed out, the pace of judicial replacement dictates that the Court is unlikely to lag the governing majority for very long.[36] Under most circumstances, the affiliated leader can expect to find a Court whose personnel were largely selected and/or confirmed by his own political coalition. Moreover, the Court can be expected to be operating under the ideological assumptions of the constitutional vision established by the last reconstruction.[37] Not only is it likely that subsequent judges have been forced to pass an either implicit or explicit litmus test of their constitutional philosophy, but a successful reconstruction is likely to have altered the ideological environment and shifted basic understandings of constitutional meaning. "Mainstream" judicial selections would now mean "consistent with the basic constitutional commitments of the established regime." Unlike a reconstructive president, an affiliated president will not find the Court a fundamental threat to his agenda; he will probably find it fairly supportive of that agenda. The threat of the judicial veto being relatively low, the affiliated president is likely to find little to fault with the Court.

The second of the two presidential imperatives—that of maintaining a political coalition—becomes more relevant for judicial supremacy during affiliated administrations. The general ideological and political environment is relatively supportive of affiliated leaders, but that environment places more constraints on the affiliated leader than it does on the reconstructive leader. The reconstructive leader's first task is negative: to tear down the prior regime that has lost credibility. As a consequence, there is substantial support for the reconstructive leader to take independent action in this temporarily unoccupied political space. Affiliated leaders, by contrast, inherit a set of commitments that they are expected to uphold.

The fundamentals of the regime are fixed and serve as hard constraints on the freedom of movement of the affiliated president. The agenda of the affiliated leader is substantially less his own than that of his coalition. The president has political support only so long as he serves the coalition. In contrast to the demand of reconstructive periods, the demands of established coalitions are likely to be relatively specific and positive.

Yet the demands of coalition maintenance can also be difficult. A political coalition may be delicate, even if it is dominant. As politics settles into its more normal patterns, it becomes more difficult to satisfy all coalition members at the same time and to do so without mobilizing the opposition. The coalition leader faces two central difficulties. First, the demands of some coalition members may be in tension with the demands of others. These tensions may be relatively minimal, arising from scarce resources and opportunity costs and the necessity of prioritizing among competing demands. They may also be relatively severe, as when some coalition members are actually opposed to the central goals of other coalition members. Second, the demands of some coalition members may be in tension with the electoral base. Thus, even if members of the governing coalition were able to compromise among themselves, their actions could well antagonize critical segments of the electorate. In this case, a willingness to respond to some of the demands of important members of the coalition could threaten the coalition's majority status.

The relationship of an affiliated president with the Court is one of partnership. Dahl likewise characterized the Court's relationship to the majority political coalition as one of partnership. But the implications of a regime perspective for the Court are more complex than Dahl suggested. Assuming that the Court's role turned on its willingness to enforce statutes, Dahl thought an affiliated Court was a dependent Court. The Court would not strike down the legislation of its coalition partners, and thus its normal role was the ministerial one of applying majoritarian statutes. The governing coalition could be expected to brook no independence from the Court, and it had few incentives to support judicial independence. But the Court need not be prostrate in order to be a partner in governing.

An affiliated Court can be expected to articulate the constitutional commitments of the dominant coalition. To that extent, judicial authority is an important asset to the dominant coalition. The Court helps to naturalize the achievements of the reconstruction, reinforcing recent constitutional changes by emphasizing their authority and continuity, a role Dahl also recognized.[38] More importantly, the Court helps enforce and extend those commitments. The American constitutional system is highly decentralized and offers many openings for dissidents to advance their own ideological and political agendas. The Court offers an efficient vehicle for monitoring those efforts and keeping them within the constraints of the new constitutional framework.[39] Judicial authority operates in the service of the dominant coalition in such circumstances, and the coalition therefore has reasons for supporting it. The judiciary can help assure that the states and the bureaucracy keep in line with the new regime.

Somewhat differently, the affiliated president and an affiliated Court draws on similar sources of authority. Once we recognize that partisan regimes involve ideological principles as well as electoral victories, then the role of the Court within the political system becomes more serious. Reconstructive presidents are authorized to articulate a new constitutional vision. They are, in that sense, true leaders, defining the constraints under which others will operate. Affiliated leaders, by contrast, are authorized only to articulate, interpret, and apply that preexisting set of commitments. As an interpreter of the inherited regime, the president is hardly alone. Indeed, other interpretations can be a source of difficulty for affiliated presidents, who are often accused of bad faith by other coalition members who offer alternative interpretations of the regime's founding commitments. Even in breaking his "no new taxes" pledge, George Bush claimed to be acting in a manner faithful to the Reagan legacy, but his interpretation of that legacy was readily open to challenge by others. The affiliated president's authority is derived from the regime, and thus his authority can be challenged on the basis of that regime. The Court is likewise a paramount interpreter of inherited regimes. When the inherited regime is collapsing under the force of a reconstructive president's challenge, then the Court is vulnerable. When the regime itself is resilient, however, the Court's interpretive authority can be a source of strength. The affiliated president can only challenge the Court by demonstrating that he offers a more accurate interpretation of common commitments, rather than by demonstrating that he is the sole representative of preferred commitments. Affiliated presidents can be measured against regime commitments and found wanting. Thus, even though an affiliated president may have an incentive to undermine judicial authority to protect himself from judicial challenge, he does not have an independent basis of support for doing so.

The complexities of coalition maintenance suggest a different reason for supporting an independent judicial authority. A dominant coalition can expect the Court to be in basic agreement on the substantive commitments of the regime. The Court, however, is not an explicit member of the governing coalition and it does not face an electoral check. As a consequence, the Court is unburdened by many of the political constraints that face an affiliated president, while sharing many of the same substantive goals. Coalition goals can therefore be served by bolstering judicial authority to take independent action and encouraging wider deference to an independent judiciary. Although an independent judiciary may occasionally impose costs on coalition members, credible judicial independence also offers substantial benefits to elected officials.

An affiliated but independent judiciary offers solutions to both of the coalition maintenance problems mentioned above. First, the judiciary offers a vehicle for overcoming impasses within the governing coalition. Disagreements among members of the governing coalition can prevent action from being taken on central regime commitments, frustrating dominant substantive goals and potentially threatening coalitional stability. An independent judiciary can cut through those deadlocks. The Court can sometimes act on behalf of its version of central regime commitments, without requiring that elected coalition members take positive action themselves. In doing so, the Court independently makes important constitutional judgments, but within a range delimited by regime boundaries. The Court can also act on low priority commitments that have diffuse support among coalition members but could not command scarce legislative resources. An affiliated judiciary is unlikely to take actions that are not favored by a substantial segment of the dominant coalition. Moreover, if the Court were to take actions that were actively opposed by most of the governing coalition, the latter has the tools to rein in the Court.[40] Minority rights within the New Deal Democratic coalition illustrate this dynamic. The Democratic coalition significantly included a variety of minority groups. In the specific case of blacks, however, Southern members of the coalition blocked actions that were seen as important regime commitments by more progressive members of the coalition. The Court's decisions in favor of black civil rights, therefore, overcame internal coalition disagreements in order to realize what were arguably basic regime commitments.[41]

Second, the Court offers a vehicle for acting on regime commitments while minimizing potential electoral costs. The Court does not have to stand for election; it cannot be directly punished for taking unpopular actions. Moreover, even though the Court is ultimately responsive to political influence, the linkages between elections and judicial behavior are attenuated and indirect. As a result, few voters are likely to hold elected officials accountable for the actions of the Court.[42] Elected officials have an incentive to bolster judicial authority not only to encourage the judiciary to take independent action but also to weaken the voter's ability to trace responsibility back to elected officials. The relatively obscure "traceability chain" between elected officials and judicial action allows coalition members to pursue certain substantive goals while distancing themselves from accountability to the electorate. Again, civil rights for blacks provide an illustration. The Warren Court's decisions sparked bitter denunciations from the Southern wing of the Democratic Party. Warren

Court rulings became opportunities for Southern Democrats to claim credit for standing up for their electorates, insuring their reelection. At the same time, Northern Democrats achieved substantive goals without having to take any positive action of their own, thus avoiding electoral fallout. The Court itself was secure in its rulings, since Southerners did not have sufficient support to seriously threaten the judiciary. By relying on the judiciary, the Democratic Party was less likely to be electorally punished for decisions on desegregation, defendant rights, prayer in school, or pornography, even though these decisions were consistent with basic party commitments.[43]

Less successfully, antebellum Democrats sought to bolster judicial authority and encourage deference to the judiciary in order that the courts could resolve the slavery issue.[44] Although Democrats could not afford to back off a defense of slavery, they also increasingly could not afford to take positive pro-slavery action given the growth of antislavery sentiments in the North. The Taney Court offered a vehicle for advancing substantive Democratic goals on slavery without requiring that elected officials take positive action that might be electorally risky for the coalition as a whole. Democratic leaders, such as President Buchanan, were active in emphasizing the independent nature of the judiciary and encouraging deference to its rulings. He could do so comfortable in the knowledge that the affiliated Court would take actions that were consistent with the substantive values of the Democratic coalition.[45] But at the same time, Democrats sought to deny responsibility for a "legal" decision that everyone was equally bound to obey. Regardless of his "individual opinion," Buchanan insisted, he had no choice but to enforce the dictates of the Court, to which "with all good citizens, I will cheerfully submit."[46] To the Democrat's misfortune, Buchanan was eventually forced to take the positive action he had hoped to avoid by favoring the pro-slavery faction in Kansas, shattering the Democratic coalition and bringing to a close the Jacksonian regime.[47] At the same time, however, the collapsing credibility of the Democratic ideological vision allowed Republicans to draw the connections between the actions of the Court and those of individual elected officials. Lincoln's "slave power conspiracy" highlighted the linkages between Stephen Douglas, Buchanan, and Taney.[48] As the constitutional consensus on slavery broke down, the Court was not autonomous enough, and its actions could be too readily traced to electorally vulnerable politicians. The politics of reconstruction is built on the failure of the politics of affiliation.

Affiliated presidents are powerful, but they operate under constraints. The twin imperatives of pursuing their substantive goals and maintaining their political coalition are increasingly in tension. Moreover, the ideological constraints of the inherited regime limit the options of affiliated presidents. These characteristics of affiliated politics favor judicial independence and power in constitutional interpretation. When constitutional politics is primarily interpretive rather than creative, the Court can claim a larger space of operations, and affiliated leaders have strong incentives to bolster judicial authority. An independent judiciary helps secure regime commitments and solve problems of coalitional maintenance.

But the strategy of deference to the judiciary is neither foolproof nor absolute. Judicial authority cannot hold together a regime that is ideologically divided and vulnerable, and judicial actions may hasten the rise of a reconstructive leader who can refound the polity on firmer foundations. Moreover, support for judicial authority is contingent. Affiliated leaders expect the Court to act in an affiliated fashion. Operating too far outside the framework of regime commitments puts the Court in danger of losing political support. Within that framework, however, the Court has substantial autonomy to shape its own agenda and elaborate constitutional meaning.[49]

Preemptive Presidents and Constitutional Ambivalence

Not every oppositional president is as well positioned to remake the inherited order as were Jefferson, Jackson, Lincoln, and Franklin Roosevelt. Other oppositional presidents, who "preempt" a continuing partisan order, come to office with relatively little authority and few resources with which to increase their authority. The regime that they oppose is still vibrant, popular, and resilient to pressure. Preemptive presidents must learn to accommodate themselves to the dominant regime in order to be successful. For many preemptive presidents, that accommodation probably occurred before they reached office. Presidential candidates such as Woodrow Wilson, Dwight Eisenhower, and Bill Clinton are reformers within their parties, either through long internal activism or through an outside path to the nomination.[50] These presidents come to power representing moderation and pragmatism, not as an ideological alternative to the dominant order. Still other preemptive presidents, such as John Tyler and Andrew Johnson, are in fact recent converts to their parties, rising to power through presidential tickets designed to blur partisan distinctions. Once in office, these presidents often return to their old party commitments and severely fragment their newfound parties, crippling their administrations.[51] A few presidents, such as Grover Cleveland and Richard Nixon, come to power with a sharper partisan image and a more defined agenda, but prove unable or unwilling to build a political movement with sufficient strength to upset the old regime. Despite the sharper partisan rhetoric, these presidents still accommodate themselves to the old regime, opportunistically exploiting available issues but not threatening the core commitments of the established order.

Preemptive presidents have unusually wide latitude in conducting their office, for their oppositional status carries few partisan commitments or political expectations that they must satisfy during their administration. The preemptive president seeks to be elected and complete his term without incident; other priorities take a backseat to this minimalist imperative. Though pragmatism may give flexibility, it provides few political resources upon which to build a strong presidency. As accommodationists, preemptive presidents are unlikely to be fully trusted by their own partisans. Preemptive presidents fit uneasily within the dominant order, lacking sufficient support for pursuing an ideological agenda. The dominant order may tolerate and even embrace preemptive presidents. Indeed, an administration like Eisenhower's can represent the hegemonic strength of the regime. But, preemptive success is contingent on respecting the limits and demands of the new political climate. The disasters of Johnson's resistance to Reconstruction or Clinton's health care reform are cautionary tales about these limits and demands.[52]

The continued strength of the old regime ensures that preemptive presidents cannot expect to advance their oppositional agenda very directly. Their supporters in Congress are likely to be in the minority or be part of an unstable coalition and unable to unite behind a positive agenda. The loyalty of the executive branch is likely to be questioned, as both its defining programmatic mission and the majority of its personnel were put in place by earlier presidents affiliated with the established regime. In extreme cases, the longevity of the administration itself may be threatened by presidential efforts to gain control over or to circumvent the executive branch that they inherited from their ideological foes, as in the cases of Andrew Johnson and Richard Nixon. Party and popular support are likely to be thin and unreliable, given the preemptive president's uncertain relationship to dominant policies and powerful constituencies. In short, the very features that make the old regime resilient remove possible political resources from a preemptive president.

The preemptive president is likely to be in opposition to the Court as well as to other elected officials and the dominant ideology. The Court will primarily be shaped by affiliated leaders, who will generally control appointments. In addition, the Court's basic agenda and constitutional understandings will be defined in terms of the dominant regime. Like other political institutions, the Court will help articulate the tenets of the dominant regime. As a result, preemptive presidents are likely to find themselves in disagreement with the much of the Court's output.

At the same time, however, the Court is a relatively autonomous institution. Its membership is less partisan and less involved in daily political struggles than most elected officials. Moreover, a major concern of the Court is articulating the constitutional norms of the dominant regime. Given the tenuous nature of most preemptive presidencies, such leaders are unlikely to advance legislation seriously at odds with the fundamentals of the dominant regime. To the extent that this is true, the judiciary is not a primary concern for a preemptive president; he faces more immediate obstacles. Likewise, the dominant regime is too resilient for the preemptive president to make significant progress in articulating an alternative constitutional vision. The preemptive president does not have the authority to call into question the foundations of the dominant regime; he cannot seriously challenge the Court's primacy as the interpreter of constitutional commitments.

In this context, the judiciary may be an important resource to the president. In their political weakness, preemptive presidents may seek alliances with the courts. Despite their particular disagreements with judicial doctrine, preemptive presidents may find themselves attempting to bolster judicial authority in order to save themselves. In a hostile political environment, the law and the judiciary may be the best defense that the president has. The judiciary's advantage, from the president's perspective, is only comparative. The presidential embrace of judicial authority arises out of political necessity, not sincere enthusiasm. But an appeal for help from the judicial branch may slow or defeat partisan foes of the president who control the legislative branch, the electorate, and other powerful interests.

The judiciary is valuable to the president because of the complicated nature of law. When the regime is strong, the political context is likely to be inhospitable to the preemptive president. Political opponents have few reasons to support the preemptive president and many reasons to oppose him. The relationship between the president and his political opponents is relatively pure in its antagonism. In the political arena, actors are partisan, and the president is on the wrong side. The law is much more ambiguous. The law, especially constitutional law, is likely to have a relatively long history, its origins predating the rise of the currently dominant regime. As a consequence, the law is not a simple reflection of current commitments, but rather contains elements of older and crosscutting concerns and interests. The law is intertemporal and partially incongruent with the current regime, and as such it may provide shelter from the prevailing political winds.[53] In addition, the law often falls far short of specific directions for the conduct of public affairs. Neither normal legislation nor the constitutional text itself speaks often in clear and unequivocal terms. This is especially true where, as in the United States, political compromise is essential to legislative success. Party discipline is often weak, and governmental institutions are too fragmented to allow legislative action based on narrow majorities. The multitude of political access points into the legislative process ensures that any given law will reflect numerous interests to a lesser or greater degree. As a consequence, the law that is the object of judicial examination is likely to contain elements within it that are incongruent with the dominant tendencies of the existing regime. The law contains concessions to opposition forces, despite their minority status. Further, the law is intended to endure into an uncertain future. This uncertainty necessarily affects the calculations of legislators. The possibility that the opposition may eventually control the government prevents the law from being purely partisan and overwhelmingly favor a single side in the political struggle. The dominant party must ultimately hedge its legislative bets, given an expectation that the law may endure into a time when they are no longer dominant (perhaps only temporarily and partially—as in the case of a preemptive president). The principle of generality that is a key feature of the rule of law is reinforced by political calculation.[54] Thus, the law will provide resources to the preemptive president, even in an otherwise hostile political environment. To the extent that the judiciary represents the law, and the impartial interpretation of the law is central to its institutional practice, then the president is likely to find support within the judiciary against his political opponents.

The preemptive president's interest in bolstering judicial authority reflects the institutional nature of the courts. Preemptive presidents can ally with the courts only because the courts take the law seriously. The relative insulation of the judiciary from normal political pressures—that is, the relative independence of the judiciary—prevents it from being a mere instrument of the dominant regime. Although judges are likely to be generally sympathetic with the basic assumptions and commitments of an enduring political order for the reasons Dahl and others suggest, judges are not immediately accountable to electoral and political interests and are less responsive to transitory political pressures. Judges are not immediately involved in the particular disputes that arise between legislators and preemptive presidents, for example. They are rarely appointed with those disputes in mind and they are likely to have little stake in their outcomes. The institutional role and norms of the judiciary further insulate the courts from partisan pressures. Judges are *supposed* to worry about the law, and the individuals selected to be judges are usually socialized into that role. The particular procedures of the courts reinforce that orientation, putting lawyers, texts, and precedents in the foreground of judicial operations. The daily working environment of judges distinguishes them from their legislative colleagues.[55]

Preemptive presidents cannot always be expected to support the Court, but they have powerful reasons to avoid challenging judicial authority in the fashion of reconstructive presidents. For reconstructive presidents, the judiciary is an isolated and antagonistic institution that the president can afford to weaken. For preemptive presidents, the judiciary is both an irritant and a potential ally. With few other allies available, the president cannot afford to undermine a potentially helpful institution. Preemptive presidents are therefore likely to be supportive of the judiciary or oscillate between an antagonistic and supportive stance, depending on the issue. In either case, preemptive presidencies are not a significant threat to judicial authority and may be a positive aid. Andrew Johnson, for example, found himself elevating the status of the judiciary in his struggle against Congress. Although the Republicans already controlled the Supreme Court by the time Johnson came to power, Johnson could not afford to attack the Court, for Congress represented a much graver threat to his power. As Congress combatted Johnson's interference with Reconstruction, Johnson called upon the Court to uphold the president's prerogatives. Even if the judiciary was ultimately unlikely to be very sympathetic to Johnson, the president was nonetheless better off in the hands of the Court than in the hands of the Radical Republicans in Congress. As his impeachment proceeded, Johnson repeatedly elevated the judiciary as the appropriate institution to decide constitutional questions. He was willing to subordinate the presidency to the courts in order to place the legislature under the same constraints.[56]

Somewhat differently, Nixon's anti-judicial rhetoric was tempered by his highly legalistic defense of presidential actions. Ultimately unable to take the ideological offensive and aggressively justify presidential actions in such varied areas as the conduct of the war, the impoundment of appropriations, or the investigation of political enemies, Nixon defended himself in terms of precedent and text. When challenged, he repeatedly produced lists of instances in which previous presidents had exercised similar powers. These highly formal defenses of the presidency were seldom accompanied by substantive justifications, precisely because in the politics of preemption substantive justifications are seldom persuasive. If Nixon could not persuasively claim that his powers were being used for the good, then he had to claim those powers as a right. In the end, Nixon was also unsuccessful in his legalistic appeals. The courts rarely accepted his arguments, and the issues were ultimately resolved in the political arena. Nonetheless, the substantive weakness of Nixon's position left little recourse other than the discourse of proceduralist legalisms.[57] The judicial authority was thus reinforced, even if the president ultimately lost.

The fragile status of preemptive presidents need not prevent them from criticizing particular aspects of the constitutional law as interpreted by the courts. It does tend to prevent elevating that criticism into a more general attack on judicial authority. The Court may not be a policy-making partner with the dominant political coalition, but it will probably be broadly sympathetic to the existing regime. To that degree, preemptive presidents can be expected to have disagreements with the Court. The question is how extensive or intense those disagreements will be and how the president will act on those disagreements.

For reconstructive presidents, conflicts with the Court quickly escalate into crises of judicial authority. Reconstructive presidents welcome such challenges and are willing and able to ignore the Court and denigrate judicial authority, with potentially enduring consequences. For preemptive presidents, disagreements with the Court must be contained skirmishes. Any escalation of the conflict is likely to result in unfavorable outcomes for the president, since the Court is in greater conformity with the dominant regime than the president himself. Thus, preemptive presidents are likely to accept the legalistic discourse that the courts favor. Where reconstructive presidents shift the conflict into the political arena and deny that the lagging judiciary is faithful to the law, preemptive presidents are more likely to accept judicial rulings and engage the Court in its own terms. Preemptive presidents become advocates before the bench, petitioners asking the Court to change its mind, rather than constitutional challengers threatening to displace the Court's right to decide the issue at all. Preemptive presidents may dislike judicial rulings, but they raise no question as to who will have the final say.

Preemptive presidents, in contrast to reconstructive presidents, have been much more deferential toward the Court, even when personally disagreeing with judicial actions. Although Eisenhower's support for the Warren Court's desegregation cases has often been underestimated, he certainly would have preferred to avoid the confrontation in Little Rock. Southern resistance to judicial desegregation orders created significant political difficulties for national politicians. Southern voters had clear and intense preferences regarding school desegregation, whereas the strength of the Northern commitment to the desegregation of elementary and secondary schools was not at all clear. Eisenhower's immediate private reaction to *Brown* was to complain that the Court was overreaching, attempting to legislate morality in a futile way. Despite his private concerns, however, Eisenhower carefully refrained from criticizing the Court. He repeatedly deflected questions regarding *Brown*, urging merely that people remain "calm" and "reasonable."[58] Regardless of his feelings about *Brown*, however, Eisenhower felt compelled to defend judicial authority. In private correspondence, he explained that "there must be respect for the Constitution—which means the Supreme Court's interpretation of the Constitution—or we shall have chaos."[59] In public, he asserted that his own view of *Brown* was irrelevant, for "the Supreme Court has spoken, and I am sworn to uphold the constitutional processes in this country; and I will obey."[60] Such an approach to the desegregation cases left Eisenhower with little leeway when Governor Orval Faubus defied court orders in Arkansas. After an initial private effort to convince Faubus to obey the Court, Eisenhower chose to throw the presidency forcefully behind the Court. Unlike Andrew Jackson, for example, who was willing to allow the Georgia state government to circumvent and violate a Court order regarding Indian tribes, Eisenhower was willing to shed blood in support of judicial authority to determine constitutional meaning.[61] When subsequently challenged over the use of federal troops in Little Rock, Eisenhower justified himself by defending the value and authority of the courts.[62] The episode illustrates how the ambiguity of the politics of preemption places a premium on the president's responsibility to enforce, rather than to articulate, the law. Presidential power was thus wrapped in the mantle of judicial authority, and Eisenhower sought to bolster that authority, in word and deed. Though Eisenhower bestowed little presidential support to the substance of the Warren Court rulings, he felt compelled to support the Court's prerogatives.

Nixon was both personally inclined and politically better situated to attack the Court. Eisenhower's calm and moderate demeanor and strong sense of executive duty were clearly on display in the Little Rock crisis, and these were key qualities of his preemptive stance—the mature acceptance and competent administration of the New Deal regime. Nixon represents a different face of preemptive presidential politics, the more strident oppositional figure testing the strength of the inherited order. Although Nixon raised few challenges to the core aspects of New Deal order, he did question its more recent supplements, especially in his popular "law and order" campaign and "Southern strategy" that specifically played off of the activism of the Warren Court.[63] Despite the centrality to his political strategy of attacks on the Warren Court, Nixon refrained from encouraging, legitimating, or engaging in disobedience to the Court. The Nixon administration's rhetoric was, in fact, deeply legalistic, embracing the discursive field of the law and the courts that interpreted it. Although the administration was frequently willing to push the boundaries of settled law, with presidential impoundments and sweeping claims of executive privilege, it mounted very traditional defenses of its innovations and always proved willing to submit presidential authority to judicial scrutiny. In the extreme case, Nixon proved willing to obey the Court and resign, rather than defy the Court and test his claims to executive privilege and presidential power in an impeachment inquiry. Nixon's behavior was undoubtedly partly a function of his own lawyerly instincts, but it was also a function of his political situation. Ultimately, the administration was politically too weak to support stronger claims to define constitutional meaning. The president could make provocative claims about constitutional meaning, but he did not have the political resources to act on those claims. He needed a judicial imprimatur to legitimate his claims, and the administration repeatedly sought that endorsement, in vain. The president had sufficient political strength to criticize the Court, but not to defy it. Despite the substantive disagreements that are likely to arise between them and affiliated courts, preemptive presidents are likely to temper their criticisms of particular decisions with a more general acceptance of the judiciary's institutional authority.

As these examples suggest, preemptive presidents will not simply embrace the substantive policies of the dominant regime, including the activities of the Court. Preemptive presidents may be constrained, but they are still oppositional. Their political commitments are generally contrary to those of the established order, even if they have few opportunities to act on their commitments and little support for significant change. Preemptive presidencies are not caretaker administrations; they are domesticated opponents. This means that preemptive presidents will exploit opportunities to advance their oppositional agenda, and the judiciary may provide a vehicle for doing so. As already noted, the judiciary is likely to be less hostile to the preemptive presidency than is the legislative and perhaps even the executive branch. As a result, the judiciary can be an outlet for presidential ambitions to alter policy. Moreover, presidents have relatively close contact with the judiciary. The president plays the leading, though not exclusive, role in selecting judicial personnel. Further, the president has nearly a free hand in determining the official position of the federal government on issues that come before the bench. Through control over the Justice Department, the president can exercise significant influence over what cases are moved through the appellate process and what arguments are presented before the Court. In other words, the federal government is a powerful and often successful litigant, and the president has almost exclusive control over that dimension of the government. These two aspects of presidential power allow preemptive presidents to introduce further tensions and contradictions into the existing regime, perhaps furthering its ultimate collapse.

Unlike reconstructive presidents, however, preemptive presidents are unlikely to dominate the judiciary or fully advance an oppositional constitutional vision through the courts. Nor are preemptive presidents likely to be as oppositional as later reconstructive presidents are. Oppositional figures who come to power during a vibrant regime must survive a difficult nomination and election process that ensures relative moderation. Preemptive presidents would therefore not want to pursue, or feel much political pressure to pursue, a harshly oppositional strategy in their dealings with the courts. In addition, the preemptive president faces constraints within the government. In nominating new judges and justices, for example, the president must still secure confirmation from the Senate. Preemptive presidents must reassure members of the dominant regime that their judicial choices are not a serious threat.[64] The appointment power of preemptive presidents is significantly constrained.

Eisenhower, Ford, and Clinton responded to this constraint by pursuing a strategy that favored well-regarded professionals with substantial expertise and politically neutral support. In the aftermath of Watergate, Ford largely delegated the task of judicial selection to his professionally respected attorney general, set broad criteria emphasizing experience and professional qualifications, and reintegrated the American Bar Association into the nomination process.[65] Clinton did much the same. Despite highly public lingering over more politically charged candidates, Clinton nominated quiet and relatively moderate candidates to the high court.[66] Nixon demonstrated the consequences of a preemptive president pursuing a more ideologically motivated and fully oppositional appointment strategy: the Senate rejected his specifically "Southern" nominees as unqualified and "too political."[67] Andrew Johnson, by contrast, was denied even this opportunity, as Congress eliminated two seats from the Court upon the death of Justice Catron (and later Justice Wayne) rather than allow Johnson to select replacements. The Court regained a seat when Johnson's affiliated successor gained the White House in the next election.[68] Nixon has been perhaps the most aggressive of any preemptive president in nominating candidates who would advance his oppositional vision from the bench. Nixon specifically placed judicial philosophy high on his list of considerations in choosing justices, and his choices were notably more conservative in their concern with precedent and criminal justice, which were the core issues of concern to him. As later commentators pointed out, however, the "Nixon" Court did not launch a "counter-revolution." His choices were relatively conservative, but not radical. Significantly, as the counter-revolution label suggests, the Burger Court did not challenge the central aspects of the New Deal regime. Nixon altered the course of New Deal jurisprudence, but could not hope to reverse it.[69] Similarly if less obviously, Eisenhower used the appointment power to drive additional wedges into the Democratic coalition on issues of race and civil rights, advancing Republican concerns in the context of a divided Democratic Senate.[70]

Preemptive presidents are also likely to use the judiciary for strategic lawmaking. Petitioning the Court is generally a low-profile activity. As a result, there are few political or electoral consequences of a more stridently oppositional line in lobbying the Court. The more significant constraint on the president in this regard is the justices themselves. A pre-

emptive president will likely face a Court that is only marginally responsive to the oppositional understanding of the Constitution, and the presidential power as a litigant comes only through the persuasiveness of government attorneys in convincing the Court to change direction.
Although there may be few political costs to offering a strongly oppositional argument to the Court, there is also little chance of a substantive
payoff. Instead, presidents must seek to exploit existing cleavages on the
Court and in established doctrine in order to nudge the Court in the
favored direction. Presidential choices here are strategic in a generally
unfavorable environment. After some initial hesitation, the Eisenhower
Justice Department took a leadership role, for example, in the civil rights
cases of the 1950s, signaling presidential support for the desegregation
decisions of the Warren Court despite likely opposition from Southern
Democrats.[71]

Overall, preemptive presidents have had some reason to support the
Court and relatively little ability to undermine the Court. Preemptive
presidents may be oppositional, but they are highly constrained and politically weak. In the politics of preemption, the independence of the
judiciary may offer the president a relatively safe haven. Certainly, the
political environment within which the president normally operates is
likely to be less hospitable than the legal environment of the judiciary.
Despite their particular disagreements with the Court, preemptive presidents have been careful to contain their conflicts with the judiciary. Preemptive presidents have accepted judicial authority to determine constitutional meaning and have often embraced the legalistic discourse that
amplifies judicial authority. These presidents have refrained from attack-
ing the Court as an institution, even if they have petitioned the Court to
change direction. Preemptive presidents cannot determine the course of
judicial doctrine, but they can be an important influence on its ultimate
development. To this degree, these presidents contribute to the further
complication of the regime, introducing discordant elements into established constitutional law, exacerbating the tensions in the dominant order, and bolstering the relative autonomy of the law and the Court to
diverge from dominant political preferences.

Presidential Support for Judicial Autonomy

The Court must compete with other political actors for the authority to
define the terms of the Constitution. For the Court to compete successfully, other political actors must have reasons for allowing the Court
to "win." The president, among others, must see some political value in
deferring to the Court and helping to construct a space for judicial au-

tonomy. Judicial supremacy makes the strongest claims on other political institutions. It asserts that the Court has a role not only in applying the Constitution in legal disputes but also in defining the nation's fundamental values and basic governmental structures. This is a strong claim, and we can easily imagine why other political actors might not wish to accede to such a claim. We can easily imagine presidents dismissing the authority of the Court and ignoring its opinions, if not its decisions. We can easily imagine a Court reduced to political subservience, inactive in the exercise of its power of review and incapable of acting independently. But judicial supremacy has grown and become more secure over time. Despite occasional voices of dissent, crucial government officials have generally supported the judiciary and recognized its claim to be the ultimate interpreter of the Constitution.

I have indicated here a political logic that accounts for our historical experience with Court and Constitution. Judicial supremacy has not been uncontested, and when it has been contested many see threats to judicial independence and constitutionalism itself. But challenges to judicial supremacy are historically limited. They arise only in particular and rare political circumstances, and are necessarily transitory. Moreover, they have generally been made in the name of constitutionalism itself. The presidents who have questioned judicial supremacy have done so not out of some hostility to constitutional values or rejection of the limits on government power. Presidents have challenged judicial supremacy in the course of establishing their own warrants to maintain the constitutional order. Such presidents have gone beyond a dialogue with the Court over the specifics of constitutional law because the nature of their divergence from the Court is too fundamental for dialogue. Their concern is with reconstructing the regime itself, with laying new foundations of political authority that go beyond constitutional technicalities and focus on basic constitutional purposes. Judicial supremacy has given way not when we need it most, but when it is needed least.

The historical presence of reconstructive leaders who have successfully challenged judicial supremacy does not imply that autonomous judicial action is politically unsustainable. Few political actors have been able to displace the judiciary. For most government officials, an autonomous judiciary exercising decisive interpretive authority is both a fact of life and a useful thing politically. For affiliated leaders who enjoy political dominance in the government and the electorate, problems of coalitional maintenance dictate maintaining a prominent place for the Court. An unelected judiciary can independently advance regime commitments, while protecting other government officials from potential electoral fallout. An autonomous judiciary can be politically more valuable than a judicial puppet. Moreover, a general acceptance of the virtue of constitutional interpretation empowers the Court by providing it with a real political resource that does not rest on immediate electoral approval. For all of those affiliated with the constitutional regime, the interpretive task is an essential and respected one. For an unaffiliated leader, an independent Court presents valuable strategic opportunities. In a hostile political climate, the judiciary offers an alternative forum within which oppositional leaders can seek refuge and pursue their agenda.

Judicial supremacy remains conditioned on political circumstances. The Court cannot expect to violate the basic constitutional assumptions of its contemporaries and be influential. Within those boundaries, however, the Court can have substantial autonomy in developing the implications of the constitutional regime. The constitutional legacy is always controversial, and that very controversy creates room for judicial interpretation. Within that context, the Court can develop the political resources to act in a distinctly nonmajoritarian and even countermajoritarian fashion. The judiciary can have an important role to play in maintaining our constitutional commitments across time, but only if those commitments are genuine. The Court can never be the sole guardian of our constitutional traditions, even if it can be the ultimate interpreter of them.

Notes

1. *Marbury v. Madison*, 5 U.S. (1 Cranch) 137, 177 (1803).
2. Ibid., p. 180.
3. *Cooper v. Aaron*, 358 U.S. 1, 18 (1958).
4. *U.S. v. Nixon*, 418 U.S. 683, 704 (1974).
5. A countermajoritarian role for the Court also raises a "countermajoritarian difficulty," however. In the modern context, in which democracy is the only generally accepted ground of authority, an institution that resists the majority will faces serious legitimacy problems. Alexander M. Bickel, *The Least Dangerous Branch* (Indianapolis: Bobbs-Merrill, 1962), pp. 14–23.
6. See, most prominently, Ronald Dworkin, *A Matter of Principle* (Cambridge: Harvard University Press, 1985), pp. 33–71.
7. *Cooper v. Aaron*, 358 U.S. 1, 18 (1958).
8. Alexander Hamilton, James Madison, and John Jay, *Federalist* No. 78, in *The Federalist Papers*, ed. Clinton Rossiter (New York: Mentor, 1961), p. 465.
9. E.g., Jack Knight and Lee Epstein, "On the Struggle for Judicial Supremacy," *Law and Society Review* 30 (1996): 87; Lee Epstein and Jack Knight, *The Choices Justices Make* (Washington, DC: CQ Press, 1998), pp. 138–81; Rafael Gely and Pablo T. Spiller, "The Political Economy of Supreme Court Constitutional Decisions: The Case of the Court-Packing Plan," *International Review of Law and Economics* 12 (1992): 45. But cf. Jeffrey A. Segal, "Separation-of-

Powers Games in the Positive Theory of Law and Courts," *American Political Science Review* 91 (1997): 28.

10. Gerald Rosenberg, "Judicial Independence and the Reality of Political Power," *Review of Politics* 54 (1992): 394, 398. The characterization of the Court as "constrained" comes from Rosenberg, *The Hollow Hope* (Chicago: University of Chicago Press, 1991), pp. 9–21. See also Stuart S. Nagel, "Court-Curbing Periods in American History," *Vanderbilt Law Review* 18 (1965): 925; Roger Handberg and Harold F. Hill, Jr., "Court Curbing, Court Reversals, and Judicial Review: The Supreme Court versus Congress," *Law and Society Review* 14 (1980): 309.

11. Robert Dahl, "Decision-Making in a Democracy: The Supreme Court as National Policy-Maker," *Journal of Public Law* 6 (1957): 293. See also Richard Funston, "The Supreme Court and Critical Elections," *American Political Science Review* 69 (1975): 795; Jonathan D. Casper, "The Supreme Court and National Policy Making," *American Political Science Review* 70 (1976): 50; David Adamany, "The Supreme Court's Role in Critical Elections," in *Realignment in American Politics*, ed. Bruce Campbell and Richard Trilling (Austin: University of Texas Press, 1980); William Lasser, *The Limits of Judicial Power* (Chapel Hill: University of North Carolina Press, 1988); John B. Taylor, "The Supreme Court and Political Eras: A Perspective on Judicial Power in a Democratic Polity," *Review of Politics* 54 (1992): 345; Barry Friedman, "Dialogue and Judicial Review," *Michigan Law Review* 91 (1993): 577; Girardeau A. Spann, *Race against the Court* (New York: New York University Press, 1993), pp. 9–35.

12. Dahl, "Decision-Making," 291.

13. The Court can do a great deal to influence those incentives through its own actions, but in this chapter I largely lay aside the Court's own efforts to build authority and concentrate on the strategic situation facing the president. Developing the political context of presidential actions should indicate the strategic opportunities that might be exploited by the judiciary. For a thoughtful analysis of such judicial action by the early Court, see Mark A. Graber, "The Passive-Aggressive Virtues: *Cohens v. Virginia* and the Problematic Establishment of Judicial Review," *Constitutional Commentary* 12 (1995): 67; Graber, "Establishing Judicial Review? *Schooner Peggy* and the Early Marshall Court," *Political Research Quarterly* 51 (1998): 221.

14. E.g., Walter Dean Burnham, *Critical Elections and the Mainsprings of American Politics* (New York: W.W. Norton, 1970); James L. Sundquist, *Dynamics of the Party System* (Washington, DC: Brookings Institution, 1983); Samuel P. Huntington, *American Politics* (Cambridge: Harvard University Press, 1981); James A. Morone, *The Democratic Wish* (New York: Basic Books, 1990); David R. Mayhew, *Divided We Govern* (New Haven: Yale University Press, 1991).

15. Stephen Skowronek, *The Politics Presidents Make* (Cambridge: Harvard University Press, 1993), pp. 34–52.

16. Ibid., p. 18.

17. The difference between these two perspectives is illustrated in the divergent ways that Stephen Skowronek and Bruce Ackerman use the term "constitutional politics." Skowronek uses the term to refer to the presidential exploitation

of his constitutional office in pursuit of other, non-constitutional goals, whereas Ackerman uses the term to refer to extraordinary efforts to change the Constitution. Skowronek, *Politics*, p. 12; Bruce Ackerman, *We the People*, vol. 1, *Foundations* (Cambridge: Harvard University Press, 1991), p. 7.

18. Skowronek, *Politics*, pp. 39, 38.

19. Ackerman, *We the People*, 1:59.

20. See also Louis Fisher, *Constitutional Dialogues* (Princeton: Princeton University Press, 1988); Neal Devins, *Shaping Constitutional Values* (Baltimore: Johns Hopkins University Press, 1996).

21. Keith E. Whittington, *Constitutional Construction* (Cambridge: Harvard University Press, 1999); Bruce Ackerman, *We the People*, vol. 2, *Transformations* (Cambridge: Harvard University Press, 1998); Howard Gillman, "Reconnecting the Modern Supreme Court to the Historical Evolution of Capitalism," in *The Supreme Court in American Politics*, ed. Howard Gillman and Cornell Clayton (Lawrence: University Press of Kansas, 1999).

22. Mary E. Stuckey, *The President as Interpreter-in-Chief* (Chatham, NJ: Chatham House, 1991), p. 1.

23. Such coalitional obligations are not historically constant. Nineteenth-century presidents were more beholden to their parties than twentieth-century presidents are. In addition, affiliated presidents are likely to be more obligated to their parties than are other types of presidents.

24. Sylvia Snowiss, *Judicial Review and the Law of the Constitution* (New Haven: Yale University Press, 1990); Paul W. Kahn, *Legitimacy and History* (New Haven: Yale University Press, 1992), pp. 9–64.

25. See also, Keith E. Whittington, "Presidential Challenges to Judicial Supremecy and the Politics of Constitutional Meaning," *Polity* 33 (2001): 365.

26. Lance Banning, *The Jefferson Persuasion* (Ithaca: Cornell University Press, 1978); Forrest McDonald, *The Presidency of Thomas Jefferson* (Lawrence: University Press of Kansas, 1976), pp. 1–52.

27. Franklin Roosevelt, *Public Papers and Addresses of Franklin D. Roosevelt*, ed. Samuel I. Rosenman, vol. 5 (New York: Random House, 1938), 236. See also Ackerman, 2:279–311.

28. E.g., Edward S. Corwin, *Court over Constitution* (Gloucester, MA: Peter Smith, 1957), pp. 1–84; Walter F. Murphy, "Who Shall Interpret? The Quest for the Ultimate Constitutional Interpreter," *Review of Politics* 48 (1986): 406; Louis Fisher, *Constitutional Dialogues* (Princeton: Princeton University Press, 1988), pp. 231–74; Robert Scigliano, *The Supreme Court and the Presidency* (New York: Free Press, 1971), pp. 23–60; Susan Burgess, *Contest for Constitutional Authority* (Lawrence: University Press of Kansas, 1992), pp. 3–28; Michael Stokes Paulsen, "The Most Dangerous Branch: Executive Power to Say What the Law Is," *Georgetown Law Journal* 83 (1994): 217; John Agresto, *The Supreme Court and Constitutional Democracy* (Ithaca: Cornell University Press, 1984), pp. 77–95.

29. *Marbury v. Madison*, 5 U.S. (1 Cranch) 137, 178 (1803).

30. Ackerman, *We the People*, 2:279–382; Lasser, *Limits of Judicial Power*, pp. 111–60; William E. Leuchtenberg, *The Supreme Court Reborn* (New York: Oxford University Press, 1995); Robert H. Jackson, *The Struggle for Judicial Supremacy* (New York: Vintage, 1941).

31. The "Court's hold over public opinion" at issue is not the narrow question of whether the mass public is aware of and understands specific cases, but the broader question of whether the Court has articulated a generally believed perspective on what the Constitution requires. The general public shows little specific awareness of the Court's work. Pioneering work in this regard by Walter Murphy and Joseph Tanenhaus, "Public Opinion and the Supreme Court: A Preliminary Mapping of Some Prerequisites for Court Legitimation of Regime Changes," in *Frontiers of Judicial Research*, ed. Joel Grossman and Joseph Tanenhaus (New York: John Wiley and Sons, 1969). See, generally, Thomas R. Marshall, *Public Opinion and the Supreme Court* (Boston: Unwin Hyman, 1989).

32. Skowronek, *Politics*, 37–38.

33. Nagel, "Court-Curbing Periods," pp. 925–28; Corwin, *Court over Constitution*, pp. 68–76; Scigliano, *Supreme Court*, pp. 23–50; Burgess, *Contest for Constitutional Authority*, pp. 3–7; Agresto, *Supreme Court*, pp. 78–95, 128–29; Fisher, *Constitutional Dialogues*, pp. 238–44.

34. Abraham Lincoln, *Abraham Lincoln: His Speeches and Writings*, ed. Roy P. Basler (New York: Da Capo Press, 1990), pp. 585–86.

35. Skowronek distinguishes between two types of affiliated leaders, those in a politics of articulation and those in a politics of disjunction. As we will see, that distinction is relevant to judicial authority as well. But I find the differences between affiliated leaders to be less important than their similarities for purposes of examining the logic of their relationship to the Court.

36. Dahl, "Decision-Making," pp. 284–85.

37. See also Howard Gillman, *The Constitution Besieged* (Durham: Duke University Press, 1993); Ackerman, *We the People*, 1:131–62.

38. Dahl, "Decision-Making," p. 294.

39. See also Lucas A. Powe, Jr., *The Warren Court and American Politics* (Cambridge: Harvard University Press, 2000).

40. See also Walter F. Murphy, *Congress and the Court* (Chicago: University of Chicago Press, 1962).

41. See also Michael J. Klarman, "*Brown*, Racial Change, and the Civil Rights Movement," *Virginia Law Review* 80 (1994): 13–71.

42. On this dynamic generally, see R. Douglas Arnold, *The Logic of Congressional Action* (New Haven: Yale University Press, 1990).

43. The party could be, and was, punished for publicly acting on those commitments through traceable legislation, however. E.g., Sundquist, *Dynamics of the Party System*, pp. 352–411; Edward G. Carmines and James A. Stimson, *Issue Evolution* (Princeton: Princeton University Press, 1989), pp. 27–58.

44. See also Mark A. Graber, "The Nonmajoritarian Difficulty: Legislative Deference to the Judiciary," *Studies in American Political Development* 7 (1993): 35; Whittington, "Reconstructive Presidents."

45. In Buchanan's case, that knowledge was explicit, since members of the Court told Buchanan privately the outcome of the *Dred Scott* case before the decision was made known publicly. *The Works of James Buchanan*, ed. John Bassett Moore, vol. 10 (Philadelphia: J.B. Lippincott, 1910), p. 106, n. 1.

46. Ibid., 106–7.

47. Kenneth M. Stampp, *America in 1857* (New York: Oxford University Press, 1990), pp. 295–331.

48. Lincoln, *Speeches*, p. 377.

49. See also David Rohde's concept of "conditional party government." Rohde, *Parties and Leaders in the Postreform House* (Chicago: University of Chicago Press, 1991).

50. Arthur S. Link, *Woodrow Wilson and the Progressive Era* (New York: Harper & Row, 1954), pp. 6–8; John Milton Cooper, Jr., *The Warrior and the Priest* (Cambridge: Harvard University Press, 1983), pp. 229–47; Elmo Richardson, *The Presidency of Dwight Eisenhower* (Lawrence: University Press of Kansas, 1979), pp. 16–19, 45–46; Fred I. Greenstein, *The Hidden-Hand Presidency* (New York: Basic Books, 1982), pp. 51–52; Stephen Skowronek, "President Clinton and the Risks of 'Third-Way' Politics," *Extensions* (Spring 1996): 11.

51. Norma Lois Peterson, *The Presidencies of William Henry Harrison and John Tyler* (Lawrence: University Press of Kansas, 1989), pp. 77–93; Eric L. McKitrick, *Andrew Johnson and Reconstruction* (Chicago: University of Chicago Press, 1960), pp. 85–92.

52. See also Skowronek, "'Third-Way' Politics."

53. See also Karen Orren and Stephen Skowronek, "Beyond the Iconography of Order: Notes for a 'New Institutionalism,'" in *The Dynamics of American Politics*, ed. Lawrence C. Dodd and Calvin Jillson (Boulder, CO: Westview Press, 1994); Ackerman, *We the People*, 1:140–62.

54. See also Terry Moe, "The Politics of Bureaucratic Structure," in *Can the Government Govern?*, ed. John Chubb and Paul Peterson (Washington, DC: Brookings Institution, 1989).

55. See also Rogers M. Smith, "Political Jurisprudence, the 'New Institutionalism,' and the Future of Public Law," *American Political Science Review* 82 (1988): 89; Ronald Kahn, *The Supreme Court and Constitutional Theory, 1953–1993* (Lawrence: University Press of Kansas, 1994); Howard Gillman, "The Court as an Idea, Not a Building (or a Game): Interpretive Institutionalism and the Analysis of Supreme Court Decision-Making," in Cornell W. Clayton and Howard Gillman, *Supreme Court Decision-Making* (Chicago: University of Chicago Press, 1999).

56. See also Whittington, *Constitutional Construction*, pp. 132–36.

57. See also ibid., 163–64, 180–84.

58. Richardson, *Dwight Eisenhower*, p. 110.

59. Ibid., p. 116.

60. Ibid., p. 110.

61. On Jackson and the Indian case, see Richard E. Ellis, *The Union at Risk* (New York: Oxford University Press, 1987), 28–32; Scigliano, *Supreme Court*, pp. 36–39.

62. Richardson, *Dwight Eisenhower*, pp. 120–21.

63. Sundquist, *Dynamics of the Party System*, pp. 369–70, 383–87; Carmines and Stimson, *Issue Evolution*, pp. 52–54; Donald Grier Stephenson, Jr., *Campaigns and the Court* (New York: Columbia University Press, 1999), pp. 179–82.

64. On Senate confirmation of judicial appointments, see generally Albert D.

Cover and Jeffrey A. Segal, "Senate Voting on Supreme Court Nominees: A Neo-institutional Model," *American Political Science Review* 84 (1990): 524; Jeffrey A. Segal, Charles M. Cameron, and Albert D. Cover, "A Spatial Model of Roll Call Voting: Senators, Constituents, Presidents, and Interest Groups in Supreme Court Confirmations," *American Journal of Political Science* 36 (1992): 96.

65. David M. O'Brien, "The Politics of Professionalism: President Gerald Ford's Appointment of John Paul Stevens," *Presidential Studies Quarterly* 21 (1991): 103.

66. Mark Silverstein and William Haltom, "You Can't Always Get What You Want: Reflections on the Ginsburg and Breyer Nominations," *Journal of Law and Politics* 12 (1996): 459.

67. Henry J. Abraham, *Justices and Presidents* (New York: Oxford University Press, 1992), pp. 13–23.

68. Ibid., pp. 124–27.

69. Vincent Blasi, ed., *The Counter-Revolution That Wasn't* (New Haven: Yale University Press, 1983); Ronald Kahn, *The Supreme Court and Constitutional Theory, 1953–1993* (Lawrence: University Press of Kansas, 1994).

70. Michael A. Kahn, "Shattering the Myth about President Eisenhower's Supreme Court Appointments," *Presidential Studies Quarterly* 22 (1992): 47; Stephen J. Wermiel, "The Nomination of Justice Brennan: Eisenhower's Mistake? A Look at the Historical Record," *Constitutional Commentary* 11 (1994–95): 515.

71. Richardson, *Dwight Eisenhower*, 108–9; Mark V. Tushnet, *Making Civil Rights Law* (New York: Oxford University Press, 1994), pp. 172–73.

13

Constitutionalism and Constitutional Failure

MARK E. BRANDON

CONSTITUTIONAL failure is not a popular topic among constitutional theorists or among Americans. To speak of failure is to speak about unhappy things, and, whatever one might say about the propensities of academics, Americans in general do not like to be made to feel unhappy, especially about their Constitution. At the risk of violating that sensibility in this essay, I want to sketch the contours of the concept of constitutional failure. I offer not a full-blown theory here, but a typology and some reflections that might facilitate the development of such a theory. The topic is an important one for constitutional theory, and I hope this discussion, if incomplete, is nonetheless useful.[1]

My claims are basically these: traditionally, constitutionalism posited natural law or natural rights as a solution to the problem of constraining and directing political power; that solution, however, was fraught with difficulties, including the recognizability and enforceability of the "higher" principles to which it appealed. In order to address those difficulties, especially those related to enforceability, the Constitution of the United States offered a new arrangement of answers to old problems of power. In doing so, the Constitution also suggested a new and more positive way of thinking about constitutionalism itself. This new way presented the possibility of conceiving of constitutionalism in terms other than higher moral and political principles. But at that moment, the new constitutionalism threatened to undermine the possibility of perceiving standards by which we might measure constitutional failure and hence to undermine the very possibility of constitutionalism. I argue, however, that the new constitutionalism actually pointed to a robust, complex, and multilayered account of constitutional failure.[2]

The Necessity of Failure

We are accustomed to thinking of constitutions as devices for creating and holding together a political world. That customary mode of thought makes a certain sense. After all, making and maintaining a politics are central objectives of constitutionalism. They are not only part of what a constitution ostensibly does, but also part of what it should do, or must do, if it is to succeed. But this sensible notion has taken on perverse forms, especially since the Civil War of the United States, where constitutional success has sometimes come to be viewed strictly in terms of the *perpetuation* of a constitution or a regime.[3] It is almost as if longevity itself were sufficient evidence of constitutional success.[4]

Such a view of things is unsatisfactory, however, for reasons other than the simple fact that constitutions can and do fail. Constitutional failure is more than an empirical reality. It is also a theoretical necessity. But the theoretical necessity arises from empirical fact. Constitutions are "made" things. The very facts that they appear on the scene at a particular time and displace existing forms of politics—perhaps even existing constitutions—subvert most claims to perpetuity as a constituent element of any constitutional regime. Of course, those facts need not prohibit a constitution or constitutional order from *aiming* at perpetuity. But they do mean that the manner in which constitutions are born and justified leaves them normatively defenseless against some forms of fundamental alteration or even displacement. Just as a constitution displaces a prior constitution or order, it too may be displaced under certain circumstances.

But constitutional failure is not always so grand as the dissolution of an order or a constitution. Constitutional failure can occur in subtler, smaller ways. These subtle forms of failure arise from the very character of constitutionalism, which is insensible without a theory or set of standards that give the political world form and limits. Of course, the "character of constitutionalism" is a tricky matter, for constitutionalism is multifaceted. For example, constitutionalism may aim at one or more basic objectives. It may take as its purpose the making of a people, sustaining ways of life, or creating or authorizing political power. But constitutionalism arises in history primarily as an attempt to solve a persistent problem in human experience: how to constrain and direct political power.[5] That is, it is fundamentally, though not exclusively, concerned with the problem of limits.

The problem of limits presents itself to Western thought (as we have inherited it) in the form of a dialogue between Socrates and Thrasymachus in Plato's *Republic*. There Thrasymachus claimed that justice is nothing more than the rule of the stronger.[6] The significance of such a claim is not simply that its logical ethical corollary is that might makes right, but also that it empties the very idea of justice of any normative force in the ordering and operation of political societies. Much of Western political thought from Plato to Nietzsche has represented an attempt to meet the challenge of Thrasymachus. (It is not clear that Socrates succeeded in doing so.) One reason for the persistence and normative power of constitutionalism is that it has represented an especially useful strategy for dealing with the problem of limiting political power. Its strategy is encapsulated in the notion "higher law," a law binding not only subjects and citizens, but even the ruler (eventually, the state).

But in order for higher law to be successful—that is, practically useful—it must include the possibility of failure. This is not merely to claim that a constitution or order carries within itself the seeds of its own destruction. It is also to make a more straightforward claim about constitutionalism, which, because it embraces the idea of higher law, must posit or presuppose standards against which to measure constitutional limits. But if those standards are to genuinely limit political power, it must be possible not to attain them. Thus, constitutional failure must be a real possibility. Without that possibility, constitutionalism itself could not succeed.[7]

Edward S. Corwin observed that the notion of higher law has a long pedigree in the West, extending back through Rome at least as far as pre-Socratic Greece and, though Corwin barely mentioned it, ancient Israel.[8] Whatever the form of higher law in these primordial times, by the time of the hegemonic rise of Christianity in Europe, the higher law was unquestionably metaphysical. That orientation owed a great deal to Plato's transformation of philosophy and to Aristotle's subsequent systematic revision of Plato's metaphysics. The aim of this metaphysical higher law was to discover transcendental moral principles. In this connection, "principles" connoted general rules, "moral" connoted bindingness, and "transcendental" connoted some source outside the ruler or state.

If higher law were to succeed in constraining political authority, however, it would have to answer a series of questions: First, from where does higher law come? (What is its source?) Second, what makes it binding? (What is its authority?) Third, how do we know what it tells us to do? (How do we discern the principles at a level of abstraction that permits us to solve problems in the world?) Fourth, how is higher law to be enforced?

In the West, the most durable theoretical framework for answers has been natural law, which has presented to the world a number of faces, including Aristotelian teleology, the rationalism of Medieval Christian theology, and the contractarianism that arose with greatest force in seventeenth-century England in the wake of the fracturing of Christian institutions. These theories are individually complex and collectively diverse, and it is beyond the scope of this essay to survey them. But I might offer some provisional claims whose demonstration requires another forum. All these versions of natural-law (or, in the case of Locke, natural right) constitutionalism shared an important characteristic: they were rooted in transcendental sources of authority and value. Hence, the standards for evaluating the success or failure of a regime derived not from the particular character of a society, regime, or constitution, but at least partly from universal standards or transcendental sources. That is, they derived either from a source above or outside human will or from a universal human nature transcending any particular form of politics.[9]

Determining what counted as constitutional failure under natural-law constitutionalism was as easy or difficult as discerning and applying the *a priori* principles that governed human beings and their institutions. Although their merits were and continue to be substantial, I believe that, with the rise of ethnically and ethically diverse nation-states, the various forms of natural-law constitutionalism failed to supply adequate answers to at least one of the four basic questions. Even in homogeneous polities, moreover, the old forms of constitutionalism had persistent difficulty with the question of enforcement.

A "New" Constitutionalism?

On one view, the Constitution of the United States was a modest attempt to build upon established principles of politics in order to answer the longstanding fourth question concerning the enforcement of higher law. But in taking a quantum step toward answering that question, the Constitution's framers supplied innovative answers to the first three questions as well.

In *Federalist* No. 1, Alexander Hamilton implicitly acknowledged the shadow of Thrasymachus. He suggested there that the Constitution was an experiment in whether it was possible to establish government through reflection and choice instead of through accident and force. But how was this government of reflection and choice to be enforced (assuming the very idea of *enforcing* reflection and choice is not oxymoronic)? How was this experiment in constraining political power to succeed? Even a rudimentary answer to those questions is complex, resting partly on institutional design (including, perhaps, some version of judicial review) and partly on social organization.[10] But neither element would have had quite the same meaning or effectiveness had it not been for two other innovations, which were crucial to the legitimation of the proposed institutional and social solutions.

The first was a reconception of the source of political authority—specifically, that the ultimate practical source of political power was neither God nor nature, but the people.[11] Of course, the doctrine of popular sovereignty did not originate in North America, as versions of it could trace their roots at least as far as ancient Greece. Moreover, there is an offshoot (or new seed) of the notion in John Locke's contractarianism. But whatever its origins, popular sovereignty, standing alone, would not solve the problem of enforcing limits, as Socrates knew too well. If the sovereignty of the people were to establish *effective* limits to political power, even to power exercised through quasi-democratic institutions, something more was required. A crucial additional ingredient, largely indigenous to North America, was the novel use of a *written* constitution.

Representative institutions were constrained, not simply because they derived their power from the consent of the governed (the people who elected representatives),[12] nor simply because their processes permitted them to make decisions reflectively and rationally instead of precipitously and passionately,[13] nor simply because they were engaged in a limited war with one another.[14] They were constrained because their origin, authority, and purpose derived from and were articulated in a written constitution, whose own authority derived from the constituent act of the people— not the "governed" people, but a sovereign people who could create and destroy government itself.

Still, how was this new instrument for constraining political power to be enforced? Plainly, the new constitution would not be self-enforcing.[15] It needed an effective institutional means for enforcing the positively embodied principles of higher law within the polity. In practice, there were several such means, but one would turn out to be deeply important. It was judicial review, the authority of judges to declare acts of government unconstitutional. Corwin made much of the English common-law roots for this judicial power,[16] and there can be no denying that the example of common-law judges, attempting to stand up to monarch and Parliament in England, was important to the development of American constitutional theory.[17] But as Corwin recognized, the experiment in judicially enforced limits failed in England, largely because the common law was too weak to overcome the institutional resistance to limiting English political power.

It would take other innovations to achieve an institutional solution to the problem of enforcing limits. So John Marshall's explanation and justification for the power of judicial review in *Marbury v. Madison* invoked not the common law, of which we have some reason for thinking Marshall was aware, but the new theory of constitutionalism implied in the Constitution and institutional arrangements of the United States.[18]

Thus, in attempting to solve the problem of enforcing higher law, the Constitution—or a particular theory of the Constitution—ingeniously reconfigured the answers to the remaining questions concerning the source, authority, and recognition of higher law. And its ingenuity laid the foundation for transforming the very idea of constitutionalism. Stated most boldly, the Constitution was a point of departure that led constitutionalism out of the old paradigm of natural law and into a new paradigm. Within the new paradigm, constitutionalism has come to embrace the extent and ways in which people might establish, maintain, and constrain a political life using a written constitution.[19]

In making such a claim, I do not suggest that the Constitution's framers had clearly in mind that their proposed solution to the problems of constraining and directing political power departed so substantially from older notions of higher law as to step into a new paradigm. Nor do I intend that constitutionalism is exhausted or captured by the notion of "interpretation" or that institutional arrangements, social organization, and norms are immaterial to the new constitutionalism.

The emphasis on writtenness does not eliminate institutions, society, or values from constitutionalism, but does transform their place and function. The new constitutionalism is a substantial conceptual departure from the old in that it possesses a distinct operating logic that leads to distinct conclusions about what it might mean to be a "constitutional" society. These conclusions, I believe, reflect our current conceptions of what a constitution and constitutional government are. Moreover, they modify what we might mean when we speak of constitutional failure.

Constitutionalism and Constitutional Failure

If the constitutional founding of the United States presented an opportunity to strip constitutionalism of its metaphysical baggage, it also threatened to undermine the moral objectivity of higher law. Without that objectivity, the argument might go, we have lost the possibility of applying binding, principled limits to governmental power. And without such limits, we have lost the capacity to talk sensibly about constitutional failure. And without that capacity, constitutionalism itself must fail, for it cannot do what it purports to do. In short, the problem became whether it is possible to conceive of a practical higher law without concessions to the old constitutionalism. Can the new constitutionalism accommodate the possibility of constitutional failure?

A comprehensive treatment of the problem of objectivity in constitutionalism is beyond the scope of this exploratory essay; however, I shall venture the following preliminary claims: First, it is possible to conceive of binding, non-metaphysical standards of constitutionalism, outside the paradigm of the old constitutionalism, that effectively preserve some notion of constitutional failure. Second, in the new constitutionalism, constitutional failure is multidimensional. That is, it exists in four distinct but related domains (or at four levels of abstraction). The types of constitutional failure that reside in those domains are a failure of *constitutionalism*, a failure of *a constitution*, a failure of *constitutional order*, and a failure of *constitutional discourse*. Third, constitutional failure sometimes operates in ironical or counterintuitive ways, precisely because it may reside in different domains. And failure of one kind may indicate or permit constitutional *success* along other dimensions, just as success in one may incite failure in another.

Failure of Constitutionalism

A failure of *constitutionalism* is a failure to employ basic principles of constitutionalism within a regime or in moving into or out of a regime. But how can we speak of a failure of constitutionalism—a failure with respect to principles of constitutionalism—if we have jettisoned the transcendental principles of the old constitutionalism? Alexander Hamilton may have pointed toward an answer to the question. As we have already seen, he described the Constitution as an experiment. It is an experiment in a particular mode of establishing, directing, and limiting political power. That is, it is an experiment regarding a particular *enterprise*. An essential element of that enterprise is a written constitution.

The very character and purpose of the enterprise imply the existence of standards that define and direct the enterprise. They make it sensible and useful. To depart from them is to abandon the enterprise and to render it, in a fundamental fashion, a failure. Although they are not objective in the sense of being universal, they are objective—or better, supply a firm ground for evaluation and criticism—because they are constitutive of the enterprise at hand, because they are part of what it means to be engaged in that enterprise.[20]

Thus, drawing on Hamilton, a constitution possesses the possibility of failure not simply because it is a human creation and therefore fallible according to transcendental standards, but because it is an experiment and therefore fallible according to the standards or principles implied by the character of the enterprise itself. That is, it is fallible according to the standards that inhere in the enterprise of attempting to constrain political power by written constitution. When one abandons those standards, one abandons the enterprise. The enterprise—or a particular iteration of the enterprise—has failed from the standpoint of constitutionalism.

What is the substance of those standards or principles? Again, a complete exposition is beyond the scope of this essay, but Hamilton suggested one fundamental principle in the passage I have cited. The basic aim of the Constitution was to attempt to establish (and constrain) government through reflection and choice instead of through accident and force. Any scheme that purports to aim at government by reflection and choice depends for its success on its ability to engage reflective choice. Specifically, it must act on the mind in a way that it permits those who would be subjects (or citizens) voluntarily to accept its authority and attach themselves to its regime.[21] That attachment, in turn, generates certain expectations among potential constitutional subjects.

Those expectations are a double-edged sword from the standpoint of the regime, for while they form part of the glue that holds any constitutional society together, they also imply certain obligations that the regime is bound to fulfill or principles it is bound to recognize. The specific content of those principles may take many forms and be present in varying intensities, depending on the character and experience of the people doing the attaching and on the precise form and origin of the regime itself.

But there are (at least) five general expectations or principles that may pertain to any constitutional regime. First, the regime should follow its own procedures. Second, procedures for establishing the regime (or for ratifying its constitution) should reflect the fundamental aim of the regime. That is, they themselves should embody a degree of reflection and choice. Third, "normal" procedures for operating the regime should also embody reflection and choice, though perhaps in ways different from those of constitutive procedures. Fourth, policies pursued by the regime should be "rational." That is, their validity should be subject to testing by reference to public, constitutional standards and to a general standard or requirement of coherence. Fifth, the regime is estopped from challenging the constitutional legitimacy of other regimes that claim authority by the same modes of creation as it claims for its own existence and authority.

Some scholars might criticize these expectations as being exclusively procedural and therefore substantively empty. This criticism is not trivial, but I think it is misplaced. My conception of constitutionalism is not normatively empty, but it is substantively thin. That is, the substantive content for many (not all) norms that authorize, evaluate, direct, and limit a regime comes largely from the people themselves. This applies to norms that are "means" and, to a constrained but nonetheless meaningful extent, to those that are "ends." This state of things may be troubling—for locating the authoritative source of many constitutive values in the people, for ignoring a power over the people themselves, for making important norms historically contingent, or for other reasons—but I suspect it is simply an aspect of the human condition. If "thin" constitutionalism remains troubling, however, it may also be desirable, in that it permits people to imagine, perhaps to execute, fundamental political change, which, on some accounts, was a basic aim of the American Revolution.

Using these thin and rudimentary criteria of constitutionalism, we might consider two examples of failure of constitutionalism. I shall draw both examples from the American constitutional experience, though one might point to examples drawn from other regimes. The first example was plain and present at the very founding of the order. The Constitution failed to supply the means by which slaves could attach themselves and construct their political identities by reference to the Constitution. Simply, the Constitution placed slaves outside the bounds of political membership, of citizenship. It also failed with respect to constitutionalism when it denied full citizenship to women. The constitutional order acted on both women and blacks in ways that were inconsistent with the principles of government by reflection and choice.

Notice that this claim does not rest on the notion that the Constitution violated the principle of "human dignity." It may well have done so, but within the assumptions of the new constitutionalism, invoking a standard of human dignity is problematic, not least because of its metaphysical roots. Human dignity evokes natural law or natural rights, which are off limits in the new constitutionalism. Thus, even if we can give meaningful constitutional content to the notion, as Walter Murphy has so artfully begun to do,[22] the form of the failure that I have suggested does not rest on *a priori* assumptions about the character, worth, or rights of human beings as human beings. It holds rather that if a constitution is to succeed on terms consistent with the new constitutionalism, it must presuppose that those who are to be constitutional subjects—or citizens—possess capacities for reflection and choice. Moreover, the constitutional order must treat those citizens with respect for those capacities. Otherwise the constitution or the order does not constitute those persons *as constitutional subjects.* Again, this is not because of any innate ontological status enjoyed by human beings, but because of what a constitution must be and a constitutional order must do if they are to comport with the principles that inhere in the constitutional enterprise.

A second example of failure of constitutionalism, again taken from the antebellum experience of the United States, was the Civil War. I assume here what may well be subject to debate—that a regime may fight a war in a constitutional manner for constitutional purposes. What I want to argue is that the decision by proponents of Union to forcibly resist the secession of the Southern states—putting to one side the responsibility of firebrands in South Carolina and elsewhere for military hostility—was inconsistent with principles of constitutionalism. One might of course claim the aim of the Confederacy to preserve slavery was itself a failure of constitutionalism, but the Confederate Constitution raised no more problems in that respect than did the original Constitution of the United States, and Lincoln's justification for the war was to preserve the Union, not to end slavery. By the fifth general test of constitutionalism, the Union was estopped from challenging the constitutional legitimacy of the emerging Confederacy, because the authority of the seceding states was consistent with the authority of Union; that is, both were authorized by similar iterations of "the people." In fact, at least on one prominent account of the origins of Union, the secessionist states' claim to authority mirrored precisely the authority that the Union claimed. To that extent, the Southern states were constitutionally justified in seceding, because they successfully invoked the very authority on which the Union itself rested. Vaclav Havel's Czech and Slovak Republic, from which the present state of Slovakia seceded peaceably, was far more constitutionalist in this regard than was Lincoln's United States.

Failure of a Constitution

The failure of *a constitution* is the second kind of constitutional failure. This form of failure may involve discarding, abandoning, or ignoring a particular constitution and may include a contemporaneous reconstitution by new constitution. In the latter case, the failure of one constitution is the success of another, at least to the extent that mere birth can be termed a success. For example, in seceding from the United States, the states of the South rescinded their prior ratifications of the Constitution, and in doing so rejected the Constitution, or rejected what they feared it had become. In subsequently ratifying a constitution for the Confederate States of America, the South replaced the old constitution with a new one. Clearly, however, one need not adopt a new constitution when discarding the old. The failure of the old is the same either way.

The failure of a constitution may be for reasons compatible with the principles of constitutionalism or for reasons incompatible. Hence, it may or may not represent a simultaneous failure of constitutionalism. The polity may discard or abandon its constitution for any number of reasons: because society wants to make specific substantive choices that are different from those in the former constitution, because it wants to devise new institutions or procedures for enacting choices, or because it is motivated by other, less noble impulses (by our lights). But if the failure is a self-conscious discarding or abandonment, and especially if it involves a contemporaneous reconstitution, the failure almost by definition must be compatible in some form or fashion with principles of constitutionalism. It must be so because it involves the exercise of some form of choice, perhaps a degree of reflection. According to principles of constitutionalism, the original choosing of a constitution must presuppose the possibility of choosing to reject that constitution, either in the beginning or later.[23]

On the other hand, one can imagine a society that rejects and adopts constitutions with such rapidity that neither the rejections nor the subsequent adoptions can plausibly be considered consistent with principle of constitutionalism. Such appears to have been the case for a time in some countries in Latin America, where there seemed simply to be an insufficiently stable sense of the possibility of constitutional politics, at least of politics *within* a constitution. There was insufficient reflection, even though there might have seemed to be some sort of choice.

Alternatively, a polity might discard its constitution without even the appearance of choice. For example, the polity might evolve out of its constitution or simply ignore it to death. In either case, there is no formal rejection, no self-consciousness, no reflection or choice. Thus, there will have been a failure of the constitution and of constitutionalism. For the foreseeable future, there seems to be little danger of such a combination of failures in the United States.

Failure of Constitutional Order

A failure of *constitutional order* is signified by the breakdown of a political regime established or authorized by a constitution. As is the case with the failure of a constitution, the failure of a constitutional order can be unreflective and unself-conscious, perhaps gradual, even almost imperceptible. To that extent, it might simultaneously implicate a failure of constitutionalism. In some ways, the failure of any regime that was once stable and plausibly "constitutional" is accompanied by forces insidious and even invisible. Such forces are present in the most reflective and self-conscious of polities. But sometimes such forces are so substantial, the breakdown so unreflective, that the failure of the order must be considered a failure of constitutionalism as well, though it need not be so considered.

It is clear that the constitutional order that had been the United States had failed by 1861. Civil war is an excellent indicator of such failure. And in one sense the Civil War signaled a simultaneous failure of constitutionalism, for it signified both sides' unwillingness to pursue constitutional processes for resolving the crisis over secession. But the failure of the order was not a failure of constitutionalism in all respects, for it was partly the consequence of a sustained deliberative process.

The failure of a constitutional order may well leave the existing constitution in place and therefore need not occur in conjunction with a failure of that constitution. In fact, the failure of a constitutional order may well grow out of or be caused by *adherence* to a constitution. Sotirios A. Barber notes an argument widely used to justify deviating from conceded constitutional rights in times of threat to national security. Such times, the argument goes, justify the polity's departing from the text: a constitution is not a suicide pact.[24] One can easily imagine circumstances in which a society is faced with a choice between its survival as a political order and the survival of its constitution. Abraham Lincoln chose the former at the expense of the latter, and backed his choice with guns.[25] Hugo Black, on the other hand, may well have embraced, at least in one case, a theory that reversed Lincoln's values and thus revised what might count as the survival of the order.[26]

In discussing the failure of a constitution, I suggested that Southern secession represented the failure of the Constitution of the United States, and in one sense it obviously did. But on the Southern view of things, secession and the formation of the Confederacy under a new constitution were not a *rejection* of the former Constitution, but an attempt to *preserve* its essential principles in a new political order. One can uncover evidence for this view in the Southern rhetoric of the day and in the fact that the Confederate Constitution was strikingly similar to the Constitution of the United States.[27] On the Southern view, then, the failure of the order was not accompanied by the failure of the Constitution, though on the Unionist view it was or would have been had secession succeeded.

Failure of Constitutional Discourse

A failure of *constitutional discourse* occurs when a constitutional order is unable to speak coherently or, more seriously, to sustain itself through constitutional interpretation or through discourse pertaining to its constitution. This form of failure might seem precious to one who doubts the capacity of language to constrain politics. As long ago as the fourth century B.C.E., however, Thucydides noted language's power in this regard in his chronicle of the demise of democratic Athens in the wake of the Peloponnesian War.[28]

A vivid and serious example of this form of failure occurred in the two to three decades preceding the American Civil War. During that period, an interpretive schism between Northern and Southern states—mainly in the context of disputes over the extension of slavery into the territories—deepened and widened to such an extent that the two regions evolved into distinctive interpretive paradigms that could not accommodate one another. There was a sense in which each was faithful to the Constitution in its own way. Hence, there was no failure of the Constitution in the mere presence of distinctive interpretive paradigms. But the conflict between the two did precipitate the breakdown of the constitutional order when the South eventually abandoned the order and seceded from the

Union in a manner (though not for a purpose) that was consistent with the principles of constitutionalism.

One can perceive discursive failures, however, that do not precipitate a breakdown of the order. For example, the deep divisions in our own time over the constitutional status of abortion reflect a kind of discursive breakdown in which neither side can speak meaningfully to the other, because each maintains a position possessing its own premises and logical structure that are, in important respects, incompatible with those of the other. In some respects, such divisions may well indicate the success of the Constitution, as each side sees itself as faithful to the values of the Constitution. Because the battle is incapable of being resolved happily for all sides, the stakes are sufficiently high that social disruption can and does occur. One of two things may be occurring with respect to this issue: either the lines of division are sufficiently complex and crosscutting that they do not threaten the failure of the order itself, or factions whose beliefs are strong enough to rationalize disruption are too weak to convulse the larger political order.

But if they did precipitate such a failure, it would not necessarily signify a failure of constitutionalism. Because it includes a set of principles, constitutionalism does not guarantee harmony, unity, or happy endings.[29]

Notes

1. Portions of this essay originally appeared in Mark E. Brandon, *Free in the World: American Slavery and Constitutional Failure* (Princeton: Princeton University Press, 1998), and Mark E. Brandon, "Constitutionalism and Constitutional Failure," *The Good Society* 9 (1999): 61. Thanks to Princeton University Press and to the Committee on the Political Economy of the Good Society for permission to use those portions. I presented earlier versions of the essay at the Annual Meeting of the Southwestern Political Science Association (San Antonio, Texas, March 30–April 2, 1994) and at the Conference in Honor of Walter F. Murphy (Princeton University, May 12–13, 1995).

2. I should offer a few words about usage. By "constitutions" I intend *written* constitutions. This deviates, of course, from Aristotelian usage, in which "constitution" refers roughly to the institutions and values of a political society, not to texts. When referring to the two elements of the Aristotelian constitution, I call them "institutions" (or "government" or "polity" or "order") and "values" (or "norms" or "ethos").

3. Abraham Lincoln contended that perpetuity was fundamental to constitutional government. See, e.g., his "First Inaugural Address—Final Text," in *The Collected Works of Abraham Lincoln*, ed. Roy P. Basler (New Brunswick: Rutgers University Press, 1953), IV:264.

4. Bruce Ackerman acknowledges some of the complexity of the longevity of the Constitution. That complexity presents itself when we recognize the norma-

tive dissonance that occurs in moving from the antebellum order to Reconstruction to the "Lochner era" to the post-Depression regime. Problematically, however, Ackerman sees each new constitutional moment (or paradigm) as embodying an episode in which "We the People" confront a critical juncture in our history by reconstituting ourselves around the Constitution. At each juncture, according to Ackerman, the reconstitution takes the form of a new constitutional ethic, which the "People" ratify in a variety of ways. Ackerman's version of the people's two bodies—i.e., the people of normal democratic politics and the constitutional people—is theoretically useful, even if some of his analysis is empirically suspect. Ackerman, *We the People:* vol. 1: *Foundations* (Cambridge: Harvard University Press, 1991).

5. Compare Stephen L. Elkin, "Constitutionalism: Old and New," in *A New Constitutionalism: Designing Political Institutions for a Good Society*, ed. Elkin and Karol E. Soltan (Chicago: University of Chicago Press, 1993), pp. 20–21. In citing Elkin for this proposition, I do not intend to incorporate his meanings for "old" and "new" constitutionalism. Compare also Sue Hemberger, ch. 6 in this volume, who focuses on authority as fundamental to constitutionalism. My disagreement with her, if there be a disagreement, is not of principle but of emphasis.

6. Plato, *The Republic* (trans. Allan Bloom, New York: Basic Books, 1968), Book I, 338a–339a. Compare the position of Plato's Callicles: he did not repudiate natural law, but formulated it as a law without limits. In nature, he said, "right has been decided to consist in the sway and advantage of the stronger over the weaker." The pursuit of this precept in human relations constitutes "natural justice." Plato, *The Gorgias*, in *Plato in Twelve Volumes* (trans. W.R.M. Lamb, Cambridge: Harvard University Press, 1925), 483d–484b.

7. For an insightful justification for constitutionalism's need to posit the possibility of constitutional failure, see Sotirios A. Barber, *On What the Constitution Means* (Baltimore: Johns Hopkins University Press, 1984).

8. Edward S. Corwin, "The 'Higher Law' Background of American Constitutional Law," in *Corwin on the Constitution* ed. Richard Loss (Ithaca: Cornell University Press, 1981), 1:79. For a glimpse at a non-Western regime that successfully anticipated aspects of the problem of limits, compare Amartya Sen, "East and West: The Reach of Reason," 47 *New York Review of Books*, July 20, 2000, p. 33.

9. With respect to Aristotle, at least, and perhaps to Medieval Christian theology as well, this claim is controversial. Stephen G. Salkever, for example, insists that at the highest level of abstraction Aristotle posited not "law" (in the sense of binding rules whose outcomes are predictable), but a general "theory of the human good." This theory, says Salkever, informs or participates in decisions about human action in particular situations, but does not determine it, for Aristotle's human goods must adapt to the structural constraints and practical limitations of particular political institutions and policies. Stephen G. Salkever, *Finding the Mean: Theory and Practice in Aristotelian Philosophy* (Princeton: Princeton University Press, 1990), p. 7. I take Salkever's points, but they do not undermine my claim that Aristotle incorporated a metaphysical approach to human action. On Salkever's own account, Aristotle's human goods are "objective" and "commen-

surable." They constitute human beings as human and thus transcend any particular forms of human enterprise. If the application of these goods must take into
account the circumstances of human experience, its method and aim involve
"seeing the universal in the particulars before us." Ibid., pp. 105–22.

10. See, e.g., *Federalist* Nos. 10, 14, 38, 51, and 78.

11. Who the people were was problematic. Compare John Marshall's national-
ist account in *M'Culloch v. Maryland*, 17 U.S. 316 (1819), with James Madison's
localist account in *Federalist* No. 39.

12. See Madison, *Federalist* No. 39, on the "republican principle."

13. See, e.g., Madison, *Federalist*, No. 10.

14. See Madison, *Federalist* Nos. 48 and 51.

15. Compare Justice Bradley, dissenting in the *Slaughter-House Cases*, 83 U.S.
(16 Wall.) 36 (1872). He claimed that the Fourteenth Amendment, properly
understood, "would execute itself." This claim, of course, presupposed the presence of courts to enforce the amendment and perhaps of legislation aiming to
reinforce it. Ibid., pp. 123–24.

16. See Corwin, "'Higher Law,'" pp. 94–117. See also Charles Howard McIl-
wain, *Constitutionalism: Ancient and Modern* (Ithaca: Cornell University Press,
1947).

17. See, for example, the *Ship Money Case* (1637), discussed in W. J. Jones,
Politics and the Bench: The Judges and the Origins of the English Civil War (London, New York: Barnes and Noble, 1971), pp. 123–30; *Dr. Bonham's Case*, 8 Co.
107a (1610).

18. *Marbury v. Madison*, 5 U.S. 137 (1803). Marshall's theory was a revision
of Hamilton's theory of democratic limits to democratic political institutions in
Federalist No. 78. But see *Fletcher v. Peck*, 10 U.S. 87 (1810), which relied explicitly on common law to underwrite the constitutional status of property. On
the subtle but significant differences between Hamilton's and Marshall's approaches to judicial review, see Sanford Byron Gabin, *Judicial Review and the
Reasonable Doubt Test* (Port Washington, NY: Kennikat Press, 1980), ch. 1.

19. Compare William F. Harris II, *The Interpretable Constitution* (Baltimore:
Johns Hopkins University Press, 1993).

20. The stratagem suggested by the notion of an "enterprise" is not new. John
Marshall's opinion in *M'Culloch v. Maryland*, 17 U.S. 316 (1819), was an early
example. For two competing non-judicial arguments that employ the notion, see
Ronald Dworkin, *Taking Rights Seriously* (Cambridge: Harvard University Press,
1977, 1978), p. 81; and H.L.A. Hart, *The Concept of Law* (Oxford: Oxford University Press, 1961, 1994). For a later iteration of Dworkin's position, see his
Law's Empire (Cambridge, MA: Belknap Press, 1986). See also Harris, *Interpretate Constitution*.

21. See Harris, *Interpretate Constitution*, p. 114.

22. Walter F. Murphy, "An Ordering of Constitutional Values," *Southern California L. Rev.* 53 (1980): 703.

23. See Barber, *On What the Constitution Means*, ch. 3. Compare John Finn,
Constitutions in Crisis: Political Violence and the Rule of Law (New York: Oxford
University Press, 1991), discussing ways by which a regime might reassert consti-

tutionalist authority in the wake of a constitutional crisis—that is, a crisis in which the survival of the regime itself was threatened.

24. For criticism of the "suicide-pact argument," see Barber, *On What the Constitution Means*, pp. 108–13.

25. Lincoln sometimes denied there was a contradiction between the two. At other times he claimed that he was not obliged to adhere to constitutional text when doing so risked the demise of perpetual union. "Message to Congress in Special Session" (July 4, 1861), in *Collected Works*, IV:421ff.

26. *Barenblatt v. U.S.*, 360 U.S. 109 (1960), Black, J., dissenting. See also Justice Davis's opinion for the Court in *Ex Parte Milligan*, 71 U.S. (4 Wall.) 2 (1866).

27. For an argument that the Confederate States of America actually got the "original" Constitution right, see James M. McPherson, *Battle Cry of Freedom: The Civil War Era* (New York: Oxford University Press, 1988), ch. 1.

28. Thucydides, *The Peloponnesian War*, trans. Richard Crawley, intro. by T. E. Wick (New York: Random House, 1982).

29. On the notion of (un-)happy endings, see Sanford Levinson, *Constitutional Faith* (Princeton: Princeton University Press, 1988).

14

Justice, Legitimacy, and Allegiance: "The End of Democracy?" Symposium Revisited

ROBERT P. GEORGE

MY CONTRIBUTION to the *First Things* symposium, "The End of Democracy? The Judicial Usurpation of Politics," was a commentary on the encyclical letter, *Evangelium Vitae* ("The Gospel of Life"), by Pope John Paul II.[1] That letter, which had been issued a year and a half earlier, forcefully reasserted the Catholic Church's firm and constant teaching regarding the value and inviolability of human life.[2] Thus, it condemned abortion and euthanasia as "crimes which no human law can claim to legitimize."[3] Moreover, the encyclical argued against use of the death penalty, stating that criminal punishment "ought not go to the extreme of executing the offender except in cases of absolute necessity: in other words, when it would not be possible otherwise to defend society."[4] The print and broadcast media duly recorded the Pope's vigorous reaffirmation of the Church's teachings on the moral wrongfulness of abortion and euthanasia and took particular note of what Joseph Cardinal Ratzinger, prefect of the Congregation for the Doctrine of the Faith, described as the Pope's development of the Church's doctrine in opposition to capital punishment.[5] What received scant attention, however, was the Pope's philosophical analysis of legally sanctioned injustice and its implications for the authority of laws and the legitimacy of political regimes.[6]

The principal purpose of this essay is to highlight the Pope's analysis and consider its relevance to the concrete circumstances of the United States, where the abortion license, among other evils, has been imposed on the nation by judicial fiat and where, at the time of my writing in *First Things*, the Supreme Court was considering whether to uphold decisions by lower federal courts establishing a constitutional right to physician-assisted suicide.[7] Although the Pope did not consider the question of judicial authority in relation to the authority of legislators and other elected officials, much less address the scope and limits of constitutional judicial review in the United States (or anywhere else), the editors of *First Things* commissioned my essay for the symposium precisely because *Evangelium Vitae* addressed so directly, and with such a high degree of philosophical sophistication, the issues of legal authority and political legitimacy in modern constitutional democracies. The editors believed, as I believe, that the Pope's teaching on these issues is highly pertinent to circumstances in which a judiciary, charged to interpret and apply the fundamental law of a democratic republic, has, under the pretext of performing that function, usurped the authority of the people to act through the institutions of representative democracy to protect the unborn and other potential victims of injustice and to secure the overall common good.

The first thing to notice about the Pope's teaching is that it is pro-democratic.[8] Perhaps it goes without saying that not every pope has been an admirer of democracy. Critics of democracy, including some popes, have worried that belief in the superiority of democratic institutions in some sense presupposes or entails the denial of objective moral truth. Even some who sympathize with democracy as an ideal have been concerned that, in practice, democratic institutions subtly inculcate in the people living under them the spirit of moral relativism or subjectivism. Certain critics of the subjectivist or relativist spirit of this age suggest that the sources of society's pathology are precisely in the democratic institutions bequeathed to the public by the nation's founders.[9] Throughout his pontificate, however, John Paul II has robustly defended the principles and institutions of democratic governance.[10] And his defense of these principles and institutions has been neither halfhearted nor merely pragmatic. John Paul II enthusiastically promotes democracy not as some sort of lesser evil, "but as a system which more perfectly than any other embodies the great moral truth of the fundamental dignity of each human person."[11] It is for this reason, the Pope says in *Evangelium Vitae*, that the "almost universal consensus with regard to the value of democracy is to be considered a positive 'sign of the times.'"[12]

At the same time, and this is the second thing to notice about the teaching of *Evangelium Vitae*, the Pope warns against making a fetish of democracy, or "idoliz[ing] [it] to the point of making it a substitute for morality or a panacea for immorality."[13] After all, democratic institutions are *procedures for* making political decisions; they cannot guarantee substantive justice. As the Pope reminds us:

> Fundamentally, democracy is a "system" and as such is a means and not an end. Its "moral" value is not automatic, but depends on conformity to the moral law to which it, like every other form of human behaviour, must be subject: in other words, its morality depends on the morality of the ends which it pursues and of the means which it employs.[14]

What is interesting about human positive law, from the moral point of view, is not merely that laws enforce obligations that already exist as a matter of moral law, but that laws sometimes create moral obligations that would otherwise not exist.[15] The moral obligation to obey the law is, however, conditional and, as such, defeasible.[16] The justice of a law or a system of laws can destroy its power to bind the consciences of those ostensibly subject to it. This is the central core of truth in the oft-misunderstood statement *lex iniusta non est lex* ("an unjust law is not law"), a proposition taught not only by St. Augustine[17] and St. Thomas Aquinas,[18] but also in substance by Plato,[19] Aristotle,[20] and Cicero.[21] And, as the Pope affirms, the democratic provenance of a law does not render its obligation-imposing power indefeasible.[22] Even a law enacted by impeccably democratic procedures can be unjust, and insofar as it is unjust it can fail to create an obligation to obey.[23]

Indeed, certain sorts of unjust laws may not licitly be obeyed. For example, it is morally wrong to comply with laws requiring people to perform actions that are themselves unjust or otherwise immoral. From the moral point of view, people subject to such laws do not have the option of obeying them. The fulfillment of their moral responsibilities requires people to disobey the laws. So, for example, a conscientious physician would simply refuse to comply with a law requiring him to administer a lethal injection to any patient whom he diagnoses as carrying HIV. Not only is there no moral obligation to obey such a law, there is a strict moral obligation not to obey it. It matters not whether the law in question was put into place by a military junta, a judicial oligarchy, or a democratically elected legislature.

But what of laws, such as those permitting abortion and euthanasia, which do not require anybody to do anything, but are, rather, *permissive* of gravely unjust actions? The Pope says that such laws are "radically opposed not only to the good of the individual but also to the common good; as such they are completely lacking in authentic juridical validity."[24] The wholesale legal permission of evils such as abortion and euthanasia constitutes a failure of government to fulfill its primary responsibility, that is, to protect the weak and vulnerable against unjust physical assaults. Moreover, such a permission is gravely unjust inasmuch as it denies the unborn, the handicapped, the frail elderly, and other vulnerable persons their right to the equal protection of the laws. Where such a denial of equality is worked by democratic means, as with the abortion license in most European countries for example, it damages the integrity of democracy itself for, as the Pope has so clearly seen, the principle of equality is itself central to the democracy's moral justification.[25] By the same token, where the denial of equal protection is worked by judicial action, as in the United States, it constitutes not only a usurpation of democratic authority, but an an assault on democracy's core principle.

Certain critics of the *First Things* symposium have alleged that the symposium was driven not by a concern about judicial usurpation as such, but by opposition to abortion and euthanasia. Writing in *Commentary* magazine's *On the Future of Conservatism: A Symposium*, Peter Berger argued that the concern of the editors of *First Things* and most of the contributors to its symposium on judicial usurpation "has been not so much the power the courts have improperly assumed but rather what they have done with this power. And at the center of this concern is the issue of abortion."[26] To illustrate what he referred to as "the problem here," Berger proposed a thought-experiment:

> Imagine that abortion in the United States had achieved its present legal status through an act of Congress rather than a Supreme Court decision. Imagine further that the Supreme Court had then ruled this action to be unconstitutional. I doubt very much that most of the *First Things* contributors would have viewed the latter action as a serious usurpation of power.[27]

Berger is correct that I and, I suspect, others involved in the *First Things* symposium (with the possible exception of Robert Bork, despite his firm pro-life convictions[28]) would have applauded a decision by the Supreme Court invalidating an act of Congress or, to make Berger's point more sharply than he did, acts of state legislatures to deprive the unborn of legal protection against abortion. But, if we attend to the Pope's analysis of democracy and its moral presuppositions in *Evangelium Vitae*, we can see that this is not the "problem" for the *First Things* symposiasts that Berger thinks it is.

I had occasion in my contribution to the symposium to contrast the Pope's analysis of the moral presuppositions of democracy with extra-curial remarks by Justice Antonin Scalia.[29] Scalia, of course, is a passionate and relentless critic of *Roe v. Wade*[30] who has long argued that the Court's invalidation of state laws restricting abortion was a gross usurpation by the judicial branch of democratic legislative authority.[31] He is also firmly committed to the pro-life cause.[32] Yet, Scalia's view is that the Constitution commits the nation to neither pro-life nor pro-choice principles; rather, he maintains, abortion is a political and not a constitutional issue.[33] And the Constitution leaves such issues entirely to democratic resolution by Congress or the state legislatures. So, Scalia declared to an apparently scandalized audience at the Pontifical Gregorian University in Rome, "if the people want abortion, the state should permit abortion in a democracy."[34]

But if, as I think, and as the Pope teaches, and as Justice Scalia agrees, abortion is the unjust killing of innocent human beings who, as a matter of right, are entitled to the equal protection of the laws, then there is a problem for a democracy in permitting abortion. (Of course, whether it is a problem that judges in any particular democratic society are empowered to do anything about is another question.) Since it is the principle of equality that provides the moral justification for democratic rule in the first place, the denial of equality, even if effected by democratic means, is inconsistent with democratic principles. In this sense, democracy is not a morally neutral mechanism for deciding disputed questions. Its own moral presuppositions exclude certain outcomes even where these outcomes represent the preferences (or, for that matter, the considered but gravely mistaken moral judgments) of a majority.

As I suggested a moment ago, to understand the moral basis of democracy in this way is not, by itself, to decide in every or any particular case that judges should invalidate legislation (including permissive abortion legislation) that conflicts with their views-however sound-of what equality requires. The existence and scope of judicial power to invalidate democratically enacted laws, including laws whose injustice compromises the principles of democracy itself, is settled not by natural law (i.e., the moral law), but by the positive constitutional law of a given democratic polity.[35] On this important point, Justice Scalia is plainly correct. But to adopt this understanding is to begin to see the dubiousness of the simple symmetry presupposed by Berger's criticism of the *First Things* symposium. And we can go much further toward undermining belief in this alleged symmetry if we consider the commitment to the principle of equality concretely embodied in the Constitution of the United States.

The Fourteenth Amendment expressly forbids the states from denying to any person within their jurisdiction the equal protection of the laws.[36] So, a court exercising judicial review of abortion laws must decide the following two questions: (1) Are the unborn "persons" within the meaning of that term as it is used in the Fourteenth Amendment, and, if so, (2) does the abortion law under review deny to unborn persons the "equal protection of the laws"?

Justice Harry Blackmun, in his opinion for the Court in *Roe v. Wade*,[37] purported to deal with the question of whether the unborn are persons within the meaning of the Fourteenth Amendment, noting that if the unborn are persons, then their right not to be killed is specifically protected by the Fourteenth Amendment.[38] Thus, the Court's duty would be to strike down permissive abortion laws as violative of the constitutional rights of unborn persons.[39] In the end, however, Blackmun effectively dismissed the question by simply observing that in places in the Constitution outside the Fourteenth Amendment where the term "person" is used (as, for example, in the provision that says that "persons" must have attained the age of thirty-five in order to serve as President of the United States[40]) it applies only postnatally.[41] He also argued, famously, that the Court could not and, therefore, need not "resolve the difficult question when life begins" given that the matter is "at this point in the development of man's knowledge" disputed by scientists, philosophers, theologians, and other experts.[42] Of course, Blackmun went on implicitly to resolve precisely this question quite against the proposition that "life begins" anytime prior to birth. Yet this is absurd from the scientific viewpoint, and indefensible philosophically.[43] And it set Blackmun up for precisely the criticism he received, namely, that *Roe* was an utterly unprincipled decision, an exercise, as Justice Byron White said in dissent, of "raw judicial power" in which the Court merely substituted its own policy preferences for the contrary judgment of the elected representatives of the people.[44]

Could the matter have been decided otherwise? Can a principled argument for the outcome in *Roe* be constructed? Blackmun's manifest failure to identify a principled ground for the decision has sparked a massive industry, now in its twenty-eighth year, of "rewriting Roe" to put it on an intellectually secure constitutional footing. Many of the best and brightest in the legal academy have joined in this effort, all to no avail. It is not merely that there is no specifically enumerated constitutional right to abortion. It is that there simply is no principle in the Constitution by whose affirmation the American people have committed themselves to a regime of abortion-on-demand. The matter is not even close. The best that plausibly can be said for the cause of abortion as a constitutional matter is what Justice Scalia says, namely, that though the Constitution does not forbid the States to restrict abortion, it does not require them to do so.[45]

By contrast, a genuinely principled argument can be made that the American people have, by ratifying the Fourteenth Amendment's guarantee of equal protection, committed themselves to a proposition which is inconsistent with the regime of abortion-on-demand. One way of stating the argument is to observe that "person," in ordinary language, connotes what logicians call a "substance sortal," that is to say, an essential property, which implies that whatever has it *has it necessarily* and never exists without it. Human beings come to be and become persons at the same time; they do not become persons at some point after coming to be (nor do they cease being persons without ceasing to be).[46] The thirty-nine- (or so) year-old person who is now, say, Professor Sotirios Barber is indistinguishable from the being (or, in philosophical terms, the "substance") who was at an earlier stage of his life a twenty-six-year-old graduate student, an eighteen-year-old undergraduate, a thirteen-year-old adolescent, a six-year-old child, a one-year-old infant, a five-month-old fetus, a four-week-old embryo, and a newly conceived human being. Professor Barber progressed from his conception through the embryonic, fetal, infant, and adolescent stages of his life into his adult stage as a distinct, unified, self-integrating organism without undergoing substantial change, that is, without ceasing to be one kind of being or substance (possessing one kind of nature) and becoming a different sort of being.[47] Of course, there was a time when he did not exist. *He* was never a sperm cell or an ovum, much less a twinkle in his father's eye. But when he came into existence, he came into existence as a person. There was no stage in his life at which he existed but was not yet a person. Just as *he* was once an adolescent and before that an infant, the very same *he* was once a fetus and before that an embryo. And in this respect Professor Barber is just like the rest of us.

John Finnis summed up the matter nicely in his critique of John Rawls's argument that restrictions on abortion violate the liberal principle of public reason which, according to Rawls, ought to govern legislative decision-making on questions of constitutional essentials and matters of basic justice.[48] Any justification for denying unborn human beings the right to the equal protection of the laws, Finnis argues,

> will have to have abandoned the one real basis of human equality and equality rights, namely the fact that each living human being possesses, actually and not merely *potentially*, the radical capacity to reason, laugh, love, repent, and choose *as this unique, personal* individual, a capacity which is not some abstract characteristic of the species but rather consists in the unique, individual, organic functioning of the organism which comes into existence as a new substance at the conception of that new human being and subsists until his or her death whether 90 minutes, ninety days, or ninety years later—a capacity, individuality and personhood which subsists as real and precious even while its operations come and go with many changing factors such as immaturity, injury, sleep, and senility.[49]

But someone may object: Is it not possible that the framers and ratifiers meant something very different by "person" when they used that term in the Fourteenth Amendment? Indeed, it is possible. Whether the framers really did have something very different in mind is certainly relevant to whether a court would now be justified in striking down a legislatively enacted regime of abortion-on-demand as a violation of the equal protection rights of the unborn. Important questions of the proper role of "original understanding" for example, would immediately be put into play. As yet, however, the argument has not been made. Although the ratifiers of the Fourteenth Amendment did not have the question of abortion in mind but were concerned, rather, about racial bias against the recently freed slaves, they very deliberately framed the Equal Protection (and Due Process) Clause(s) in general terms to forbid the denial of equal protection (and due process) to any person or class of persons, and all the evidence from the ratification debates is consistent with the proposition that by "persons" the framers and ratifiers meant (and meant to protect) all human beings, all living members of homo sapiens.

In any event, I am not here arguing that Justice Scalia is certainly wrong to suggest that courts could not be justified in striking down liberal abortion laws. To make that argument, I would have to address the panoply of reasons militating in favor of judicial restraint when it comes to an issue such as abortion.[50] I am here interested merely in showing that, unlike the Court's decision in *Roe*, a decision outlawing or substantially restricting abortion could be supported by a plausible and truly principled constitutional argument. Thus, the symmetry presupposed by Berger's criticism of the *First Things* symposium does not in fact exist.

The conception of democracy, and the understanding of America's democratic institutions, which the symposiasts had in mind when expressing their concerns about the possible "end of democracy" and offering their criticisms of "the judicial usurpation of politics," were not conceptions according to which democracy is (as Justice Scalia supposes) a simple, morally neutral mechanism of majority rule, whereby fifty-one percent of the people do as they please. Rather, it is a conception of democracy which, as the Pope's analysis in *Evangelium Vitae* brings to light, is shaped by its own justifying moral principle of the equality-in-dignity of all human beings, a conception which, I and others connected with *First Things* believe, was operative in the central proposition of the Declaration of Independence ("all men are created equal") and enshrined in our Constitution (particularly, though not exclusively, in the Equal Protection Clause of the Fourteenth Amendment). Under our conception of democracy, the function of democratic institutions is to serve as the mechanisms by which the people act to fulfill their moral-political responsibilities to protect the weak and innocent, preserve and promote public health, safety, and morals, and secure the overall common good.

In engaging the question of the legitimacy of the regime of judicial rule, a point that I and other participants in the *First Things* symposium should have made more explicitly is that apart from the most tyrannical regimes (which conscientious citizens may rightly, and where possible should, work to subvert), the question of legitimacy is a matter of degree, rather than an either-or proposition. Consider the case of non-tyrannical but authoritarian regimes. Because democracy, as the Pope teaches, embodies the principle of human equality, a regime that fails to adopt, or move in the direction of, democratic rule will necessarily implicate itself in a measure of injustice. And insofar as a regime implicates itself in injustice, it weakens the citizens' reasons for giving their loyalty or allegiance to the regime. In a word, it weakens, even if it does not destroy, a regime's legitimacy. However, no regime this side of God's sovereign rule in the kingdom of heaven is perfectly just, utterly free of injustice. But that certainly does not mean that every regime is simply illegitimate and may rightly be subverted. Even nondemocratic regimes can deserve the allegiance of their citizens. Citizens of nondemocratic regimes are certainly justified in working by peaceful means toward the goal of democratic rule; however, if their government is not a tyrannical one, they have reasons for obeying the laws enacted by their rulers, serving in the military, and treating the official acts of government as politically authoritative. In short, they have reasons for giving the regime their allegiance.

So, even if we are correct in arguing that the regime of judicial rule in the United States is doubly unjust, first, in its usurpation of democratic authority, and second, and not unrelatedly, in the wicked ends it has sometimes, as in *Roe*, served, that does not mean that we should support revolutionary action against the government of the United States. While these injustices weaken the legitimacy of the regime, they do not render our whole government simply illegitimate. The unjust and unconstitutional acts of the judiciary should be resisted; loyal citizens of the United States should work to restore those aspects of constitutional self-government that have been undermined by usurping judges. But, the means used to resist judicial usurpation and restore democratic rule must themselves be constitutionally and morally pure. The identification and use of such means will itself require careful democratic deliberation—what Mary Ann Glendon, writing in response to the *First* Things symposium, called "the hard work of citizenship."[51]

But the courts, and the Supreme Court in particular, should recognize the profound dilemma in which their usurpations have placed many conscientious and loyal American citizens. It would be bad enough for citizens who recognize the equality-in-dignity of unborn human beings to find themselves on the losing side of a democratic debate over the question of abortion. (This is the position in which pro-life citizens of the United Kingdom or Sweden find themselves.) It is even worse, however, when citizens are deprived of any right to work through normal democratic processes to preserve or restore legal protection for the unborn. It is not merely that the judicial manufacture of a constitutional right to abortion-on-demand makes the political task of protecting the unborn especially difficult, but that the institution claiming the ultimate authority to specify the meaning of the nation's fundamental moral-political commitments, namely the Supreme Court, tells the nation that the Constitution to which citizens are asked to give their allegiance includes so grave an injustice as the abortion license. Thus, citizens are asked to be loyal not only to a constitution that fails to protect the basic right to equality of the unborn, but also to one that denies them any democratic means to effect the protection of that basic right short of amending the Constitution.

Even prior to the *Dred Scott* decision in 1856,[52] the legitimacy of the regime of government in the United States was weakened by the grave injustice of slavery. Still, conscientious citizens such as Abraham Lincoln, who opposed that monstrous evil, could, he and many others believed (and I believe), honestly swear to uphold the Constitution because, whatever its inadequacies, it did not contain a strict right to own slaves. True, it failed to secure the moral right of every human being not to be enslaved, but it did not remove the authority of democratic institutions to abolish slavery and secure the moral right against it. The people in their states retained the authority to act through democratic means to effect abolition within their jurisdictions, and the people of the northern states chose to exercise this authority. Congress, in its exercise of general jurisdiction in the federal territories, had (or so it was thought) the authority to act against slavery, albeit in a limited way, and did so act. Of course, inasmuch as the southern states permitted slavery, they were guilty of grave injustice, and insofar as the United States Constitution permitted slavery in states that chose to retain "the peculiar institution," and even facilitated it in certain ways, it failed to protect the right of those enslaved to the equal protection of the laws.[53] But as bad as this situation was, no citizen was asked to pledge allegiance to a regime whose basic constitutional principles included something so unjust as a right of some human beings to buy, sell, use, and use up other human beings.

Then came *Dred Scott*.[54] According to the understanding of the Constitution by which Roger Brooke Taney and those justices joining him sent Dred Scott back into slavery, the American people, acting through the constitutionally established institutions of democracy at the federal level, had no authority to interfere with the right of slaveholding, even where, as in the territories, general jurisdiction was in the hands of the federal government.[55] This was, in effect, to manufacture a constitutional right to slaveholding.[56] Indeed, it is difficult to see how the practical import of this decision was not to deprive even the free states of their effective power to prohibit slavery within their borders. So not only was *Dred Scott*'s central holding unjust, but it was also a gross usurpation of the people's authority to act through their democratic institutions to prohibit or, at least, contain slavery. And, in these respects, *Dred Scott* resembles nothing so much as *Roe v. Wade*,[57] creating for many morally conscientious citizens of the antebellum era precisely the dilemma that *Roe* creates for many such citizens today.

When it comes to cases such as *Dred Scott* and *Roe*, there seem to be but two options available to citizens who recognize the profound injustices these decisions work: either citizens are to treat the legitimacy of the Constitution as gravely weakened, or they are to deny that the Court has the authority to settle definitively the meaning of the Constitution—in other words, either the Constitution is illegitimate or the Court is behaving illegitimately. In reaction to the *Dred Scott* case, a not insignificant number of abolitionists chose the former option, some going so far as to denounce the Constitution as a "covenant with death and agreement with hell"[58] and even to burn copies of it. Lincoln, however, chose the latter option. While recognizing the authority of the Court to resolve the particular case (despite the incorrectness and injustice of its ruling), he refused to concede to the justices the right to lay down a rule permanently binding the other branches of government to recognize a constitutional right of slaveholding.[59] Plainly referring to the decision in *Dred Scott*, Lincoln stated:

> I do not forget the position assumed by some that constitutional questions are to be decided by the Supreme Court, nor do I deny that such decisions must be binding in any case upon the parties to a suit as to the object of that suit, while they are also entitled to very high respect and consideration in all parallel cases by other departments of the Government. And while it is obviously possible that such decision may be erroneous in any given case, still the evil effect following it, being limited to that particular case, with the chance that it may be overruled and never become a precedent for other cases, can better be borne than could the evils of a different practice. At the same time, the candid citizen must confess that if the policy of the government, upon vital questions affecting the whole people is to be irrevocably fixed by decisions of the Supreme Court, the instant they are made in ordinary litigation between parties in personal actions, the people will have ceased to be their own rulers, having to that extent practically resigned their government into the hands of that eminent tribunal.[60]

I would suggest that the proper response of pro-life citizens to the call by Supreme Court Justices Sandra Day O'Connor, Anthony Kennedy, and David Souter in *Casey* to end the debate over abortion and "[accept] a common [pro-abortion] mandate rooted in the Constitution,"[61] is to reassert Lincoln's argument in response to judicial usurpation and injustice in *Dred Scott*. We should say, in effect, that while we could not in conscience give our unfettered allegiance to a regime committed in its very constitution to abortion-on-demand, any more than we could give wholehearted allegiance to a regime constitutionally committed to chattel slavery, we do not accept the authority of judges to read into the Constitution a right to abortion. On the contrary, we reject the justices' claim to have their ruling treated as a legitimate and authoritative interpretation of the Constitution. And we will resist their usurpation of our authority, as a people, to act through the institutions of representative democracy to protect the rights of the unborn. In other words, our response to judicial usurpation and injustice in our own time should not be to denounce the Constitution or to withdraw our allegiance from the United States, but rather to reassert the true principles of the Constitution, and to reaffirm our allegiance to this nation, under God,[62] in its aspiration to secure true liberty and justice for all.

Notes

1. Robert P. George, "The Tyrant State," in *The End of Democracy? The Judicial Usurpation of Politics*, ed. Mitchell S. Muncy (Dallas: Spence Publishing Company, 1997).

2. Pope John Paul II, *Evangelium Vitae* (March 25, 1995), p. 2.

3. Ibid., p. 73.

4. Ibid., p. 56. This language seems clearly to exclude the possibility of a purely retributive justification for the death penalty. In the sentence immediately following it, the encyclical also seems to rule out as a matter of moral principle, and not merely on the basis of sociological considerations, a justification based on the belief that punishing some criminals with death deters others: "Today however, as a result of steady improvements in the organization of the penal system, such cases [i.e., cases in which the execution of a wrongdoer is absolutely necessary for the protection of society] are very rare, if not practically non-existent." Ibid.

5. See "The Authoritative Catechism, and . . . ," *Catholic World Report* (Oct. 1997): 6–7.

6. See Pope John Paul II, *Evangelium Vitae*, pp. 68–74.

7. Ibid., p. 70.

8. On these critics, see Richard John Neuhaus, "The Liberalism of John Paul II," *First Things* (May 1997): 16.

9. See Pope John Paul II, *Centesimus Annus* (May 1, 1991), p. 46.

10. Ibid.

11. Pope John Paul II, *Evangelium Vitae*, p. 70.

12. Ibid.

13. Ibid.

14. Ibid.

15. See John M. Finnis, "Law as Co-ordination," *Ratio Juris* 2 (1989).

16. Ibid.

17. See Augustine, *The Problem of Free Choice: De Libero Arbitrio*, trans. Dom. Mark Pontifex (London: Newman Press, 1955), 1.5.11 (stating that an unjust law seems not to be law).

18. See Thomas Aquinas, *Summa Theologiae*, trans. Fathers of the English Dominican Province (London: Benziger Bros., 1947), I-II, q. 95, a. 2 (stating that an unjust law is not a law but a corruption of law); ibid., I-II, q. 96, a. 4 (stating that unjust laws are not so much laws as they are acts of violence).

19. See Plato, *The Laws*, trans. A. E. Taylor (London: Aidine Press, 1966), 4.715.

20. See Aristotle, *The Politics*, trans. Ernest Barker (Oxford: Oxford University Press, 1995), 3.6.1279a8.

21. See Cicero, *Laws: De Legibus*, trans. Clinton Walker Keyes (Cambridge: Harvard University Press, 1996), 2, v. 11–13.

22. See Pope John Paul II, *Evangelium Vitae*, p. 72.

23. Ibid.

24. Ibid., p. 72. John Paul II goes on to argue that such laws call for disobedience and even "conscientious objection" (p. 73). On the necessarily indirect nature of the disobedience and conscientious objection demanded by unjust laws which are permissive in nature, see George, "The Tyrant State," p. 58.

25. Pope John Paul II, *Evangelium Vitae*, p. 71.

26. Peter L. Berger, in *The End of Democracy? The Judicial Usurpation of Politics*, ed. Mitchell S. Muncy (Dallas: Spence Publishing Company, 1997), p. 72. A similar point is made by Gertrude Himmelfarb in her contribution to the same symposium. See Gertrude Himmelfarb in *The End of Democracy? The Judicial Usurpation of Politics*, ed. Mitchell S. Muncy (Dallas: Spence Publishing Company, 1997), pp. 87–92.

27. Berger, *The End of Democracy?* p. 72.

28. See Robert H. Bork, *Slouching towards Gomorrah: Modern Liberalism and American Decline* (New York: Regan Books, 1996), pp. 173–85.

29. See Justice Antonin Scalia, "Of Democracy, Morality, and the Majority," *Origins* 26 (1996): 81.

30. *Roe v. Wade*, 410 U.S. 113 (1973).

31. *Planned Parenthood v. Casey*, 505 U.S. 997–1000 (1992) (Scalia, J., concurring in part and dissenting in part); *Webster v. Reproductive Health Services*, 492 U.S. 490, 532–37 (1989) (Scalia, J., concurring).

32. See Scalia, "Of Democracy," p. 87.

33. See *Webster v. Reproductive Health Services*, pp. 532–37.

34. See Scalia, "Of Democracy," p. 87.

35. See Robert P. George, "Natural Law and Positive Law," in *The Autonomy of Law: Essays on Legal Positivism*, ed. Robert P. George (Oxford: Clarendon Press, 1996), pp. 330–32.

36. U.S. Constitution,Fourteenth Amendment, para. 1.

37. *Roe v. Wade*, p. 113.

38. *Roe v. Wade*, p. 113.

39. *Roe v. Wade*, pp. 156–57.

40. U.S. Constitution, Art. II, Sec. 1, Cl. 5; *Roe v. Wade*, p. 157.

41. *Roe v. Wade*, p. 157.

42. *Roe v. Wade*, p. 159.

43. See Dianne N. Irving, "Scientific and Philosophical Expertise: An Evaluation of the Arguments on 'Personhood,'" *Linacre Quarterly* Feb. 1993: 18.

44. *Roe v. Wade*, p. 222.

45. See *Planned Parenthood v. Casey*, p. 979.

46. See Germain Grisez, "When Do People Begin?" *Proc. of the Amer. Cath. Phil Assoc.* 63 (1989): 31.

47. See Patrick Lee, *Abortion and Unborn Human Life* (Washington, DC: Catholic University of America Press, 1996).

48. See John Rawls, *Political Liberalism* (New York: Columbia University Press, 1993), p. 243, n. 32.

49. John Finnis, "Abortion, Natural Law, and Public Reason" (paper presented at the panel on Natural Law, Liberalism and Public Reason sponsored by the American Public Philosophy Institute at the American Political Science Association 1997 Annual Convention, Washington, DC, Aug. 30, 1997, on file with author).

50. For a valuable account of such reasons, see generally Cass R. Sunstein, *Legal Reasoning and Political Conflict* (New York: Oxford University Press, 1996).

51. Mary A. Glendon, "Comment" in "The End of Democracy? A Discussion Continued," *First Things* 69 (Jan. 1997): 23.

52. *Dred Scott v. Sanford*, 60 U.S. 393 (1856).

53. It was to secure fully this protection that the Fourteenth Amendment, after the abolition of slavery throughout the nation by the Thirteenth Amendment, was introduced into the Constitution as a guarantee of equal protection to be enforced by Congress against the states.

54. *Dred Scott v. Sanford*, p. 393.

55. *Dred Scott v. Sanford*, pp. 400–403.

56. See Robert H. Bork, *The Tempting of America: The Political Seduction of the Law* (New York: Free Press, 1990), pp. 28–34 (discussing the political climate surrounding the *Dred Scott* decision).

57. *Roe v. Wade*, p. 113.

58. Archibald H. Grimke, *William Lloyd Garrison: The Abolitionist* (New York: Funk and Wagnalls, 1891), p. 310.

59. See Abraham Lincoln, "First Inaugural Address," in *Lend Me Your Ears: Great Speeches in History* (New York: W.W. Norton & Company, 1997), p. 882.

60. Ibid., pp. 171–72.

61. *Planned Parenthood v. Casey*, p. 867.

62. This familiar phrase, which was inserted into the Pledge of Allegiance in the 1950s, derives from President Abraham Lincoln's Gettysburg Address. See Abraham Lincoln, "Gettysburg Address," in *Lend Me Your Ears*, p. 49.

Notes on Contributors

WALTER F. MURPHY is McCormick Professor of Jurisprudence, Emeritus, Princeton University. His forthcoming book is *Constitutional Democracy*.

JOHN E. FINN is professor of government at Wesleyan University. His books include *Constitutions in Crisis*.

CHRISTOPHER L. EISGRUBER is Director, Program in Law and Public Affairs, and Laurance S. Rockefeller Professor of Public Affairs in the Woodrow Wilson School and the University Center for Human Values, Princeton University. He is the author of *Constitutional Self-Government*.

JAMES E. FLEMING is professor of Law at Fordham University. His next book will be titled *Securing Constitutional Democracy*.

JEFFREY K. TULIS is professor of government at the University of Texas, Austin. His next book is tentatively titled *Constitutional Deference*.

SUZETTE HEMBERGER lives in Washington, D.C. Her forthcoming book will be titled *Creatures of the Constitutions*.

SOTIRIOS A. BARBER is professor of government at the University of Notre Dame. His next book will be titled *Welfare and the Constitution*.

STEPHEN MACEDO is Laurance S. Rockefeller Professor of Politics and the University Center of Human Values at Princeton University. His latest book is *Diversity and Distrust: Civic Education in a Multicultural Democracy*.

SANFORD LEVINSON holds the W. St. John Garwood & W. St. John Garwood, Jr. Regents Chair in Law at the University of Texas, Austin. His latest book is *Written in Stone: Public Monuments and Changing Societies*.

H. N. HIRSCH is Mitau Professor of Political Science at Macalester College. His latest book is *A Theory of Liberty: The Constitution and Minorities*.

WAYNE D. MOORE is associate professor of political science at the Virginia Polytechnic Institute and State University. He is the author of *Constitutional Rights and Powers of the People*.

KEITH E. WHITTINGTON is assistant professor of politics, Princeton University. His latest book is *Constitutional Construction: Divided Powers and Constitutional Meaning*.

MARK E. BRANDON is Professor of Law at Vanderbilt University. He is the author of *Free in the World*.

ROBERT P. GEORGE is McCormick Professor of Jurisprudence and Director of the James Madison Program in American Ideals and Institutions at Princeton University. His latest book is *In Defense of Natural Law*.

Index

view of, 118; relation of, to the Constitution, 116–19, 129

Dees, Morris: and vicarious liability, 224–26

Democracy: *See* Representative Democracy

Departmentalism: *See* Interpretation, of the Constitution

Diversity: benefits of, 185, 195–97; limits of, in liberal regimes, 183–84, 220 n.47. *See also* Multiculturalism

Douglas, Frederick: claim of, to citizenship, 252–53; Robert Cover on, 243; criticism of Dred Scott Case, 247; early view of Constitution as proslavery, 239–41; electoral strategy of, 246, 249–51; as exemplar of constitutional citizenship, 254–55; and William Lloyd Garrison, 239–40, 242, 246, 249; as influenced by Garritt Smith, 240–42; later approach to constitutional interpretation, 240–45, 251, 254–55; as unofficial constitution maker, 238, 254; William Wiecek on, 240, 245

Douglas, William O.: Opinion in *Griswold v. Connecticut*, 81

Dred Scott v. Sanford, 75, 245, 247, 252, 323–24

Dworkin, Ronald: on civil disobedience, 185; and the Constitution as discursive practice, 48–49; on principled solutions to social issues, 207

Eisenhower, Dwight: reaction of, to *Brown v. Board of Education*, 286–87

Elkin, Stephen: approach of, to constitutional studies, 163

Ely, John Hart: on judicial review, 20

Engel v. Vitale, 205–7, 211

Establishment Clause (U.S. Constitution): and aid to parochial schools, 199–203; and school prayer, 205–11, 214

Everson v. New Jersey, 195

Federalism: and the American Civil War, 71; as consociationalism, 23; and the Fourteenth Amendment, 75–76

Federalist Party: on defects of Articles of Confederation, 135; depreciation of local juries, 146; on popular interests and national power, 133–34; political knowledge as scientific and universal, 138,

144–48, 158 n.69; on power to tax, 135–36, 143; preference for standing army, 135, 138–39; on government as guarantor of liberty and security, 129–33; Jackson Turner Main on, 158 n.69; on tenure of constitutional offices, 147; on term limits, 147–48; on threat to liberty as external, 130–33; on unlimited power and sovereignty, 134–36; view of Constitution as empowering (not limiting) government, 134. *See also The Federalist*

The Federalist on amending process, 123; and Federalist constitution making, 165; on the Constitution's nationalizing tendencies, 123; on constitutional maintenance, 163–65; on defects of the Articles of Confederation, 123, 165

Fidelity, to the Constitution: and constitutional ends, 163, 165

First Amendment: and advocacy of violence, 225–26; and civil liability for speech, 224–25; and constitution maintenance, 223; and constitution making, 223; and Critical Race Theory, 223, 231–32; Catharine MacKinnon on, 223, 228–30; Alexander Meiklejohn on, 232; and religious freedom, 227; and right to privacy, 81–82; Cass Sunstein on, 223, 232–33; and value of social equality, 229–32

Fourteenth Amendment: and common-law rights, 77–79, 82; and the Constitution as an instrument of justice, 85; as distorted by legalistic view of the Constitution, 74, 82

Fourteenth Amendment (U.S. Constitution): Congress's authority under, 72–73; as distorted by judicial supremacy, 71–75

Frankfurter, Felix: dissent in *West Virginia Board of Education v. Barnette*, 209–10; on the judiciary's role in constitutional interpretation, 78–79

Freedom of Speech: *See* First Amendment

General Welfare: and constitutional maintenance, 166; as end of government, 166

German Basic Law: practices under, as compared to American practice, 92–96,